ENGLISH POETRY

ENGLISH POETRY

a poetic record, from
Chaucer to Yeats

Selected, arranged, edited,
annotated, and introduced

by

DAVID HOPKINS

London and New York

First published 1990 by Routledge
11 New Fetter Lane, London EC4P 4EE

Simultaneously published in the USA and Canada
by Routledge
a division of Routledge, Chapman and Hall, Inc.
29 West 35th Steet, New York, NY 10001

© 1990 David Hopkins

Printed in Great Britain by T. J. Press (Padstow) Ltd, Padstow, Cornwall

All rights reserved. No part of this book may be reprinted or
reproduced or utilized in any form or by any electronic,
mechanical, or other means, now known or hereafter invented,
including photocopying and recording, or in any information
storage or retrieval system, without permission in writing from
the publishers.

British Library Cataloguing in Publication Data
English Poetry: poetic record from Chaucer to Yeats.
1. Poetry in English. Critical studies
I. Hopkins. David, *1948–*
821'.009

Library of Congress Cataloging in Publication Data
English Poetry: a poetic record from Chaucer to Yeats / edited by
David Hopkins
p.   cm.
Includes bibliographical references.
1. English poetry—History and criticism—Theory, etc. 2. Poetry-
-Authorship.   3. Poetry   I. Hopkins, David, 1948–
PR503.E53   1990
821.009–dc20   89-71347
ISBN 0-415-05239-4

CONTENTS

Acknowledgements	vii
Preface	ix
Introduction	1
PART ONE: ON POETRY	19
PART TWO: ON POETS	
Poets of the 14th and 15th Centuries	71
Geoffrey Chaucer (c.1343–1400)	72
The ballads	83
The early Tudor poets	84
Sir Thomas Wyatt (1503–42)	84
Henry Howard, Earl of Surrey (?1517–47)	85
Edmund Spenser (c.1552–99)	86
Sir Philip Sidney (1554–86)	93
Sir Philip Sidney (1554–86) and Mary Herbert, Countess of Pembroke (1561–1621)	95
George Chapman (?1559–1634)	96
Edward Fairfax (d. 1635)	98
Christopher Marlowe (1564–93)	98
William Shakespeare (1564–1616)	100
The 'metaphysical' poets	116
John Donne (1572–1631)	118
Ben Jonson (1572–1637)	124
George Sandys (1578–1644)	133
George Herbert (1593–1633)	135
Edmund Waller (1606–87)	136
Sir Richard Fanshawe (1608–66)	138
John Milton (1608–74)	139
Richard Crashaw (?1612–49)	156
Samuel Butler (1612–80)	157
Sir John Denham (1615–69)	158
Abraham Cowley (1618–67)	158
Richard Lovelace (1618–57)	164
Poets of the later 17th and early 18th centuries	165
John Dryden (1631–1700)	168
Thomas Shadwell (?1642–92)	175
John Wilmot, Earl of Rochester (1647–80)	176
John Oldham (1653–83)	177
Anne Finch, Countess of Winchilsea (1661–1720)	178
Jonathan Swift (1667–1745)	178
Thomas Parnell (1679–1718)	179
Edward Young (1683–1765)	179
Alexander Pope (1688–1744)	181
John Dyer (1699–1757)	190
James Thomson (1700–48)	190
Poets of the mid-18th century	193
Samuel Johnson (1709–84)	193
William Shenstone (1714–63)	194
Thomas Gray (1716–71)	194
Mark Akenside (1721–70)	197
William Collins (1721–59)	197
Christopher Smart (1722–71)	198
Thomas Warton (1728–90)	199
William Cowper (1731–1800)	199
Charles Churchill (1732–64)	202
Thomas Chatterton (1752–70)	203
George Crabbe (1754–1832)	204
William Blake (1757–1827)	207
The Regency and 'Lake' Poets	209
William Wordsworth (1770–1850)	211
Sir Walter Scott (1771–1832)	227
Samuel Taylor Coleridge (1772–1832)	228
Robert Southey (1774–1843)	230
James Henry Leigh Hunt (1784–1859)	231
The post-Wordsworth generation	232
George Gordon, Lord Byron (1788–1824)	233
Percy Bysshe Shelley (1792–1822)	238
John Clare (1793–1864)	244
John Keats (1795–1821)	247
Alfred, Lord Tennyson (1809–92)	252
Robert Browning (1812–89)	254
Emily Brontë (1818–48)	257
Arthur Hugh Clough (1819–61)	258
George Meredith (1828–1909)	258

William Morris (1834–96)	259	Robert Bridges (1844–1930)	262
Algernon Charles Swinburne		Gerard Manley Hopkins (1844–89)	262
(1837–1909)	260	William Butler Yeats (1865–1939)	263
Thomas Hardy (1840–1928)	261	Index	267

ACKNOWLEDGEMENTS

Thanks are due to the following for permission to reproduce material in this book: Baylor University for Browning's epigram on Swinburne from Robert Secor, 'Swinburne at his lyre; a new epigram by Browning', *Studies in Browning and His Circle*, (1974) 2,2, pp.58–60; Collins Publishers for Edmund Blunden's 'The Death Mask of John Clare' from *Poems of Many Years* (1957); the executors and estate of C. Day Lewis and The Hogarth Press and Jonathan Cape for C. Day Lewis's 'Birthday Poem for Thomas Hardy' from *Complete Poems* (1954); Faber & Faber Ltd for W.H. Auden's 'New Year Letter' from *Collected Poems* and 'In Memory of W.B. Yeats' from *The English Auden*, for quotations from T.S. Eliot's 'The Metaphysical Poets' in *Selected Essays* and from Ted Hughes's *Poetry in the Making* and his 'Note' in *A Choice of Shakespeare's Verse*; *London Magazine* for the interview between Philip Larkin and John Haffenden from *London Magazine* (1980) n.s. 20; Longman for Roger Lonsdale's text of William Collins's 'Ode on the Popular Superstitions of the Highlands' from the Longman Annotated English Poets series; Macmillan Publishing Company, New York for Thomas Hardy's 'A Singer Asleep (Algernon Charles Swinburne, 1837–1909)' and 'George Meredith (1828–1909)' – both from *The Complete Poems of Thomas Hardy*, edited by James Gibson (New York, Macmillan, 1978) – for W.B. Yeats's 'The Symbolism of Poetry', 'The Philosophy of Shelley's Poetry', 'The Tragic Theatre', 'Edmund Spenser', 'William Blake and the Imagination', and 'The Happiest of Poets' – all from W.B. Yeats, *Essays and Introductions* (New York, Macmillan, 1961) and *Autobiography* (New York, Macmillan, 1970); Professor Eric Robinson and Curtis Brown for John Clare's 'Shadows of Taste' and 'Lines on Cowper' from *John Clare* (Oxford Authors) and his 'To the Rural Muse' from *The Later Poems of John Clare* (Oxford English Texts) and 'To the Memory of Keats' from *The Early Poems of John Clare* (Oxford English Texts); Stanley Thornes (Publishers) Ltd for Ted Hughes's Introduction to *Here Today*.

PREFACE

This volume contains a collection of poetic responses by the English poets to one another's work. It does not attempt to represent the full range of remarks which English poets have made about their fellow practitioners, but, rather, concentrates on those moments when, in reflecting on their art in general, on their own work, or on the work of one or more of their peers, they have been prompted to exhibit some features of the very activity which they are describing or commending. The majority of the items included are full-dress poems, or extracts from larger poems, but I have included poets' prose comments in those instances where the writing seems, in whole or in part, to be 'aspiring to the condition of poetry' – where the writer is deploying rhythmical and metaphorical effects, verbal colouring, heightened diction, or impassioned rhetoric to a degree that one would not normally expect to find in discursive prose. In the Introduction, I attempt to suggest the particular interest of poets' specifically poetic responses to their art and to their fellow artists.

Any anthologist (particularly one faced with a body of material as large as that potentially eligible for the present volume) must establish clear and reasoned principles of selection if the end-product is to seem a coherent book, rather than merely an arbitrarily assembled collection of snippets. But an anthologist must also recognise that, however unified he can make his collection, however much each of his extracts is freshly illuminated by the new environment in which it finds itself, an anthology can never be more than a provisional holding-together of a selective body of material, each item of which is temporarily 'on loan' from a number of other contexts in which it has slightly different kinds of significance.

Many items in this anthology are excerpted from larger works – the most immediate and important of all the contexts in which they live. Beyond that, they form parts of their authors' total *oeuvres*. But they are also parts of other larger wholes. The English poets' responses to one another's work can be only very partially represented by collecting their explicit *statements*. To gain a complete sense of what the English poets meant to one another, one would have to take stock of the numerous and diverse ways in which the work of one poet is present in others' work: in translation, adaptation, imitation, parody, allusion, echo – modes which often reveal poets' reactions to their peers more fully and intimately than their explicit comments.

English poets have, moreover, been sometimes more deeply inspired and influenced by foreign poets than by their own compatriots. And the work of some poets shows that they were deeply affected by peers on whom they left either little or no direct commentary, or commentary which gives a very misleading or imperfect sense of the nature of their interest. A comprehensive presentation of the subject covered by the present volume could therefore only be achieved by reprinting large sections – perhaps, in some cases, virtually the whole – of the poets' complete works, together with large sections of the work of those poets, English and foreign, to whom each of their works was most intimately related. In restricting myself to the more manageable topic of English poets' explicit commentary on their English peers, I am fully conscious that I am presenting the tips of numerous icebergs whose full shape might not always be adequately suggested by what appears above surface level.

Though the main body of the anthology presents a chronological collection of English poets' reflections on particular peers, a preliminary section has been included which contains a selection of the poets' more general reflections on their art. This seemed desirable for two reasons. First, a number of those general passages contain within them important passing (and therefore not easily excerptible) mentions of specific poets. Second, many of the poets' particular comments on their fellow practitioners take on a greater significance when seen in the light of the more general claims which the community of poets down the centuries has made for its art.

The chronological section includes comment on English narrative, dramatic and lyric poets from Chaucer to W.B. Yeats. Chaucer seemed the obvious starting-point, since he was from early on acknowledged as the 'father of English poetry', the effective instigator of a long and continuous tradition whose members all recognised him as their ultimate ancestor. The decision to end with Yeats is inevitably more controversial. It was arrived at for a number of overlapping reasons. First among them was a general conviction that the tradition of poetic criticism (though by no means entirely dead) has substantially declined both in quantity and quality over the last century. Second, Yeats is the last major English poet to have consistently written about poetry in his own prose in a way that is undeniably 'poetical'. It seems broadly true that since Yeats a dissociation of sensibility has set in, as a result of which most poets have tended to keep their poetic and critical selves in more or less separate compartments. A typical critical essay by T.S. Eliot, for example, is at a much further imaginative and linguistic distance from *Four Quartets* than Shelley's *Defence of Poetry* is from *Prometheus Unbound* or Wordsworth's *Lyrical Ballads* Preface is from *The Prelude*. Third, Yeats is the last English poet to have had a poetic tribute paid to him which is a celebrated poem in its own right. Fourth, there seemed to be good arguments for ending the book with a poet whose reputation is by now fairly 'settled'; those sections of anthologies which include material from the anthologist's own time are, notoriously, the parts which date most rapidly. It seemed, for all these reasons, that (though such a decision could never be entirely satisfactory) there was a certain aptness in making Yeats the final subject in a collection of English poetic responses to poetry, and in ending the volume on a strong note with Auden's famous elegy on his older contemporary.

My reference above to Yeats as an 'English' poet was not merely a piece of inadvertent chauvinism. In general, this anthology concentrates on English poetry in the narrowest sense; Irish, Welsh, Scots, American, and Commonwealth poets have generally been excluded, both as subjects and commentators. But exceptions have occasionally been made, in instances where an Irish or Scots poet has had such intimate connections with, or made such an obvious impact upon, the English poetic tradition that his exclusion would seem merely pedantic.

In making the selection, I have sought to include items which are both of some intrinsic merit and which either shed direct critical light on their subject or provide indications as to why that subject was admired in the past. Parodies and imitations have been excluded, except in instances where a critical comment is cast in a partially parodic or imitative form. I have generally excluded material which focuses on the life of a poet rather than his work, but I have included general tributes to a poet's memory in cases where the reverence expressed for an author's character or personality is inextricable from the homage paid to his work. Though no extracts are included purely for their 'representative' quality, I have tried to keep a balance between familiar and more out-of-the-way items, and have attempted to include a variety of tones and styles in the passages selected. I have also tried to avoid merely selecting items which reflect the priorities and emphases of modern literary historians. Many of the poets who are the subjects of their peers' comments are, of course, the same poets who are most admired by modern critics. But I hope the anthology might prompt some readers both to sample a number of poets who have been much admired by their peers but who are now generally neglected, and to look at the work of a number of established classics in slightly different lights from those to which they are accustomed.

The arrangement of the book is, I hope, largely self-explanatory. Items are numbered for ease of cross-reference in a single sequence, but arranged in two parts. Part One ('On Poetry') presents poets' reflections on poetry in general, and on more particular topics and problems related to the arts of poetry. The items in Part One are arranged chronologically, by their authors' dates of birth. Part Two of the book ('On Poets') contains poets' reflections on the work of specific peers. The arrangement is again chronological, this time by the poets or groups of poets who are the subject of their fellow artists' comment. Entries on groups or schools of poets, or on poets whose date of birth is uncertain, are inserted at what seemed to be appropriate places in the chronology. Within the entry for each poet/subject, the arrangement is chronological by poet/ critic: thus, for example, Jonson-on-Shakespeare is followed by Milton-on-Shakespeare, then Dryden-on-Shakespeare, and so on, up to Swinburne-on-Shakespeare. Then the Shakespeare entry is followed by one on the 'metaphysical' poets, then by one on Donne, and so on, up to the final entry on Yeats. In instances where a poet's reflections on his own work have been included, they are placed at the beginning of that poet's entry. In both parts of the book, where several extracts are taken from a single work, they are not necessarily printed in the same order in which they occurred in their original setting, or taken from the same edition of the work.

Since the book is designed for general readers (both within and outside universities), and since it is, by its very nature, unlikely to be consulted or cited for its texts as such, all items have been edited with a view to maximum ease of readability. Consequently, spelling, punctuation, capitals, italics and paragraphing have been modernised throughout, even in the medieval items. Capital letters have sometimes been silently supplied at the beginning of items, and a full stop at the end. Each item has a title, to indicate its broad subject. The great majority of these titles are editorial, and are given in italics. Where the author's original title has been used, it is printed in roman type. Each item is dated immediately after the text. The date given is normally that of the item's first publication, but this should not be taken to indicate that the text printed always strictly follows that of the first edition. Readings from later editions are sometimes silently incorporated, when there is no likelihood of the reader's being thereby misled. Significant discrepancies between the date of each item's composition and that of its first publication have been noted wherever possible. Editorial omissions within items, of whatever length, are indicated by the insertion of an ellipsis (three full stops). In notes and captions, wr. = written, pub. = published, rev. = revised.

The notes are designed to provide such information as will answer ordinary readers' immediate queries about the meaning and significance of each item. Thus, archaic or difficult words are glossed, references and quotations are identified, and concise contextual information is provided wherever an item's significance cannot be readily appreciated without it. Extensive cross-referencing (using item numbers) is designed to prevent unnecessary duplication. The notes also provide information about the many lesser-known poets who appear either as subjects or commentators and about lesser-known aspects of major poets' work on which the intelligibility of specific items depends. It has, however, been assumed that readers requiring more general data about the better-known English poets will obtain it from the standard works of reference. The indexes at the end of the volume list (i) main treatments of general topics in both parts of the anthology and (ii) mentions of particular poets outside the main author entries in Part Two.

In selecting material for inclusion and when preparing the annotation, I have drawn on the work of numerous scholars to whom, in the nature of the case, it is not possible to express formal acknowledgement. I should, however, like to thank those friends and colleagues who have directly assisted me by suggesting items for inclusion and by providing other kinds of advice: Stuart Gillespie, George Myerson, Myra Stokes, Charles Tomlinson, and, above all, Catherine Bradley, who commissioned the anthology and gave me guidance and encouragement in its early stages, and Tom Mason, with whom I have, fortunately, been able to discuss every aspect of the project from inception to conclusion. My wife, Sandra, has, as always, provided much valuable advice and assistance throughout the making of the book.

Bristol
April 1989

INTRODUCTION

'To judge of poets is only the faculty of poets; and not of all poets, but the best'. Most of us would, I think, be inclined – after perhaps a few moments' hesitation – to dissent from Ben Jonson's famous pronouncement. The hesitation might perhaps stem partly from a supposition that there *must* be ways in which poets' pronouncements on their art carry some special weight and authority, and partly from a recognition that many of the most memorable and frequently quoted comments on the arts of poetry have, indeed, been made by poets. But such factors would probably be soon outweighed by counter-considerations – not least among them, our awareness that our own understanding and appreciation of poetry had been undoubtedly enhanced in countless ways by the writing of men and women who were not poets at all, let alone 'of the best'.

It is probable that such feelings would be confirmed rather than undermined by a casual perusal of the present collection. Those who have been brought up on the writings of modern literary critics are likely to find a number of features of the poets' reponses to their art strange and offputting. Moreover, they are likely to be struck by the extent to which these offputting features are common to the writings of poets of widely different temperaments, backgrounds, and historical periods. First-time readers of this anthology might thus soon begin to feel that they were confronting a body of convictions about poetry and the criticism of poetry that flew in the face of everything that their own literary education and experience had led them to expect.

Poets' reflections on poetry differ most obviously from those of modern critics in that they are predominantly general and predominantly enthusiastic – or more than enthusiastic. Poets, characteristically, write in a tone of excited reverence (and occasionally of exasperated hatred), and are far more often concerned to celebrate their art in a general way, or to capture in words the 'animating spirit', 'informing soul' or 'characteristic genius' which pervades the total *oeuvre* of one or more of their peers, than they are to debate particular critical problems, or to discuss particular passages in detail. Their writing is highly figurative and unashamedly emotional. They frequently employ large, sounding phrases which must rely for any effectiveness they may have on their evocative resonance rather than on any technical exactness.

Modern critics, in contrast, tend to see their activity as a rigorous analytical discipline, in the exercise of which it is their duty to accumulate detailed evidence to support specific and clear lines of argument. The tone of most modern criticism is, consequently, rational and cool. It generally avoids both metaphorical flights and large celebratory phrases, and seeks for a technical clarity in its vocabulary similar to that aspired to by philosophers and natural scientists. Modern critics may express preferences (though the habit is becoming increasingly unfashionable), but they seldom write as if they revered, or were in awe of, or even passionately loathed, their chosen author. Indeed, the maintenance of an imaginative and emotional distance from their subject often seems to be thought of as an essential means of achieving the analytical objectivity which is the critic's goal.

The modern critics' methods and procedures command a great deal of respect. For while most of us are delighted when our favourite lecturer or broadcaster manages to convey, in his spoken words, an infectious enthusiasm for his subject, we soon tend to become uneasy when a critic begins to display his emotional engagement with his author too openly in print. Many of us, encountering for the first time the poets' exuberant metaphors and resounding affirmations, are likely to suspect that we are being subjected to a display of the kind of impressionistic amateurism which has been long since discredited by literary academics as 'belletrism'. Moroever, we are liable to be disappointed by the poets' surprising reticence in those very areas where they might most obviously be thought to possess special expertise. For, compared to musicians and painters, the poets have relatively little to say on the specifically technical aspects of their art. It is in vain that one looks to them for much sustained and detailed discussion of diction, versification, and poetic form. Moreover, those larger comments which poets have made on the essential nature and characteristics of their art are nearly always occasional, prompted by particular pressures and circumstances, and thus treating their subject in an oblique and partial, rather than a judiciously systematic, manner.

Another major difference between the poets' writings on poetry and those to which we are accustomed lies in their view of literary history. Most current textbooks invite us to view the history of English poetry as a succession of epochs, movements and schools: The Augustan Age, the Romantic Period, Modernism, etc. We are increasingly encouraged to think of the political, social, theological, aesthetic, and economic events and ideas of each 'period' as the prime context in which that period's poetry should be understood. The stress of the poets themselves, in contrast, is on the continuity of the arts of poetry across period boundaries, and on the power of poetic writing to speak beyond the time and place in which it was originally composed. The poets feel themselves to be joined one to another by a pattern of lineal descent as strong and demonstrable as the biological ties which link the generations of a human family. They believe that their common membership of a community of thought and feeling across the centuries is ultimately of far greater importance than any differences of convention, idiom, or emphasis which might seem to divide them.

To some modern critics and readers, such a stance will inevitably seem naïve and self-deluded. For such readers, poetry, like all other cultural phenomena, must be seen as the product of the value-systems, ideologies and socio-economic arrangements which were dominant at the moment of that poetry's composition. Some modern academics, indeed, would deny the very existence of 'poetry' or 'literature' as discrete categories, and would advocate the assimilation of literary study, along with that of politics, religion, ideas, and the other arts, to a more general study of 'discourse' or 'cultural practices'. For them, the poets' assertion of the unique, autonomous, and trans-historical nature of their art is an act of dangerous mystification. In their view, the critic's proper purpose is precisely to resist, subvert and undermine the poets' avowed intentions, and their claim to present 'truth'. Critics should unmask the ideological assumptions which lurk behind the poets' work. It is their duty to expose the contradictions which are inherent in those assumptions, and which are unwittingly revealed by the 'tensions', 'silences' and 'gaps' in the poets' texts. To acquiesce in the poets' claims that their work stands, in important senses, free of the historical moment which gave it birth, and that it can properly be read only in a spirit of emotional and imaginative engagement, would be to render oneself altogether incapable of understanding poetry's true cultural significance. To collaborate with the poets in the way they demand would be to disqualify oneself from perceiving the real nature of their activity.

A final factor which might make modern readers wary of the poets' pronouncements on their art is the suspicion that practitioners will inevitably have personal axes to grind; that, rather than offering disinterested comment on their fellow artists, they will be secretly propagandising on their own behalf, or colouring their characterisations of their peers with their own ambitions, preoccupations, anxieties and jealousies. Readers are likely to suspect that poets' comments will be likely to reveal the presence of The Burden of the Past and The Anxiety of Influence rather than to provide genuine illumination of its ostensible subject.

Faced with such doubts, suspicions and hostilities, what kind of explanation or description of their practice might the poets themselves have to offer? For the remainder of this Introduction, I shall attempt to sketch an answer, drawing chiefly on evidence presented later in the book. (References in square brackets are to item numbers in the anthology.) This evidence suggests that, while much may seem to divide poets of different schools and periods in their more prosaic, theorising moods, they share a remarkable amount of common ground and common assumption when writing about their art poetically.

The poets' recurrent impulse to write about their art either in full-dress poetry or in poetic prose has been directly prompted by their conception of the art itself. For the poets, poetry is an act of *creation*; the power which effects that creation must consequently be seen as nothing short of *godlike*. The poet is a creator-god [62 (Shelley)] at whose command 'a new world leaps forth' [15–16 (Cowley)]. The poet's sphere of activity is larger than the Nature experienced by humans in the normal course of their lives [36 (Akenside)]. The poet 'doth grow in effect another Nature' [2 (Sidney)], both by depicting places and beings which cannot ordinarily be said to exist, and by making Nature seem somehow more comprehensible and beautiful than it is in our ordinary experience. The poet 'approximates the remote and familiarises the wonderful' [135 (Johnson)]; he makes plausible situations and personages that would otherwise have seemed merely fanciful or whimsical; the poet 'gives to airy nothing/A local habitation and a name' [7 (Shakespeare)]. He creates 'forms more real than living man' [59 (Shelley)]. Wordsworth, it was said, 'new-created all he saw' [317 (Shelley)]. Shakespeare 'exhausted worlds, and then imagined new' [133 (Johnson)]. Milton's 'delight was to sport in the wide regions of possibility; reality was a scene too narrow for his mind. He sent his faculties out upon discovery, into worlds where only imagination can travel' [199 (Johnson)]. The 'force' of poetry is one which 'calls new powers into being' [32 (Johnson)]. The poet 'creates anew the universe' [62 (Shelley)]. He 'sees all *new*' [67 (Elizabeth Barrett Browning)]. The creating power of poetic genius is a surging, potent 'energy', which is 'ambitious and adventurous, always investigating, always aspiring ... always imagining something greater than it knows' [267 (Johnson)]. Beside the 'brazen' world we know, that created by the poets seems, uniquely, 'golden' [2 (Sidney)]. Poets' language can thus legitimately be described as 'the speech of heaven' [5 (Daniel)].

Though the poets might differ in detail over the proportion of 'wit' (natural talent, intuitive intelligence) to 'judgement' (skill, craftsmanship, discriminatory power) which is ideal in the act of poetic composition, they are all agreed that poetry is not 'a power to be exerted according to the determination of the will' [62 (Shelley)]. Poetry cannot be written to order; nor can it be conceived at the tepid mental temperature in which people conduct their daily lives. To create as a god, a poet needs powers which are not normally afforded to mortals – even to the poet himself outside the practice of his art. Thus, poets of all periods have constantly returned to the ancient metaphor of inspiration: the notion that poetic composition must result from the intervention in human affairs of some power that seems more-than-human – perhaps one of the Muses, the nine female deities who have jurisdiction over the arts, or Apollo, the god of poetry. Dryden, often thought of as a poet who valued 'judgement' above 'wit', wrote (in phrases which would have pleased Shelley) that poets 'have not the inspiration when [they] please, but must wait till the god comes rushing on [them], and invades [them] with a fury which [they] are not able to resist' [19]. Pope [23] followed his predecessor Cowley [17] in describing the power which brings poetry into being as a mysterious force which 'like the power divine/We only can by negatives define'. The greater the poetic task at hand, the greater the poets' sense of their need for inspiration, and the more intense are their calls for preternatural aid. It is no accident that the most lengthy and eloquent invocations to the Muse contained in this volume [189; 307] come from the two most self-consciously ambitious English poets: Milton and Wordsworth.

The poets believe that, when inspired by the Muse, they have the power to defy the normal laws of Nature and give permanence and solidity to phenomena which are normally hopelessly fitful and transient. Poetry 'arrests the vanishing apparitions which haunt the interlunations of life' [62 (Shelley)]. It 'solidates and crystallises' the 'ice' of the present which would otherwise 'melt so soon away' [15 (Cowley)]: 'A face of beauty, in a city crowd/Met, passed, and vanished like a summer cloud,/ In poesy's vision more refined and fair' [64 (Clare)]. On a larger scale, poets preserve the events of history so that they can survive and live on in the memory of posterity. Those 'chiefs' and 'sages' whose acts were not celebrated by a poet have faded from human consciousness [30 (Pope)]. Chaucer deserves special praise because he was one of those 'born to record and eternise' the acts of men [89 (Blake)].

For the poets, what differentiates their kind of writing from all others is its power of reconciling, conjoining, and fusing in a single compound, sentiments, capacities and phenomena which in any other kind of discourse would seem merely paradoxical or contradictory. This is true both of the faculties and qualities of mind employed in the process of composition itself, and of the matter which is the end-result of that process. Large sections of Pope's *Essay on Criticism* are devoted to celebrating the state of equipose, or armed neutrality, between competing mental powers which is the prerequisite for successful poetic composition. Poets seem miraculously able to combine in their work the freshness of youthful perception with the wise maturity of old age [242 (Jabez Hughes); 310 (Coleridge); 324 (Arnold)]. Poetic wit is able to join widely disparate phenomena 'without force or strife' [17 (Cowley)]. Poetry allows neither writer nor reader to compartmentalise the various parts of himself. It 'brings the whole soul of man into activity' [52 (Coleridge)]. It 'subdues to union under its light yoke all irreconcilable things' [62 (Shelley)]. Poetry is characterised by a 'balance or reconciliation of opposite or discordant qualities: of sameness with difference; of the general with the concrete; the idea with the image; the individual with the representative; the sense of novelty and freshness with old and familiar objects; a more than usual state of emotion with more than usual order; judgement ever awake and steady self possession with enthusiasm and feeling profound or vehement' [52 (Coleridge)]. In a poem, 'meaning' and 'music', 'form' and 'content', 'craftsmanlike control' and 'emotional commitment' form an indissoluble unity.

This unity resembles that of a living creature. The force of poetry 'embodies sentiment and animates matter' [32 (Johnson)]. A poem is 'a living organism, not a dead aggregate, and its music is the expression of the law of its growth' [73 (Thomson)]. Metre is 'a fellow-growth from the same life' as that of the whole poem 'even as the bark is to the tree' [50 (Coleridge)]. The contemporary poet Ted Hughes has written that a poem is 'an assembly of living parts moved by a single spirit. The living parts are the words, the images, the rhythms. The spirit is the life which inhabits them when they all work together. It is impossible to say which comes first, parts or spirit'.[1] Homer, the first great European poet to have been continuously remembered, 'found out "living words" ' [28 (Pope)]. His vocabulary lives with the life of its subject : 'an arrow is "impatient" to be on the wing, a weapon "thirsts" to drink the blood of an enemy, and the like' [28 (Pope)]. In Homer's poetry 'every thing moves, every thing lives, and is put in action' [27 (Pope)]. A poet's words are the 'incarnation' of his thought [43 (Wordsworth)]. The poet 'bodies forth' his imaginings [7 (Shakespeare)]. Those imaginings then live in the reader's mind as fully as they lived in the mind of their creator. 'When [Shakespeare] describes any thing', writes Dryden [128], 'you more than see it, you feel it too'. Poetic discourse admits, and exploits, the inextricability of the perceived and the perceiver. Homer's attribution of human life to arrows and weapons is but one tiny example of poets' perpetual propensity to imbue their creations with a human life, and to extend our sense of what human life might be by linking it with the activities of the 'outside' world. The poet 'rejoices more than other men in the spirit of life that is in him; delighting to contemplate similar volitions and passions as manifested in the goings-on of the universe, and habitually impelled to create them where he does not find them' [38 (Wordsworth)].

When readers' minds are filled with the poet's imaginings, they are transported out of their normal, everyday, state. The greater the poetry, the more fully it demands a 'perpetual activity of attention' [147 (Coleridge)]. For Pope, 'no man of a true poetical spirit is master of himself while he reads' Homer; 'the reader is hurried out of himself by the force of the poet's imagination' [27]. Johnson is equally passionate about the experience of reading *King Lear*. The events of the play, he writes, 'fill the mind with a perpetual tumult of indignation, pity, and hope'; 'the mind, which once ventures within it, is hurried irresistibly along' [141]. Keats [154], reflecting on his own experience of reading the same play, speaks of 'burning through' Shakespeare's text. Not all poetry, of course, is compelling to quite this degree, but even lesser specimens of the art have a hold over the reader's mind which is deep and direct. Poetry speaks not to the mind alone, but to 'the whole man – blood, imagination, intellect, running together' [Yeats[2]].

Even poetical works which deal with subject-matter as harrowing as that of *The Iliad* or *King Lear* are experienced as profound *pleasure*. Indeed, one of the most striking things about poetry is that it can put us in a frame of mind where we can tolerate – indeed, enjoy – phenomena which in life would be unbearably and overwhelmingly painful. The most extraordinary of all the reconciliations of opposites which poetry can perform is its capacity to transform the most incomprehensibly brutal of life-situations (without simply censoring or prettifying them) into imaginative creations in which we can take genuine delight. Poetry 'turns all things to loveliness ... it adds beauty to that which is most deformed' [62 (Shelley)]. Poetic form and metre are essential ingredients in 'tempering and restraining' the pain of the 'excitement' produced by 'more pathetic situations and sentiments' [42 (Wordsworth)]. Of crucial importance, also, is our consciousness of the very fictionality of the poets' fictions. What they offer us are 'useful lies' [15 (Cowley)]; 'if we thought murders and treasons real, they would please no more' [34 (Johnson)]. What we are offered is not a slice of raw life, but life-situations transformed by the chemistry of poetic art into something rich and strange.

'Poetry is ever accompanied by pleasure'; it 'acts in a divine and unapprehended manner, beyond and above consciousness'; the poet's 'auditors are as men entranced by the melody of an unseen musician, who feel that they are moved and softened, yet know not whence or why' [59 (Shelley)]. The poet writes, says Wordsworth, under 'one restriction only, namely the necessity of giving immediate pleasure to a human being possessed of that information which may be expected from him, not as a lawyer, a physician, a mariner, an astronomer, or a natural philosopher, but as a man' [39 (Wordsworth)]. Some might object that the poet's pleasure-giving renders his activity superficial when compared with, say, the scientist's sober transmission of factual knowledge. To such people, Wordsworth retorts that *all* human knowledge worthy of the name, including scientific knowledge, is grounded in, and transmitted through, the medium of pleasure, the sheer delight of discovery. The poet's recognition of that fact, and his avowed *intent* to provide pleasure gives his enterprise the soundest of bases; it is 'a homage paid ... to the grand elementary principle of pleasure, by which [Man] knows, and feels, and lives, and moves' [39 (Wordsworth)].

The poet 'entices' [3 (Sidney)] where other kinds of writer perplex us with tortuous logic, or confound us with strenuous technicality. His is a 'dulcet and gentle philosophy' which leads us on 'with a ravishing delight and incredible sweetness' [10 (Jonson)]. The poet's truths are 'carried alive into the heart by passion' [39 (Wordsworth)]. Poetry (in a phrase of Johnson's) 'finds the passes of the mind'.[3] It engages more than our merely rational selves, and 'compels us to feel that which we perceive, and to imagine that which we know' [62 (Shelley)]. In a poem, writes Ted Hughes, 'besides being told a string of facts, we are made to dance them out inwardly and sing out the feelings behind them inwardly. As a result, the facts go more deeply into our minds and affect us more strongly than if they were just counted off to us in prose.'[4] In this way, poets' moral teachings, because they have penetrated our being more fully and wholly than any purely intellectual arguments, can be more lastingly effective than those of the great divines and theologians [103 (Milton)]. But poetry is by no means always straightforwardly supportive of established morality. The poet is also a beguiler and subverter; he 'holds in his grasp the rod of the enchanter, Pleasure, and with a touch he unnerves the joints that would seize and drag him before the seat of an ordinary police' [55 (John Wilson)].

Given the nature of the poets' general convictions about the creativity, grandeur and comprehensiveness of their art, it is perhaps not surprising that their responses to the work of their fellow poets are so consistently coloured by excitement, awe, wonder, and reverence. To write coolly or impassively about an art with such power to create new, living, imaginative worlds and to transport readers out of their ordinary habits of thought and feeling would clearly be to give a fundamentally misleading impression of poetry's most essential characteristics. To write in ordinary prose about an art which so thoroughly transcends the habits and categories of thought and feeling with which ordinary prose is associated would be to risk undermining the poets' work in the most basic way. To talk about an art which speaks to the whole person in an idiom which appeals to the mind and intellect alone would be radically inappropriate. The poets' decision to display in their writings on poetry some of the very features of the art which they are describing is an indication that, for them, full-dress poetry, or prose which aspires to the condition of poetry, is the only idiom adequate to the task.

It is for this reason that poets are so frequently and so passionately scornful of prose critics. Tennyson once referred to a critic-contemporary as a 'louse on the locks of literature'. And Pope, in Book IV of *The Dunciad*, makes the literary scholar Richard Bentley proudly proclaim:

> Turn what they will to verse, their toil is vain;
> Critics like me shall make it prose again.

The dangers of a critic 'murdering to dissect' the texts on which he is writing are clear and obvious to every poet.

Ted Hughes has described how a poem derives directly from its author's *excitement* with his subject:

> Something has so excited him that he is mentally dancing and singing ... [B]ecause he is a poet, and full of words, his song-dance does not break into real song, as it would if he were a musician, or into real dancing, as it would if he were a dancer. It breaks into words. And the dance and the song come out somehow within the words. The dance makes the words move in a pattern, which we call metre and versification. The song makes the sound of the lines rise and fall against each other, which we call the music of poetry, or the cadence.[5]

Poets' excitement at the contemplation of their art can take a variety of forms, many of which are represented in this anthology. Their responses can be expressed at various levels of intensity, from ardent reverence to lighthearted banter. They can become excited at communicating and celebrating the significance and pleasure of poetry in the largest and most general ways. They can become stirred when contemplating the lineal succession of poets down the ages. Their excitement is sometimes prompted by the qualities of particular works. Sometimes they take delight in simply letting their mind play back over some aspect of a famous story, as told by a favourite poet.

Perhaps the most frequent circumstance in which poets register their excitement with their art is when they attempt to characterise the creative spirit or artistic personality that informs the work of one or more of their peers. Obvious and famous examples are Surrey's poem on Wyatt [96], Jonson's on Shakespeare [125], Carew's on Donne [165], and Coleridge's on Wordsworth [308]. But the great majority of the items in Part Two of this anthology come, more or less, into this category. These are perhaps the passages which are likely to cause the modern reader most difficulty, since, after the detailed and specific analyses and arguments of modern academic critics, such passages might be thought to contain little more than bland, generalised eulogy.

However, an interest in the spirit or artistic personality which informs the work of a particular poet is not as uncommon or unnatural as the staple of modern criticism might lead one to suppose. It is manifested at the simplest and most naïve level whenever one person proclaims, 'I can't stand Browning!' or asks, 'Do you like Donne?' Such speakers are not usually thinking of particular *poems* by Browning or Donne, let alone particular *details* in particular poems, but are alluding to the general impression that the cumulative effect of reading a number of poems by Browning or Donne has produced, or might produce, in them. For every reader of poetry is conscious that, whatever poets' common preoccupations, and however much they might draw on one another's work, each speaks with a voice, and from a perspective, that is distinctively his own. And every reader instinctively recognises that a poet's voice and outlook is located not merely in particular parts or particular details of individual works, but is diffused throughout each poem, and thence throughout the poet's total *oeuvre*. Most readers have a vague sense of the overall 'feel' of the work of their favourite poet, but would find it difficult to describe that poet's distinctive character in words, and thus to know it fully and surely.

When writing about their peers, poets are constantly endeavouring to define and revere the distinctive contribution which each individual talent has made to the larger poetic tradition – Donne's dazzling force of mind, Milton's heroic independence, Dryden's philosophical acuteness, Wordsworth's capacity to new-create familiar objects, Shelley's lofty idealism and musical virtuosity, and so on. The pleasure afforded to readers by such eulogies is the pleasure of having their own vague impressions of each poet's distinctive voice and stance distilled, epitomised, deepened, and extended, in language which has something of the same living quality and potent appeal to the whole person as the work of the poets themselves. The poets' eulogies invite assent because they are able to combine great precision with great inclusiveness – yet another example of the power of poetic language to effect a reconciliation of otherwise incompatible qualities. In a few potent and telling phrases, poets can suggest and evoke, and thus allow readers to apprehend, those essential characteristics of their peers' work which might otherwise be lost sight of through the haze of miscellaneous, fragmentary and contradictory impressions which constitutes most peoples' impression of a poet's complete works. Only the poets have the force and comprehensiveness of mind and language to penetrate to the centre, and to hold all the detail in a single imaginative compass. Only poets are able to 'survey the whole' and thus to convey how, in a poet's whole *oeuvre*, as in individual poems,

> what affects our hearts
> Is not the exactness of peculiar parts;
> 'Tis not a lip or eye we beauty call,
> But the joint force and full result of all.[6]

The poets' eulogies have, in a way, become a victim of their own success. Many of them have proved so memorable, have struck common chords in so many readers' hearts down the centuries, that they are now in danger of sounding like clichés, or statements of the obvious. One of the purposes of the notes in this anthology is to remind readers of the point and aptness of the poets' phrases and images, and thus to restore to their encomia some of their original edge and precision.

Just as the poets' general comments on the work of their peers concentrate on distilling the essential spirit of their fellow artists' work, rather than on analysing particular works and local details, so their remarks on form, metre, and diction present the *upshot* of their more technical deliberations, rather than the *process* by which their formal, metrical and linguistic decisions were arrived at. Poets regularly allude to the range of skills and to the sheer amount of hard work and devotion which their profession necessitates [11 (ii) (Jonson); 24 (Pope); 33 (Johnson); 71 (Arnold); 222 (Cowley)]. Wordsworth (sometimes thought of as a poet who valued spontaneity at the expense of craftsmanship) specifically praised Shelley (the most passionate of believers in poetic inspiration) for being 'one of the best *artists* of us all: I mean in workmanship of style'.[7]

A number of poets have written or planned technical manuals on their art. Ben Jonson's dialogue on poetry – in which John Donne and himself appeared as principal interlocutors – was burnt in a fire; Dryden never produced his promised treatise on prosody. And poets' letters and recorded conversations give some hints of the intensive technical discussion and advice which occurs in private deliberations and consultations between practitioners. But when writing for the general reader, poets have usually not thought it appropriate to invite the reader directly into the artist's workshop or to expound their technical principles for the layman's benefit, but have, rather, offered finished poetry which exemplifies its own precepts, and from which the poet's technical decisions and priorities must be *deduced*. Thus, writing about the sonnet [47], Wordsworth, in a rapid survey of the various uses to which that slender poetic form has been put, demonstrates the sonnet's capacity to encompass much in little (the subject of his poem). Writing of the mellifluous seductiveness of the courtier-poet Sir Charles Sedley [239], Rochester manifests a similar seductiveness in his own verse. Carew [165] celebrates Donne with a string of the very 'conceits' and 'strong lines' which he celebrates as that poet's great glory. Denham's expressed desire [221] that his verse should 'flow' like the River Thames achieves its own ambition. In our own time, Ted Hughes writes a poem ('The Thought-Fox') which simultaneously evokes a fox outside in the darkness and the first stirrings, in the darkness of the mind, of the matter which will become a poem – the poem we are reading. In the most extensive 'technical' passage included in this anthology [26], Pope provides, in thirty-seven lines, a complete manual on how to write (and how not to write) heroic couplets. Pope's precepts are more deeply and fully felt, because they are implicit and self-illustrative; every reader has to dance and sing each of them out inwardly. When we read that

> True ease in writing comes from art, not chance,
> As those move easiest who have learned to dance,

we realise that Pope is manifesting, not merely stating, the truth which he enunciates. The effortless-seeming limpidity of the poetic 'movement' in these lines has, we recognise, been hard won, and is the end-product of much offstage labour exerted in mastering the complexities of numerous poetical 'dance steps'. The kind of 'technical' discussion which Pope is here providing requires to be received and understood at more than the merely cerebral level.

The fact that poets constantly stress the immortality of their art, its capacity to speak beyond the moment of its birth is nowadays, as we have seen, sometimes interpreted as revealing their ideological naïveté, their obliviousness to the degree to which every work of art is bound by the historical context of which it is a 'product'. But critics who argue thus often forget that it is, surprisingly, those poets who insist most vehemently on the trans-historical dimension of poetry who both display the acutest historical sense and the most active involvement with the ideas and events of their own times. Shelley, in many ways the most 'idealist' of poet-critics, both rested his *Defence of Poetry* on a historical framework of great range and precision, and engaged vigorously as pamphleteer and propagandist in the revolutionary politics of his day. Dryden and Pope, often supposed (as good 'Augustans') to have valued the general over the particular, and to have believed in a simple uniformity of human nature across historical and geographical boundaries, wrote satires which are dense in topical allusion, and researched the historical contexts of the poets they translated with an imaginative thoroughness which would put many an antiquarian to shame. Thus, when Dryden writes [87] that 'mankind is ever the same, and nothing lost out of Nature, though every thing is altered', he must not be thought to be manifesting a naïve obliviousness to the immense changes in human beliefs, values, and institutions which are brought about by historical change. For Dryden, both halves of his paradox must carry equal weight. It is precisely *because* he is so acutely aware of the degree to which 'every thing is altered' that he feels prompted to note Chaucer's extraordinary power to discover that which is permanent in human nature. Chaucer has immortalised the 'general characters' of men precisely by attending to the 'monks, and friars, and canons, and lady abbesses, and nuns' who surrounded him in his own fourteenth century. But his artist's eye has penetrated beyond the merely documentary, and has discerned the continuities of human nature which manifest themselves *within* the contingent circumstances of the world in which he lived.

Modern readers' suspicions that poets' comments on their predecessors will inevitably involve personal axe-grinding and/or an element of (perhaps unconscious) envy often seem to derive from two main sources: from the pronouncements and practice of a number of recent poets, and from the writings of academic critics who have recast the subjects of their study in their own image. Some twentieth-century poets do, indeed, seem to have used their writing on other poets as an occasion to reflect on their own artistic concerns. A reader who encounters, for example, T.S. Eliot's evocations of Webster and Donne in 'Whispers of Immortality' is more likely to be struck by their similarity, in terms of subject-matter, imagery and ethos, to other poems in Eliot's 1920 volume, than by their power to evoke the distinctive qualities of those Jacobean writers. And Eliot's account (in his essay 'The Metaphysical Poets') of how a poet's mind 'is constantly amalgamating disparate experience' has frequently reminded readers of Eliot's own 'Love Song of J. Alfred Prufrock' or 'Preludes', to which it might be thought to have more relevance than to the poems of Donne, Herbert, or Marvell:

> The ordinary man's experience is chaotic, irregular, fragmentary. The latter falls in love, or reads Spinoza, and these two experiences have nothing to do with each other, or with the noise of the typewriter or the smell of cooking; in the mind of the poet these experiences are always forming new wholes.[8]

Similarly, when we read in the 'Note' which accompanies Ted Hughes's *A Choice of Shakespeare's Verse* that Shakespeare's works are animated by a single 'great recurrent dream' in which an ancient goddess 'of natural law and of love ..., of all sensation and organic life' fights it out with 'the puritan mind – a mind desensitized to the true nature of nature',[9] we may more readily recall some of Hughes's own leading concerns in his poem *Gaudete* or his essay 'Myth and Education' than the plays of Shakespeare which are Hughes's ostensible subject.

It is perhaps not surprising that academics, oppressed by their obligation to publish or perish, and constantly on the lookout for 'new ideas' and for research projects which have not already been 'done', should have been subconsciously tempted to imbue the poets with their own malaise, attributing to them an 'anxiety of influence' and a consciousness of 'the burden of the past' which are so characteristic of their own profession. For the late Philip Larkin, however, the poetic past was no burden, because it was of no consequence whatsoever :

> Poems don't come from other poems, they come from being oneself, in life. Every man is an island, entire of himself [sic], as Donne said. This American idea – it is American, isn't it? Started with Pound and Eliot? – that somehow every new poem has to be the sum of all old poems, like the latest Ford, well, it's the sort of idea lecturers get, if you'll excuse my saying so. Makes sense and so on. Only it's not how poetry works.[10]

The evidence collected in this anthology suggests that Eliot's and Hughes's appropriation of older poets for the purposes of self-defence and self-examination, the academics' attribution to the poets of oedipal envy and disquiet, and Larkin's wholesale dismissal of past poetry as useless to the present practitioner, are all, historically speaking, anomalies and aberrations. For the overwhelming majority of the items in this book affirm the poets' felt need to study and revere their predecessors, and stress the enabling and enriching power which the poetry of the past has on the poetry of the present.

The major English poets are all steeped in the works of their predecessors. Usually, this is clearly apparent. On occasions, a poet's need to assert the distinctiveness of his own voice can conceal the depth and intimacy of his knowledge of his forebears' work. Pope's poetry occupied a considerably lower place in the affections of Wordsworth than that of Chaucer, Spenser, Shakespeare, or Milton, but he nevertheless once declared that he 'could repeat ... several thousand lines of Pope' from memory.[11] The poets have three main reasons for valuing and treasuring their predecessors. First, the study of past poetry is the fundamental way in which a poet learns his craft. For Ben Jonson [11 (iii)], the capacity to distil and transform nutritious substance from one's predecessors, 'to draw forth out of the best and choicest flowers with the bee, and turn all into honey', is one of the prime requirements for any poet. For Pope [27], the work of Homer was 'like a copious nursery, which contains the seed and first productions of every kind, out of which those who followed him have but selected some particular plants, each according to his fancy, to cultivate and beautify'; Homer was [28] 'the father of poetic diction; the first who taught that "language of the gods" to men'.

Second, poets are convinced that, since their predecessors are godlike creators, their works are as much a part of Nature as any other phenomena or personages in the sublunary world. For Shelley [56], therefore, 'one great poet is a masterpiece of nature which another poet not only ought to study but must study'. Pope registers the impossibility, for a poet, of distinguishing between the Nature which he apprehends directly, and that which he discovers in the works of his peers; when Virgil studied his greatest predecessor, Pope records, 'Nature and Homer, were, he found, the same'.[12]

Third, poets have experienced the work of their predecessors with such intensity, that they have felt to be in their great forebears' presence – even, in some instances, to have been possessed by the spirits of those forebears. For Daniel [4], poetry is the place where dialogue is achieved across the ages; it is the means by which 'we do confer with who are gone,/ And the dead-living unto counsel call'. Other poets have felt such a 'sympathetic bond' [20 (Roscommon)] with a fellow artist of the past that they have spoken of themselves as a virtual reincarnation of that earlier poet. Dryden claimed a 'soul congenial' to Chaucer's. Spenser [83] felt an 'infusion sweet' of Chaucer's spirit into his own. Landor [359] thought Keats 'cognate' to both Spenser and Chaucer. Such patterns of congeniality have been felt to transcend national frontiers. Cowley's affinity with Virgil inclined Denham [223] to believe Pythagoras' doctrine of the transmigration of souls. Pope's translation of Homer made the same doctrine attractive to Christopher Pitt [265].

The poets' characteristic attitude to their predecessors is epitomised by Pope [25]. The young poet, perusing the works of his great forebears, 'Glows while he reads, but trembles as he writes'. The trembling is partly humility at the formidable prospect of treading where Homer, Virgil, Ovid, Chaucer, Spenser, Shakespeare and Milton have trodden before. It is partly excitement at the thrill of his own talents, talents which might equip him to become a member of such august company. The poets' attitude is simultaneously self-assertive and and self-abasing. Chaucer [79] sends his *Troilus and Criseyde* out into the world, hoping that it will be read and understood widely, and that no one will tamper with its wording, but simultaneously instructing his poem to be 'subject' to 'allè poesy' [humble in the face of the great classical poets] and to 'kiss the steppès were as thou seest pace/Virgil, Ovid, Homer, Lucan, and Stace'. Keats [154] prays that, having been 'consumèd in the fire' of Shakespeare's *King Lear* he might be given 'new phoenix-wings' for poetical flights of his own.

The poets' feelings of reverence towards and indebtedness to their predecessors derive from their sense that, whatever their particular differences of style or emphasis, all members of the community of poets are united in their common pursuit of a species of truth which is unique and irreplaceable. When commenting on the effect of their art on readers, poets of widely different periods and backgrounds are in agreement that a proper response to poetry involves feelings of *recognition* and *assent*. The poet seems to have put into words something which, once uttered, seems ungainsayably true. For Pope [158], true poetic wit is 'Something whose truth convinced at sight we find,/That gives us back the image of our mind'. Johnson speaks of the poet's ability to 'awaken those ideas that slumber in the heart'.[13] Wordsworth remarks that his poetry was designed 'to remind men of their knowledge, as it lurks inoperative and unvalued in their minds'.[14] Keats [358] writes that poetry 'should strike the reader as a wording of his own highest thoughts, and appear almost a remembrance'. Recently, Ted Hughes has described poetic thinking as 'whatever kind of trick or skill it is that enables us to catch [our] elusive or shadowy thoughts, and collect them together, and hold them still so we can get a really good look at them'.[15]

But if poetry produces a spark of recognition, that which is recognised is not anything that readers were conscious that they already knew. The passages in this anthology show that poetry-readers' feelings of assent and recognition are characteristically accompanied by feelings of discovery, amazement, wonder and awe – and sometimes of extreme disquiet. The truth captured by the poets strikes the reader as, in Johnson's phrase, 'at once natural and new'.[16] When Shakespeare provokes us to tears, notes Pope [129], our first reaction is one of surprise; it is only later that we realise that the tears were inevitable. Shakespeare's talent was to 'light up' the hitherto 'unknown' regions of the human heart [152 (Landor)]. It is precisely the function of poetry, observes Coleridge [309], to direct us to 'loveliness' and 'wonders' 'for which, in consequence of the film of familiarity and selfish solicitude, we have eyes, yet see not, ears that hear not, and hearts that neither feel nor understand'. To be shaken out of our normal mental habits is not always a comfortable experience. It is therefore not surprising that great poets are seldom instantly popular [45 (Wordsworth)]. But the truths which the poets tell have the power to survive, and to make us realise how partial, fragmentary, and superficial a view we normally have of the world which we inhabit. Poetry 'makes us the inhabitants of a world to which the familiar world is a chaos' [62 (Shelley)]. Far from leaving us comfortably cosseted by the values of our own culture, it 'defeats the curse which binds us to be subjected to the accident of surrounding impressions' [62 (Shelley)]. Poetry does not simply 'reflect faithfully' men's feelings as we know them from everyday life; it also 'rectifies' them by rearranging and ordering them in accordance with 'eternal Nature, and the great moving spirit of things' [306 (Wordsworth)]. It is precisely the poet's duty, even when writing about contemporary ideas, persons, and events, to 'divest himself of the prejudices of his age and country' and to 'disregard present laws and opinions', thus rising 'to general and transcendental truths, which will always be the same' [33 (Johnson)].

Such 'transcendental truths' are not summarisable pieces of portable wisdom, didactic platitudes or 'eternal verities' which somehow float free of the particular language in which they are articulated, or the particular imaginative situations in which they are embodied. The poets discover general truths which are *immanent in* the local and the particular, and inseparable from the particular circumstances in which they find expression. It is still frequently assumed that poetry merely depicts or records an outer world (of facts and phenomena) and an inner world (of feelings and emotions) that are already available to us. The poets assert that their work reveals to us facets of a permanent Nature that would otherwise be invisible and inaccessible [23 (Pope)]. The poet has a more 'comprehensive soul'; he has, somewhere within him, more of the sum total of human propensities and susceptibilities, than ordinary men and women [87, 128 (Dryden); 38 (Wordsworth)]; he reveals to humans what they *might* feel, not merely what they *do* feel. Without the aid of poetic thought, writes Ted Hughes, even our own minds 'lie in us like the fish in the pond of a man who cannot fish'.[17] It is thus in poetry that we actually *discover* what the world, and human nature, are like, or might be like. Our feelings of assent and recognition, with their concomitant feelings of amazement and awe, are a register of the fact that the poets are able (in Coleridge's word) to 'find' a depth in us which we previously were not aware even existed; that they can make contact with, shape, and activate, dim intuitions, and fragmentary perceptions about ourselves and our world which we were previously not conscious that we possessed. The poets reveal to us a world more truly wonderful and more truly terrible than any we could have imagined without them. It is on such grounds that the poets can claim that poetry is a source of matchless insight, a 'lance' 'brandished at the eyes of ignorance' [125 (Jonson)], or a star-like inspiration for the benighted [307 (Wordsworth)]. It is on such grounds that they can claim that poetic genius 'widen[s] the sphere of human sensibility' and introduces 'a new element into the intellectual universe' [44 (Wordsworth)].

It is because they discover and reveal the possible and the potential in human nature, rather than merely recording what seems 'natural' from the perspective of one time and one place, that poems have more significance than is ever apparent at the moment of their first appearance. Poems *accrue* meaning and potency, the more their implications become apparent to successive generations of readers. The 'honours' due to the company of poets thus 'with increase of ages grow,/ As streams roll down, enlarging as they flow' [25 (Pope)]. Poets can be thought to divine the future in embryo [15 (Cowley)]. Poets are 'the hierophants of an unapprehended inspiration; the mirrors of the gigantic shadows which futurity casts upon the present' [63 (Shelley)]. Chaucer epitomises the poet's distinctive gifts, in being [86 (Dryden)] a 'perpetual fountain of good sense'; his genius is ever-flowing, to sustain and refresh, in slightly different ways, all those readers who have come, down the centuries, to drink from his spring. Chaucer is thus justly 'time-honoured' [91 (Wordsworth)]. When experiencing the poets' imaginings we are transported from the prison of our own personality, time and place, and are allowed, with all others who read the same work, to 'repose on the stability of truth' [134 (Johnson)]. Nothing less than the kind of truth provided by the poets will be found ultimately satisfying. Their godlike conjoining powers allow us imaginative access to events, experiences and sentiments which would, in any other conceivable circumstances, be either altogether inaccessible or deeply, and merely, disturbing. Poetry is thus inestimably valuable, and the name of poet justly 'reverend', since 'nothing can more adorn humanity' [9 (Jonson)]. A nation with poetry is a nation to be greatly honoured. Poetry can 'do much more with one poor pen/ Than all the powers of princes can effect' [5 (Daniel)].

The poets would be likely to regard those academic commentators who, for whatever reason, withhold their sympathy and refuse to surrender to the transporting power of the poets' imaginings as the modern equivalents of the critics described by Wordsworth [46]:

> critics too petulant to be passive to a genuine poet, and too feeble to grapple with him; men who take upon them to report of the course which *he* holds whom they are utterly unable to accompany – confounded if he turn quick upon the wing, dismayed if he soar steadily 'into the region'; men of palsied imaginations and indurated hearts, in whose minds all healthy action is languid, ... judges whose censure is auspicious, and whose praise ominous!

Such critics regard their analytical objectivity and their refusal to collaborate with the poets or to succumb to their charms, as the essential means whereby they can alert us to the real significance of what the poets are saying. In the poets' view, these critics would have, wilfully, rendered themselves utterly incapable of assimilating, or even comprehending, the uniquely precious revelations which poetic art has to offer.

Notes

1. Ted Hughes, *Poetry in the Making* (London, 1967), p. 17.
2. W.B.Yeats, *Essays and Introductions* (London, 1961), p. 266.
3. 'Life of Pope', G. Birkbeck Hill, (ed.) *Lives of the Poets*, (3 vols., Oxford, 1905), III, 227.

4. 'Introduction: Listening to Poetry', *Here Today* (London, 1963), p. [12].
5. ibid., pp. [11]–[12].
6. Alexander Pope, *An Essay on Criticism*, 243–6.
7. Markham L. Peacock (ed.) *The Critical Opinions of William Wordsworth* (Baltimore, Md, 1950), p. 349.
8. *Selected Essays* (1932; rpt. London, 1944), p. 287.
9. Hughes, *A Choice of Shakespeare's Verse* (London, 1971), pp. 182, 187, 193.
10. Interview with John Haffenden, *London Magazine*, n.s., 20 (April/May 1980), p. 89.
11. *The Critical Opinions of William Wordsworth*, p. 246.
12. *An Essay on Criticism*, 135.
13. 'Life of Dryden', *Lives of the Poets*, I, 459.
14. *The Critical Opinions of William Wordsworth*, p. 444.
15. *Poetry in the Making*, p. 58.
16. 'Life of Cowley', *Lives of the Poets*, I, 20.
17. *Poetry in the Making*, p. 58.

Part One

ON POETRY

1 *Poetic immortality*

One day I wrote her name upon the strand,[1]
   But came the waves, and washèd it away;
   Again I wrote it, with a second hand,
   But came the tide, and made my pains his prey.
'Vain man,' said she, 'that dost in vain assay[2]
   A mortal thing so to immortalise;
   For I myself shall like to this decay,
   And eke[3] my name be wipèd out likewise.'
'Not so,' quoth I. 'Let baser things devise[4]
   To die in dust, but you shall live by fame;
   My verse your virtues rare shall éternise,
   And in the heavens write your glorious name.
Where, whenas death shall all the world subdue,
   Our love shall live, and later life renew.'
      ((1595) Edmund Spenser (c. 1552–99), Sonnet 75 from *Amoretti*)

1. beach. 2. try. 3. also. 4. contrive.

2 *The poet as creator*

There is no art delivered to mankind that hath not the works of Nature for his principal object, without which they could not consist, and on which they so depend as they become actors and players, as it were, of what Nature will have set forth. So doth the astronomer look upon the stars, and, by that he seeth, setteth down what order Nature hath taken therein. So do the geometrician and arithmetician in their diverse sorts of quantities. So doth the musician in times[1] tell you which by nature agree, which not. The natural philosopher[2] thereon hath his name, and the moral philosopher standeth upon[3] the natural virtues, vices, and passions of man; and 'follow Nature', saith he, 'therein, and thou shalt not err.' The lawyer saith what men have determined,[4] the historian what men have done. The grammarian speaketh only of the rules of speech; and the rhetorician and logician, considering what in Nature will soonest prove and persuade, thereon give artificial rules, which still are compassed[5] within the circle of a question according to the proposed matter. The physician weigheth the nature of a man's body, and the nature of things helpful or hurtful unto it. And the metaphysic,[6] though it be in the second[7] and abstract notions, and therefore be counted supernatural, yet doth he indeed build upon the depth of Nature. Only the poet, disdaining to be tied to any such subjection, lifted up with the vigour of his own invention, doth grow in effect another Nature, in making things either better than Nature bringeth forth, or, quite anew, forms such as never were in Nature, as the heroes, demi-gods, Cyclops, Chimeras,[8] Furies, and such like; so as he goeth hand in hand with Nature, not enclosed within the narrow warrant of her gifts,[9] but freely ranging only within the zodiac[10] of his own wit.

Nature never set forth the earth in so rich tapestry as divers poets have done, neither with pleasant rivers, fruitful trees, sweet-smelling flowers, nor whatsoever else may make the too much loved earth more lovely. Her world is brazen;[11] the poets only deliver a golden.

((wr. ?1581–3; pub. 1595) Sir Philip Sidney (1554–86), from *An Apology for Poetry*)

1. in the measures of his music. 2. scientist. 3. takes as his province. 4. made decisions about. 5. circumscribed. 6. metaphysician; a student of matters lying beyond the physical world. 7. because these notions are mental concepts *abstracted from* Nature. 8. in Greek mythology, fire-breathing monsters with lions' heads, goats' bodies and dragons' tails. 9. dependent on her limited sphere of patronage. 10. range, scope. 11. made of brass; classical myth had depicted the world as passing through several ages, of which the age of brass represented a deterioration after those of gold and silver.

3 The poet as enchanter

Now therein of all sciences (I speak still of human, and according to the human conceits[1]) is our poet the monarch. For he doth not only show the way, but giveth so sweet a prospect into the way, as will entice any man to enter into it. Nay, he doth, as if your journey should lie through a fair vineyard, at the first give you a cluster of grapes, that, full of that taste, you may long to pass further. He beginneth not with obscure definitions which must blur the margent with interpretations,[2] and load the memory with doubtfulness;[3] but he cometh to you with words set in delightful proportion, either accompanied with, or prepared for, the well-enchanting skill of music; and with a tale, forsooth, he cometh unto you, with a tale which holdeth children from play, and old men from the chimney corner.

((wr. ?1581–3; pub. 1595) Sir Philip Sidney (1554–86), from *An Apology for Poetry*)

1. understanding. 2. as in scholarly works, the pages of which have their margins offputtingly crammed with erudite commentary. 3. ambiguity.

4 Poetry as communion across time

O blessed letters,[1] that combine in one
  All ages past, and make one live with all;
By you we do confer with who are gone,
  And the dead-living unto counsel call;
By you the unborn shall have communion
  Of what we feel, and what doth us befall.
Soul of the world, Knowledge, without thee,
  What hath the earth that truly glorious is?
Why should our pride make such a stir to be,
  To be forgot? What good is like to this,
  To do worthy the writing, and to write
Worthy the reading, and the world's delight?

((1599) Samuel Daniel (1562–1619),[2] from 'Musophilus')

1. literature. 2. Daniel, court poet to both Elizabeth I and James I, wrote in a variety of genres, from the sonnet sequence (*Delia*, 1592) to the epic (*The Civil Wars*, 1595–1609). Among his admirers have been Lamb, Wordsworth, and Coleridge.

5 Poetry in England

Power above powers, O heavenly Eloquence,
    That with the strong rein of commanding words
    Dost manage, guide, and master the eminence
    Of men's affections[1] more than all their swords,
    Shall we not offer to thy excellence
    The richest treasure that our wit affords?
Thou that canst do much more with one poor pen,
    Than all the powers of princes can effect;
    And draw, divert, dispose and fashion men
    Better than force or rigour can direct.
    Should we this ornament of glory then,
    As the unmaterial fruits of shades[2] neglect?
Or should we, careless, come behind the rest
    In power of words, that go before in worth?
    Whenas our accent's equal to the best,
    Is able greater wonders to bring forth?
    When all that ever hotter spirits expressed
    Comes bettered by the patience of the north.
And who, in time, knows whither we may vent
    The treasure of our tongue, to what strange shores
    This gain of our best glory shall be sent,
    To enrich unknowing nations with our stores?
    What worlds in the yet unformèd occident
    May come refined with the accents that are ours?
Or who can tell for what great work in hand
    The greatness of our style is now ordained?
    What powers it shall bring in, what spirits command,
    What thoughts let out, what humours[3] keep restrained?
    What mischief it may powerfully withstand,
    And what fair ends may thereby be attained?
And as for Poesy, mother of this force,
    That breeds, brings forth, and nourishes this might,
    Teaching it in a loose yet measured course,
    With comely motions how to go upright;
    And fostering it with bountiful discourse,
    Adorns it thus in fashions of delight,
What should I say? since it is well approved
    The speech of heaven, with whom they have commérce,
    That only seem out of themselves removed,
    And do with more than human skills converse;
    Those numbers, wherewith heaven and earth are moved,
    Show weakness speaks in prose, but power in verse.
        ((1599) Samuel Daniel (1562–1619),[4] from 'Musophilus')

1. men's most potent passions. 2. the immaterial products of phantasms. 3. eccentricities. 4. see 4 n.2.

6 In praise of rhyme

I see not how that can be taken for an ill custom, which Nature hath thus ratified, all nations received, time so long confirmed, the effects such as it performs those offices of motion for which it is employed: delighting the ear, stirring the heart, and satisfying the judgement in such sort, as I doubt whether ever single numbers[1] will do in our climate, if they show no more work of wonder than yet we see. And if ever they prove to become any thing, it must be by the approbation of many ages that must give them their strength for any operation, or before the world will feel where the pulse, life, and energy lies, which now we are sure where to have in our rhymes, whose known frame hath those due stays for the mind, those encounters of touch,[2] as makes the motion certain, though the variety be infinite. Nor will the general sort for whom we write (the wise being above books) taste these laboured measures but as an orderly prose when we have all done. For this kind acquaintance and continual familiarity ever had betwixt our ear and this cadence is grown to so intimate a friendship, as it will now hardly ever be brought to miss it. For be the verse never so good, never so full, it seems not to satisfy nor to breed that delight, as when it is met and combined with a like sounding accent;[3] which seems as the jointure,[4] without which it hangs loose, and cannot subsist, but runs wildly on, like a tedious fancy,[5] without a close.[6]

((1603) Samuel Daniel (1562–1619),[7] from *A Defence of Rhyme*)

1. lines of verse not joined by rhyme. 2. meetings/correspondences of note/tone. 3. tone. 4. connection. 5. piece of improvisatory music. 6. concluding cadence. 7. see 4 n.2.

7 *Poetic frenzy*

The poet's eye, in a fine frenzy[1] rolling,
Doth glance from heaven to earth, from earth to heaven;
And, as imagination bodies forth
The forms of things unknown, the poet's pen
Turns them to shapes, and gives to airy nothing
A local habitation and a name.

((wr. ?1595–6; pub. 1600) William Shakespeare (1564–1616), from Theseus's speech in *A Midsummer Night's Dream* (V.i))

1. wild excitement.

8 *Poetry a lasting monument*

Not marble, nor the gilded monuments
Of princes, shall outlive this powerful rhyme;
But you shall shine more bright in these conténts[1]
Than unswept stone,[2] besmeared with sluttish time.
When wasteful[3] war shall statues overturn,
And broils root out the work of masonry,[4]
Nor Mars his sword, nor war's quick[5] fire shall burn
The living record of your memory.
'Gainst death and all-oblivious enmity[6]
Shall you pace forth; your praise shall still find room
Even in the eyes of all posterity,
That wear this world out to the ending doom.[7]

So, till the judgement that yourself arise,
You live in this, and dwell in lovers' eyes.
((1609) William Shakespeare (1564–1616), Sonnet 55)

1. the contents of my poems about you. 2. a neglected tombstone. 3. destructive. 4. the art of the mason. 5. fierce. 6. the enmity of being altogether forgotten. 7. that will last till doomsday.

9 *In defence of poetry*

If it may stand with your most wished content,
I can refell opinion[1] and approve
The state of poesy, such as it is,
Blessèd, eternal, and most true divine.
Indeed, if you will look on Poesy
As she appears in many, poor and lame,
Patched up in remnants and old worn rags,
Half starved for want of her peculiar food,
Sacred invention; then, I must confirm
Both your conceit[2] and censure of her merit.
But view her in her glorious ornaments,
Attirèd in the majesty of art,
Set high in spirit, with the precious taste
Of sweet philosophy, and, which is most,
Crowned with the rich traditions of a soul
That hates to have her dignity profaned
With any relish of an earthly thought;
Oh, then how proud a presence doth she bear!
Then is she like herself, fit to be seen
Of none but grave and consecrated eyes;
Nor is it any blemish to her fame,
That such lean, ignorant, and blasted wits,
Such brainless gulls, should utter their stolen wares
With such applauses in our vulgar ears;
Or that their slubbered[3] lines have current pass
From the fat judgements of the multitude,
But that this barren and infected age
Should set no difference 'twixt these empty spirits
And a true poet – than which reverend name
Nothing can more adorn humanity.
((1601) Ben Jonson (1572–1637), from Lorenzo junior's speech in
Every Man in his Humour (Quarto edition, V.iii.))

1. refute popular prejudice; the speaker is defending poetry against the low esteem in which his father says it is currently held. 2. conception. 3. sloppy, slovenly.

10 *The uses of poetry*

It nourisheth and instructeth our youth; delights our age; adorns our prosperity; comforts our adversity; entertains us at home; keeps us company abroad; travels with us; watches; divides the times of our earnest[1] and sports; shares in our country recesses[2] and recreations; insomuch as the wisest and best learned have thought her the absolute mistress of manners, and nearest of kin to virtue. And whereas they entitle philosophy to be a rigid and austere poesy, they have, on the contrary, styled poesy a dulcet and gentle philosophy, which leads on and guides us by the hand to action, with a ravishing delight and incredible sweetness.

((1640) Ben Jonson (1572–1637), from *Timber*)

1. serious activities. 2. retreats.

11 Qualities required of a poet

(i) *Natural wit*

First, we require in our poet or maker (for that title our language affords him, elegantly, with the Greek[1]) a goodness of natural wit. For, whereas all other arts consist of doctrine and precepts, the poet must be able by nature and instinct to pour out the treasures of his mind; and, as Seneca saith, 'Aliquando secundum Anacreontem insanire, iucundum esse' ['Sometimes Anacreon finds it pleasurable to rave'],[2] by which he understands the poetical rapture. And according to that of Plato, 'Frustra poeticas fores sui compos pulsavit' ['The sane man knocks in vain at the portals of poetry'];[3] and of Aristotle, 'Nullum magnum ingenium sine mixtura dementiae fuit. Nec potest grande aliquid, et supra ceteros loqui, nisi mota mens' ['No great mind has ever existed without a touch of madness. Nor is the mind able to speak loftily and above others, unless it is inspired'].[4] Then it riseth higher, as by a divine instinct, when it contemns common and known conceptions. It utters somewhat above a mortal mouth. Then it gets aloft, and flies away with his rider, whither, before, it was doubtful to ascend. This the poets understood by their Helicon,[5] Pegasus,[6] or Parnassus.[7]

(ii) *Practice of his art*

To this perfection of nature in our poet, we require exercise of those parts, and frequent. If his wit will not arrive suddenly at the dignity of the ancients, let him not yet fall out with it, quarrel, or be over-hastily angry; offer to turn it away from study, in a humour;[8] but come to it again upon better cogitation; try another time, with labour. If then it succeed not, cast not away the quills yet; nor scratch the wainscot, beat not the poor desk; but bring all to the forge, and file, again; turn it anew. There is no statute law of the kingdom bids you be a poet against your will, or the first quarter. If it come, in a year or two, it is well. The common rhymers pour forth verses, such as they are, extempore, but there never comes from them one sense worth the life of a day.

(iii) *The power of imitation*

The third requisite in our poet or maker is imitation: to be able to convert the substance or riches of another poet to his own use; to make choice of one excellent man above the rest, and so to follow him as the copy may be mistaken for the principal; not as a creature that swallows what it takes in, crude, raw or indigested; but that feeds with an appetite, and hath a stomach to concoct,[9] divide,[10] and turn all into nourishment; not to imitate servilely, as Horace saith,[11] and catch at vices for virtue; but to draw forth out of the best and choicest flowers with the bee, and turn all into honey, work it into one relish and savour.

((1640) Ben Jonson (1572–1637), from *Timber*)

1. 'Poiētēs' is Greek for both 'poet' and 'maker'. 2. *On Tranquillity of Mind*, 17. 10–11; for Anacreon, see 165 n.11; for Seneca, see 17 n.13. 3. *Phaedrus*, 245a. 4. *Problems*, 30.1; as well as being the two greatest Greek philosophers, Plato and Aristotle were two of the most often-quoted literary critics of antiquity. 5. a mountain home of the Muses. 6. the Muses' winged horse. 7. another mountain seat of Apollo, god of poetry, and the Muses. 8. bad temper. 9. digest. 10. break down. 11. *Ars Poetica*, ll. 131–5; Horace's poem, which Jonson translated, was the most famous of all ancient literary critical writings during the Renaissance.

12 Mirth and poetry

Then to the well-trod stage anon,
If Jonson's learnèd sock[1] be on,
Or sweetest Shakespeare, fancy's child,
Warble his native[2] wood-notes wild,
And ever against eating cares,
Lap me in soft Lydian airs,[3]
Married to immortal verse
Such as the meeting soul[4] may pierce[5]
In notes, with many a winding bout[6]
Of linkèd sweetness long drawn out,
With wanton heed[7] and giddy cunning,[8]
The melting voice through mazes running;
Untwisting all the chains that tie
The hidden soul of harmony.[9]
That Orpheus'[10] self may heave his head
From golden slumber on a bed
Of heaped Elysian[11] flowers, and hear
Such strains as would have won the ear
Of Pluto, to have quite set free
His half-regained Euridice.[12]
These delights, if thou canst give,
Mirth, with thee I mean to live.

((1645) John Milton (1608–74), from 'L'Allegro'[13])

1. the slipper worn by comic actors on the Greek and Roman stage; Jonson constantly evoked Greek and Roman precedent for his own dramatic practice. 2. natural, untutored. 3. the Lydian mode, in Greek music, was renowned for its soft tenderness, bordering on effeminacy. 4. the soul which responds to the music. 5. penetrate. 6. coil, hence passage (in music). 7. attention. 8. skill. 9. as the singer's voice runs through the mazes of sound, so all the chains which entangle the hidden soul (the essence of harmony) are loosed. 10. the archetypal poet-musician of Greek myth, who could charm the beasts with his songs. 11. Elysium, in Greek mythology, was the realm of the happy dead. 12. when Orpheus' wife Eurydice died, he followed her to the Underworld; his music so charmed Pluto and Persephone (Roman form: Proserpina), king and queen of Hades, that he was allowed to lead her back to the daylight, on condition that he did not look back; he did, however, and Eurydice consequently had to return to the Underworld. 13. 'The Cheerful Man'.

13 Poetry and the melancholy man

Sometime[1] let gorgeous[2] Tragedy
In sceptred pall[3] come sweeping by,
Presenting Thebes' or Pelops' line,
Or the tale of Troy divine,[4]
Or what, though rare, of later age
Ennobled hath the buskined[5] stage.
But, O sad virgin! that thy power
Might raise Musaeus[6] from his bower,
Or bid the soul of Orpheus sing
Such notes as, warbled to the string,
Drew iron tears down Pluto's cheek,
And made hell grant what love did seek;[7]
Or call up him that left half-told
The story of Cambuscan bold,
Of Camball, and of Algarsife,
And who had Canace to wife,
That owned the virtuous ring and glass
And of the wondrous horse of brass
On which the Tartar king did ride;[8]
And if ought else great bards beside
In sage and solemn tunes have sung,
Of tourneys, and of trophies hung,[9]
Of forests and enchantments drear,
Where more is meant than meets the ear.

((1645) John Milton (1608–74), from 'Il Penseroso'[10])

1. sometimes. 2. in stately dress. 3. regal cloak. 4. Greek legends, the subjects of plays by the three extant Greek tragedians, Aeschylus, Sophocles and Euripides. 5. the buskin was the high boot thought (erroneously) to have been worn by Greek tragic actors to enhance their stature. 6. a legendary Greek poet. 7. see 12 n.12. 8. the story alluded to is that of Chaucer's 'Squire's Tale', a fable of magic and fantasy, left unfinished. 9. spoils of battle hung up as offerings to the gods; Milton alludes to Spenser's *Fairy Queen* (see 103). 10. 'The Thoughtful Man'.

14 Sacred music and poetry

Blest pair of sirens,[1] pledges[2] of heaven's joy,
Sphere-borne harmonious sisters, Voice and Verse,
Wed your divine sounds, and mixed power employ
Dead things with imbreathed sense able to pierce,[3]
And to our high-raised fantasy[4] present,
That undisturbèd song of pure concent,[5]
Ay[6] sung before the sapphire-coloured throne
To him that sits thereon
With saintly shout and solemn jubilee,[7]
Where the bright seraphim[8] in burning row
Their loud uplifted angel trumpets blow,
And the cherubic[9] host in thousand choirs

Touch their immortal harps of golden wires,
With those just spirits that wear victorious palms,[10]
Hymns devout and holy psalms
Singing everlastingly;
That we on earth with undiscording[11] voice
May rightly answer that melodious noise,[12]
As once we did, till disproportioned[13] sin
Jarred against nature's chime,[14] and with harsh din
Broke the fair music that all creatures made
To their great Lord, whose love their motion swayed[15]
In perfect diapason,[16] whilst they stood
In first obedience, and their state of good.
O may we soon again renew that song,
And keep in tune with heaven, till God ere long
To his celestial consort[17] us unite,
To live with him, and sing in endless morn of light.
((1645) John Milton (1608–74), 'At a Solemn Music')

1. in Plato (*Republic*, X.616–17), a siren (singing maiden) is said to stand on each of the eight concentric spheres which constitute the universe; the concerted sound of the sirens' voices produces a perfect harmony. 2. (i) offspring, children (ii) assurances, promises (because earthly music reminds us of the music of heaven). 3. just as Orpheus' music (see 12 ns.10 and 12) could attract trees, stones, and rocks. 4. imagination. 5. harmony. 6. for ever. 7. rejoicing. 8. the highest order of angels. 9. those angels who lived in the contemplation of divine beauty and wisdom, and excelled in knowledge. 10. the chaste spirits redeemed from earth and allowed to enter heaven (see Rev. 7 and 14). 11. harmonising. 12. music. 13. ugly (disrupting, at the Fall, the perfect harmony of God's original creation). 14. concord. 15. ruled. 16. complete concord. 17. choir, ensemble.

15. The Muse

Go, the rich chariot instantly prepare;
    The Queen, my Muse, will take the air;
Unruly Fancy with strong Judgement trace,[1]
    Put in nimble-footed Wit,
    Smooth-paced[2] Eloquence join with it,
Sound Memory with young Invention place,
    Harness all the wingèd race.
Let the postilion[3] Nature mount, and let
    The coachman Art be set.
And let the airy footmen, running all beside,
    Make a long row of goodly pride.
Figures,[4] Conceits,[5] Raptures,[6] and Sentences,[7]
    In a well-worded dress.
And innocent Loves, and pleasant Truths, and useful Lies,
    In all their gaudy liveries.
Mount, glorious Queen, thy travelling throne,
    And bid it to put on;[8]
    For long, though cheerful, is the way,
And life, alas, allows but one ill winter's day.

Where never foot of man, or hoof of beast
    The passage pressed,
  Where never fish did fly,
And with short silver wings cut the low, liquid sky.[9]
  Where bird with painted oars did ne'er
Row through the trackless ocean of the air.
    Where never yet did pry
  The busy[10] Morning's curious eye,
The wheels of thy bold coach pass quick and free,
  And all's an open road to thee.
  Whatever God did say,[11]
Is all thy plain and smooth, uninterrupted way.
Nay even beyond his works thy voyages are known,
  Thou hast thousand worlds, too, of thine own.
Thou speak'st, great Queen, in the same style as he,
And a new world leaps forth when thou say'st, 'Let it be.'

Thou fathom'st[12] the deep gulf of ages past,
  And can pluck up with ease
The years which thou dost please,
Like shipwrecked treasures by rude tempests cast
  Long since into the sea,
Brought up again to light and public use by thee.
  Nor dost thou only dive so low,
    But fly
With an unwearied wing the other way on high,
  Where fates among the stars do grow;[13]
There into the close[14] nests of time dost peep,
  And there with piercing eye,
Through the firm shell and the thick white dost spy,
  Years to come a-forming lie,
Close in their sacred secondine[15] asleep,
  Till hatched by the sun's vital heat
  Which o'er them yet does brooding set
  They life and motion get,
  And ripe at last with vigorous might
Break through the shell, and take their everlasting flight.

  And sure we may
  The same too of the present say,
If past and future times do thee obey.
  Thou stop'st this current, and dost make
This running river settle like a lake;
Thy certain hand holds fast this slippery snake.[16]
  The fruit which does so quickly waste,
  Men scarce can see it, much less taste,
Thou comfitest[17] in sweets, to make it last.
  This shining piece of ice
  Which melts so soon away
  With the sun's ray,
Thy verse does solidate and crystallise,
  Till it a lasting mirror be.

> Nay, thy immortal rhyme
> Makes this one short point of time
> To fill up half the orb of round eternity.[18]
>
>   ((1656) Abraham Cowley (1618–67)[19])

1. harness. 2. evenly-stepping. 3. driver (of the first pair of coach-horses). 4. figures of speech. 5. ingenious analogies. 6. 'uncommon heats of imagination' (Johnson, *Dictionary*). 7. epigrams. 8. hurry on. 9. the sea. 10. meddling, prying. 11. at the creation. 12. penetrate. 13. an allusion to the popular belief that the stars control men's fortunes. 14. secret. 15. the sack within which an embryo develops in the womb. 16. the year (thus represented in Egyptian hieroglyphics). 17. preserve in sugar. 18. 'There are two sorts of eternity; from the present backwards to eternity, and from the present forwards,...These two make up the whole circle of eternity, which the present time cuts like a diameter, but poetry makes it extend to all eternity to come, which is the half-circle' (Cowley's note). 19. Cowley is nowadays thought of (if he is thought of at all) as a 'transitional' poet, between the 'metaphysicals' and 'Augustans', but for well over a century after his death he was admired (see 30 n.3 and 222–9) for qualities that were felt to be distinctively his own.

16 *Music and poetry*

> As first a various, unformed hint we find
> Rise in some godlike poet's fertile mind,
> Till all the parts and words their places take,
> And with just marches verse and music make;
> Such was God's poem, this world's new essay;
> So wild and rude in its first draft it lay;
> The ungoverned parts no correspondence[1] knew,
> An artless war from thwarting motions[2] grew,
> Till they to number and fixed rules were brought
> By the Eternal Mind's poetic thought.
> Water and air he for the tenor chose,
> Earth made the bass, the treble flame arose,[3]
> To the active moon a quick, brisk stroke he gave,
> To Saturn's string a touch more soft and grave,
> The motions straight, and round, and swift, and slow,
> And short, and long, were mixed and woven so,
> Did in such artful figures smoothly fall,
> As made this decent,[4] measured dance of all.
> And this is music, sounds that charm our ears,
> Are but one dressing that rich science[5] wears.
> Though no man hear it, though no man it rehearse,[6]
> Yet will there still be music in my verse.
> In this great world[7] so much of it we see;
> The lesser, Man, is all-o'er harmony.
> Storehouse of all proportions! Single choir!
> Which first God's breath did tunefully inspire!
> From hence blest music's heavenly charms arise,
> From sympathy[8] which them and Man allies.
>
>   ((1656) Abraham Cowley (1618–67),[9] from *The Davideis*, Bk. 1)

1. (i) congruity (ii) harmony; Cowley plays throughout on God's dual role as creator/maker and poet/musician. 2. (i) movements (ii) melodic progressions. 3. Cowley associates the variously pitched voices in a choir with the elements making up the world. 4. fitting. 5. knowledge, skill. 6. recite. 7. the universe. 8. consonance, harmony. 9. see 15 n.19.

17 *Poetic wit*

Tell me, O tell, what kind of thing is wit,
   Thou who master art of it.[1]
For the first matter[2] loves variety less,
Less women love it, either in love or dress.
    A thousand different shapes it bears,
    Comely in thousand shapes appears.
Yonder we saw it plain; and here 'tis now,
Like spirits[3] in a place, we know not how.

London, that vents of false ware so much store,
   In no ware deceives us more.
For men, led by the colour and the shape,
Like Zeuxis' birds fly to the painted grape;[4]
    Some things do through our judgement pass
    As through a multiplying[5] glass.
And sometimes, if the object be too far,
We take a falling meteor for a star.

Hence 'tis a wit, that greatest word of fame,
   Grows such a common name;
And wits by our creation they become,
Just so as titular bishops made at Rome.[6]
    'Tis not a tale, 'tis not a jest
    Admired with laughter at a feast,
Nor florid talk which can that title gain;
The proofs of wit for ever must remain.

'Tis not to force some lifeless verses meet
   With their five gouty feet.
All everywhere, like Man's, must be the soul,
And reason the inferior powers control.
    Such were the numbers which could call
    The stones into the Theban wall.[7]
Such miracles are ceased; and now we see
No towns or houses raised by poetry.

Yet 'tis not to adorn and gild each part;
   That shows more cost than art.
Jewels at nose and lips but ill appear;
Rather than all things wit, let none be there.
    Several[8] lights will not be seen,
    If there be nothing else between.
Men doubt, because they stand so thick i'the sky,
If those be stars which paint the galaxy.

'Tis not when two like words make up one noise,
   Jests for Dutch men and English boys;[9]
In which who finds out wit, the same may see
In anagrams and acrostics[10] poetry.
    Much less can that have any place
    At which a virgin hides her face;

Such dross the fire must purge away; 'tis just
The author blush there, where the reader must.

'Tis not such lines as almost crack the stage
    When Bajazet[11] begins to rage;
Nor a tall[12] metaphor in the Oxford way,
Nor the dry chips of short-lunged Seneca;[13]
    Nor upon all things to obtrude,
    And force some odd similitude.
What is it, then, which like the Power Divine
We only can by negatives define?

In a true piece of wit all things must be,
    Yet all things there agree.
As in the Ark, joined without force or strife,
All creatures dwelt; all creatures that had life.
    Or as the primitive forms[14] of all
    (If we compare great things with small)
Which without discord or confusion lie,
In that strange mirror[15] of the Deity.

But Love that moulds one man up out of two,
    Makes me forget and injure you.
I took you for myself, sure, when I thought
That you in any thing were to be taught.
    Correct my error with thy pen;
    And if any ask me then,
What thing right wit, and height of genius is,
I'll only show your lines, and say, "Tis this.'
        ((1656) Abraham Cowley (1618–67),[16] 'Ode: Of Wit')

1. the poem's addressee has never been identified. 2. the primal chaos. 3. ghosts who were supposed to appear in bodies of condensed air. 4. Zeuxis, the Greek painter, was said to have painted grapes so life-like that the birds came to pick at them. 5. magnifying. 6. a 'titular bishop' in the Roman Catholic Church was one whose supposed sphere of jurisdiction actually lay outside the domain of Rome, and was thus merely notional. 7. Amphion, a ruler of Thebes in Greek legend, was said to have been a harpist of such skill that the stones of the city wall were drawn into place by his music. 8. separate. 9. both seen as likely connoisseurs of feeble puns. 10. puzzle-poems in which one or more letters of each line, taken in order, spell a word or group of words. 11. a ranting tyrant in Marlowe's play *Tamburlaine the Great*. 12. high-flown, far-fetched. 13. the style of the Roman philosopher Seneca (c.4 BC – AD 65) was renowned for its pithy concentration. 14. Cowley alludes to Plato's notion of a realm of purely intellectual and ideal 'forms', of which the objects of the everyday world are inferior copies. 15. pattern or model; in Cowley's Christian thought, the ideal realm of the Platonic forms is identified with the mirror of truth, in which God sees both himself and futurity (the two being synonymous, since everything that is or will be derives from him). 16. see 15 n.19.

18 *Verse-translation and civilisation*

Whether the fruitful Nile, or Tyrian shore,[1]
The seeds of arts and infant science bore,
'Tis sure the noble plant, translated first,
Advanced its head in Grecian gardens[2] nursed.

> The Grecians added verse; their tuneful tongue
> Made Nature first, and Nature's god their song.
> Nor stopped translation here; for conquering Rome
> With Grecian spoils brought Grecian numbers home,
> Enriched by those Athenian Muses more
> Than all the vanquished world could yield before;
> Till barbarous nations, and more barbarous times,
> Debased the majesty of verse to rhymes;[3]
> Those rude at first, a kind of hobbling prose,
> That limped along, and tinkled in the close.
> But Italy, reviving from the trance
> Of Vandal, Goth, and monkish ignorance,
> With pauses, cadence, and well-vowelled words,
> And all the graces a good ear affords,
> Made rhyme an art, and Dante's[4] polished page
> Restored a silver, not a golden age.[5]
> Then Petrarch[6] followed, and in him we see
> What rhyme improved in all its height can be;
> At best a pleasing sound, and fair barbarity.
> The French pursued their steps; and Britain, last,
> In manly sweetness all the rest surpassed.
>
> ((1684) John Dryden (1631–1700), from 'To the Earl of Roscommon,[7] on his Excellent *Essay on Translated Verse*')

1. Phoenicia. 2. the traditional home of Greek philosophy, and thus, by extension, of poetry. 3. rhyme was first introduced into European verse in the early Middle Ages. 4. Dante Alighieri (1265–1321), best known as the author of *The Divine Comedy*. 5. see 2 n.11. 6. Francesco Petrarca [Petrarch] (1304–74), renowned for his lyrics in praise of Laura. He and Dante Alighieri (see n.4) were generally regarded as the two principal founding fathers of Italian poetry. 7. see 20 n.7.

19 *Poetic fury*

We, who are priests of Apollo,[1] have not the inspiration when we please, but must wait till the god comes rushing on us, and invades us with a fury which we are not able to resist; which gives us double strength while the fit continues, and leaves us languishing and spent at its departure.

((1692) John Dryden (1631–1700), from the Dedication to *Eleonora*)

1. the sun god; also god of music and poetry.

20 *Advice to the translator of poetry*

> Each poet with a different talent writes,
> One praises, one instructs, another bites;
> Horace[1] did ne'er aspire to epic bays,[2]
> Nor lofty Maro[3] stoop to lyric lays.
> Examine how your humour[4] is inclined,
> And which the ruling passion of your mind;
> Then seek a poet who your way does bend,
> And choose an author as you choose a friend;
> United by this sympathetic bond,
> You grow familiar, intimate, and fond;

Your thoughts, your words, your styles, your souls agree,
No longer his interpreter, but he. ...
Take pains the genuine meaning to explore,
There sweat, there strain, tug the laborious oar.
Search every comment[5] that your care can find,
Some here, some there may hit the poet's mind.
Yet be not blindly guided by the throng;
The multitude is always in the wrong.
When things appear unnatural or hard,
Consult your author, with himself compared;
Who knows what blessing Phoebus[6] may bestow,
And future ages to your labour owe?
Such secrets are not easily found out,
But, once discovered, leave no room for doubt.
Truth stamps conviction in your ravished breast,
And peace and joy attend the glorious guest.

((1684) Wentworth Dillon, Earl of Roscommon (?1633–85),[7] from
An Essay on Translated Verse)

1. the Roman poet Horace (65–8 BC) was particularly renowned for his lyric *Odes*, as well as for his literary criticism (see 11 n.11). 2. laurels, used ceremonially to wreathe poets. 3. Virgil, the chief Roman epic poet. 4. temperament. 5. commentary. 6. see 19 n.1. 7. author of a blank-verse translation of Horace's *Ars Poetica* (1685), and an early admirer of Milton (see 192); Roscommon was involved, in the early 1680s, in conversations and projects with Dryden and others, designed to explore the ways in which poetic translation might contribute to the general literary life of the nation.

21 *Poetry and the passions*

Here[1] all the passions, for their greater sway,
In all the power of words themselves array;
And hence the soft pathetic gently charms,
And hence the bolder fills the breast with arms.
Sweet Love in numbers finds a world of darts,
And with desirings wounds the tender hearts.
Fair Hope displays its pinions to the wind,
And flutters in the lines, and lifts the mind.
Brisk Joy with transport fills the rising strain,
Breaks in the notes, and bounds in every vein.
Stern Courage, glittering in the sparks of ire,
Inflames those lays that set the breast on fire.
Aversion learns to fly with swifter will,
In numbers taught to represent an ill.
By frightful accents Fear produces fears;
By sad expression Sorrow melts to tears;
And dire Amazement and Despair are brought
By words of horror through the wilds of thought.
'Tis thus tumultuous passions learn to roll;
Thus, armed with poetry, they win the soul.

((1713) Thomas Parnell (1679–1718),[2] from 'An Essay on the
Different Styles of Poetry')

1. the speaker is an imaginary Greek poet, who shows the writer a vision of the various aspects of the poetic domain. 2. friend of Swift and Pope; most of his verse was published posthumously by Pope in 1721.

22 Advice to a satirist

If satire charms, strike faults, but spare the man;
'Tis dull to be as witty as you can.
Satire recoils whenever charged too high;[1]
Round your own fame the fatal splinters fly.
As the soft plume gives swiftness to the dart,
Good breeding sends the satire to the heart.
   Painters and surgeons may the structure[2] scan;
Genius[3] and morals be with you the man;
Defaults in those alone should give offence;
Who strikes the person, pleads his innocence.
My narrow-minded satire can't extend
To Codrus'[4] form; I'm not so much his friend;
Himself should publish that (the world agree)
Before his works, or in the pillory.
Let him be black, fair, tall, short, thin, or fat,
Dirty or clean, I find no theme in that.
Is that called humour?[5] It has this pretence,
'Tis neither virtue, breeding, wit, or sense.
Unless you boast the genius of a Swift,[6]
Beware of humour, the dull rogue's last shift.
   ((1730) Edward Young (1683–1765),[7] from 'Epistle II : To Mr Pope, from Oxford')

1. pressed too far. 2. the physical form. 3. disposition, character. 4. a butt of the satire of the Roman poet Juvenal; here used to denote any victim of a satirist's attack. 5. the faculty of depicting the ludicrous. 6. Jonathan Swift, friend of Pope, renowned for the grotesque physicality of his satire. 7. author of *Love of Fame: The Universal Passion* (a series of satires, 1725–8), and, more famously, *Night Thoughts* (1742–5), a poem of melancholy reflection on human mortality; see 257 and 258.

23 Poetry and nature

First follow Nature,[1] and your judgement frame
By her just standard, which is still[2] the same;
Unerring Nature, still divinely bright,
One clear, unchanged, and universal light,
Life, force, and beauty must to all impart,
At once the source, and end, and test of art.
Art from that fund each just supply provides,
Works without show, and without pomp presides;
In some fair body thus the informing[3] soul
With spirits feeds, with vigour fills the whole,
Each motion guides, and every nerve[4] sustains;
Itself unseen, but in the effects remains.
Some, to whom heaven in wit[5] has been profuse,
Want as much more, to turn it to its use;
For wit and judgement[6] often are at strife,
Though meant each other's aid, like man and wife.
'Tis more to guide than spur the Muse's steed;[7]

ON POETRY

    Restrain his fury, than provoke his speed;
    The wingèd courser, like a generous[8] horse,
    Shows most true mettle[9] when you check his course.
        ((wr. 1709; pub. 1711) Alexander Pope (1688–1744), from *An Essay on Criticism*)

1. the mysterious unchanging reality to which our eyes are normally blind, but which the work of a great artist allows us to glimpse; Pope's advice in this passage applies equally to the would-be poet and to the would-be critic of poetry. 2. always. 3. giving form to, animating. 4. muscle. 5. the inventive, imaginative power. 6. the power by which an artist sifts, shapes, and orders the promptings of his imagination. 7. Pegasus (see 11 n.6). 8. well-bred. 9. spirit, vigour.

24 *The perils of a poetic career*

(i)

    Unhappy wit,[1] like most mistaken things,
    Atones not for that envy which it brings.
    In youth alone its empty praise we boast,
    But soon the short-lived vanity is lost!
    Like some fair flower the early spring supplies,
    That gaily blooms, but even in blooming dies.
    What is this wit which must our cares employ?
    The owner's wife, that other men enjoy,
    Then most our trouble still when most admired,
    And still the more we give, the more required;
    Whose fame with pains we guard, but lose with ease,
    Sure some to vex, but never all to please;
    'Tis what the vicious fear, the virtuous shun;
    By fools 'tis hated, and by knaves undone!

(ii)

I believe if any one, early in his life, should contemplate the dangerous fate of authors, he would scarce be of their number on any consideration. The life of a wit is a warfare upon earth, and the present spirit of the learned world is such, that to attempt to serve it any way one must have the constancy of a martyr, and a resolution to suffer for its sake.
        (((i) wr. 1709; pub. 1711; (ii) 1717) Alexander Pope (1688–1744), from *An Essay on Criticism* and Preface to *The Works of Mr Alexander Pope*)

1. poetic talent.

25 *The immortal poets of the past*

    Still green with bays[1] each ancient altar stands,
    Above the reach of sacrilegious hands,
    Secure from flames, from Envy's fiercer rage,
    Destructive war, and all-involving age.[2]

See, from each clime[3] the learned their incense bring;
Hear in all tongues consenting paeans[4] ring!
In praise so just let every voice be joined,
And fill the general chorus of mankind!
Hail bards triumphant, born in happier days!
Immortal heirs of universal praise!
Whose honours with increase of ages grow,
As streams roll down, enlarging as they flow!
Nations unborn your mighty names shall sound,
And worlds applaud that must not yet be found!
Oh may some spark of your celestial fire
The last, the meanest of your sons inspire
(That on weak wings, from far, pursues your flights;
Glows while he reads, but trembles as he writes),
To teach vain wits a science[5] little known,
To admire superior sense, and doubt their own!
   ((wr. 1709; pub. 1711) Alexander Pope (1688–1744), from *An Essay on Criticism*)

1. see 20 n.2. 2. the passing of time, which causes all to decay. 3. part of the world. 4. hymns of praise. 5. knowledge.

26 Versification

But most by numbers[1] judge a poet's song,
And smooth or rough,[2] with them, is right or wrong;
In the bright Muse though thousand charms conspire,
Her voice is all these tuneful fools admire,
Who haunt Parnassus[3] but to please their ear,
Not mend their minds; as some to church repair,
Not for the doctrine, but the music there.
These equal[4] syllables alone require,
Though oft the ear the open[5] vowels tire,
While éxpletives[6] their feeble aid *do* join,
And ten low words oft creep in one dull line,[7]
While they ring round the same unvaried chimes,[8]
With sure returns of still-expected rhymes.
Where-e'er you find 'the cooling western breeze',
In the next line, it 'whispers through the trees';
If 'crystal streams with pleasing murmurs creep',
The reader's threatened (not in vain) with 'sleep'.
Then, at the last and only couplet fraught
With some unmeaning thing they call a thought,
A needless alexandrine[9] ends the song,
That like a wounded snake drags its slow length along.
Leave such to tune their own dull rhymes, and know
What's roundly smooth, or languishingly slow;
And praise the easy vigour of a line,
Where Denham's strength and Waller's sweetness join.[10]
True ease in writing comes from art, not chance,
As those move easiest who have learned to dance.
'Tis not enough no harshness gives offence,

> The sound must seem an echo to the sense.
> Soft is the strain when Zephyr[11] gently blows,
> And the smooth stream in smoother numbers flows;
> But when loud surges lash the sounding shore,
> The hoarse, rough verse should like the torrent roar.
> When Ajax[12] strives some rock's vast weight to throw,
> The line too labours, and the words move slow;
> Not so, when swift Camilla[13] scours the plain,
> Flies o'er the unbending corn, and skims along the main.
> ((wr. 1709; pub. 1711) Alexander Pope (1688–1744), from *An Essay on Criticism*)

1. versification alone. 2. metrically regular, or irregular. 3. see 11 n.7. 4. regular. 5. vowels pronounced with the mouth wide open. 6. redundant or superfluous words or phrases. 7. here, as elsewhere in the passage, Pope's verse mimics its subject. 8. Pope mocks phrases and gambits commonly used in the verse of the period (including some of his own). 9. the six-foot, twelve-syllable, iambic line often used to 'vary' iambic pentameter lines, particularly at the end of a paragraph (the effect is mimicked by Pope in the line that follows). 10. Sir John Denham (1615–69) was praised by Dryden for the 'majesty' of his style, particularly in the topographical poem *Cooper's Hill* (see 221); Edmund Waller (1606–87) was celebrated for the flowing elegance of his lyric and complimentary verse (see 185–7). 11. a mild and gentle wind. 12. in Homer's *Iliad* (XII.378–86), the mighty warrior Ajax crushes one of his opponents with a rock which is too heavy for anyone else even to lift. 13. the maiden-warrior who is one of Aeneas' opponents in the latter part of Virgil's *Aeneid*, and who, Virgil says, might have skimmed over a cornfield without even harming the ears of corn (*Aeneid*, VII.808–11).

27 Homer as poet par excellence

Our author's work is a wild paradise, where, if we cannot see all the beauties so distinctly as in an ordered garden, it is only because the number of them is infinitely greater. 'Tis like a copious nursery, which contains the seed and first productions of every kind, out of which those who followed him have but selected some particular plants, each according to his fancy, to cultivate and beautify. If some things are too luxuriant, it is owing to the richness of the soil; and if others are not arrived to perfection or maturity, it is only because they are overrun and oppressed by those of a stronger nature.

It is to the strength of this amazing invention we are to attribute that unequalled fire and rapture which is so forcible in Homer, that no man of a true poetical spirit is master of himself while he reads him. What he writes is of the most animated nature imaginable; every thing moves, every thing lives, and is put in action. If a council be called, or a battle fought, you are not coldly informed of what was said or done as from a third person; the reader is hurried out of himself by the force of the poet's imagination, and turns in one place to a hearer, in another to a spectator. The course of his verses resembles that of the army he describes, ... 'They pour along like a fire that sweeps the whole earth before it'. 'Tis, however, remarkable that his fancy, which is everywhere vigorous, is not discovered immediately at the beginning of his poem in its fullest splendour; it grows in the progress both upon himself and others, and becomes on fire, like a chariot wheel, by its own rapidity. Exact disposition,[1] just thought, correct elocution,[2] polished numbers,[3] may have been found in a thousand; but this poetical fire, this 'vivida vis animi' ['living power of the mind'],[4] in a very few. Even in works where all those are imperfect or neglected, this can overpower criticism, and make us admire, even while we disapprove. Nay, where this appears, though attended with absurdities, it brightens all the rubbish about it, till we see nothing but its own splendour. This fire is discerned in Virgil,[5] but discerned as through a glass, reflected from Homer, more shining than fierce, but everywhere equal and constant; in Lucan[6] and Statius[7] it bursts out in sudden, short, and interrupted flashes; in Milton it glows like a furnace kept up to an uncommon ardour by the force of art; in Shakespeare it strikes before we are aware, like an accidental fire from heaven; but in Homer, and in him only, it burns everywhere clearly and everywhere irresistibly.

((1715) Alexander Pope (1688–1744), from Preface to *The Iliad of Homer*)

1. arrangement of materials. 2. apt expression. 3. versification. 4. in his *De Rerum Natura* ['On the Nature of Things'], 1.72, the Roman poet Lucretius (94–55 BC) uses the phrase to describe the fearless imaginative vigour of his idol, the Greek philosopher Epicurus. 5. Virgil's *Aeneid*, the greatest Roman epic, draws heavily on Homer's *Iliad* and *Odyssey*. 6. Roman poet (AD 39–65), author of *Pharsalia*, an epic on the Roman civil wars. 7. Roman poet (AD 40–c.96), author of two epics, the *Thebaid* and the unfinished *Achilleid*, both on themes from Greek legend.

28 Homer as the father of poetic diction

We acknowledge him the father of poetic diction; the first who taught that 'language of the gods' to men. His expression is like the colouring of some great masters, which discovers itself to be laid on boldly, and executed with rapidity. It is, indeed, the strongest and most glowing imaginable, and touched with the greatest spirit. Aristotle[1] had reason to say he was the only poet who had found out 'living words'; there are in him more daring figures[2] and metaphors than in any good author whatever. An arrow is 'impatient' to be on the wing, a weapon 'thirsts' to drink the blood of an enemy, and the like; yet his expression is never too big for the sense, but justly great in proportion to it. It is the sentiment[3] that swells and fills out the diction, which rises with it, and forms itself about it, for in the same degree that a thought is warmer, an expression will be brighter; as that is more strong, this will become more perspicuous;[4] like glass in the furnace, which grows to a greater magnitude, and refines to a greater clearness, only as the breath within is more powerful, and the heat more intense.

((1715) Alexander Pope (1688–1744), from Preface to *The Iliad of Homer*)

1. *Poetics*, Ch. IV. 2. rhetorical devices. 3. feeling. 4. clear, lucid.

29 Bad poetry

Here she[1] beholds the chaos dark and deep,
Where nameless somethings in their causes sleep,
'Till genial Jacob,[2] or a warm[3] third day,[4]

Call forth each mass, a poem, or a play;
How Hints, like spawn, scarce quick[5] in embryo lie,
How new-born Nonsense first is taught to cry,
Maggots[6] half-formed in rhyme exactly meet,
And learn to crawl upon poetic feet.
Here one poor word an hundred clenches[7] makes,
And ductile[8] Dullness new meanders takes;
There motley Images her fancy[9] strike,
Figures ill-paired, and Similes unlike.
She sees a mob of Metaphors advance,
Pleased with the madness of the mazy dance;
How Tragedy and Comedy embrace;
How Farce and Epic get[10] a jumbled race;
How Time himself stands still at her command,
Realms shift their place, and Ocean turns to land.
Here gay Description Egypt glads with showers,
Or gives to Zembla[11] fruits, to Barca[12] flowers;
Glittering with ice here hoary hills are seen,
There painted vallies of eternal green,
In cold December fragrant chaplets[13] blow,
And heavy harvests nod beneath the snow.
    ((1728) Alexander Pope (1688–1744), from *The Dunciad Variorum*)

1. the goddess Dullness, patroness of all those whose activities threaten the well-being of art and of the life of the mind; here she surveys her creation in a manner comically analogous to God surveying his creation in Milton's *Paradise Lost*. 2. Jacob Tonson (?1656-1736), the leading literary publisher of his day. 3. (i) profitable (ii) apt for incubation. 4. the profits from the third day of a play's run were set aside for the author's benefit. 5. alive. 6. (i) grubs (ii) perverse whimsies. 7. puns. 8. easily-channelled. 9. imagination. 10. beget. 11. a bleak group of islands in the Arctic. 12. a desert region of Libya. 13. wreaths of flowers.

30 *Poetry and civilisation*

Lest you should think that verse shall die,
　　Which sounds the silver Thames along,
Taught on the wings of truth, to fly
　　Above the reach of vulgar song;

Though daring Milton sits sublime,
　　In Spenser native Muses play;[1]
Nor yet shall Waller[2] yield to time,
　　Nor pensive Cowley's moral lay.[3]

Sages and chiefs long since had birth
　　Ere Caesar[4] was, or Newton[5] named,
These raised new empires o'er the earth,
　　And those new heavens and systems framed;

Vain was the chief's and sage's pride;
　　They had no poet, and they died!
In vain they schemed, in vain they bled;
　　They had no poet, and are dead!
    ((wr. ?1737; pub. 1751) Alexander Pope (1688–1744), 'Part of the
            Ninth Ode of the Fourth Book of Horace')

1. in the rustic pastoral of *The Shepherd's Calendar*, and in the numerous references to English history and landscape throughout *The Fairy Queen*. 2. see 26 n.10. 3. Abraham Cowley (see 222–9) treats questions of morality and the good life most extensively in his *Essays in Verse and Prose* (1668). 4. Julius Caesar, who extended the Roman Empire as far as the English Channel. 5. Sir Isaac Newton (1642–1727), the great mathematician and astronomer.

31 *Mock-epic satire*

Each other satire humbler arts has known,
Content with meaner beauties, though its own;
Enough for that, if, rugged in its course,
The verse but rolls with vehemence and force;
Or nicely pointed in the Horatian[1] way,
Wounds keen, like sirens[2] mischievously gay.
Here[3] all has wit, yet must that wit be strong
Beyond the turns of epigram or song.
The thought must rise exactly from the vice,
Sudden, yet finished; clean, and yet concise.
One harmony must first with last unite,
As all true paintings have their place and light.
Transitions must be quick, and yet designed,
Not made to fill, but just retain the mind;
And similes, like meteors of the night,
Just give one flash of momentary light.
  As thinking makes the soul, low things expressed
In high-raised terms define a *Dunciad*[4] best.
Books and the man demand as much, or more,
Than he who wandered on the Latian[5] shore;
For here (eternal grief to Duns's[6] soul,
And B――'s[7] thin ghost) the part contains the whole;
Since in mock-epic none succeeds, but he
Who tastes the whole of epic poesy.
    ((1730) Walter Harte (1709–74),[8] from 'An Essay on Satire,
                                Particularly on *The Dunciad*')

1. the satires of Horace were particularly admired for the relaxed urbanity with which they made their points. 2. mythical maidens whose songs were said to draw men to destruction. 3. in mock-epic. 4. Pope's mock-epic satire on Dullness (see 29 n.1). 5. Virgil's Aeneas (the *Aeneid* begins, 'Arms and the man ...'). 6. Duns Scotus, the medieval theologian whose name (as here) became synonymous with hair-splitting and unintelligent pedantry. 7. possibly Sir Richard Blackmore (d.1729), physician to Queen Anne and author of tedious epic poems. 8. a clergyman and miscellaneous writer who was helped considerably by Pope in his earlier career; he later became a friend of Dr Johnson.

32 *The force of poetry*

When Macbeth is confirming himself in the horrid purpose of stabbing his king, he breaks out amidst his emotions into a wish natural to a murderer:

> Come, thick night!
> And pall thee in the dunnest smoke of hell,
> That my keen knife see not the wound it makes;
> Nor heaven peep through the blanket of the dark,
> To cry, hold, hold![1]

In this passage is exerted all the force of poetry, that force which calls new powers into being, which embodies[2] sentiment, and animates[3] matter.

((1751) Samuel Johnson (1709–84), from *The Rambler*, No. 168)

1. *Macbeth*, I.v.50–4 (the speaker is actually Lady Macbeth). 2. endows with a physical existence. 3. breathes a living spirit into.

33 The poet's task

'The business of a poet,' said Imlac,[1] 'is to examine not the individual but the species; to remark general properties and large appearances. He does not number the streaks of the tulip, or describe the different shades in the verdure of the forest. He is to exhibit in his portraits of nature such prominent and striking features as recall the original to every mind, and must neglect the minuter discriminations which one may have remarked[2] and another have neglected, for those characteristics which are alike obvious to vigilance and carelessness.

But the knowledge of nature is only half the task of a poet; he must be acquainted likewise with all the modes of life. His character requires that he estimate the happiness and misery of every condition, observe the power of all the passions in all their combinations, and trace the changes of the human mind as they are modified by various institutions and accidental influences of climate or custom, from the sprightliness of infancy to the despondence of decrepitude. He must divest himself of the prejudices of his age or country; he must consider right and wrong in their abstracted and invariable state; he must disregard present laws and opinions, and rise to general[3] and transcendental truths, which will always be the same. He must therefore content himself with the slow progress of his name, contemn the applause of his own time, and commit his claims to the justice of posterity. He must write as the interpreter of nature, and the legislator of mankind, and consider himself as presiding over the thoughts and manners of future generations, as a being superior to time and place.

His labour is not yet at an end. He must know many languages and many sciences; and, that his style may be worthy of his thoughts, must, by incessant practice, familiarise to himself every delicacy of speech and grace of harmony.'

((1759) Samuel Johnson (1709–84), from *Rasselas*, Ch. 10)

1. the much-travelled sage who, in Johnson's tale, guides and advises Prince Rasselas and his young companions. 2. noted. 3. universal.

34 How poetic drama moves

It will be asked how the drama moves, if it is not credited.[1] It is credited with all the credit due to a drama. It is credited, whenever it moves, as a just[2] picture of a real original; as representing to the auditor what he would himself feel if he were to do or suffer what is there feigned to be suffered or to be done. The reflection that strikes the heart is not that the evils before us are real evils, but that they are evils to which we ourselves may be exposed. If there be any fallacy, it is not that we fancy the players, but that we fancy ourselves unhappy for a moment; but we rather lament the possibility than suppose the presence of misery, as a mother weeps over her babe, when she remembers that death may take it from her. The delight of tragedy proceeds from our consciousness of fiction; if we thought murders and treasons real, they would please no more.

Imitations produce pain or pleasure, not because they are mistaken for realities, but because they bring realities to mind. When the imagination is recreated by a painted landscape, the trees are not supposed capable to give shade, or the fountains coolness; but we consider how we should be pleased with such fountains playing beside us, and such woods waving over us. We are agitated in reading the history of Henry the Fifth, yet no man takes his book for the field of Agincourt.

((1765) Samuel Johnson (1709–84), from Preface to *The Works of Shakespeare*)

1. believed in literally. 2. apt, telling.

35 *Religious poetry*

Let no pious ear be offended if I advance, in opposition to many authorities, that poetical devotion cannot often please. The doctrines of religion may indeed be defended in a didactic poem, and he who has the happy power of arguing in verse will not lose it because his subject is sacred. A poet may describe the beauty and the grandeur of nature, the flowers of the spring, and the harvests of autumn, the vicissitudes of the tide, and the revolutions of the sky, and praise the Maker for his works in lines which no reader shall lay aside. The subject of the disputation is not piety, but the motives to piety; that of the description is not God, but the works of God.

Contemplative piety, or the intercourse between God and the human soul, cannot be poetical. Man admitted to implore the mercy of his Creator and plead the merits of his Redeemer is already in a higher state than poetry can confer.

The essence of poetry is invention; such invention as, by producing something unexpected, surprises and delights. The topics of devotion are few, and, being few, are universally known; but, few as they are, they can be made no more; they can receive no grace from novelty of sentiment,[1] and very little from novelty of expression.

Poetry pleases by exhibiting an idea more grateful[2] to the mind than things themselves afford. This effect proceeds from the display of those parts of nature which attract, and the concealment of those which repel the imagination; but religion must be shown as it is; suppression and addition equally corrupt it, and such as it is, it is known already.

From poetry the reader justly expects, and from good poetry always obtains, the enlargement of his comprehension[3] and elevation of his fancy;[4] but this is rarely to be hoped by Christians from metrical devotion.

Whatever is great, desirable, or tremendous, is comprised in the name of the Supreme Being. Omnipotence cannot be exalted; Infinity cannot be amplified; Perfection cannot be improved.

The employments of pious meditation are faith, thanksgiving, repentance, and supplication. Faith, invariably uniform, cannot be invested by fancy with decorations. Thanksgiving, the most joyful of all holy effusions, yet addressed to a Being without passions, is confined to few modes, and is to be felt rather than expressed. Repentance, trembling in the presence of the Judge, is not at leisure for cadences[5] and epithets.[6] Supplication of man to man may diffuse itself through many topics of persuasion, but supplication to God can only cry for mercy.

Of sentiments purely religious, it will be found that the most simple expression is the most sublime.[7] Poetry loses its lustre and its power, because it is applied to the decoration of something more excellent than itself. All that pious verse can do is to help the memory and delight the ear, and for these purposes it may be very useful; but it supplies nothing to the mind. The ideas of Christian theology are too simple for eloquence, too sacred for fiction, and too majestic for ornament; to recommend them by tropes and figures[8] is to magnify by a concave mirror the sidereal[9] hemisphere.

((1779) Samuel Johnson (1709–84), from 'Waller' in *Lives of the Poets*)

1. thought, opinion. 2. pleasing, delightful. 3. 'knowledge; power of the mind to admit and contain many ideas at once' (Johnson, *Dictionary*). 4. imagination. 5. poetic shapings and modulations. 6. adjectives. 7. for Johnson's definition of 'the sublime', see 159. 8. rhetorical embellishments in which words and expressions are diverted from their original, literal, significations. 9. starry.

36 *The poet the chief of artists*

          But the chief
Are poets; eloquent men, who dwell on earth
To clothe whate'er the soul admires[1] or loves
With language and with numbers. Hence to these
A field is opened wide as Nature's sphere;
Nay, wider; various as the sudden acts
Of human wit, and vast as the demands
Of human will. The bard, nor length, nor depth,
Nor place, nor form controls. To eyes, to ears,
To every organ of the copious mind,
He offereth all its treasures. Him the hours,
The seasons him obey; and changeful Time
Sees him at will keep measure with his flight,
At will outstrip it. To enhance his toil,
He summoneth, from the uttermost extent
Of things which God hath taught him, every form
Auxiliar,[2] every power; and all beside
Excludes, imperious. His prevailing hand
Gives to corporeal essence life, and sense,
And every stately function of the soul.

The soul itself, to him obsequious, lies
Like matter's passive heap; and, as he wills,
To reason and affection he assigns
Their just alliances, their just degrees;
Whence his peculiar honours, whence the race
Of men who people his delightful world,
Men genuine and according to themselves,
Transcend as far the uncertain sons of earth,
As earth itself to his delightful world,
The palm of spotless beauty doth resign.
((1770) Mark Akenside (1721–70),[3] from *The Pleasures of the Imagination*, Bk. IV)

1. views with awe. 2. helpful. 3. physician and poet; this extract is from his major work, an unfinished philosophical poem in blank verse.

37 *Rhyming couplets v. blank verse*

Some, Milton-mad (an affectation
Gleaned up from college education),
Approve no verse, but that which flows
In epithetic,[1] measured prose,
With trim expressions daily dressed
Stolen, misapplied, and not confessed,
And call it writing in the style
Of that great Homer of our isle.
'Whilom', 'what time', 'eftsoons', and 'erst',[2]
(So prose is oftentime be-versed)
Sprinkled with quaint fantastic phrase,
Uncouth to ears of modern days,
Make up the metre which they call
Blank, classic blank, their all-in-all.
   Can only blank admit sublime?
Go read and measure Dryden's rhyme.
Admire the magic of his song,
See how his numbers roll along,
With ease and strength and varied pause,[3]
Nor cramped by sound nor metre's laws.
   Is harmony the gift of rhyme?
Read, if you can, your Milton's chime;
Where taste, not wantonly severe,[4]
May find the measure, not the ear.
   As rhyme, rich rhyme, was Dryden's choice,
And blank has Milton's nobler voice,
I deem it as the subject's lead,
That either measure will succeed;
That rhyme will readily admit
Of fancy, numbers, force, and wit;
But though each couplet has its strength,
It palls in works of epic length.
((1762) Robert Lloyd (1733–64),[5] from 'On Rhyme')

1. abounding in epithets. 2. Spenserian archaisms, employed by 18th-century blank verse poets. 3. resting-places for the ear, breaking the monotony of over-regular verse. 4. if not unwarrantedly pedantic. 5. singled out by William Cowper as the natural heir to Matthew Prior (1664–1721) as the leading author of 'easy jingles' (short-line light verse).

38 *What is a poet?*

What is a poet? To whom does he address himself? And what language is to be expected from him? He is a man speaking to men; a man, it is true, endowed with more lively sensibility, more enthusiasm[1] and tenderness, who has a greater knowledge of human nature, and a more comprehensive soul, than are supposed to be common among mankind; a man pleased with his own passions and volitions,[2] and who rejoices more than other men in the spirit of life that is in him; delighting to contemplate similar volitions and passions as manifested in the goings-on of the universe, and habitually impelled to create them where he does not find them. To these qualities he has added a disposition to be affected more than other men by absent things as if they were present; an ability of conjuring up in himself passions, which are indeed far from being the same as those produced by real events, yet (especially in those parts of the general sympathy which are pleasing and delightful) do more nearly resemble the passions produced by real events than anything which, from the motions of their own minds merely, other men are accustomed to feel in themselves; whence, and from practice, he has acquired a greater readiness and power in expressing what he thinks and feels, and especially those thoughts and feelings which, by his own choice, or from the structure of his own mind, arise in him without immediate external excitement.

((1802) William Wordsworth (1770–1850), from Preface to *Lyrical Ballads*)

1. passionate intensity of feeling. 2. wishes, resolves.

39 *Poetry, nature, and pleasure*

Aristotle, I have been told, has said that poetry is the most philosophic of all writing.[1] It is so. Its object is truth, not individual and local but general and operative;[2] not standing upon external testimony, but carried alive into the heart by passion; truth which is its own testimony, which gives competence and confidence to the tribunal to which it appeals, and receives them from the same tribunal. Poetry is the image of man and nature. The obstacles which stand in the way of the fidelity of the biographer and historian, and of their consequent utility, are incalculably greater than those which are to be encountered by the poet who comprehends the dignity of his art. The poet writes under one restriction only, namely the necessity of giving immediate pleasure to a human being possessed of that information which may be expected from him, not as a lawyer, a physician, a mariner, an astronomer, or a natural philosopher,[3] but as a man. Except this one restriction, there is no object standing between the poet and the image of things; between this, and the biographer and historian, there are a thousand.

Nor let this necessity of producing immediate pleasure be considered as a degradation of the poet's art. It is far otherwise. It is an acknowledgement of the beauty of the universe, an acknowledgement the more sincere, because not formal but indirect. It is a task light and easy to him who looks at the world in the spirit of love. Further, it is a homage paid to the native and naked dignity of man, to the grand elementary principle of pleasure, by which he knows, and feels, and lives, and moves.

((1802) William Wordsworth (1770–1850), from Preface to *Lyrical Ballads*)

1. *Poetics*, Ch II; Aristotle actually says that poetry is more philosophical than history. 2. productive, exercising energy. 3. scientist.

40 *The poet as upholder and preserver*

The knowledge both of the poet and the man of science is pleasure; but the knowledge of the one cleaves to us as a necessary part of our existence, our natural and unalienable inheritance; the other is a personal and individual acquisition, slow to come to us, and by no habitual and direct sympathy connecting us with our fellow-beings. The man of science seeks truth as a remote and unknown benefactor; he cherishes and loves it in his solitude; the poet, singing a song in which all human beings join with him, rejoices in the presence of truth as our visible friend and hourly companion. Poetry is the breath and finer spirit of all knowledge; it is the impassioned expression which is in the countenance of all science.[1] Emphatically may it be said of the poet, as Shakespeare hath said of man, that he looks before and after.[2] He is the rock of defence for human nature; an upholder and preserver, carrying everywhere with him relationship and love. In spite of difference of soil and climate, of language and manners, of laws and customs; in spite of things silently gone out of mind, and things violently destroyed, the poet binds together by passion and knowledge the vast empire of human society, as it is spread over the whole earth, and over all time. The objects of the poet's thoughts are everywhere; though the eyes and senses of man are, it is true, his favourite guides, yet he will follow wheresoever he can find an atmosphere of sensation in which to move his wings. Poetry is the first and last of all knowledge. It is as immortal as the heart of man.

((1802) William Wordsworth (1770–1850), from Preface to *Lyrical Ballads*)

1. just as the expression gives purpose and unity to the otherwise disparate features of a face, so poetry gives purpose and unity to the materials of the scientist's study. 2. *Hamlet*, IV.iv.37.

41 *Poetry and prose*

There neither is, nor can be, any *essential* difference between the language of prose and metrical composition. We are fond of tracing the resemblance between poetry and painting, and accordingly we call them sisters; but where shall we find bonds of connection sufficiently strict to typify the affinity between metrical and prose composition? They both speak by and to the same organs. The bodies in which both of them are clothed may be said to be of the same substance. Their affections are kindred, and almost identical, not necessarily differing even in degree. Poetry sheds no tears 'such as angels weep',[1] but natural and human tears. She can boast of no celestial ichor[2] that distinguishes her vital juices from those of prose. The same human blood circulates through the veins of them both.

((1800) William Wordsworth (1770–1850), from Preface to *Lyrical Ballads*)

1. *Paradise Lost*, I.620. 2. the fluid said, in Greek myth, to run like blood in the veins of the gods.

42 Metre

The end of poetry is to produce excitement in co-existence with an overbalance of pleasure; but, by the supposition, excitement is an unusual and irregular state of mind; ideas and feelings do not, in that state, succeed each other in accustomed order. If the words, however, by which this excitement is produced be in themselves powerful, or the images and feelings have an undue proportion of pain connected with them, there is some danger that the excitement may be carried beyond its proper bounds. Now the co-presence of something regular, something to which the mind has been accustomed in various moods and in a less excited state, cannot but have great efficacy in tempering and restraining the passion by an intertexture of ordinary feeling, and of feeling not strictly and necessarily connected with the passion. This is unquestionably true; and hence, though the opinion will at first appear paradoxical, from the tendency of metre to divest language, in a certain degree, of its reality, and thus to throw a sort of half-consciousness of unsubstantial existence over the whole composition, there can be little doubt but that more pathetic situations and sentiments, that is, those which have a greater proportion of pain connected with them, may be endured in metrical composition, especially in rhyme, than in prose.

((1800) William Wordsworth (1770–1850), from Preface to *Lyrical Ballads*)

43 The power of poetic language

Words are too awful an instrument for good and evil to be trifled with. They hold above all other external powers a dominion over thoughts. If words be not ... an incarnation of the thought, but only a clothing for it, then surely will they prove an ill gift; such a one as those poisoned vestments, read of in the stories of superstitious times,[1] which had power to consume and to alienate from his right mind the victim who put them on. Language, if it do not uphold, and feed, and leave in quiet, like the power of gravitation or the air we breathe, is a counter-spirit, unremittingly and noiselessly at work, to subvert, to lay waste, to vitiate, and to dissolve.

((wr. 1812; pub. 1876) William Wordsworth (1770–1850), from *Essays Upon Epitaphs*, III)

1. e.g. the poisoned shirt of the centaur Nessus which killed Hercules (the story is told in Sophocles' play, *The Women of Trachis*).

44 Poetic genius

Of genius the only proof is the act of doing well what is worthy to be done, and what was never done before. Of genius in the fine arts, the only infallible sign is the widening of the sphere of human sensibility, for the delight, honour, and benefit of human nature. Genius is the introduction of a new element into the intellectual universe.

((1815) William Wordsworth (1770–1850), from 'Essay Supplementary to the Preface')

45 Great poetry never instantly popular

But in everything which is to send the soul into herself to be admonished of her weakness or to be made conscious of her power; wherever life and nature are described as operated upon by the creative or abstracting virtue of the imagination; wherever the instinctive wisdom of antiquity and her heroic passions uniting, in the heart of the poet, with the meditative wisdom of later ages, have produced that accord of sublimated humanity which is at once a history of the remote past and a prophetic enunciation of the remotest future, *there* the poet must reconcile himself for a season to few and scattered hearers. Grand thoughts (and Shakespeare must often have sighed over this truth), as they are most naturally and most fitly conceived in solitude, so can they not be brought forth in the midst of plaudits without some violation of their sanctity. Go to a silent exhibition of the productions of the sister art,[1] and be convinced that the qualities which dazzle at first sight and kindle the admiration of the multitude, are essentially different from those by which permanent influence is secured. Let us not shrink from following up these principles as far as they will carry us, and conclude with observing that there never has been a period, and perhaps never will be, in which vicious[2] poetry, of some kind or other, has not excited more zealous admiration, and been far more generally read, than good. But this advantage attends the good, that the *individual*, as well as the species, survives from age to age; whereas, of the depraved, though the species be immortal, the individual quickly perishes; the object of present admiration vanishes, being supplanted by some other as easily produced; which, though no better, brings with it at least the irritation of novelty, with adaptation more or less skilful, to the changing humours[3] of the majority of those who are most at leisure to regard poetic works when they first solicit their attention.

((1815) William Wordsworth (1770–1850), from 'Essay Supplementary to the Preface')

1. painting. 2. faulty, flawed, debased. 3. moods.

46 False critics of poetry

To be mistaught is worse than to be untaught; and no perverseness equals that which is supported by system,[1] no errors are so difficult to root out as those which the understanding has pledged its credit to uphold.² In this class are contained censors who, if they be pleased with what is good, are pleased with it only by imperfect glimpses, and upon false principles; who, should they generalise rightly, to a certain point, are sure to suffer for it in the end; who, if they stumble upon a sound rule, are fettered by misapplying it, or by straining it too far; being incapable of perceiving when it ought to yield to one of higher order. In it are found critics too petulant to be passive to a genuine poet, and too feeble to grapple with him; men who take upon them to report of the course which *he* holds whom they are utterly unable to accompany – confounded if he turn quick upon the wing, dismayed if he soar steadily 'into the region'; men of palsied imaginations and indurated³ hearts, in whose minds all healthy action is languid, who therefore feed as the many direct them, or, with the many, are greedy after vicious provocatives;⁴ judges whose censure is auspicious, and whose praise ominous!

((1815) William Wordsworth (1770–1850), from 'Essay Supplementary to the Preface')

1. doctrine. 2. staked its credibility or reputation on defending. 3. hardened. 4. stimulants.

47 *The sonnet*

Scorn not the sonnet; critic, you have frowned,
Mindless of its just honours; with this key
Shakespeare unlocked his heart;¹ the melody
Of this small lute gave ease to Petrarch's wound;²
A thousand times this pipe did Tasso³ sound;
With it Camoëns⁴ soothed an exile's grief;
The sonnet glittered, a gay myrtle leaf
Amid the cypress with which Dante crowned
His visionary brow;⁵ a glow-worm lamp,
It cheered mild Spenser, called from Fairyland
To struggle through dark ways;⁶ and, when a damp
Fell round the path of Milton, in his hand
The thing became a trumpet,⁷ whence he blew
Soul-animating strains – alas, too few!

((1827) William Wordsworth (1770–1850), 'Scorn not the Sonnet')

1. Shakespeare's 154 sonnets have often been interpreted as if they revealed intimate secrets of their author's personal life. 2. many of Petrarch's sonnets (see 18 n.6) express the pain of the poet's love for his mistress, Laura. 3. as well as the epic *Jerusalem Delivered* (see 60 n.6), Torquato Tasso wrote many sonnets, upon some of which Spenser drew when composing his *Amoretti* (see n.6). 4. the Portuguese poet Luis de Camoëns (1524–80) was banished from court and spent two years in military service in North Africa. 5. the myrtle denotes love, in contrast to the cypress, which is symbolic of mourning, and thus a fitting emblem of the sombre vision of *The Divine Comedy*. 6. Spenser's sonnets, the *Amoretti*, appeared in 1595, between the two instalments of *The Fairy Queen* (1590 and 1596), while Spenser was acting as a public servant in Ireland (which he regarded as a place of exile). 7. some of Milton's most famous sonnets are grand addresses to parliamentary leaders, or comments on public events of a momentous nature.

48 Artificial poetry and true poetry[1]

A poet! he hath put his heart to school,
Nor dares to move unpropped upon the staff
Which Art hath lodged within his hand – must laugh
By precept only, and shed tears by rule.
Thy art be Nature; the live current quaff,
And let the groveller sip his stagnant pool,
In fear that else, when critics grave and cool
Have killed him, Scorn should write his epitaph.
How does the meadow-flower its bloom unfold?
Because the lovely little flower is free
Down to its root, and, in that freedom, bold;
And so the grandeur of the forest-tree
Comes not by casting in a formal mould,
But from its *own* divine vitality.
((1842) William Wordsworth (1770–1850), 'A poet ...')

1. 'I was impelled to write this sonnet by the disgusting frequency with which the word "artistical", imported with other impertinences from the Germans, is employed by writers of the present day. For "artistical" let them substitute 'artificial', and the poetry written on this system, both at home and abroad, will be for the most part much better characterised' (Wordsworth's own note).

49 The ode[1]

Peculiar, not far-fetched; natural, but not obvious; delicate, not affected; dignified, not swelling; fiery, but not mad; rich in imagery, but not loaded with it – in short, a union of harmony and good sense, of perspicuity and conciseness. Thought is the body of such an ode, enthusiasm the soul, and imagery the drapery.
((wr. 1795–6; pub. 1895) Samuel Taylor Coleridge (1772–1834), from a notebook (published in *Anima Poetae*))

1. in this passage, Coleridge freely adapts some of Edward Young's remarks about the Ode in his essay 'On Lyric Poetry' (1728).

50 The organic nature of poetry

The spirit of poetry, like all other living powers, must of necessity circumscribe itself by rules, were it only to unite power with beauty. It must embody, in order to reveal itself. But a living body is of necessity an organised one; and what is organisation but the connection of parts to a whole, so that each part is at once end and means? This is no discovery of criticism. It is a necessity of the human mind, and all nations have felt and obeyed it, in the invention of metre and measured sounds, as the vehicle and *involucrum*[1] of poetry – itself a fellow-growth from the same life, even as the bark is to the tree!
((wr. 1812; pub. 1836) Samuel Taylor Coleridge (1772–1834), from a lecture on Shakespeare (published in *Literary Remains*))

1. organic casing.

51 *The inner genesis of poetry*

One character attaches to all true poets; they write from a principle within, independent of everything without. The work of a true poet in its form, its shapings, and its modifications, is distinguished from all other works that assume to belong to the class of poetry, as a natural from an artificial flower, or as the mimic[1] garden of a child from an enamelled meadow. In the former, the flowers are broken from their stems and stuck into the ground; they are beautiful to the eye, and fragrant to the sense; but their colours soon fade, and their odour is transient as the smile of the planter; while the meadow may be visited again and again with renewed delight, its beauty is innate in the soul, and its bloom is of the freshness of nature.

((wr. 1812; pub. 1836) Samuel Taylor Coleridge (1772–1834), from a lecture on Shakespeare (published in *Literary Remains*))

1. imitation, toy.

52 *The poet's 'fusing' power*

The poet, described in ideal perfection, brings the whole soul of man into activity, with the subordination of its faculties to each other according to their relative worth and dignity. He diffuses a tone and spirit of unity that blends, and (as it were) *fuses*, each into each, by that synthetic[1] and magical power to which we have exclusively appropriated the name of imagination. This power, first put into action by the will and understanding, and retained under their irremissive,[2] though gentle and unnoticed, control ... reveals itself in the balance or reconciliation of opposite or discordant qualities: of sameness with difference; of the general with the concrete; the idea with the image; the individual with the representative; the sense of novelty and freshness with old and familiar objects; a more than usual state of emotion with more than usual order; judgement ever awake and steady self-possession with enthusiasm and feeling profound or vehement; and while it blends and harmonises the natural and the artificial, still subordinates art to nature; the manner to the matter; and our admiration of the poet to our sympathy with the poetry. 'Doubtless,' as Sir John Davies[3] observes of the soul (and his words may with slight alteration be applied, and even more appropriately, to the poetic imagination) :

> Doubtless this could not be, but that she turns
>   Bodies to spirit by sublimation strange,
> As fire converts to fire the things it burns,
>   As we our food into our nature change.
>
> From their gross matter she abstracts their forms,
>   And draws a kind of quíntessence[4] from things;
> Which to her proper nature she transforms,
>   To bear them light on her celestial wings.

> Thus does she, when from individual states
> She doth abstract the universal kinds,
> Which then, re-clothed in divers names and fates,
> Steal access through our senses to our minds.

Finally, good sense is the body of poetic genius, fancy its drapery, motion its life, and imagination the soul that is everywhere, and in each; and forms all into one graceful and intelligent whole.

((1817) Samuel Taylor Coleridge (1772–1834), from *Biographia Literaria*, Ch. 14)

1. combining. 2. unremitting. 3. Sir John Davies (1569–1626), Elizabethan poet; Coleridge quotes from the section 'On the Soul of Man' from Davies's philosophical poem *Nosce Teipsum* ['Know Thyself'] (1599). 4. refined essence (an alchemical term).

53 *The poet's musicality*

'The man that hath not music in his soul'[1] can indeed never be a genuine poet. Imagery (even taken from nature, much more when transplanted from books, as travels, voyages, and works of natural history), affecting incidents, just thoughts, interesting personal or domestic feelings, and with these the art of their combination or intexture in the form of a poem, may all by incessant effort be acquired as a trade by a man of talents and much reading who ... has mistaken an intense desire of poetic reputation for a natural poetic genius, the love of the arbitrary end for a possession of the peculiar means. But the sense of musical delight, with the power of producing it, is a gift of imagination; and this, together with the power of reducing multitude into unity of effect, and modifying a series of thoughts by some one predominant thought or feeling, may be cultivated and improved, but can never be learned. It is in these that 'poeta nascitur, non fit' ['a poet is born, not made'].[2]

((1817) Samuel Taylor Coleridge (1772–1834), from *Biographia Literaria*, Ch. 15)

1. *The Merchant of Venice*, V.i.83 (Coleridge prints 'his soul' for Shakespeare's 'himself'). 2. proverbial.

54 *Live poetic words*

The rules of the imagination are themselves the very powers of growth and production. The words to which they are reducible, present only the outlines and external appearances of the fruit. A deceptive counterfeit of the superficial form and colours may be elaborated; but the marble peach feels cold and heavy, and children only put it to their mouths.

((1817) Samuel Taylor Coleridge (1772–1834), from *Biographia Literaria*, Ch. 18)

55 *The poet's enchanting powers*

All nations and times have agreed in not judging him by the prosaic laws to which we who write and speak prose are amenable. His is a playful part, and he has a knack of slipping from under the hand of serious judgement. He is a Proteus,[1] and feels himself bound to speak the bare truth only when he is reduced to his proper person, not whilst he is exercising his preternatural powers of illusion. He holds in his grasp the rod of the enchanter, Pleasure, and with a touch he unnerves the joints that would seize and drag him before the seat of an ordinary police.

((1845) 'Christopher North' (John Wilson) (1785–1854),[2] from *North's Specimens of the British Critics*)

1. in Greek myth, the 'old man of the sea', who could assume different shapes to avoid being questioned. 2. friend and early champion of Wordsworth, joint-editor of *Blackwood's Edinburgh Magazine*, and later Professor of Moral Philosophy at Edinburgh University; his first volume of verse, *The Isle of Palms*, appeared in 1812.

56 *The poet as imitator*

As to imitation, poetry is a mimetic[1] art. It creates, but it creates by combination and representation. Poetical abstractions are beautiful and new, not because the portions of which they are composed had no previous existence in the mind of man or in nature, but because the whole produced by their combination has some intelligible and beautiful analogy with those sources of emotion and thought, and with the contemporary condition of them; one great poet is a masterpiece of nature which another not only ought to study but must study. He might as wisely and as easily determine that his mind should no longer be the mirror of all that is lovely in the visible universe, as exclude from his contemplation the beautiful which exists in the writings of a great contemporary. The pretence of doing it would be a presumption in any but the greatest; the effect, even in him, would be strained, unnatural, and ineffectual. A poet is the combined product of such internal powers as modify the nature of others, and of such external influences as excite and sustain these powers; he is not one, but both. Every man's mind is, in this respect, modified by all the objects of nature and art; by every word and every suggestion which he ever admitted to act upon his consciousness; it is the mirror upon which all forms are reflected, and in which they compose one form.

((1820) Percy Bysshe Shelley (1792–1822), from Preface to *Prometheus Unbound*)

1. imitative.

57 *The poet's created forms*

On a poet's lips I slept
Dreaming like a love-adept[1]
In the sound his breathing kept;
Nor seeks nor finds he mortal blisses,
But feeds on the aërial kisses
Of shapes that haunt thought's wildernesses.
He will watch from dawn to gloom
The lake-reflected sun illume
The yellow bees i'the ivy-bloom,
Nor heed nor see what things they be;
But from these create he can
Forms more real than living man,

Nurslings of immortality!

((1820) Percy Bysshe Shelley (1792–1822), from a speech by
The Fourth Spirit in *Prometheus Unbound*)

1. one skilled and experienced in the ways of love.

58 *The eternal truth of poetry*

A poem is the very image of life expressed in its eternal truth. There is this difference between a story and a poem, that a story is a catalogue of detached facts which have no other connection than time, place, circumstance, cause, and effect; the other is the creation of actions according to the unchangeable forms of human nature, as existing in the mind of the Creator, which is itself the image of all other minds. The one is partial, and applies only to a definite period of time, and a certain combination of events which can never again recur; the other is universal, and contains within itself the germ of a relation to whatever motives or actions have place in the possible varieties of human nature. Time, which destroys the beauty and the use of the story of particular facts, stripped of the poetry which should invest them, augments that of poetry, and for ever develops new and wonderful applications of the eternal truth which it contains. Hence epitomes have been called the moths of just history;[1] they eat out the poetry of it. A story of particular facts is as a mirror which obscures and distorts that which should be beautiful. Poetry is a mirror which makes beautiful that which is distorted.

((wr. 1821; pub. 1840) Percy Bysshe Shelley (1792–1822), from *A Defence of Poetry*)

1. by Sir Francis Bacon, in *The Advancement of Learning*, II.ii.4.

59 *Poetry, pleasure, and fame*

Poetry is ever accompanied with pleasure. All spirits on which it falls open themselves to receive the wisdom which is mingled with its delight. In the infancy of the world, neither poets themselves nor their auditors are fully aware of the excellence of poetry, for it acts in a divine and unapprehended manner, beyond and above consciousness; and it is reserved for future generations to contemplate and measure the mighty cause and effect in all the strength and splendour of their union. Even in modern times, no living poet ever arrived at the fullness of his fame; the jury which sits in judgement upon a poet, belonging as he does to all time, must be composed of his peers; it must be impanelled by time from the selectest of the wise of many generations. A poet is a nightingale, who sits in darkness and sings to cheer its own solitude with sweet sounds; his auditors are as men entranced by the melody of an unseen musician, who feel that they are moved and softened, yet know not whence or why.

((wr. 1821; pub. 1840) Percy Bysshe Shelley (1792–1822), from *A Defence of Poetry*)

60 Poetry and morality

Ethical science arranges the elements which poetry has created, and propounds schemes and proposes examples of civil and domestic life; nor is it for want of admirable doctrines that men hate, and despise, and censure, and deceive, and subjugate one another. But poetry acts in another and diviner manner. It awakens and enlarges the mind itself by rendering it the receptacle of a thousand unapprehended combinations of thought. Poetry lifts the veil from the hidden beauty of the world, and makes familiar objects be as if they were not familiar; it reproduces all that it represents, and the impersonations clothed in its Elysian[1] light stand thenceforward in the minds of those who have once contemplated them, as memorials of that gentle and exalted content which extends itself over all thoughts and actions with which it coexists.

The great secret of morals is love; or, a going-out of our own nature, and an identification of ourselves with the beautiful which exists in thought, action, or person, not our own.[2] A man, to be greatly good, must imagine intensely and comprehensively; he must put himself in the place of another and of many others; the pains and pleasures of his species must become his own. The great instrument of moral good is the imagination; and poetry administers to the effect by acting upon the cause. Poetry enlarges the circumference of the imagination by replenishing it with thoughts of ever new delight, which have the power of attracting and assimilating to their own nature all other thoughts, and which form new intervals and interstices[3] whose void for ever craves fresh food. Poetry strengthens that faculty which is the organ of the moral nature of man, in the same manner as exercise strengthens a limb.

A poet therefore would do ill to embody his own conceptions of right and wrong, which are usually those of his place and time, in his poetical creations, which participate in neither. By this assumption of the inferior office of interpreting the effect, in which perhaps, after all, he might acquit himself but imperfectly, he would resign the glory in a participation in the cause. There was little danger that Homer, or any of the eternal poets, should have so far misunderstood themselves as to have abdicated this throne of their widest dominion. Those in whom the poetical faculty, though great, is less intense, as Euripides,[4] Lucan,[5] Tasso,[6] Spenser,[7] have frequently affected a moral aim, and the effect of their poetry is diminished in exact proportion to the degree in which they compel us to advert to[8] this purpose.

((wr. 1821; pub. 1840) Percy Bysshe Shelley (1792–1822), from *A Defence of Poetry*)

---

1. glorious, blessed (for Elysium, see 12 n.11) 2. Shelley's sentiment is here close to that expressed by Socrates in Plato's *Symposium*, a work which Shelley translated. 3. openings, gaps. 4. (480–406 BC), the Greek tragedian who had been criticised for the lengthy philosophical disquisitions in some of his plays. 5. see 27 n.6 6. Torquato Tasso (1544–95), Italian poet, author of the epic *Gerusalemme Liberata* ['Jerusalem Delivered'], based on the story of the First Crusade; Tasso has sometimes been criticised for the supposed conflict between his epic's pious purpose and the sensuous fancifulness of its poetry. 7. Spenser had written in his Dedicatory Letter to Sir Walter Raleigh that his aim in *The Fairy Queen* was 'to

fashion a gentleman or noble person in virtuous and gentle discipline'. 8. take notice of, heed.

61 *The inexhaustible nature of poetry*

All high poetry is infinite; it is as the first acorn, which contained all oaks potentially. Veil after veil may be undrawn, and the inmost naked beauty of the meaning never exposed. A great poem is a fountain for ever overflowing with the waters of wisdom and delight; and after one person and one age has exhausted all its divine effluence which their peculiar relations enable them to share, another and yet another succeeds, and new relations are ever developed, the source of an unforeseen and an unconceived delight.

((wr. 1821; pub. 1840) Percy Bysshe Shelley (1792–1822), from *A Defence of Poetry*)

62 *The nature of poetry*

Poetry is indeed something divine. It is at once the centre and circumference of knowledge; it is that which comprehends all science, and that to which all science must be referred. It is at the same time the root and blossom of all other systems of thought; it is that from which all spring, and that which adorns all; and that which, if blighted, denies the fruit and the seed, and withholds from the barren world the nourishment and the succession of the scions[1] of the tree of life. It is the perfect and consummate surface and bloom of all things; it is as the odour and the colour of the rose to the texture of the elements which compose it; as the form and splendour of unfaded beauty to the secrets of anatomy and corruption. What were virtue, love, patriotism, friendship; what were the scenery of this beautiful universe which we inhabit, what were our aspirations beyond it, if poetry did not ascend to bring light and fire from those eternal regions where the owl-winged faculty of calculation dare not ever soar? Poetry is not like reasoning, a power to be exerted according to the determination of the will. A man cannot say, 'I will compose poetry.' The greatest poet even cannot say it; for the mind in creation is as a fading coal, which some invisible influence, like an inconstant wind, awakens to transitory brightness. This power arises from within, like the colour of a flower which fades and changes as it is developed, and the conscious portions of our natures are unprophetic either of its approach or its departure. ...

Poetry is the record of the best and happiest moments of the happiest and best minds. We are aware of evanescent visitations of thought and feeling sometimes associated with place or person, sometimes regarding our own mind alone, and always arising unforeseen and departing unbidden, but elevating and delightful beyond all expression, so that even in the desire and regret they leave, there cannot but be pleasure, participating as it does in the nature of its object. It is, as it were, the interpenetration of a diviner nature through our own; but its footsteps are like those of a wind over the sea, which the coming calm erases, and whose traces remain only, as on the wrinkled sand which paves it. These and corresponding conditions of being are experienced principally by those of the most delicate sensibility and the most enlarged imagination; and the state of mind produced by them is at war with every base desire. The enthusiasm of virtue, love, patriotism, and friendship is essentially linked with these emotions; and whilst they last, self appears as what it is, an atom to a universe. Poets are not only subject to these experiences as spirits of the most refined organisation, but they can colour all that they combine with the evanescent hues of this ethereal world. A word, a trait in the representation of a scene or a passion, will touch the enchanted chord, and reanimate, in those who have ever experienced these emotions, the sleeping, the cold, the buried image of the past. Poetry thus makes immortal all that is best and most beautiful in the world. It arrests the vanishing apparitions which haunt the interlunations[2] of life, and, veiling them or in language or in form, sends them forth among mankind, bearing sweet news of kindred joy to those with whom their sisters abide – abide, because there is no portal of expression from the caverns of the spirit which they inhabit, into the universe of things. Poetry redeems from decay the visitations of the divinity in man.

Poetry turns all things to loveliness. It exalts the beauty of that which is most beautiful, and it adds beauty to that which is most deformed. It marries exultation and horror, grief and pleasure, eternity and change. It subdues to union under its light yoke all irreconcilable things. It transmutes all that it touches, and every form moving within the radiance of its presence is changed by wondrous sympathy to an incarnation of the spirit which it breathes. Its secret alchemy turns to potable[3] gold the poisonous waters which flow from death through life. It strips the veil of familiarity from the world, and lays bare the naked and sleeping beauty, which is the spirit of its forms.

All things exist as they are perceived, at least in relation to the percipient. 'The mind is its own place, and of itself can make a heaven of hell, a hell of heaven.'[4] But poetry defeats the curse which binds us to be subjected to the accident of surrounding impressions. And whether it spreads its own figured curtain, or withdraws life's dark veil from before the scene of things, it equally creates for us a being within our being. It makes us the inhabitants of a world to which the familiar world is a chaos. It reproduces the common universe of which we are portions and percipients, and it purges from our inward sight the film of familiarity which obscures from us the wonder of our being. It compels us to feel that which we perceive, and to imagine that which we know. It creates anew the universe, after it has been annihilated in our minds by the recurrence of impressions blunted by reiteration. It justifies the bold and true word of Tasso, 'Non merita nome di creatore, se non Iddio ed il Poeta' ['No one deserves the name of creator, save God and the poet'].[5]

((wr. 1821; pub. 1840) Percy Bysshe Shelley (1792–1822), from *A Defence of Poetry*)

---

1. shoots. 2. period between the old and new moons. 3. drinkable. 4. *Paradise Lost*, I.254–5.

5. for Tasso, see 60 n.6; Shelley is paraphrasing, rather than quoting verbatim, a remark in Tasso's 'Discourses on the Heroic Poem'.

63 *Poets and the future*

It is impossible to read the compositions of the most celebrated writers of the present day without being startled with the electric life which burns within their words. They measure the circumference and sound the depths of human nature with a comprehensive and all-penetrating spirit, and they are themselves perhaps the most sincerely astonished at its manifestations; for it is less their spirit than the spirit of the age. Poets are the hierophants[1] of an unapprehended inspiration; the mirrors of the gigantic shadows which futurity casts upon the present; the words which express what they understand not; the trumpets which sing to battle, and feel not what they inspire; the influence which is moved not, but moves. Poets are the unacknowledged legislators of the world.

((wr. 1821; pub. 1840) Percy Bysshe Shelley (1792–1822), from *A Defence of Poetry*)

1. inspired priestly expounders.

64 *Taste, fashion, and poetry*

In poesy's spells some all their raptures find,
And revel in the melodies of mind.
There nature o'er the soul her beauty flings,
In all the sweets and essences of things.
A face of beauty, in a city crowd
Met, passed, and vanished like a summer cloud,
In poesy's vision more refined and fair,
Taste reads o'erjoyed and greets her image there.
Dashes of sunshine and a page of May
Live there a whole life long one summer's day.
A blossom in its witchery of bloom
There gathered dwells in beauty and perfume;
The singing bird, the brook that laughs along,
There ceaseless sing and never thirsts for song.
A pleasing image to its page conferred
In living character and breathing word
Becomes a landscape heard and felt and seen,
Sunshine and shade one harmonising green,
Where meads and brooks and forests basking lie,
Lasting as truth and the eternal sky.
Thus truth to nature, as the true sublime,
Stands a Mount Atlas, overpeering[1] time.
   Styles may with fashions vary; tawdry, chaste,
Have had their votaries,[2] which each fancied taste,
From Donne's old homely gold, whose broken feet
Jostles the reader's patience from its seat,[3]
To Pope's smooth rhymes that regularly play
In music's stated periods[4] all the way,

That starts and closes, starts again, and times
Its tuning gamut[5] true as minster chimes.
From these old fashions stranger metres flow,
Half-prose, half-verse, that stagger as they go.
One line starts smooth, and then, for room perplexed,
Elbows along and knocks against the next,
And half its neighbour; where a pause marks time,
There the clause ends; what follows is for rhyme.
Yet truth to nature will in all remain
As grass in winter glorifies the plain,
And over fashion's foils[6] rise proud and high
As light's bright fountain in a cloudy sky.
   ((wr. 1812–31; pub. 1908) John Clare (1793–1864), from 'Shadows of Taste')

1. looking down upon. 2. disciples. 3. see 165 n.15. 4. with exact observance of metrical propriety. 5. musical scale. 6. defeats.

65 *The poet's power of empathy*

(i)

As to the poetical character itself – I mean that sort of which, if I am anything, I am a member; that sort distinguished from the Wordsworthian or egotistical sublime, which is a thing *per se* and stands alone – it is not itself; it has no self; it is everything and nothing. It has no character; it enjoys light and shade; it lives in gusto, be it foul or fair, high or low, rich or poor, mean or elevated. It has as much delight in conceiving an Iago as an Imogen.[1] What shocks the virtuous philosopher, delights the chameleon poet. It does no harm from its relish of the dark side of things, any more than from its taste for the bright one, because they both end in speculation. A poet is the most unpoetical of any thing in existence, because he has no identity. He is continually informing and filling some other body. The sun, the moon, the sea, and men and women who are creatures of impulse are poetical, and have about them an unchangeable attribute; the poet has none, no identity. He is certainly the most unpoetical of all God's creatures.

(ii)

Where's the poet? show him, show him,
Muses nine, that I may know him!
'Tis the man who with a man
   Is an equal, be he king,
Or poorest of the beggar clan,
   Or any other wondrous thing
A man may be 'twixt ape and Plato;[2]
'Tis the man who with a bird,
Wren or eagle, finds his way to
   All its instincts; he hath heard
The lion's roaring, and can tell
What his horny throat expresseth,

>   And to him the tiger's yell
>   Comes articulate, and presseth
>   On his ear like mother-tongue.
>   (((i) wr. 1819; (ii) wr. 1818; pub. 1848) John Keats (1795–1821),
>   from a letter to Richard Woodhouse, 27 October, and 'Where's
>   the poet ...')

1. in *Othello* and *Cymbeline* respectively. 2. Plato's emphasis on a realm of purely intellectual 'ideas' or 'forms' (see 17 n.14) makes him an apt emblem for the extreme reach of man's mental or spiritual ambitions.

66 False Poets and True

> Look how the lark soars upward and is gone,
> Turning a spirit as he nears the sky!
> His voice is heard, but body there is none
> To fix the vague excursions of the eye.
> So, poets' songs are with us, though they die
> Obscured, and hid by death's oblivious shroud,
> And earth inherits the rich melody
> Like raining music from the morning cloud.
> Yet, few there be who pipe so sweet and loud
> Their voices reach us through the lapse of space;
> The noisy day is deafened by a crowd
> Of undistinguished birds, a twittering race;
> But only lark and nightingale[1] forlorn
> Fill up the silences of night and morn.
>   ((1846) Thomas Hood (1799–1845)[2])

1. Shelley (author of 'To a Skylark') and Keats (author of 'Ode to a Nightingale') respectively. 2. literary editor and friend of the essayists Lamb, Hazlitt, and De Quincey; much of his verse is comic, satiric, or parodic in nature; his more serious poems include 'The Song of the Shirt' (1843), which is cast in the form of an embittered protest from an exploited seamstress.

67 *The poet's childlike vision*

> The poet hath the child's sight in his breast
> And sees all *new*. What oftenest he has viewed
> He views with the first glory. Fair and good
> Pall never on him, at the fairest, best,
> But stand before him holy, and undressed
> In weekday false conventions, such as would
> Drag other men down from the altitude
> Of primal types, too early dispossessed.
> Why, God would tire of all his heavens, as soon
> As thou, O godlike, childlike, poet, didst
> Of daily and nightly sights of sun and moon!
> And therefore hath he set thee in the midst,
> Where men may hear thy wonder's ceaseless tune,
> And praise his world for ever, as thou bid'st.
>   ((1850) Elizabeth Barrett Browning (1806–61),[1] 'The Poet')

1. married Robert Browning, 1846; her most famous poem is *Aurora Leigh*, a novel in blank verse, telling the life-story of its eponymous heroine, a writer.

68 The poet as truth-teller

                    As the earth
Plunges in fury, when the internal fires
Have reached and pricked her heart, and, throwing flat
The marts and temples, the triumphal gates
And towers of observation, clears herself
To elemental freedom – thus, my soul,
At poetry's divine first finger-touch,
Let go conventions and sprang up surprised,
Convicted of the great eternities
Before two worlds.
            What's this, Aurora Leigh,[1]
You write so of the poets, and not laugh?
Those virtuous liars, dreamers after dark,
Exaggerators of the sun and moon,
And soothsayers in a tea-cup?
                        I write so
Of the only truth-tellers now left to God;
The only speakers of essential truth,
Opposed to relative, comparative,
And temporal truths; the only holders by
His sun-skirts, through conventional grey glooms;
The only teachers who instruct mankind,
From just a shadow on a charnel[2] wall,
To find man's veritable stature out,
Erect, sublime, the measure of a man –
And that's the measure of an angel, says
The apostle.[3] Ay, and while your common men
Lay telegraphs, gauge railroads, reign, reap, dine,
And dust the flaunty carpets of the world
For kings to walk on, or our president,
The poet suddenly will catch them up
With his voice like a thunder: 'This is soul,
This is life, this word is being said in heaven,
Here's God down on us! What are you about?'
How all those workers start amid their work,
Look round, look up, and feel, a moment's space,
That carpet-dusting, though a pretty trade,
Is not the imperative labour after all.
        ((1857) Elizabeth Barrett Browning (1806–61)[4], from *Aurora Leigh*,
                                                                Bk. 1)

1. see 67 n.1. 2. cemetery. 3. St John the Divine; see Rev. 21:17. 4. see 67 n.1.

69 The Poet's Song

  The rain had fallen, the poet arose,
    He passed by the town and out of the street,
  A light wind blew from the gates of the sun,
    And waves of shadow went over the wheat;
  And he sat him down in a lonely place,
    And chanted a melody loud and sweet,

That made the wild swan pause in her cloud,
    And the lark drop down at his feet.

The swallow stopped as he hunted the fly,
    The snake slipped under a spray;
The wild hawk stood with the down on his beak,
    And stared, with his foot on the prey;
And the nightingale thought, 'I have sung many songs,
    But never a one so gay;
For he sings of what the world will be
    When the years have died away.'

((1842) Alfred, Lord Tennyson (1809–92))

70 *The poet and 'general life'*

The poet, to whose mighty heart
Heaven doth a quicker pulse impart,
Subdues that energy to scan
Not his own course, but that of man.
Though he move mountains, though his day
Be passed on the proud heights of sway,
Though he hath loosed a thousand chains,
Though he hath borne immortal pains,
Action and suffering though he know,
He hath not lived, if he lives so.
He sees, in some great-historied land,
A ruler of the people stand,
Sees his strong thought in fiery flood
Roll through the heaving multitude,
Exults – yet for no moment's space
Envies the all-regarded place.
Beautiful eyes meet his, and he
Bears to admire uncravingly;
They pass; he, mingled with the crowd,
Is in their far-off triumphs proud.
From some high station he looks down,
At sunset, on a populous town;
Surveys each happy group which fleets,
Toil ended, through the shining streets,
Each with some errand of its own,
And does not say, 'I am alone.'
He sees the gentle stir of birth
When morning purifies the earth;
He leans upon a gate and sees
The pastures, and the quiet trees.
Low, woody hill, with gracious bound,
Folds the still valley almost round;
The cuckoo, loud on some high lawn,
Is answered from the depth of dawn;
In the hedge straggling to the stream,
Pale, dew-drenched, half-shut roses gleam;
But, where the farther side slopes down,

He sees the drowsy new-waked clown[1]
In his white, quaint-embroidered frock
Make, whistling, toward his mist-wreathed flock;
Slowly, behind his heavy tread,
The wet, flowered grass heaves up its head.
Leaned on his gate, he gazes; tears
Are in his eyes, and in his ears
The murmur of a thousand years.
Before him he sees life unroll,
A placid and continuous whole;
That general life, which does not cease,
Whose secret is not joy, but peace;
That life, whose dumb wish is not missed,
If birth proceeds, if things subsist;
The life of plants, and stones, and rain,
The life he craves – if not in vain
Fate gave, what chance shall not control,
His sad lucidity of soul.
  ((1849) Matthew Arnold (1822–88), from 'Resignation'))

1. countryman.

71 Austerity of Poetry

That son of Italy who tried to blow,
Ere Dante came, the trump of sacred song,[1]
In his light youth amid a festal throng
Sate with his bride to see a public show.

Fair was the bride, and on her front[2] did glow
Youth like a star; and what to youth belong:
Gay raiment, sparkling gauds, elation strong.
A prop gave way! crash fell a platform![3] lo,

'Mid struggling sufferers, hurt to death, she lay!
Shuddering, they drew her garments off, and found
A robe of sackcloth next the smooth, white skin.

Such, poets, is your bride, the Muse! young, gay,
Radiant, adorned outside; a hidden ground
Of thought and of austerity within.
  ((1867) Matthew Arnold (1822–88))

1. Giacopone di Todi (c.1230–1306), Italian poet, precursor of Dante. 2. forehead. 3. Giacopone's wife was killed when the stand collapsed from which she had been invited to view the public festivities at Todi in 1268; when trying to resuscitate her, her husband found that she wore an ascetic's hair shirt beneath her rich robes.

72 *Poetry: a criticism of life*

It is important ... to hold fast to this: that poetry is at bottom a criticism of life; that the greatness of a poet lies in his powerful and beautiful application of ideas to life, to the question: How to live? Morals are often treated in a narrow and false fashion; they are bound up with systems of thought and belief which have had their day; they are fallen into the hands of pedants and professional dealers; they grow tiresome to some of us. We find attraction, at times, even in a poetry of revolt against them; in a poetry which might take for its motto Omar Kheyam's[1] words: 'Let us make up in the tavern for the time which we have wasted in the mosque.' Or we find attractions in a poetry indifferent to them; in a poetry where the contents may be what they will, but where the form is studied and exquisite. We delude ourselves in either case; and the best cure for our delusion is to let our minds rest upon that great and inexhaustible word *life*, until we learn to enter into its meaning. A poetry of revolt against moral ideas is a poetry of revolt against *life*; a poetry of indifference towards moral ideas is a poetry of indifference towards *life*.

((1879) Matthew Arnold (1822–88), from 'Wordsworth')

1. the *Rubáiyát*, a philosophical poem by the 12th-century Persian poet Omar Khayyám, is best known in the free English rendering (1859) by Edward Fitzgerald (1809–83); Arnold read the poem in the fuller French prose version (1867) by J.B. Nicolas.

73 *True poetry*

The only true or inspired poetry is always from within, not from without. The experience contained in it has been spiritually transmuted from lead into gold. It is severely logical, the most trivial of its adornments being subservient to and suggested by the dominant idea, any departure from whose dictates would be the 'falsifying of a revelation'. It is unadulterated with worldly wisdom, deference to prevailing opinions, mere talent or cleverness. Its anguish is untainted by the gall of bitterness; its joy is never selfish; its grossness is never obscene. It perceives always the profound identity underlying all surface differences. It is a living organism, not a dead aggregate, and its music is the expression of the law of its growth; so that it could no more be set to a different melody than could a rose tree be consummated with lilies or violets. It is most philosophic when most enthusiastic, the clearest light of its wisdom being shed from the keenest fire of its love. It is a synthesis not arithmetical, but algebraical; that is to say, its particular subjects are universal symbols, its predicates universal laws; hence it is infinitely suggestive. It is ever-fresh wonder at the infinite mystery, ever-young faith in the eternal soul. Whatever be its mood, we feel that it is not self-possessed but god-possessed; whether the god came down serene and stately as Jove, when, a swan, he wooed Leda;[1] or with overwhelming might insupportably burning, as when he consumed Semele.[2]

((1860) James Thomson ('B.V.') (1834–82),[3] from 'Shelley')

1. Zeus is said to have ravished Leda, wife of the Queen of Sparta, in the form of a swan. 2. Semele prayed to Zeus to visit her in all his splendour; he did so, but she was consumed by his lightning. 3. wrote initially under the pseudonym 'B.V.' ('Byssshe Vanolis'), thus testifying to his dual admiration for Percy Bysshe Shelley and the German Romantic poet 'Novalis' (Friedrich Leopold von Hardenberg [1772–1801]); his most famous poem is 'The City of Dreadful Night' (1874), a nightmare vision of an imaginary city of misery and horror, presided over by the figure of Melancholia.

74 Rhythm

The purpose of rhythm, it has always seemed to me, is to prolong the moment of contemplation, the moment when we are both asleep and awake, which is the one moment of creation, by hushing us with an alluring monotony, while it holds us waking by variety, to keep us in that state of perhaps real trance, in which the mind, liberated from the pressure of the will, is unfolded in symbols. If certain sensitive persons listen persistently to the ticking of a watch, or gaze persistently on the monotonous flashing of a light, they fall into the hypnotic trance; and rhythm is but the ticking of a watch made softer, that one must needs listen, and various, that one may not be swept beyond memory or grow weary of listening; while the patterns of the artist are but the monotonous flash woven to take the eyes in a subtler enchantment.

((1900) William Butler Yeats (1865–1939), from 'The Symbolism of Poetry')

75 Poetry and philosophy

I thought that whatever of philosophy has been made poetry is alone permanent, and that one should begin to arrange it in some regular order, rejecting nothing as the make-believe of the poets. I thought, so far as I can recollect my thoughts after so many years, that if a powerful and benevolent spirit has shaped the destiny of this world, we can better discover that destiny from the words that have gathered up the heart's desire of the world, than from historical records, or from speculation, wherein the heart withers. Since then I have observed dreams and visions very carefully, and am now certain that the imagination has some way of lighting on the truth that the reason has not, and that its commandments, delivered when the body is still and the reason silent, are the most binding we can ever know.

((1900) William Butler Yeats (1865–1939), from 'The Philosophy of Shelley's Poetry')

76 Tragedy

Tragic art, passionate art, the drowner of dykes, the confounder of understanding, moves us by setting us to reverie, by alluring us almost to the intensity of trance. The persons upon the stage, let us say, greaten till they are humanity itself. We feel our minds expand convulsively or spread out slowly like some moon-brightened image-crowded sea. That which is before our eyes perpetually vanishes and returns again in the midst of the excitement it creates, and the more enthralling it is, the more do we forget it.

((1910) William Butler Yeats (1865–1939), from 'The Tragic Theatre')

Part Two

ON POETS

Poets of the 14th and 15th centuries

77 *Medieval poets and the English language*

Our natural tongue is rude,
And hard to be ennewed,[1]
With polished termès lusty;[2]
Our language is so rusty,
So cankered,[3] and so full
Of frowards,[4] and so dull,
That if I would apply[5]
To write ornatèly,[6]
I wot[7] not where to find
Termès[8] to serve my mind.
    Gower's[9] English is old,
And of no value told;[10]
His matter is worth gold,
And worthy to be enrolled.[11]
    In Chaucer I am sped,[12]
His *Talès* I have read:
His matter is delectable,
Solacious[13] and commendable;
His English well allowed,[14]
So as it is enprowed,[15]
For as it is employed,
There is no English void,[16]
At those days much commended;
And now men would have amended
His English, whereat they bark,
And mar all they wark.[17]
Chaucer, that famous clerk,[18]
His termès were not dark,[19]
But pleasant, easy, and plain;
No word he wrote in vain.
    Also John Lydgate[20]
Writeth after an higher rate;[21]
It is diffuse[22] to find
The sentence[23] of his mind,
Yet writeth he in his kind,
No man that can amend
Those matters that he hath penned;
Yet some men find a fault,
And say he writeth too haut.[24]

    ((wr. *c*.1505; pub. *c*.1545) John Skelton (?1460–1529),[25]
from *Philip Sparrow*)

1. revived, made fresh; the imagined speaker is Jane Scrope, a young woman lamenting the death of Philip, her pet sparrow. 2. pleasing. 3. corrupted, diseased. 4. awkward, inelegant words. 5. attempt. 6. with deliberate rhetorical embellishment. 7. know. 8. means of expression. 9. John Gower (?1330–1408), friend of Chaucer and dedicatee of his *Troilus and Criseyde*; his principal English work (dating from the 1390s) is *Confessio Amantis*, a collection

of love-stories in verse drawn from classical myth and medieval romance. 10. reckoned to be. 11. copied out. 12. skilled, knowledgeable. 13. affording pleasure and consolation. 14. approved of. 15. used to advantage. 16. lacking. 17. say, write. 18. scholar. 19. obscure. 20. John Lydgate (?1370–?1449), a prolific poet in many different genres, many of whose works are modelled on those of Chaucer. 21. in a loftier manner. 22. rambling, long-winded. 23. sense (Skelton's point is illustrated by item 81). 24. in too elevated a style. 25. tutor to Henry VIII when prince, and author of poetry of widely various kinds, from the court satire of *The Bouge of Court* to the allegorical vision of *The Garland of Laurel* (a poem which imagines the crowning of Skelton himself among the great poets) and the morality-play *Magnificence*; Skelton is chiefly renowned for his metre, the rough, short-line, so-called 'Skeltonics', which have been described as 'a headlong, voluble, breathless doggerel'; Pope referred to him as 'beastly Skelton' and commented on his 'ribaldry, obscenity, and scurrilous language'.

Geoffrey Chaucer (c.1343–1400)

78 *Chaucer and his 'Legend of Good Women'*

Alas, that I ne had English, rhyme or prose,
Sufficiént this flower[1] to praise aright!
But helpeth, ye that han cunning[2] and might,[3]
Ye lovers that can make of sentiment,[4]
In this case oughtè ye be diligent
To furthren me somewhat in my labour.
Whether ye been with the leaf or with the flower.[5]
For well I wot that ye have here-before
Of making ropen,[6] and led away the corn,
And I come after, gleaning here and there,
And am full glad if I may find an ear
Of any goodly word that ye han left.
And though it happen me rehearsen eft[7]
That ye han in your freshè songes said,
Forbeareth me, and beth not evil apayd,[8]
Sin that ye see I do it in the honour
Of love, and eke[9] in service of the flower,
Whom that I serve as I have wit or might.
  ((wr. ?1385–6) Geoffrey Chaucer (c.1343–1400), from Prologue F
        to *The Legend of Good Women*)

1. the daisy, in which the poet has said he takes particular delight. 2. have knowledge. 3. ability. 4. who can write about matters of feeling. 5. perhaps a reference to contemporary courtly debates between supporters of The Flower (?representing transient beauty and love) and The Leaf (?representing constancy and virtue). 6. you have reaped the harvest of poetry. 7. even though I repeat. 8. displeased. 9. also.

79 *Chaucer's wishes for his 'Troilus'*

Go, little book, go, little my tragedy,
There God thy maker yet, ere that he die,
So sendè might to make in some comedy![1]
But, little book, no making thou ne envy,
But subject be to allè poesy,[2]
And kiss the steppès where as thou seest pace[3]
Virgil, Ovid, Homer, Lucan, and Stace.[4]

And for there is so great diversity
In English and in writing of our tongue,
So pray I God that none miswritè thee,[5]
Ne thee mis-metre[6] for default of tongue.[7]
And read whereso thou be, or ellès sung,[8]
That thou be understood, God I beseech!
((wr. ?1385–6) Geoffrey Chaucer (c.1343–1400), from *Troilus and Criseyde*, Bk. V)

1. may God send your author power to compose a comic poem before he dies. 2. don't envy other compositions, but show humility; 'poesy' refers specifically to unrhymed classical verse. 3. pass along. 4. see 27 ns.6–7. 5. mistranscribe. 6. scan incorrectly. 7. through ignorance of language. 8. recited aloud.

80 An admirer's lament for Chaucer

O master dear, and father reverent!
My master Chaucer, flower of eloquence,
Mirror of fructuous entendement,[1]
O universal father in science[2]!
Alas! that thou thine excellent prudénce
In thy bed mortal mightest not bequeath;[3]
What ailed Death? Alas! why would he slay thee?

O Death! thou didest not harm singular[4]
In slaughter of him, but all this land it smarteth;
But natheless, yet hast thou no powér
His namè slay; his high virtue asterteth[5]
Unslain from thee, which ay us lifely hearteth[6]
With books of his ornatè enditing,
That is to all this land illumining. ...

Alas, my worthy master honouráble
This landè's very treasure and richess,
Death, by thy death, hath harm irreparáble
Unto us done; her vengeable[7] duress
Despoilèd hath this land of the sweetnéss
Of rhetoric; for unto Tullius[8]
Was never man so like amongès us.

Also, who was higher in philosophy
To Aristotle[9] in our tongue, but thou?
The steppès of Virgil in poesy
Thou followedst eke,[10] men wot[11] well enough.
((wr. 1412) Thomas Hoccleve (?1369–1426),[12] from *Regement of Princes*)

1. fruitful significance. 2. knowledge. 3. Chaucer could not bequeath his wisdom to others on his death bed. 4. merely one single harm. 5. his lofty power escapes. 6. cheers. 7. vengeful. 8. Marcus Tullius Cicero (106–43 BC), renowned as the greatest Roman master

of oratorical style. 9. Aristotle was the most celebrated and widely read of the ancient philosophers in the Middle Ages. 10. also. 11. know. 12. clerk in the Office of the Privy Seal, and author of moral treatises and of poetry of an autobiographical nature, including a treatment of his nervous breakdown.

81 *Chaucer and the 'Canterbury Tales'*[1]

When brightè Phoebus passèd was the Ram,[2]
Mid of April, and into Bullè came,
And Saturn old with his frosty face
In Virgin[4] taken had his place,
Melánchólic[5] and slow of motíon,
And was also in the opposítíon
Of Lúcina, the moonè moist and pale,
That many a shower from heaven made avail;[6]
When Aúrora[7] was in the morrow red,
And Jupiter in the Crabbè's[8] head
Hath take his palace and his mansíon;
The lusty time and jolly fresh seasón
When that Flora,[9] the noble mighty queen,
The soil hath clad in newè tender green,
With her flowers craftily ymeint,[10]
Branch and bough with red and white depeint,
Fleting the balm[11] on hillès and on vallies;
The time in sooth when Canterbury talès
Complete and told[12] at many a sundry stage
Of estates in the pilgrimage,[13]
Every man like to his degree,[14]
Some of disport,[15] some of morality,
Some of knighthood, love and gentillesse,[16]
And some also of perfect holiness,
And some also, in sooth, of ribaldry
To makè laughter in the company
(Each admitted,[17] for none would other grieve),
Like as the Cook, the Miller and the Reeve
Acquit hemself, shortly to conclude,
Boistously,[18] in their termès rude,
When they had well drunken of the bowl,[19]
And eke also with his pillèd knoll[20]
The Pardoner, beardless all his chin,
Glassy-eyed and face of cherubin,[21]
Telling a tale to anger with the Friar,
As openly the story can you lere[22]
Word for word with every circumstance,
Each one ywrit and put in rémembrance
By him that was, if I shall not feign,
Flower of poets throughout all Britain,
Which soothly haddè most of excellence –
Read his making,[23] who list the truthè find –
Which never shall appallen[24] in my mind,

But alway fresh been in my memory;
To whom be yove[25] praise, honour and glory,
Of well-saying[26] first in our language,
Chief registrer[27] of his pilgrimage,
All that was told forgetting nought at all,
Feignèd talès, nor thing historical[28]
With many proverb diverse and uncouth,[29]
By rehearsal of his sugared mouth,
Of eachè thing keeping in substance
The sentence[30] whole, withoutè variance,
Voiding the chaff,[31] soothly[32] for to sayn,
Illumining the truè pickèd grain[33]
By crafty[34] writing of his sawès[35] sweet,
From the time that they diden meet
First the pilgrims soothly everyone,
At the Tabard[36] assembled one by one
And from Southwark, shortly for to say,
To Canterbury riding on their way,
Telling a tale, as I rehearsè[37] can,
Like as the Host assigned every man,
None so hardy[38] his bidding disobey.

((wr. c.1420) John Lydgate (?1370–1449),[39]
from *The Siege of Thebes*)

1. Lydgate's poem is cast in the form of a sequel to Chaucer's *Canterbury Tales*, relating the tales told by Chaucer's pilgrims on their return journey; his Prologue is substantially modelled on Chaucer's. 2. the first sign of the Zodiac. 3. Taurus, the second sign. 4. Virgo. 5. Saturn's influence was supposed to produce a melancholy temperament. 6. fall down. 7. goddess of dawn. 8. Cancer, fourth sign of the zodiac. 9. goddess of flowers. 10. skilfully mingled. 11. the balm wafting. 12. were told complete. 13. in the pilgrimage whose participants came from many different ranks in society. 14. each man's tale suitable to his rank. 15. diversion, amusement. 16. courtesy. 17. allowed. 18. roughly, coarsely. 19. cup. 20. bald head; Chaucer's Pardoner is not, in fact, bald. 21. Chaucer's Summoner, not his Pardoner, has a red, cherubic face. 22. with which to anger the Friar, as the story can openly teach you; again, it is the Summoner whose tale is designed to goad the Friar. 23. poetry. 24. fade, grow dim. 25. given. 26. eloquence. 27. recorder. 28. forgetting nothing of what was told, either of fiction or of historical fact. 29. strange, curious. 30. meaning. 31. getting rid of the redundant parts. 32. truly. 33. the choice grain. 34. clever, ingenious. 35. speeches, tales. 36. the inn at Southwark where Chaucer's pilgrims assembled. 37. tell. 38. daring (understand 'was'). 39. see 77 n.20.

82 *Jane Scrope[1] remembers Chaucer*

(i) *The 'Canterbury Tales'*

Yet one thing is behind
That now cometh to mind;
An epitaph I would have
For Philippè's[1] grave;
But for I am a maid,
Timorous, half-afraid,
That never yet assayed
Of Heliconè's[2] well,

Where the Muses dwell;
Though I can read and spell,
Recount, report, and tell
Of the *Tales of Canterbury*,
Some sad stories, some merry;
As Palamon and Arcite,
Duke Theseus[3] and Partelet;[4]
And of the Wife of Bath,
That worketh much scath[5]
When her tale is told
Among housewives bold,
How she controlled
Her husbands as she wold,[6]
And them to despise
In the homeliest wise,
Bring other wives in thought
Their husbands to set at nought.

(ii) *'Troilus and Criseyde'*

And though I can expound
Of Hector of Troy,
That was all their joy,
Whom Achilles slew,
Wherefore all Troy did rue;
And of the love so hot
That made Troilus to dote
Upon fair Cresseid;
And what they wrote and said,
And of their wanton wills
Pandar[7] bare the bills[8]
From one to the other;
His master's love to further,
Sometime a precious thing,
An ouch[9] or else a ring;
From her to him again
Sometime a pretty chain,
Or a bracelet of hair
Prayed Troilus for to wear
That token for her sake;
How heartily he did it take,
And much thereof did make;
And all that was in vain,
For she did but feign;
The story telleth plain,
He could not obtain,
Though his father were a king,
Yet there was a thing,
That made the male to wring;[10]
She made him to sing
The song of lover's lay;

Musing night and day,
Mourning all alone,
Comfort had he none,
For she was quite agone.
Thus in conclusíon,
She brought him in abusíon;[11]
In earnest and in game,
She was much to blame;
Disparaged is her fame,
And blemished is her name,
In manner half with shame;[12]
Troilus also hath lost
On her much love and cost,
And now must kiss the post;[13]
Pandar, that went between,
Hath won nothing, I ween,[14]
But light for summer green;[15]
Yet for a special laud,
He is named Troilus' bawd;
Of that name he is sure,
Whilès the world shall dure.

((wr. c. 1505) John Skelton (?1460–1529),[16] from *Philip Sparrow*)

1. see 77 n.1. 2. Helicon (see 11 n.5) was the site of the fountains of the Muses, Aganippe and Hippocrene. 3. in 'The Knight's Tale'. 4. in 'The Nun's Priest's Tale'. 5. does much damage. 6. wished. 7. Pandarus, Criseyde's uncle and the lovers' go-between. 8. letters, messages. 9. brooch; the reference is perhaps to the brooch recovered by Troilus from Diomedes' coat (*Troilus*, V.1661), perhaps to Criseyde's request (III.885) that Pandarus should take Troilus a 'blue ring', perhaps to the lovers' exchange of rings (III.1366–72). 10. caused trouble, suffering. 11. deceived him. 12. Jane's words here show traces of the anti-Cressida tradition which finds most memorable expression in *The Testament of Cresseid* by the Scots poet, Robert Henryson (?1424–?1506). 13. have the door slammed in his face (i.e. fail) (proverbial). 14. I think. 15. the light of summer which makes the plants grow (i.e. Pandarus won nothing substantial). 16. see 77 n.25.

83 *Chaucer and time*

Whilom,[1] as antique stories tellen us,
  Those two[2] were foes the fellonest on ground,
  And battle made the dreadest dangerous
  That ever shrilling trumpet did resound;
  Though now their acts be nowhere to be found,
  As that renownèd poet them compiled
  With warlike numbers and heroic sound,
  Dan[3] Chaucer, well of English undefiled,
On fame's eternal beadroll[4] worthy to be filed.[5]

But wicked Time that all good thoughts doth waste,
  And works of noblest wits to nought outwear,
  That famous monument hath quite defaced,[6]
  And robbed the world of treasure endless dear,
  The which might have enrichèd all us here.
  O cursèd Eld,[7] the canker-worm of writs,

How may these rhymes, so rude as doth appear,
    Hope to endure, sith[8] works of heavenly wits
Are quite devoured, and brought to nought by little bits!

Then pardon, O most sacred happy spirit,
    That I thy labours lost may thus revive,
    And steal from thee the meed of thy due merit,
    That none durst ever whilst thou wast alive,
    And, being dead, in vain yet many strive:
Ne dare I like;[9] but through infusion[10] sweet
    Of thine own spirit which doth in me survive,
    I follow here the footing of thy feet,[11]
That with thy meaning so I may the rather meet.[12]

((1596) Edmund Spenser (*c*.1552–99), from *The Fairy Queen*, Bk. IV, Canto ii)

1. formerly. 2. the knightly friends, Cambell and Triamond; Spenser based Cambell on Cambalo in Chaucer's 'Squire's Tale'; the Squire had been about to tell of Cambalo's deeds of arms when his tale ended. 3. master. 4. catalogue. 5. preserved. 6. it was uncertain whether 'The Squire's Tale' had been left unfinished, or whether the final part had been lost; in this stanza, Spenser adapts Chaucer's own complaints about the transitoriness of fame in *The House of Fame* (1136–47) and *Anelida and Arcite* (10–14). 7. antiquity. 8. since. 9. nor would I dare. 10. pouring in. 11. (i) footsteps (ii) metrical patterns. 12. accord.

84 *Chaucer's immortality*

But yet in all this interchange of all,
    Virtue, we see, with her fair grace stands fast;
    For what high races[1] hath there come to fall
    With low disgrace, quite vanishèd and past,
    Since Chaucer lived; who yet lives, and yet shall,
Though (which I grieve to say) but in his last![2]
    Yet what a time hath he wrested from Time,
    And won upon the mighty waste of days,
    Unto the immortal honour of our clime,
    That by his means came first adorned with bays!
    Unto the sacred relics of whose time,
We yet are bound in zeal to offer praise.
And could our lines, begotten in this age,
    Obtain but such a blessèd hand[3] of years,
    And 'scape the fury of that threatening rage,
    Which in confusèd clouds ghastly appears;
    Who would not strain his travails to engage,
When such true glory should succeed his cares?
But whereas he came planted in the spring,
    And had the sun before him of respect;[4]
    We, set in the autumn, in the withering
    And sullen season of a cold defect,[5]
    Must taste those sour distastes the times do bring
Upon the fullness of a cloyed neglect.[6]

((1599) Samuel Daniel (1562–1619),[7] from 'Musophilus')

1. courses of life. 2. ?in his terminal stage. 3. handful. 4. facing him. 5. failure of the sun to shine. 6. must accept the distasteful response of such times as ours, when the public neglect poetry, because their taste is cloyed with excess. 7. see 4 n.2.

85 Chaucer and the English language

That noble Chaucer, in those former times
The first enriched our English with his rhymes,
And was the first of ours that ever brake
Into the Muses' treasure, and first spake
In weighty numbers,[1] delving in the mine
Of perfect knowledge, which he could refine
And coin for current;[2] and as much as then
The English language could express to men,
He made it do, and by his wondrous skill,
Gave us much light from his abundant quill.

((1627) Michael Drayton (1563–1631),[3] from 'To ... Henry Reynolds, Esquire, Of Poets and Poesy')

1. forceful, impressive poetry. 2. in current use. 3. prolific poet whose writings include pastorals, sonnets, satires, odes, and a large number of poems on mythological and historical subjects, including a vast poem on the topography, legends, and lore of England, *The Poly-Olbion* (wr. 1598–1622).

86 Chaucer's good sense

As he is the father of English poetry, so I hold him in the same degree of veneration as the Grecians held Homer, or the Romans Virgil. He is a perpetual fountain of good sense, learned in all sciences,[1] and therefore speaks properly on all subjects.

((1700) John Dryden (1631–1700), from Preface to *Fables*)

1. branches of knowledge.

87 Chaucer's comprehensive nature

He must have been a man of a most wonderful comprehensive nature, because, as it has been truly observed of him, he has taken into the compass of his *Canterbury Tales* the various manners and humours[1] (as we now call them) of the whole English nation in his age. Not a single character has escaped him. All his pilgrims are severally distinguished from each other; and not only in their inclinations but in their very physiognomies and persons. Baptista Porta[2] could not have described their natures better than by the marks which the poet gives them. The manner and matter of their tales, and of their telling, are so suited to their different educations, humours, and callings, that each of them would be improper in any other mouth. Even the grave and serious characters are distinguished by their several sorts of gravity. Their discourses are such as belong to their age, their calling, and their breeding; such as are becoming of them, and of them only. Some of his persons are vicious, and some virtuous; some are unlearned, or (as Chaucer calls them) lewd, and some are learned. Even the ribaldry of the low characters is different. The Reeve, the Miller, and the Cook are several men, and distinguished from each other as much as the mincing Lady Prioress, and the broad-speaking gap-toothed Wife of Bath. But enough of this; there is such a variety of game springing up before me that I am distracted in my choice, and know not which to follow. 'Tis sufficient to say according to the proverb, that here is God's plenty. We have our forefathers and great-grandames all before us as they were in Chaucer's days; their general characters are still remaining in mankind, and even in England, though they are called by other names than those of monks, and friars, and canons, and lady abbesses, and nuns; for mankind is ever the same, and nothing lost out of nature, though every thing is altered.

((1700) John Dryden (1631–1700), from Preface to *Fables*)

1. temperaments, psychological types. 2. (c.1538–1615), author of the standard treatise on physiognomy.

88 For a Statue of Chaucer at Woodstock

Such was old Chaucer, such the placid mien
Of him who first with harmony informed
The language of our fathers. Here he dwelt
For many a cheerful day.[1] These ancient walls
Have often heard him while his legends blithe
He sang of love or knighthood, or the wiles
Of homely life, through each estate[2] and age,
The fashions and the follies of the world
With cunning hand portraying. Though perchance
From Blenheim's towers,[3] O stranger, thou art come,
Glowing with Churchill's trophies, yet in vain
Dost thou applaud them, if thy breast be cold
To him, this other hero, who, in times
Dark and untaught, began with charming verse
To tame the rudeness of his native land.

((1758) Mark Akenside (1721–70)[4])

1. from 1357 to 1359 Chaucer was page to Elizabeth, Countess of Ulster, who made frequent visits to Woodstock in Oxfordshire. 2. rank in society. 3. Blenheim Palace is the spectacular mansion built at Woodstock by Sir John Vanbrugh to celebrate the victory of John Churchill, 1st Duke of Marlborough over the French and Bavarians at the battle of Blenheim (1704). 4. see 36 n.3.

89 *Chaucer's Canterbury pilgrims*

The characters of Chaucer's pilgrims are the characters which compose all ages and nations. As one age falls, another rises, different to mortal sight, but to immortals only the same; for we see the same characters repeated again and again, in animals, vegetables, minerals, and in men. Nothing new occurs in identical existence. Accident ever varies; substance can never suffer change nor decay.

Of Chaucer's characters, as described in his *Canterbury Tales*, some of the names or titles are altered by time, but the characters themselves for ever remain unaltered, and consequently they are the physiognomies and lineaments of universal human life, beyond which nature never steps. Names alter; things never alter. I have known multitudes of those who would have been monks in the age of monkery, who in this deistical age are deists. As Newton numbered the stars,[1] and as Linnaeus[2] numbered the plants, so Chaucer numbered the classes of men. ...

The Knight is a true hero, a good, great, and wise man; his whole-length portrait on horseback, as written by Chaucer, cannot be surpassed. He has spent his life in the field; has ever been a conqueror, and is that species of character which in every age stands as the guardian of man against the oppressor. His son is like him with the germ of perhaps greater perfection still, as he blends literature and the arts with his warlike studies. Their dress and their horses are of the first rate, without ostentation, and with all the true grandeur that unaffected simplicity when in high rank always displays. ...

The Friar ... in his office ... is said to be a 'full solemn man' : eloquent, amorous, witty, and satirical; young, handsome, and rich; he is a complete rogue, with constitutional gaiety enough to make him a master of all the pleasures of the world. ...

Chaucer is himself the great poetical observer of men, who in every age is born to record and eternise its acts. This he does as a master, as a father, and superior, who looks down on their little follies from the Emperor to the Miller; sometimes with severity, oftner with joke and sport. ...

The Pardoner [is] the age's knave, who always commands and domineers over the high and low vulgar. This man is sent in every age for a rod and scourge, and for a blight, for a trial of men, to divide the classes of men; he is in the most holy sanctuary, and he is suffered by Providence for wise ends, and has also his great use, and his grand leading destiny. His companion, the Summoner, is also a devil of the first magnitude: grand, terrific, rich, and honoured in the rank of which he holds the destiny. ...

The Good Parson [is] an apostle, a real messenger of heaven, sent in every age for its light and its warmth. This man is beloved and venerated by all, and neglected by all. He serves all, and is served by none. He is, according to Christ's definition, the greatest of his age. Yet he is a Poor Parson of a town. Read Chaucer's description of the Good Parson, and bow the head and the knee to him, who, in every age, sends us such a burning and a shining light. Search, O ye rich and powerful, for these men and obey their counsel; then shall the golden age return. But, alas, you will not easily distinguish him from the Friar or the Pardoner! They, also, are 'full solemn men', and their counsel you will continue to follow. ...

Chaucer's characters live age after age. Every age is a Canterbury Pilgrimage. We all pass on, each sustaining one or other of these characters; nor can a child be born, who is not one of these characters of Chaucer.

((1809) William Blake (1757–1827), from *A Descriptive Catalogue of Pictures*)

---

1. see 30 n.5. 2. Linnaeus [Carl Linné] (1707–78), the Swedish naturalist, established the binomial system for the scientific classification and naming of animals and plants.

90 Wordsworth reading Chaucer

Beside the pleasant Mill of Trompington[1]
I laughed with Chaucer; in the hawthorn shade
Heard him, while birds were warbling, tell his tales
Of amorous passion.

((wr. 1804; pub. 1850) William Wordsworth (1770–1850), from *The Prelude*, Bk. III)

1. Trumpington, near Cambridge (where Wordsworth was an undergraduate), is the setting for Chaucer's 'Reeve's Tale', which tells of the amorous exploits of two Cambridge students.

91 Chaucer and the 'papal darkness'

'Sweet is the holiness of youth';[1] so felt
Time-honoured Chaucer, speaking through that lay
By which the Prioress beguiled the way,
And many a pilgrim's rugged heart did melt.
Hadst thou, loved bard, whose spirit often dwelt
In the clear land of vision, but foreseen
King, child, and seraph, blended in the mien
Of pious Edward,[2] kneeling as he knelt
In meek and simple infancy, what joy
For universal Christendom had thrilled
Thy heart! what hopes inspired thy genius, skilled
(O great precursor! genuine morning star!)
The lucid shafts of reason to employ,
Piercing the papal darkness from afar!

((1822) William Wordsworth (1770–1850), 'Sonnet 23: Edward VI', from *Ecclesiastical Sonnets*)

1. this line is spoken by Chaucer's Prioress in Wordsworth's modernised version of 'The Prioress's Tale' (pub. 1820), but does not occur in Chaucer's original. 2. King Edward VI (1537–53), brought up in the Protestant faith, was a studious and pious boy; after his premature death, the crown passed to the Catholic Mary, under whose reign Protestants were vigorously persecuted; Chaucer was often regarded as a stalwart champion of Protestantism, particularly on the strength of 'The Ploughman's Tale', a spurious work (but included in early editions of Chaucer) which contains vigorous anti-papist polemic.

92 Chaucer in his poetry

I take unceasing delight in Chaucer. His manly cheerfulness is especially delicious to me in my old age. How exquisitely tender he is, and yet how perfectly free from the least touch of sickly melancholy or morbid drooping! The sympathy of the poet with the subjects of his poetry is particularly remarkable in Shakespeare and Chaucer; but what the first effects by a strong act of imagination and mental metamorphosis, the last does without any effort, merely by the inborn kindly joyousness of his nature. How well we seem to know Chaucer! How absolutely nothing do we know of Shakespeare!

((wr.1834; pub. 1835) Samuel Taylor Coleridge (1772–1834), from *Table Talk*)

93 Chaucer old-fashioned, but a true poet

No doubt he well invented, nobly felt,
But, O ye powers, how monstrously he spelt!
His syllables confound our critic men,
Who strive in vain to find exactly ten;
And waste much learning to reduce his songs
To modish measurement of shorts and longs.[1]
His language, too, unpolished and unfixed,
Of Norman, Saxon, Latin, oddly mixed;
Such words might please the uneducated ears
That hailed the blaring trumpets of Poitiers.[2]
They shared the sable Edward's glee and glory,
And, like his conquests, they were transitory.
Then how shall such old-fashioned lingo cope
With polish, elegance, and Mister Pope?
  Yet, thou true poet, let no judgement wrong
Thy rich, spontaneous, many-coloured song;
Just mirror of a bold, ambitious age,
In passion furious, in reflection sage!
An age of gorgeous sights and famous deeds,
And virtue more than peace admits or needs;
When shivered lances were our ladies' sport,
And love itself assumed a lofty port;
When every beast, and bird, and flower, and tree,
Conveyed a meaning and a mystery;
And men in all degrees, sorts, ranks, and trades,
Knights, palmers, scholars, wives, devoted maids,
In garb, and speech, and manners, stood confessed
To outward view, by hues and signs expressed,
And told their state and calling by their vest.[3]

((1833) Hartley Coleridge (1796–1849),[4] from 'Chaucer')

1. the reference is to the attempts by 18th-century scholars, particularly Thomas Tyrwhitt (1730–86), to show that Chaucer had (contrary to earlier beliefs) written in regular, ten-syllable, iambic pentameter lines. 2. the battle of Poitiers (1356), at which Edward the Black Prince (1330–76), eldest son of Edward III and father of Richard II, defeated the French. 3. style of clothing. 4. eldest son of S.T. Coleridge, and subject of his father's poems 'Frost at Midnight' and 'The Nightingale'.

The ballads

94 Stirring qualities of the old ballads

I never heard the old song of Percy and Douglas[1] that I found not my heart moved more than with a trumpet; and yet it is sung but by some blind crowder,[2] with no rougher voice than rude style; which being so evil-apparelled in the dust and cobwebs of that uncivil age, what would it work, trimmed in the gorgeous eloquence of Pindar?[3]

((wr. c.1581–3; pub. 1595) Sir Philip Sidney (1554–86), from *An Apology for Poetry*)

1. several of the earliest English ballads (e.g. 'The Battle of Otterburn' and 'Chevy Chase') depict the rivalry between the border families of Percy (English) and Douglas (Scots). 2. fiddler. 3. Greek poet (c.518–443 BC), most of whose extant works are cast in the form of odes celebrating athletic victories; Pindar was renowned for the eloquence and grandeur of his style and for the richness and boldness of his metaphors.

The early Tudor poets

95 *Poets of Henry VIII's reign*

When after those,[1] four ages[2] very near,
They with the Muses, which conversèd were:
That princely Surrey,[3] early in the time
Of the eighth Henry, who was then the prime
Of England's noble youth; with him there came
Wyatt,[4] with reverence whom we still do name
Amongst our poets; Bryan[5] had a share
With the two former, which accounted were
That time's best makers, and the authors were
Of those small poems which the title bear
Of *Songs and Sonnets*,[6] wherein oft they hit
On many dainty passages of wit.

((1627) Michael Drayton (1563–1631),[7] from 'To ... Henry Reynolds, Esquire, Of Poets and Poesy')

1. Chaucer and Gower. 2. generations. 3. Henry Howard, Earl of Surrey (?1517–47) (see 97). 4. Sir Thomas Wyatt (1503–42) (see 96). 5. Sir Francis Bryan (d.1550), favourite of Henry VIII and friend of Wyatt, whose Third Satire is addressed to him. 6. *Tottel's Miscellany* (1557), originally entitled *Songs and Sonnets*, a famous anthology of early Tudor verse, including poems by Surrey, Wyatt, and Bryan, and mentioned by Shakespeare in *The Merry Wives of Windsor*. 7. see 85 n.3.

Sir Thomas Wyatt (1503–42)

96 *Wyatt's mind and character*

Wyatt resteth here, that quick[1] could never rest;
Whose heavenly gifts, increasèd by disdain[2]
And virtue, sank the deeper in his breast,
Such profit he of envy could obtain.
A head where wisdom mysteries did frame,
Whose hammers beat still[3] in that lively brain,
As on a stithy,[4] where some work of fame
Was daily wrought, to turn to Britain's gain.
A visage stern and mild, where both did grow
Vice to contemn, in virtue to rejoice;
Amid great storms whom grace assurèd so,
To live upright, and smile at fortune's choice.
A hand that taught what might be said in rhyme;
That reft Chaucer the glory of his wit.

A mark,⁵ the which (unpérfected for time)⁶
   Some may approach, but never none shall hit.
A tongue that served in foreign realms his king;⁷
   Whose courteous talk to virtue did inflame
   Each noble heart; a worthy guide to bring
   Our English youth by travail unto fame.
An eye whose judgement no affect⁸ could blind
   Friends to allure,⁹ and foes to reconcile;
   Whose piercing look did represent a mind
   With virtue fraught, reposèd, void of guile.
A heart where dread was never so impressed¹⁰
   To hide the thought that might the truth advance;
   In neither fortune lift,¹¹ nor yet repressed
   To swell in wealth,¹² not yield unto mischance.
A valiant corpse¹³ where force and beauty met;
   Happy, alas, too happy, but for foes,
   Lived, and ran the race that Nature set,
   Of manhood's shape where she the mould did lose.¹⁴
But to the heavens that simple¹⁵ soul is fled,
   Which left with such as covet Christ to know,¹⁶
   Witness of faith that never shall be dead;
   Sent for our wealth,¹⁷ but not receivèd so.
Thus for our guilt this jewel have we lost;
The earth his bones, the heavens possess his ghost.
      ((1542) Henry Howard, Earl of Surrey (?1517–47),¹⁸ 'An Epitaph
      on Sir Thomas Wyatt the Elder')

1. alive. 2. the disdain for Wyatt displayed by his many envious enemies in Henry VIII's court. 3. continuously. 4. anvil. 5. bullseye in an archery target. 6. because his death was premature. 7. Wyatt served Henry VIII abroad on several occasions as diplomat and ambassador. 8. strong feeling, likely to bias his judgement. 9. attract. 10. never crowded in upon. 11. buoyed up with pride. 12. prosperity. 13. body. 14. Nature has lost the mould in which she created such manly figures as Wyatt. 15. guileless. 16. desire earnestly to know Christ; Surrey here alludes to Wyatt's religious verse, his translation of the seven Penitential Psalms. 17. salvation. 18. son of Thomas Howard (afterwards Duke of Norfolk); like Wyatt, Surrey wrote sonnets on the Italian model; he also pioneered blank verse in his translation of Books II and IV of Virgil's *Aeneid*.

Henry Howard, Earl of Surrey (?1517–47)

97 *Surrey's poetic art*

What should I speak in praise of Surrey's skill,
Unless I had a thousand tongues at will?
No-one is able to depaint at full
The flowing fountain of his sacred skull;
Whose pen approved what wit he had in mew,¹
Where such a skill in making sonnets² grew.
Each word in place with such a sleight³ is couched,
Each thing whereof he treats so firmly touched,
As Pallas⁴ seemed within his noble breast
To have sojourned, and been a daily guest.

Our mother tongue by him hath got such light,
As ruder speech thereby is banished quite.
((1567) George Turberville (c.1544–c.1597),[5] from 'Verse in
Praise of Lord Henry Howard, Earl of Surrey')

1. in the process of transformation. 2. see 96 n.18. 3. skill. 4. Athene, Greek goddess of reason, and patroness of the arts and literature. 5. minor Tudor poet and translator who, like Wyatt and Surrey, imitated Italian models.

Edmund Spenser (c.1552–99)

98 An exhortation to write public poetry[1]

Piers:
Abandon then the base and viler clown;
Lift up thyself out of the lowly dust,
And sing of bloody Mars, of wars, of jousts;
Turn thee to those that wield the awful[2] crown,
To doubted[3] knights, whose woundless armour rusts,
And helms unbruisèd waxen[4] daily brown.

There may thy Muse display her fluttering wing,
And stretch herself at large from east to west;
Whether thou list in fair Eliza[5] rest,
Or if thee please in bigger notes to sing,
Advance[6] the worthy[7] whom she loveth best,
That first the white bear to the stake did bring.[8]

And when the stubborn[9] stroke of stronger stounds[10]
Has somewhat slacked the tenor of thy string,[11]
Of love and lustihead[12] then mayst thou sing,
And carol loud, and lead the Miller's round,[13]
All[14] were Eliza one of thilk[15] same ring;
So might our Cuddy's name to heaven sound.
((1579) Edmund Spenser (c.1552–99), from 'October' in *The Shepherd's Calendar*)

1. 'Piers' in this poem (cast in the form of a pastoral dialogue) has often been taken to represent the lofty idealism of Spenser himself; his addressee, Cuddy, is currently a practitioner of pastoral verse. 2. awe-inspiring. 3. dreaded. 4. become. 5. Queen Elizabeth I. 6. exalt, extol. 7. great man. 8. the Earl of Leicester, Queen Elizabeth's favourite, whose badge was a bear and rugged staff. 9. harsh. 10. noise, roar. 11. has abated and made your lyre-strings sound in a more relaxed vein. 12. pleasure, delight. 13. a kind of dance. 14. although. 15. the very.

99 Spenser and his Muse

Lo, I, the man whose Muse whilom[1] did mask,[2]
As time her taught,[3] in lowly shepherd's weeds,
Am now enforced,[4] a far unfitter task,
For trumpets stern to change mine oaten reeds,[5]
And sing of knights' and ladies' gentle deeds;

Whose praises having slept in silence long,
Me, all too mean, the sacred Muse areeds[6]
To blazon broad[7] amongst her learnèd throng;
Fierce wars and faithful loves shall moralise my song.

Help then, O holy virgin, chief of nine,[8]
Thy weaker[9] novice to perform thy will;
Lay forth out of thine everlasting scryne[10]
The antique rolls, which there lie hidden still,
Of fairy knights, and fairest Tanaquil,[11]
Whom that most noble Briton prince so long
Sought through the world, and suffered so much ill,
That I must rue his undeservèd wrong;
O, help thou my weak wit, and sharpen my dull tongue!

And thou, most dreaded imp[12] of highest Jove,
Fair Venus' son,[13] that with thy cruel dart
At that good knight so cunningly didst rove,[14]
That glorious fire it kindled in his heart;
Lay now thy deadly heben[15] bow apart,
And, with thy mother mild, come to mine aid;
Come, both; and with you bring triumphant Mart,[16]
In loves and gentle jollities arrayed,
After his murderous spoils and bloody rage allayed.

And with them eke,[17] O goddess heavenly bright,[18]
Mirror[19] of grace and majesty divine,
Great lady of the greatest isle, whose light
Like Phoebus' lamp[20] throughout the world doth shine,
Shed thy fair beams into my feeble eyne,[21]
And raise my thoughts, too humble and too vile,[22]
To think of that true glorious type[23] of thine,
The argument[24] of mine afflicted[25] style;
The which to hear vouchsafe, O dearest dread,[26] awhile.
((1590) Edmund Spenser (c.1552–99), Prefatory material to *The Fairy Queen*, Bk. 1)

1. once. 2. went in disguise; Spenser refers to his sequence of pastoral poems, *The Shepherd's Calendar* (1579) (see 98). 3. as was fitting at that stage; pastoral was thought to be fitting apprentice-work for a poet; Virgil had written his pastoral poems, the *Eclogues*, at the beginning of his career. 4. compelled to undertake. 5. pastoral pipe. 6. counsels. 7. proclaim. 8. perhaps Calliope, patron Muse of heroic poetry, or Clio, Muse of history. 9. too weak. 10. coffer containing records of eternally famous deeds. 11. the chaste wife of Tarquin, first king of Rome, identified later in the poem with Gloriana, the Fairy Queen, whom King Arthur, Spenser's hero, is seeking throughout the poem. 12. offspring. 13. Cupid. 14. shoot. 15. ebony. 16. Mars. 17. also. 18. Queen Elizabeth I. 19. the earthly reflection of. 20. the sun. 21. eyes. 22. lowly. 23. Glory; Elizabeth is here seen as the 'type' or pattern of ideal Glory. 24. subject. 25. humble. 26. object of my reverence and respect.

100 *Spenser's moral invention*

Grave moral Spenser after these[1] came on,
Than whom I am persuaded there was none,

Since the blind bard[2] his *Iliads* up did make,
Fitter a task like that to undertake,
To set down boldly, bravely[3] to invent,
In all high knowledge surely[4] excellent.
((1627) Michael Drayton (1563–1631),[5] from 'To ... Henry
Reynolds, Esquire, Of Poets and Poesy')

1. Gascoigne and Churchyard (two early Elizabethan poets whom Drayton has been discussing). 2. Homer. 3. splendidly. 4. undoubtedly. 5. see 85 n.3.

101 Spenser's music

If music and sweet poetry agree,
As they must needs, the sister and the brother,
Then must the love be great 'twixt thee[1] and me,
Because thou lov'st the one, and I the other.
Dowland[2] to thee is dear, whose heavenly touch
Upon the lute doth ravish human sense;
Spenser to me, whose deep conceit[3] is such,
As, passing all conceit,[4] needs no defence.
Thou lov'st to hear the sweet melodious sound
That Phoebus'[5] lute, the queen of music, makes;
And I in deep delight am chiefly drowned,
Whenas[6] himself to singing[7] he betakes.
  One god is god of both, as poets feign;
  One knight[8] loves both, and both in thee remain.
((1598) Richard Barnfield (1574–1627),[9] 'To his Friend,
Master R.L., in Praise of Music and Poetry')

1. the addressee of the poem ('Master R.L.') has been identified as Richard Linche, author of *Diella: Certain Sonnets* (1596). 2. John Dowland (1563–1626), the famous lutenist, composer, and song-writer. 3. Spenser described *The Fairy Queen* as 'a continued allegory, or dark conceit', alluding to its meanings which lurk subtly beneath the surface. 4. conception. 5. See 19 n.1. 6. when. 7. music involving words. 8. probably Sir George Carey, the dedicatee of Dowland's first book of airs (1597), whose wife was the dedicatee of Spenser's *Muiopotmos* (1590). 9. author of sonnets, pastorals, and lyric verse; this poem was reprinted in *The Passionate Pilgrim* (1599) and was formerly attributed to Shakespeare.

102 Spenser's eloquence

He sung[1] the heroic knights of Fairy Land
In lines so elegant, of such command,
That had the Thracian[2] played but half so well
He had not left Eurydice in hell.
But, ere he ended his melodious song,
An host of angels flew the clouds among,
And rapt this swan from his attentive mates,
To make him one of their associates
In heaven's fair choir; where now he sings the praise
Of Him that is the first and last of days.
Divinest Spenser, heaven-bred, happy Muse!
Would any power into my brain infuse

Thy worth, or all that poets had before,
I could not praise till thou deserv'st no more.
((1616) William Browne (?1590–1645), from *Britannia's Pastorals*,[3] Bk. II)

1. Browne imagines Colin Clout (i.e. Spenser) singing to the sea-nymph, Thetis. 2. Orpheus (see 12 n.12). 3. Browne's now-forgotten poem is a long narrative in couplets, interspersed with songs in lyric metres; it was admired by both Milton and Keats.

103 *Spenser as moral teacher*

I cannot praise a fugitive and cloistered virtue, unexercised and unbreathed, that never sallies out and seeks her adversary, but slinks out of the race, where that immortal garland is to be run for, not without dust and heat. Assuredly we bring not innocence into the world; we bring impurity much rather; that which purifies us is trial, and trial is by what is contrary. That virtue, therefore, which is but a youngling in the contemplation of evil, and knows not the utmost that vice promises to her followers, and rejects it, is but a blank[1] virtue, not a pure; her whiteness is but an excremental[2] whiteness; which was the reason why our sage and serious poet Spenser (whom I dare be known to think a better teacher than Scotus[3] or Aquinas[4]), describing true temperance under the person of Guyon,[5] brings him in with his palmer through the Cave of Mammon, and the Bower of Earthly Bliss, that he might see, and know, and yet abstain.

((1644) John Milton (1608–74), from *Areopagitica*)

1. colourless, ineffectual. 2. superficial. 3. see 31 n.6; Milton's reference, however, is not pejorative. 4. St Thomas Aquinas (c.1225–74), the greatest medieval scholastic theologian, author of the vast *Summa Theologica*. 5. in Cantos vii and xii of Bk. II of *The Fairy Queen*; in fact, the palmer is present when Guyon visits the Bower of Bliss, but not in the Cave of Mammon.

104 *Spenser's fancy and Chaucer's manners*

Nor shall my verse that elder bard forget,
The gentle Spenser, Fancy's[1] pleasing son,
Who, like a copious river, poured his song
O'er all the mazes of enchanted ground;
Nor thee, his ancient master, laughing sage,
Chaucer, whose native manners-painting[2] verse,
Well moralised, shines through the gothic cloud
Of time and language o'er thy genius thrown.
((1744) James Thomson (1700–48), from 'Summer' in *The Seasons*)

1. imagination. 2. able to capture a character's temperament, bearing, and conduct; for Chaucer as Spenser's 'master', see 83.

105 Ode Sent to Mr Upton on his Edition of *The Fairy Queen*

As oft, reclined on Cherwell's[1] shelving shore,
I traced romantic Spenser's moral page,
And soothed my sorrows with the dulcet lore

Which Fancy fabled in her elfin age,
Much would I grieve that envious Time so soon
O'er the loved strain had cast his dim disguise,
As lowering clouds, in April's brightest noon,
Mar the pure splendours of the purple skies.
Sage Upton[2] came, from every mystic tale
To chase the gloom that hung o'er fairy ground;
His wizard hand unlocks each guarded vale,
And opes each flowery forest's magic bound.
Thus never knight with mortal arms essayed
The castle of proud Busirane to quell,
Till Britomart her beamy shield displayed,
And broke with golden spear the mighty spell;
The dauntless maid with hardy step explored
Each room, arrayed in glistering imagery;
And through the enchanted chamber, richly stored,
Saw Cupid's stately masque come sweeping by.[3]
At this, where'er, in distant region's sheen,
She roves, embowered with many a spangled[4] bough,
Mild Una,[5] lifting her majestic mien,
Braids with a brighter wreath her radiant brow.
At this, in hopeless sorrow drooping long,
Her painted wings Imagination plumes;
Pleased that her laureate votary's[6] rescued song
Its native charm and genuine grace resumes.

((1777) Thomas Warton (1728–90)[7])

1. one of the rivers which flow through Oxford, where Warton was educated (at Trinity College) and later (1757) was elected Professor of Poetry. 2. John Upton (1707–60), clergyman and scholar, whose edition of *The Fairy Queen* (1758) is still admired for the perspicacity and erudition of its commentary. 3. see *Fairy Queen*, III. xi–xii. 4. speckled. 5. the holy maid in Bk. 1 of *The Fairy Queen*, whose purity and truth suggest that of the Church. 6. poetic devotee. 7. Poet Laureate, 1785; editor of Milton's minor poems, and author of a history of English poetry (1774–81), which is notable for its detailed coverage of medieval and renaissance literature.

106 *Spenser and the passions*

Muse of my Spenser, who so well could sing
The passions all, their bearings[1] and their ties;[2]
Who could in view those shadowy beings bring,
And with bold hand remove each dark disguise,
Wherein love, hatred, scorn, or anger lies;
Guide him to Fairy Land, who now intends
That way his flight;[3] assist him as he flies,
To mark those passions, Virtue's foes and friends,
By whom when led she droops, when leading she ascends.

((1807) George Crabbe (1754–1832), from 'The Birth of Flattery')

1. the influences they exert. 2. the links between them. 3. Crabbe's poem (this passage is the opening of its invocation, cast in Spenserian stanzas) is an allegorical fantasy depicting the birth of a daughter, Flattery, to her parents, Poverty and Cunning.

107 *Gentle Spenser*

And that gentle bard,
Chosen by the Muses for their page of state –
Sweet Spenser, moving through his clouded heaven
With the moon's beauty, and the moon's soft pace,
I called him brother, Englishman, and friend!
 ((wr.1804; pub. 1850) William Wordsworth (1770–1850), from *The Prelude*, Bk. III)

108 *Wordsworth reading Spenser*

In trellised shed with clustering roses gay,
And, Mary,[1] oft beside our blazing fire,
When years of wedded life were as a day
Whose current answers to the heart's desire,
Did we together read in Spenser's lay[2]
How Una, sad of soul, in sad attire,
The gentle Una, of celestial birth,
To seek her knight went wandering o'er the earth.

Ah, then, beloved, pleasing was the smart,
And the tear precious in compassion shed
For her who, pierced by sorrow's thrilling dart,[3]
Did meekly bear the pang unmerited;
Meek as that emblem of her lowly heart,
The milk-white lamb which in a line she led,
And faithful, loyal in her innocence,
Like the brave lion slain in her defence.[4]

Notes could we hear as of a fairy shell
Attuned to words, with sacred wisdom fraught;[5]
Free Fancy prized each specious[6] miracle,
And all its finer inspiration caught;
Till in the bosom of our rustic cell
We by a lamentable change were taught
That 'bliss with mortal man may not abide';[7]
How nearly joy and sorrow are allied!

For us the stream of fiction ceased to flow;
For us the voice of melody was mute.
But, as soft gales dissolve the dreary snow,
And give the timid herbage[8] leave to shoot,
Heaven's breathing influence failed not to bestow
A timely promise of unlooked-for fruit,
Fair fruit of pleasure and serene content
From blossoms wild of fancies innocent.

It soothed us, it beguiled us, then, to hear
Once more of troubles wrought by magic spell;
And griefs whose airy motion comes not near

> The pangs that tempt the spirit to rebel;
> Then, with mild Una in her sober cheer,
> High over hill and low adown the dell
> Again we wandered,[9] willing to partake
> All that she suffered for her dear lord's sake.
>> ((1815) William Wordsworth (1770–1850), from Dedication to
>> *The White Doe of Rylstone*)

1. Mary Hutchinson, whom Wordsworth married in 1802. 2. Bk. I of *The Fairy Queen*. 3. *Fairy Queen*, I.vii.25.2. 4. see *Fairy Queen*, I.iii.. 5. laden. 6. beautiful. 7. *Fairy Queen*, I.viii.44.9. Wordsworth refers to the deaths of his children, Catharine and Thomas, in 1812. 8. newly growing vegetation. 9. *Fairy Queen*, I.vii.28.8–9.

109 *The imaginative world of 'The Fairy Queen'*

It is in the domains neither of history or geography; is ignorant of all artificial boundary, all material obstacles; it is truly in land of Fairy, that is, in mental space.
>> ((wr. 1819; pub. 1836) Samuel Taylor Coleridge (1772–1834), from a lecture
>> (published in *Literary Remains*))[1]

1. in this edition, Coleridge's nephew, H.N. Coleridge, added: 'The poet has placed you in a dream, a charmed sleep, and you neither wish, nor have the power, to inquire where you are, or how you got there.'

110 *Spenser's 'Epithalamion'*

> Sweet Spenser, sweetest bard; yet not more sweet
> Than pure was he, and not more pure than wise,
> High priest of all the Muses' mysteries.
>
> I called to mind that mighty master's song,
>> When he brought home his beautifulest bride,
> And Mulla[1] murmured her sweet undersong,
>> And Mole[2] with all his mountain woods replied;
> Never to mortal lips a strain was given,
> More rich with love, more redolent[3] of heaven.
>
> His cup of joy was mantling[4] to the brim,
>> Yet solemn thoughts enhanced his deep delight;
> A holy feeling filled his marriage-hymn,
>> And Love aspired with Faith a heavenward flight.
>>> ((1816) Robert Southey (1774–1843),[5] from Proem to 'Carmen
>>> Nuptiale')

1. the river Awbeg, which flowed near Spenser's home near Kilcolman in Ireland, and whose nymphs are invoked in 'Epithalamion'. 2. the range of hills by the Awbeg. 3. emitting the sweet scents of. 4. frothing. 5. prolific member of the 'Lake Poets' group (see 305 and ns.), and friend of Coleridge; wrote large-scale narrative poems; originally an enthusiast for the French Revolution, Southey accepted the post of Poet Laureate in 1813, and was pilloried by Hazlitt, Byron, and others for betraying his radical principles.

111 Keats and Spenser

Spenser! a jealous honourer of thine,[1]
　A forester deep in thy midmost trees,
Did last eve ask my promise to refine
　Some English that might strive thine ear to please.
But, elfin poet, 'tis impossible
　For an inhabitant of wintry earth
To rise like Phoebus with a golden quell
　Fire-winged and make a morning in his mirth.[2]
It is impossible to escape from toil[3]
　O'the sudden, and receive thy spiriting;
The flower must drink the nature of the soil
　Before it can put forth its blossoming.
Be with me in the summer days, and I
Will for thine honour and his pleasure try.
　　((wr. 1818; pub. 1848) John Keats (1795–1821), 'Spenser! a jealous honourer ...')

1. Keats's friend, John Hamilton Reynolds (1796–1852), an admirer of Spenser who had written sonnets on Robin Hood in Sherwood Forest. 2. the rising of Apollo (god of the sun) is imagined as dispelling the night of winter. 3. the task of preparing Keats's poem *Endymion* (pub. 1818) for the press.

112 Spenser's descriptions of beauty and happiness

He seemed always to feel through the eyes, imagining everything in pictures. Marlowe's *Hero and Leander*[1] is more energetic in its sensuality, more complicated in its intellectual energy than this languid story,[2] which pictures always a happiness that would perish if the desire to which it offers so many roses lost its indolence and its softness. There is no passion in the pleasure he has set amid perilous seas, for he would have us understand that there alone could the war-worn and the sea-worn man find dateless leisure and unrepining peace.
　　((1902) William Butler Yeats (1865–1939), from 'Edmund Spenser')

1. an unfinished narrative poem (pub., with a completion by George Chapman, 1598), depicting the love-affair of Leander and Hero, the priestess of Aphrodite, to whom Leander swims across the Hellespont. 2. *The Fairy Queen*.

Sir Philip Sidney (1554–86)

113 Sidney and his Muse

Loving in truth, and fain[1] in verse my love to show,
That the dear she[2] might take some pleasure of my pain:
Pleasure might cause her read, reading might make her know,
Knowledge might pity win, and pity grace obtain,
　I sought fit words to paint the blackest face of woe,
Studying inventions fine, her wits to entertain;
Oft turning others' leaves, to see if thence would flow

Some fresh and fruitful showers upon my sunburned brain.
　　　　But words came halting forth, wanting Invention's stay,[3]
　　　Invention, Nature's child, fled step-dame Study's blows,
　　　And others' feet[4] still seemed but strangers in my way.
　　　Thus, great with child to speak, and helpless in my throes,
　　　　Biting my truant[5] pen, beating myself for spite,
　　　'Fool,' said my Muse to me, 'look in thy heart and write.'[6]
　　　　　　((wr. c.1582–3; pub. 1591) Sir Philip Sidney (1554–86), Sonnet 1
　　　　　　　　　　　　　　　　　　　from *Astrophel*[7] *and Stella*)

1. desirous. 2. Stella, the addressee of Sidney's sonnet-sequence, based upon Penelope Rich (c.1562–1607), sister of Queen Elizabeth I's favourite, the Earl of Essex; Penelope's father expressed on his death bed (in 1576) his wish that she might marry Sidney, but she was in fact married (unhappily) to Lord Rich, in 1581; the precise details of her relationship with Sidney are not known. 3. support. 4. (i) steps (ii) poetic measures. 5. idle. 6. i.e. at the image of Stella there. 7. Sidney's alter-ego in the sonnet sequence; Spenser used the name as the title of his lengthy pastoral elegy on Sidney (pub. 1595; this poem is rather too diffuse to be easily represented in the present collection).

114 *Sidney: the man and his work*

　　　He was (woe worth that word!) to each well-thinking mind
　　　A spotless friend, a matchless man, whose virtue ever shined;
　　　Declaring in his thoughts, his life, and that he writ,
　　　Highest conceits,[1] longest foresights, and deepest works of wit.
　　　　　　((wr. ?1586; pub. 1593) Anon.,[2] from 'An Epitaph upon the
　　　　　　　　　Right Honourable Sir Philip Sidney' in *The Phoenix Nest*)

1. thoughts, conceptions. 2. Charles Lamb attributed this poem, on internal evidence alone, to Fulke Greville, Lord Brooke (1554–1628), Sidney's friend, and the author of his *Life* (pub. 1652).

115 *Sidney, Lyly, and the English language*

　　　The noble Sidney with this last[1] arose,
　　　That heroë for numbers[2] and for prose,
　　　That throughly paced[3] our language as to show
　　　The plenteous English hand in hand might go
　　　With Greek or Latin; and did first reduce[4]
　　　Our tongue from Lyly's[5] writing, then in use :
　　　Talking of stones, stars, plants, of fishes, flies,
　　　Playing with words and idle similes;
　　　As the English apes and very zanies[6] be,
　　　Of everything that they do hear and see
　　　So imitating his ridiculous tricks,
　　　They spake and writ all like mere lunatics.
　　　　　　　((1627) Michael Drayton (1563–1630),[7] from 'To ... Henry
　　　　　　　　　　　Reynolds, Esquire, Of Poets and Poesy')

1. Spenser. 2. verse. 3. trained it to move. 4. lead away from. 5. John Lyly (?1554–1606), the style of whose prose romance *Euphues* (1578–80) set a fashion for writing which was characterised by elaborate wordplay and antithesis, and by recondite allusions, particularly to myth and natural history. 6. feeble mimics. 7. see 85 n.3.

Sir Philip Sidney (1554–86), and Mary Herbert, Countess of Pembroke (1561–1621)

116 Upon the Translation of the Psalms by Sir Philip Sidney, and the Countess of Pembroke his Sister[1]

Eternal God (for whom whoever dare
Seek new expressions, do the circle square,[2]
And thrust into strait corners[3] of poor wit[4]
Thee, who art cornerless and infinite[5]),
I would but bless thy name, not name thee now;
And thy gifts are as infinite as thou;
Fix we our praises therefore on this one,[6]
That, as thy blessèd spirit fell upon
These Psalms' first author[7] in a cloven[8] tongue
(For 'twas a double power by which he sung
The highest matter in the noblest form),
So thou has cleft that spirit, to perform
That work again, and shed it, here, upon
Two, by their bloods, and by thy spirit, one;
A brother and a sister, made by thee
The organ, where thou art the harmony.
Two that make one John Baptist's holy voice,[9]
And who that psalm, 'Now let the isles rejoice',[10]
Have both translated, and applied it too,[11]
Both told us what and taught us how to do.
They show us islanders our joy, our King,
They tell us why, and teach us how to sing;
Make all this all,[12] three choirs, heaven, earth, and spheres,[13]
The first, heaven, hath a song, but no man hears;
The spheres have music, but they have no tongue,
Their harmony is rather danced than sung;
But our third choir, to which the first gives ear
(For angels learn by what the Church does here),
This choir hath all. The organist is he[14]
Who hath tuned God and man, the organ we;
The songs are these, which heaven's high holy Muse
Whispered to David, David to the Jews;
And David's súccessors, in holy zeal,
In forms of joy and art do re-reveal
To us so sweetly and sincerely too,
That I must not rejoice as I would do
When I behold that these Psalms are become
So well attired abroad,[15] so ill at home,
So well in chambers,[16] in thy Church so ill,
As I can scarce call that reformed, until
This be reformed;[17] would a whole state present
A lesser gift than some one man hath sent?

And shall our Church, unto our spouse[18] and king,
More hoarse, more harsh, than any other, sing?
For that[19] we pray, we praise thy name for this,[20]
Which, by this Moses and this Miriam,[21] is
Already done; and as those Psalms we call
(Though some have other authors) David's all,
So though some have, some may some psalms translate,
We thy Sidneian Psalms shall celebrate,
And, till we come the extemporal[22] song to sing,
(Learned the first hour, that we see the King
Who hath translated[23] these translators) may
These their sweet learnèd labours, all the way
Be as our tuning, that, when hence we part,
We may fall in with[24] them, and sing our part.
((1635) John Donne (1572–1631)

1. the Sidneys' verse translation of the Psalms was not published until 1823, but circulated widely in manuscript in Donne's lifetime; Sir Philip Sidney died early in the composition of the Psalter, so much of the work was, in fact, his sister's. 2. attempt absurdity. 3. narrow constraints. 4. inadequate intelligence. 5. the circle is here taken as an emblem of divine perfection. 6. this one gift. 7. David, by tradition author of the Psalms. 8. double. 9. John the Baptist heralded the coming of Christ. 10. Psalm 97. 11. by making England rejoice. 12. the totality of creation. 13. the transparent concentric spheres in which the planets were thought to be embedded; for the music of the spheres, see 14 n.1. 14. Christ, reconciler of God and man. 15. (i) on the continent (ii) outside the Anglican Church. 16. private rooms. 17. the Church of England claimed to have 'reformed' the errors and vices of the Roman Catholic Church, but allowed inferior versions of the Psalms to be said and sung. 18. the Church is said to be the 'bride' of Christ. 19. the reformation of the Anglican psalter. 20. the Sidneys' version. 21. in Exodus, Moses sings a hymn of praise to God which is taken up by his sister, Miriam. 22. (i) unpremeditated (ii) celestial, beyond time. 23. removed to heaven. 24. (i) join in with (ii) meet.

George Chapman (?1559–1634)

117 *Chapman the translator*

Others again here livèd in my days
That have of us deservèd no less praise
For their translations than the daintiest[1] wit
That on Parnassus[2] thinks he highest doth sit,
And for a chair may 'mongst the Muses call
As the most curious[3] maker of them all;
As reverent Chapman, who hath brought to us
Musaeus,[4] Homer,[5] and Hesiodus[6]
Out of the Greek, and by his skill hath reared
Them to that height, and to our tongues endeared
That were those poets at this day alive
To see their books thus with us to survive,
They would think, having neglected them so long,
They had been written in the English tongue.
((1627) Michael Drayton (1563–1631),[7] from 'To ... Henry Reynolds, Esquire, Of Poets and Poesy')

1. most precious, most fastidious. 2. see 11 n.7. 3. particular, painstaking. 4. Greek poet of the 4th–5th century AD (not to be confused with the legendary Musaeus, for whom see 13 n.6); Chapman's version of *The Divine Poem of Musaeus* (Musaeus' *Hero and Leander*) appeared in 1616. 5. Parts of Chapman's version of the *Iliad* were printed in 1598 and 1609; the complete (revised) version appeared in 1611; Chapman's *Odyssey* was published in 1614–15. 6. Chapman's translation of the *Works and Days* (a poem dealing with the routine of a farmer's life) by the Greek poet Hesiod (8th century BC) was published in 1618. 7. see 85 n.3.

118 To My Worthy and Honoured Friend, Mr George Chapman, On his Translation of Hesiod's *Works and Days*

Whose work could this be, Chapman, to refine
Old Hesiod's ore, and give it us, but thine,
Who hadst before wrought in rich Homer's mine?[1]

What treasure hast thou brought us! And what store
Still, still, dost thou arrive with, at our shore,
To make thy honour, and our wealth, the more!

If all the vulgar tongues that speak this day
Were asked of thy discoveries, they must say,
To the Greek coast thine only knew the way.

Such passage hast thou found, such returns made,
As now, of all men, it is called thy trade;
And who make thither else, rob, or invade.

((1618) Ben Jonson (1572–1637)

1. see 117 ns.5–6.

119 On First Looking into Chapman's Homer

Much have I travelled in the realms of gold,[1]
  And many goodly states and kingdoms seen;
  Round many western islands have I been
Which bards in fealty to Apollo[2] hold.
Oft of one wide expanse had I been told
  That deep-browed Homer ruled as his demesne;[3]
  Yet did I never breathe its pure serene
Till I heard Chapman speak out loud and bold.
Then felt I like some watcher of the skies
  When a new planet swims into his ken;
Or like stout Cortez, when with eagle eyes
  He stared at the Pacific, and all his men
Looked at each other with a wild surmise,
  Silent, upon a peak in Darien.[4]

((1816) John Keats (1795–1821)

1. imaginative worlds. 2. poets are in a state of fealty (feudal vassalage) to their patron god, Apollo. 3. dominion. 4. it was, in fact, the Spanish conquistador Vasco Nuñez de Balboa (c.1475–1519) who saw the Pacific from the Isthmus of Darien; Keats confuses this incident with a description of Cortez's emotions on first seeing Mexico City.

Edward Fairfax (d. 1635)

120 *Fairfax's Tasso*[1]

In scenes like these,[2] which, daring to depart
  From sober truth, are still to Nature true,
    And call forth fresh delights to Fancy's[3] view,
The heroic Muse employed her Tasso's art.
How have I trembled when, at Tancred's stroke,
  Its gushing blood the gaping cypress poured;
When each live plant with mortal accents spoke,
  And the wild blast upheaved the vanished sword![4]
How have I sat, where piped the pensive wind,
  To hear his harp by British Fairfax strung.
Prevailing[5] poet, whose undoubting mind
  Believed the magic wonders which he sung!
Hence at each sound imagination glows;
  Hence his warm lay with softest sweetness flows;
Melting it flows, pure, numerous,[6] strong, and clear,
  And fills the impassioned heart, and lulls the harmonious ear.
    ((wr. 1749–50; pub. 1788) William Collins (1721–59),[7] from 'Ode
    on the Popular Superstitions of the Highlands of Scotland')

1. Edward Fairfax's translation (1600) of Torquato Tasso's *Jerusalem Delivered* (see 60 n.6), on which Spenser was a major influence, was widely read for over two centuries after its first appearance, and was said by Dryden to have been an important influence on the course of English versification. 2. Collins has been treating the supernatural scenes in Shakespeare. 3. imagination's. 4. see Fairfax's Tasso, XIII. 36–43; Tancred is one of the Norman heroes of the First Crusade who, in Tasso's poem, are besieging Jerusalem; in the episode referred to, Tancred has entered a grove which has been enchanted by the sorcerer Ismeno, who is assisting the Saracen forces. 5. powerful 6. harmonious in versification. 7. see 144 n.8

Christopher Marlowe (1564–93)

121 *Marlowe's poetic raptures*

Neat[1] Marlowe, bathèd in the Thespian[2] springs,
Had in him those brave[3] translunary[4] things
That the first poets had; his raptures were
All air and fire, which made his verses clear,
For that fine madness still he did retain
Which rightly should possess a poet's brain.
    ((1627) Michael Drayton (1563–1631),[5] from 'To ... Henry
    Reynolds, Esquire, Of Poets and Poesy')

1. clear, direct. 2. Thespis was the semi-legendary inventor of Greek tragedy. 3. daring. 4. visionary. 5. see 85 n.3.

122 Marlowe's dramatic verse

One higher-pitched doth set his soaring thought
On crownèd kings that Fortune hath low brought;
Or some uprearèd, high-aspiring swain,
As it might be the Turkish Tamerlain.[1]
Then weeneth[2] he his base drink-drownèd spright,[3]
Rapt to the threefold loft of heaven's height,
When he conceives upon his feignèd stage
The stalking steps of his great personage,
Graced with huf-cap[4] terms and thundering threats
That his poor hearers' hair quite upright sets.
Such soon, as some brave-minded hungry youth,
Sees fitly frame to his wide-strainèd mouth,
He vaunts his voice upon an hirèd stage,
With high-set steps, and princely carriage;
Now swooping[5] inside robes of royalty,
That erst did scrub in lousy brokery.[6]
There, if he can with terms Italianate,
Big-sounding sentences,[7] and words of state,
Fair patch me up[8] his pure iambic verse,
He ravishes the gazing scaffolders.[9]

((1597) Joseph Hall (1574–1656), from *Virgidemiarum*,[10] I.iii)

1. Tamburlaine, the eponymous hero of Marlowe's play (pub. 1590) is a Scythian shepherd who eventually defeats the Turkish emperor, Bajazet. 2. thinks. 3. spirit. 4. blustering, swaggering. 5. sweeping. 6. go meanly attired in crafty criminality. 7. aphorisms. 8. botch together. 9. occupants of the theatre gallery. 10. Hall's title refers to the sheaf of rods with which the satirist metaphorically beats his victims; Hall's satires were published while he was a student at Cambridge; he later became Bishop, successively, of Exeter and Norwich.

123 Christopher Marlowe

Crowned, girdled, garbed and shod with light and fire,
   Son first-born of the morning, sovereign star!
   Soul nearest ours of all, that wert most far,[1]
Most far off in the abysm of time, thy lyre
Hung highest above the dawn-enkindled choir
   Where all ye sang together, all that are,
   And all the starry songs behind thy car[2]
Rang sequence, all our souls acclaim thee sire.

'If all the pens that ever poets held
   Had fed the feeling of their masters' thoughts,'[3]
   And as with rush of hurtling chariots
The flight of all their spirits were impelled
   Toward one great end, thy glory – nay, not then,
   Not yet mightst thou be praised enough of men.

((1882) Algernon Charles Swinburne (1837–1909),[4] from 'Sonnets on the English Dramatic Poets')

1. of the dramatists who are the subject of Swinburne's sequence. 2. chariot. 3. quoted from Marlowe's *Tamburlaine*, I.1942–3. 4. prolific late-Victorian poet and aesthete, once admired for his musicality and metrical virtuosity, but now seldom read; he was a particular admirer of Blake, and of Elizabethan and Jacobean drama, being the author of prose studies of Blake (1868), Chapman (1875), Marlowe (1883), Middleton (1887) and Tourneur (1889).

William Shakespeare (1564–1616)

124 *Shakespeare's natural brain*

    And be it said of thee,
Shakespeare, thou had'st as smooth a comic vein,
Fitting the sock,[1] and in thy natural brain
As strong conception[2] and as clear a rage[3]
As anyone that trafficked[4] with the stage.
        ((1627) Michael Drayton (1563–1631),[5] from 'To ... Henry Reynolds, Esquire, Of Poets and Poesy')

1. see 12 n.1. 2. imaginative power. 3. inspiration. 4. had dealings with. 5. see 85 n.3.

125 To the Memory of my Beloved, the Author, Mr William Shakespeare, and What he hath Left Us

To draw no envy, Shakespeare, on thy name,
    Am I thus ample to thy book[1] and fame,
While I confess[2] thy writings to be such
    As neither man nor Muse can praise too much.
'Tis true, and all men's suffrage.[3] But these ways
    Were not the paths I meant unto thy praise;
For silliest ignorance on these may light,
    Which, when it sounds at best, but echoes right;
Or blind affection,[4] which doth ne'er advance
    The truth, but gropes and urgeth all by chance;
Or crafty malice might pretend this praise,
    And think to ruin where it seemed to raise.
These are as[5] some infamous bawd or whore
    Should praise a matron; what could hurt her more?
But thou art proof against them, and, indeed,
    Above the ill fortune of them, or the need.
I therefore will begin. Soul of the age!
    The applause, delight, the wonder of our stage!
My Shakespeare rise; I will not lodge thee by
    Chaucer, or Spenser, or bid Beaumont lie
A little further, to make thee a room;[6]
    Thou art a monument without a tomb,
And art alive still[7] while thy book doth live,
    And we have wits to read and praise to give.
That I not mix thee so,[8] my brain excuses –
    I mean with great but disproportioned[9] Muses;
For if I thought my judgement were of years,[10]
    I should commit[11] thee surely with thy peers,
And tell how far thou didst our Lyly[12] outshine,
    Or sporting Kyd,[13] or Marlowe's mighty line.
And though thou hadst small Latin and less Greek,
    From thence to honour thee I would not seek

For names, but call forth thundering Aeschylus,
    Euripides, and Sophocles[14] to us,
Pacuvius, Accius,[15] him of Cordova dead,[16]
    To life again, to hear thy buskin[17] tread,
And shake a stage; or, when thy socks[18] were on,
    Leave thee alone for the comparison
Of all that insolent Greece or haughty Rome
    Sent forth, or since did from their ashes come.
Triumph, my Britain, thou hast one to show,
    To whom all scenes[19] of Europe homage owe.
He was not of an age, but for all time!
    And all the Muses still were in their prime,
When like Apollo he came forth to warm
    Our ears, or like a Mercury[20] to charm.
Nature herself was proud of his designs,
    And joyed to wear the dressing of his lines,
Which were so richly spun, and woven so fit,
    As, since, she will vouchsafe[21] no other wit.
The merry Greek, tart Aristophanes,[22]
    Neat[23] Terence, witty Plautus,[24] now not please,
But antiquated and deserted lie,
    As they were not of Nature's family.
Yet must I not give Nature all; thy art,
    My gentle Shakespeare, must enjoy a part.
For though the poet's matter Nature be,
    His art doth give the fashion;[25] and that he
Who casts[26] to write a living line must sweat
    (Such as thine are) and strike the second heat[27]
Upon the Muses' anvil, turn the same
    (And himself with it) that he thinks to frame,
Or for[28] the laurel he may gain a scorn;
    For a good poet's made, as well as born.
And such wert thou. Look how the father's face
    Lives in his issue; even so, the race[29]
Of Shakespeare's mind and manners brightly shines
    In his well-turnèd and true-filèd lines,
In each of which he seems to shake a lance,[30]
    As brandished at the eyes of ignorance.
Sweet swan of Avon, what a sight it were
    To see thee in our waters yet appear,
And make those flights upon the banks of Thames
    That so did take Eliza and our James![31]
But stay! I see thee in the hemisphere
    Advanced, and made a constellation there!
Shine forth, thou star of poets, and with rage,
    Or influence,[32] chide, or cheer, the drooping stage;
Which, since thy flight from hence, hath mourned like night,
    And déspairs[33] day, but for thy volume's light.

((1623) Ben Jonson (1572–1637))

1. full in my praise of your volume; Jonson's poem first appeared among the preliminaries to the First Folio edition of Shakespeare's works (1623). 2. declare. 3. agreed opinion. 4. uncritical partisanship. 5. as if. 6. Jonson is jibing at a recent elegy on Shakespeare by

William Basse, which had imagined Spenser, Chaucer and Beaumont moving up in their graves to make room for Shakespeare. 7. always. 8. compare you thus. 9. not fully comparable. 10. mature. 11. compare. 12. for Lyly, see 115 n.5; Lyly's plays were written for boy actors and performed for courtly audiences. 13. Thomas Kyd (1558–94) is best remembered for *The Spanish Tragedy* (1592), one of the most popular plays on the Elizabethan stage. 14. the three greatest tragedians of ancient Athens. 15. Roman tragedians. 16. as well as being a philosopher (see 17 n.13), Seneca, who was born at Cordoba in Spain, wrote tragedies on the Greek model. 17. see 13 n.5. 18. see 12 n.1. 19. stages. 20. god of eloquence. 21. recognise. 22. (*c*.448–380 BC), the greatest comic poet of ancient Athens, whose plays abound in sharp topical satire. 23. pithy. 24. Publius Terentius Afer (*c*.190–159 BC) and Titus Maccius Plautus (*c*.254–184 BC), the two most famous comic poets of Rome, who wrote social comedies on Greek models, deploying stock characters. 25. shape, structure. 26. intends, plans. 27. mass of metal heated in a furnace for the second time. 28. instead of. 29. (i) liveliness (ii) rapidity (iii) lineage. 30. a play on the name 'Shake-spear'. 31. Queen Elizabeth I and James I, the latter of whom was Ben Jonson's patron. 32. the supposed flowing of etherial fluid from the stars which was thought to affect life on earth. 33. gives up hope of.

126 *Shakespeare's vices and virtues*

I remember the players have often mentioned it as an honour to Shakespeare that in his writing, whatsoever he penned, he never blotted out a line.[1] My answer hath been, 'Would he had blotted a thousand!' – which they thought a malevolent speech. I had not told posterity this, but for their ignorance, who choose that circumstance to commend their friend by, wherein he most faulted, and to justify mine own candour;[2] for I loved the man, and do honour his memory – on this side idolatry – as much as any. He was indeed honest, and of an open and free nature; had an excellent fancy,[3] brave notions,[4] and gentle expressions, wherein he flowed with that facility that sometime it was necessary he should be stopped; ... His wit was in his own power; would the rule of it had been so too!

((1640) Ben Jonson (1572–1637), from *Timber*)

1. in their prefatory address to the First Folio edition of Shakespeare (1623), the editors, Shakespeare's former actor-colleagues, John Heminges (1556–1630) and Henry Condell (d.1627), had commented on the neat state of Shakespeare's manuscripts. 2. partiality. 3. imagination. 4. grand ideas.

127 *Shakespeare's works his monument*

What needs my Shakespeare for his honoured bones
The labour of an age in pilèd stones?
Or that his hallowed relics should be hid
Under a star-ypointing pyramid?
Dear son of Memory,[1] great heir of Fame,
What need'st thou such weak witness of thy name?
Thou in our wonder and astonishment
Hast built thyself a livelong monument.
For whilst, to the shame of slow-endeavouring art,[2]
Thy easy numbers flow, and that each heart
Hath from the leaves of thy unvalued[3] book,
Those Delphic lines[4] with deep impression took,

Then thou our fancy[5] of itself bereaving,
Dost make us marble with too much conceiving;[6]
And so sepúlchred in such pomp dost lie,
That kings for such a tomb would wish to die.
((wr. 1630; pub. 1632) John Milton (1608–74), 'On Shakespeare')

1. Shakespeare is portrayed as the Muses' brother, since they are the 'Daughters of Memory'. 2. art which is achieved by long and strenuous application. 3. invaluable. 4. the shrine of the oracle of Apollo, god of poetry, was at Delphi. 5. imagination. 6. imagining; the reader is so rapt in his perusal of Shakespeare that he becomes, himself, like the monument on a grave.

128 *Shakespeare's comprehensive soul*

To begin ... with Shakespeare. He was the man who, of all modern, and perhaps ancient, poets, had the largest and most comprehensive soul. All the images of Nature were still[1] present to him, and he drew them not laboriously, but luckily.[2] When he describes any thing, you more than see it, you feel it too. Those who accuse him to have wanted learning give him the greater commendation. He was naturally learned. He needed not the spectacles of books to read Nature. He looked inwards and found her there. I cannot say he is everywhere alike. Were he so, I should do him injury to compare him with the greatest of mankind. He is many times flat, insipid, his comic wit degenerating into clenches,[3] his serious swelling into bombast. But he is always great when some great occasion is presented to him. No man can say he ever had a fit subject for his wit, and did not then raise himself as high above the rest of poets 'quantum lenta solent inter viburna cupressi' ['as high as cypress trees often do among the bending osiers'].[4]
((1668) John Dryden (1631–1700), from *Of Dramatic Poesy: an Essay*)

1. continuously. 2. successfully, easily. 3. feeble puns. 4. Virgil, *Eclogues*, I.25.

129 *Shakespeare the original*

If ever any author deserved the name of an original, it was Shakespeare. Homer himself drew not his art so immediately from the fountains of Nature. It proceeded through Egyptian strainers and channels,[1] and came to him not without some tincture of the learning, or some cast of the models, of those before him. The poetry of Shakespeare was inspiration indeed. He is not so much an imitator as an instrument of Nature; and it is not so just to say that he speaks from her as that she speaks through him.

His characters are so much Nature herself that 'tis a sort of injury to call them by so distant a name as copies of her. Those of other poets have a constant resemblance which shows that they received them from one another, and were but multipliers of the same image. Each picture, like a mock-rainbow,[2] is but the reflection of a reflection. But every single character in Shakespeare is as much an individual as those in life itself. It is as impossible to find any two alike; and such as from their relation or affinity in any respect appear most to be twins, will, upon comparison, be found remarkably distinct. To this life and variety of character we must add the wonderful preservation of it, which is such throughout his plays that had all the speeches been printed without the very names of the persons, I believe one might have applied them with certainty to every speaker.

The power over our passions was never possessed in a more eminent degree, or displayed in so different instances. Yet all along, there is seen no labour, no pains to raise them; no preparation to guide our guess to the effect, or be perceived to lead toward it. But the heart swells and the tears burst out just at the proper places. We are surprised the moment we weep; and yet upon reflection find the passion so just, that we should be surprised if we had not wept, and wept at that very moment.

How astonishing is it again, that the passions directly opposite to these, laughter and spleen, are no less at his command; that he is not more a master of the great than the ridiculous in human nature; of our noblest tendernesses, than of our vainest foibles; of our strongest emotions, than of our idlest sensations![3]

Nor does he only excel in the passions. In the coolness of reflection and reasoning he is full as admirable. His sentiments[4] are not only in general the most pertinent and judicious upon every subject, but by a talent very peculiar, something between penetration and felicity, he hits upon that particular point on which the bent of each argument turns, or the force of each motive depends. This is perfectly amazing from a man of no education or experience in those great and public scenes of life which are usually the subject of his thoughts; so that he seems to have known the world by intuition, to have looked through human nature at one glance, and to be the only author that gives ground for a very new opinion: that the philosopher, and even the man of the world, may be born, as well as the poet.

((1725) Alexander Pope (1688–1744), from Preface to *The Works of Shakespeare*)

1. in his 'Essay on the Life, Writings, and Learning of Homer', included in the early editions of Pope's translation of the *Iliad*, Thomas Parnell (see 21 n.2) surveyed the various legends and scholarly suggestions that Homer had visited Egypt, or that Egyptian influence is to be found in his work. 2. a secondary rainbow, 'a fainter one formed inside or outside the primary by double reflection and double refraction, and exhibiting the spectrum colours in the opposite order to that of the primary' (OED). 3. most superficial feelings. 4. thoughts, reflections.

130 *Shakespeare's motives for writing?*

Shakespeare (whom you and every playhouse bill
Style the divine, the matchless, what you will),
For gain, not glory, winged his roving flight,
And grew immortal in his own despite.

((1737) Alexander Pope (1688–1744), from 'The First Epistle of the Second Book of Horace Imitated: To Augustus')

131 *Wild Shakespeare*

For lofty sense,
Creative fancy, and inspection keen
Through the deep windings of the human heart,
Is not wild Shakespeare thine[1] and Nature's boast?
>   ((1744) James Thomson (1700–48), from 'Summer' in
>   *The Seasons*)

1. Britain's.

132 *Shakespeare's unevenness*

Pride of his own, and wonder of his age,
Who first created, and yet rules, the stage;
Bold to design, all-powerful to express,
Shakespeare each passion drew in every dress;
Great above rule, and imitating none,
Rich without borrowing, Nature was his own.
Yet is his sense debased by gross allay,[1]
As gold in mines lies mixed with dirt and clay.
Now eagle-winged his heavenward flight he takes;
The big stage thunders, and the soul awakes;
Now, low on earth, a kindred reptile creeps;
Sad Hamlet quibbles,[2] and the hearer sleeps.
>   ((1733) David Mallet (?1705–65),[3] from 'Of Verbal Criticism')

1. alloy (admixture of base metal). 2. puns, plays on words. 3. Scots author; a friend of Pope and collaborator with Thompson on the masque *Alfred* (1740), which contains the famous song, 'Rule Britannia'.

133 *Shakespeare's imagined worlds*

When Learning's triumph[1] o'er her barbarous foes
First reared the stage, immortal Shakespeare rose;
Each change of many-coloured life he drew,
Exhausted worlds, and then imagined new;
Existence saw him spurn her bounded reign,
And panting Time toiled after him in vain.
His powerful strokes presiding[2] Truth impressed,
And unresisted Passion stormed the breast.
>   ((1747) Samuel Johnson (1709–84), from 'Prologue Spoken by Mr
>   Garrick at the Opening of the Theatre in Drury Lane')

1. at the Renaissance. 2. commanding.

134 *Shakespeare as poet of nature*

Nothing can please many and please long, but just representations of General Nature.[1] Particular manners[2] can be known to few, and therefore few only can judge how nearly[3] they are copied. The irregular combinations of fanciful invention[4] may delight awhile, by that novelty of which the common satiety of life[5] sends us all in quest; but the pleasures of sudden wonder are soon exhausted, and the mind can only repose on the stability of truth.

Shakespeare is above all writers, at least above all modern[6] writers, the poet of Nature; the poet that holds up to his readers a faithful mirror[7] of manners and of life. His characters are not modified by the customs of particular places, unpractised by the rest of the world; by the peculiarities of studies or professions, which can operate but upon small numbers; or by the accidents of transient fashions or temporary opinions. They are the genuine progeny[8] of common humanity, such as the world will always supply, and observation will always find. His persons act and speak by the influence of those general passions and principles by which all minds are agitated, and the whole system of life is continued in motion. In the writings of other poets, a character is too often an individual;[9] in those of Shakespeare it is commonly a species.[10]

((1765) Samuel Johnson (1709–84), from Preface to *The Works of Shakespeare*)

1. the permanent features of human existence which (the artist can show) exist within, and express themselves through, the forms of particular societies. 2. the customs, habits, modes of behaviour, which are peculiar to one culture. 3. closely, accurately. 4. strange novelties conjured up by artists' imaginations. 5. the tedium offered by pleasures to which we are accustomed. 6. i.e. writers since those of ancient Greece and Rome. 7. Johnson echoes Hamlet's description of good acting (*Hamlet*, III,ii.22). 8. legitimate offspring. 9. *merely* peculiar, eccentric. 10. an embodiment, *in* an individual characterisation, of a recurrent principle of human behaviour.

135 *Shakespeare's drama the mirror of life*

Shakespeare has no heroes;[1] his scenes are occupied only by men who act and speak as the reader thinks that he should himself have spoken or acted on the same occasion. Even where the agency[2] is supernatural, the dialogue is level with life.[3] Other writers disguise the most natural passions and most frequent incidents; so that he who contemplates them in the book will not know them in the world. Shakespeare approximates[4] the remote and familiarises[5] the wonderful. The event which he represents will not happen, but if it were possible, its effects would probably be such as he has assigned; and it may be said that he has not only shown human nature as it acts in real exigences,[6] but as it would be found in trials to which it cannot be exposed.

This therefore, is the praise of Shakespeare: that his drama is the mirror of life;[7] that he who has mazed[8] his imagination in following the phantoms which other writers raise up before him may here be cured of his delirious extasies by reading human sentiments in human language; by scenes from which a hermit may estimate the transactions[9] of the world, and a confessor predict the progress of the passions.

((1765) Samuel Johnson (1709–84), from Preface to *The Works of Shakespeare*)

1. superhuman personages. 2. personage (but also including non-human characters, e.g. fairies, ghosts, witches, monsters). 3. of the same kind as to be found in life. 4. brings into our ken. 5. makes plausible. 6. urgent circumstances. 7. see 134 n.7. 8. bewildered. 9. happenings, going-on (hermits and priests are shut off from such 'transactions' by the circumstances of their vocation).

136 Shakespeare's mingled drama

Shakespeare's plays are not in the rigorous and critical sense either tragedies or comedies, but compositions of a distinct[1] kind, exhibiting the real state of sublunary[2] Nature, which partakes of good and evil, joy and sorrow, mingled with endless variety of proportion and innumerable modes of combination, and expressing the course of the world, in which the loss of one is the gain of another; in which, at the same time, the reveller is hasting to his wine, and the mourner burying his friend; in which the malignity of one is sometimes defeated by the frolic[3] of another, and many mischiefs and many benefits are done and hindered without design.

((1765) Samuel Johnson (1709–84), from Preface to *The Works of Shakespeare*)

1. different. 2. of this world, on earth. 3. prank, trick.

137 Shakespeare's durability

As his personages act upon principles arising from genuine passion, very little modified by particular forms,[1] their pleasures and vexations are communicable to all times and to all places; they are natural, and therefore durable; the adventitious[2] peculiarities of personal habits are only superficial dyes, bright and pleasing for a little while, yet soon fading to a dim tinct, without any remains of former lustre; but the discriminations of true passion are the colours of Nature; they pervade the whole mass, and can only perish with the body that exhibits them. The accidental compositions of heterogeneous modes[3] are dissolved by the chance which combined them; but the uniform simplicity of primitive qualities neither admits increase nor suffers decay. The sand heaped by one flood is scattered by another, but the rock always continues in its place. The stream of time, which is continually washing the dissoluble[4] fabrics of other poets, passes without injury by the adamant[5] of Shakespeare.

((1765) Samuel Johnson (1709–84), from Preface to *The Works of Shakespeare*)

1. the behaviour, rules, and customs peculiar to particular societies. 2. freak, eccentric. 3. compositions in which opposites, or things alien to one another, are arbitrarily conjoined. 4. soluble. 5. impenetrably hard stone.

138 Shakespeare's diverse plenty

The work of a correct and regular writer is a garden accurately formed and diligently planted, varied with shades and scented with flowers. The composition of Shakespeare is a forest, in which oaks extend their branches, and pines tower in the air, interspersed sometimes with weeds and brambles, and sometimes giving shelter to myrtles and to roses; filling the eye with awful[1] pomp, and gratifying the mind with endless diversity. Other poets display cabinets[2] of precious rarities, minutely finished, wrought into shape, and polished unto brightness. Shakespeare opens a mine which contains gold and diamonds in unexhaustible plenty, though clouded by incrustations, debased by impurities, and mingled with a mass of meaner minerals.

((1765) Samuel Johnson (1709–84), from Preface to *The Works of Shakespeare*)

1. awe-inspiring. 2. private jewel boxes.

139 *Shakespeare's quibbles*

A quibble[1] is to Shakespeare what luminous vapours[2] are to the traveller; he follows it at all adventures;[3] it is sure to lead him out of his way, and sure to engulf him in the mire. It has some malignant power over his mind, and its fascinations are irresistible. Whatever be the dignity or profundity of his disquisition, whether he be enlarging knowledge or exalting affection, whether he be amusing attention with incidents, or enchaining it in suspense, let but a quibble spring up before him, and he leaves his work unfinished. A quibble is the golden apple[4] for which he will always turn aside from his career, or stoop from his elevation. A quibble, poor and barren as it is, gave him such delight that he was content to purchase it by the sacrifice of reason, propriety and truth. A quibble was to him the fatal Cleopatra for which he lost the world[5] and was content to lose it.

((1765) Samuel Johnson (1709–84), from Preface to *The Works of Shakespeare*)

1. pun, play on the sound of words. 2. glowing ground-fog. 3. randomly, recklessly. 4. a reference to the story of Atalanta; Atalanta had vowed that she would only marry a man who could outrun her in a race; Hippomenes caused her to stop running by throwing golden apples in her path, and thus won her. 5. Dryden's version of the Antony and Cleopatra story (1678) is entitled *All for Love, or the World Well Lost*.

140 *Falstaff*

But Falstaff – unimitated, unimitable Falstaff – how shall I describe thee? Thou compound of sense and vice; of sense which may be admired[1] but not esteemed,[2] of vice which may be despised, but hardly detested. Falstaff is a character loaded with faults, and with those faults which naturally produce contempt. He is a thief and a glutton, a coward and a boaster, always ready to cheat the weak, and prey upon the poor; to terrify the timorous, and insult the defenceless. At once obsequious and malignant, he satirises in their absence those whom he lives by flattering. He is familiar with the Prince only as an agent of vice, but of this familiarity he is so proud as not only to be supercilious and haughty with common men, but to think his interest of importance to the Duke of Lancaster.[3] Yet the man thus corrupt, thus despicable, makes himself necessary to the Prince that despises him, by the most pleasing of all qualities: perpetual gaiety; by an unfailing power of exciting laughter, which is the more freely indulged, as his wit is not of the splendid or ambitious[4] kind, but consists in easy escapes[5] and sallies of levity,[6] which make sport, but raise no envy. It must be observed that he is stained with no enormous or sanguinary[7] crimes, so that his licentiousness is not so offensive but that it may be borne for his mirth.

((1765) Samuel Johnson (1709–84), from Notes to *2 Henry IV* in *The Works of Shakespeare*)

1. wondered at. 2. respected, valued highly. 3. see *2 Henry IV* I.ii.. 4. pretentious, designed to 'upstage' others. 5. spontaneous quips. 6. off-the-cuff frivolities. 7. cruel, murderous.

141 *'King Lear'*

The Tragedy of Lear is deservedly celebrated among the dramas of Shakespeare. There is perhaps no play which keeps the attention so strongly fixed; which so much agitates our passions and interests our curiosity. The artful involutions[1] of distinct interests, the striking opposition of contrary characters, the sudden changes of fortune, and the quick succession of events, fill the mind with a perpetual tumult of indignation, pity, and hope. There is no scene which does not contribute to the aggravation of the distress, or conduct of the action, and scarce a line which does not conduce to the progress of the scene. So powerful is the current of the poet's imagination, that the mind which once ventures within it is hurried irresistibly along.

((1765) Samuel Johnson (1709–84), from Notes to *King Lear* in *The Works of Shakespeare*)

1. ingenious interweaving.

142 *Shakespeare as Nature's darling*

Far from the sun and summer gale,
In thy green lap was Nature's darling laid,
What time, where lucid[1] Avon strayed,
To him the mighty Mother[2] did unveil
Her awful[3] face; the dauntless child
Stretched forth his little arms and smiled.
'This pencil[4] take,' she said, 'whose colours clear
Richly paint the vernal[5] year;
Thine, too, these golden keys, immortal boy!
This can unlock the gates of joy;
Of horror that, and thrilling fears,
Or ope the sacred source of sympathetic tears.'

((wr. 1751–4; pub. 1757) Thomas Gray (1716–71), from 'The Progress of Poesy: a Pindaric Ode')

1. clear. 2. Cybele, goddess of the powers of Nature. 3. awe-inspiring. 4. brush. 5. spring-like.

143 *Shakespeare defends his portrayal of his England*

What my age and climate[1] held to view,
Impartial I surveyed, and fearless drew.
And say, ye skilful in[2] the human heart,
Who know to prize a poet's noblest part,
What age, what clime, could e'er an ampler field
For lofty thought, for daring fancy[3] yield?
I saw this England break the shameful bands

Forged for the souls of men by sacred hands;[4]
I saw each groaning realm her aid implore;[5]
Her sons the heroes of each warlike shore;
Her naval standard (the dire Spaniard's bane)
Obeyed through all the circuit of the main.
Then, too, great Commerce, for a late-found world,
Around your coast her eager sails unfurled;
New hopes, new passions thence the bosom fired;
New plans, new arts the genius thence inspired;
Thence every scene which private fortune knows,
In stronger life, with bolder spirit, rose.
  Disgraced I this full prospect[6] which I drew?
My colours languid, or my strokes untrue?
Have not your sages, warriors, swains, and kings,
Confessed the living draught[7] of men and things?
What other bard in any clime appears
Alike the master of your smiles and tears?
Yet have I deigned your audience to entice
With wretched bribes to luxury and vice?
Or have my various scenes a purpose known
Which Freedom, Virtue, Glory, might not own?
        ((1749) Mark Akenside (1721–70),[8] from 'Odes II.i.: The
        Remonstrance of Shakespeare, Supposed to have been
        Spoken at the Theatre Royal, while the French
        Comedians were Acting by Subscription')

1. region of the earth. 2. knowledgeable about. 3. imaginative flights. 4. at the Reformation. 5. Elizabeth I, for example, sent help to the Netherlands in their struggle against Spanish domination. 6. scene. 7. drawn likeness. 8. see 36 n.3.

144 *Shakespeare and the sister arts*

O might some verse with happiest skill persuade
Expressive picture to adopt thine[1] aid!
What wondrous drafts might rise from every page!
What other Raphaels[2] charm a distant age!
  Methinks even now I view some free design,
Where breathing Nature lives in every line;
Chaste and subdued the modest lights decay,
Steal into shade, and mildly melt away.
  And see, where Antony, in tears approved,[3]
Guards the pale relics of the chief he loved;[4]
O'er the cold corse the warrior seems to bend,
Deep sunk in grief, and mourns his murdered friend!
Still as they press, he calls on all around,
Lifts the torn robe, and points the bleeding wound.
  But who is he, whose brows exalted bear
A wrath impatient and a fiercer air?[5]
Awake to all that injured worth can feel,
On his own Rome he turns the avenging steel.
Yet shall not war's insatiate fury fall
(So heaven ordains it) on the destined wall.
See the fond mother midst the plaintive train,

Hung on his knees, and prostrate on the plain!⁶
Touched to the soul, in vain he strives to hide
The son's affection in the Roman's pride.
O'er all the man conflicting passions rise;
Rage grasps the sword, while Pity melts the eyes.
   Thus, generous critic,⁷ as thy bard inspires,
The sister arts shall nurse their drooping fires;
Each from his scenes her stores alternate bring,
Blend the fair tints, or wake the vocal string.

((1743) William Collins (1721–59),⁸ from 'An Epistle, Addressed to Sir Thomas Hanmer, on his Edition of Shakespeare's Works')

1. Shakespeare's. 2. generally regarded in Collins's day as the greatest of all painters. 3. demonstrated to be genuine. 4. see *Julius Caesar*, III.ii. 5. Coriolanus. 6. see *Coriolanus*, V.iii. 7. Sir Thomas Hanmer (1677–1746) (editor of the 6-volume Oxford edition of Shakespeare [1743–4]), to whom the poem is addressed. 8. Collins had only just graduated from Oxford when he wrote this poem; the Odes, on which his later reputation rests, were written in the later 1740s; Collins died young, after suffering from a lengthy nervous illness.

145 *Shakespeare's transformations of reality*

In the plays of Shakespeare, every man sees himself, without knowing that he sees himself – as in the phenomena of nature, in the mist of the mountain, a traveller beholds his own figure, but the glory¹ round the head distinguishes it from a mere vulgar copy; or as a man traversing the Brocken² in the north of Germany at sunrise, when the glorious beams are shot askance the mountain; he sees before him a figure of gigantic proportions, and of such elevated dignity that he only knows it to be himself by the similarity of action; or as the Fata Morgana at Messina,³ in which all forms at determined distances are presented in an invisible mist, dressed in all the gorgeous colours of prismatic imagination and with magic harmony uniting them and producing a beautiful whole in the mind of the spectator.

((wr. 1811; pub. 1856) Samuel Taylor Coleridge (1772–1834), from a lecture on Shakespeare)

1. halo. 2. climbed by Coleridge on his German tour of 1798–9. 3. in Sicily, which Coleridge visited in 1804; the 'Fata Morgana' is the name by which a distinctive mirage effect at Messina is known.

146 *Shakespeare's organic form*

The form is mechanic when on any given material we impress a predetermined form, not necessarily arising out of the properties of the material; as when to a mass of wet clay we give whatever shape we wish it to retain when hardened. The organic form, on the other hand, is innate. It shapes, as it develops itself from within, and the fullness of its development is one and the same with the perfection of its outward form. Such is the life, such the form. Nature, the prime genial¹ artist, inexhaustible in diverse powers, is equally inexhaustible in forms; each exterior is the physiognomy² of the being within, its true image reflected and thrown out from the concave mirror; and even such is the appropriate excellence

of her chosen poet, of our own Shakespeare, himself a Nature humanised, a genial understanding directing self-consciously a power and an implicit wisdom deeper even than our consciousness.
>> ((wr. 1812; pub. 1836) Samuel Taylor Coleridge (1772–1834), from a lecture on *Romeo and Juliet* and *Hamlet* (published in *Literary Remains*))

1. creative. 2. external features.

147 'Venus and Adonis'

His Venus and Adonis seem at once the characters themselves, and the whole representation of those characters by the most consummate actors. You seem to be told nothing, but to see and hear everything. Hence it is that from the perpetual activity of attention required on the part of the reader; from the rapid flow, the quick change, and the playful nature of the thoughts and images; and above all from the alienation, and, if I may hazard such an expression, the utter *aloofness* of the poet's own feelings from those of which he is at once the painter and the analyst.
>> ((1817) Samuel Taylor Coleridge (1772–1834), from *Biographia Literaria*, Ch. 15)

148 *Shakespeare's creative power and intellectual energy*

No man was ever yet a great poet without being at the same time a profound philosopher. For poetry is the blossom and the fragrancy of all human knowledge, human thoughts, human passions, emotions, language. In Shakespeare's poems, the creative power and the intellectual energy wrestle as in a war embrace. Each in its excess of strength seems to threaten the extinction of the other. At length in the drama they were reconciled, and fought each with its shield before the breast of the other; or like two rapid streams that, at their first meeting within narrow and rocky banks, mutually strive to repel each other and intermix reluctantly and in tumult, but soon, finding a wider channel and more yielding shores, blend, and dilate, and flow on, in one current and with one voice. ...

Shakespeare, no mere child of Nature, no automaton of genius, no passive vehicle of inspiration possessed by the spirit, not possessing it, first studied patiently, meditated deeply, understood minutely, till knowledge, become habitual and intuitive, wedded itself to his habitual feelings, and at length gave birth to that stupendous power, by which he stands alone, with no equal or second in his own class; to that power which seated him on one of the two glory-smitten summits of the poetic mountain, with Milton as his compeer, not rival. While the former darts himself forth, and passes into all the forms of human character and passion, the one Proteus[1] of the fire and the flood, the other attracts all forms and things to himself, into the unity of his own ideal. All things and modes of action shape themselves anew in the being of Milton; while Shakespeare becomes all things, yet for ever remaining himself. O what great men hast thou not produced, England, my country! Truly, indeed,

> Must *we* be free or die, who speak the tongue
> Which Shakespeare spake; the faith and morals hold
> Which Milton held. In every thing we are sprung
> Of earth's first blood, have titles manifold!²

((1817) Samuel Taylor Coleridge (1772–1834), from *Biographia Literaria*, Ch.15)

1. see 55 n.1. 2. from Wordsworth's sonnet, 'It is not to be thought of that the flood...'

149 *Keynotes of Shakespeare's tragedies*

In the Shakespearian drama there is a vitality which grows and evolves itself from within, a keynote which guides and controls the harmonies throughout. What is *Lear*? It is storm and tempest; the thunder at first grumbling in the far horizon, then gathering around us, and at length bursting in fury over our heads, succeeded by a breaking of the clouds for a while, a last flash of lightning, the closing in of night, and the single hope of darkness! And *Romeo and Juliet*? It is a spring day, gusty and beautiful in the morn, and closing like an April evening with the song of the nightingale; whilst *Macbeth* is deep and earthy, composed to the subterranean music of a troubled conscience, which converts everything into the wild and fearful!

((wr. 1818; pub. 1836) Samuel Taylor Coleridge (1772–1834), from notes on Beaumont and Fletcher (published in *Literary Remains*))

150 *Mercutio*

Oh! how shall I describe that exquisite ebullience and overflow of youthful life, wafted on over the laughing wavelets of pleasure and prosperity, waves of the sea like a wanton beauty that distorted a face on which she saw her lover gazing enraptured, had wrinkled her surface in the triumph of its smoothness! Wit ever wakeful, fancy busy and procreative as insects, courage, an easy mind that, without cares of its own, was at once disposed to laugh away those of others, and yet be interested in them; these and all congenial qualities, melting into the common *copula*¹ of all, the man of quality and the gentleman, with all its excellencies and all its foibles!

((wr. 1819; pub. 1836) Samuel Taylor Coleridge (1772–1834), from a lecture on *Romeo and Juliet* (published in *Literary Remains*))

1. that which joins them.

151 *'Timon of Athens'*

It is a *Lear* of the satirical drama; a *Lear* of domestic or ordinary life; a local eddy of passion on the high road of society, while all around is the weekday goings-on of wind and weather; a *Lear*, therefore, without its soul-scorching flashes, its ear-cleaving thunderclaps, its meteoric splendours; without the contagion and the fearful sympathies of Nature, the Fates, the Furies, the frenzied Elements, dance in and out – now breaking through and scattering, now hand in hand with, the fierce or fantastic group of human passions, crimes, and anguishes, reeling on the unsteady ground, in a wild harmony to the swell and sink of the earthquake.

((wr. 1819; pub. 1836) Samuel Taylor Coleridge (1772–1834), from a lecture on *Troilus and Cressida* (published in *Literary Remains*))

152 Shakespeare and the human heart

He lighted with his golden lamp on high
The unknown regions of the human heart,
Showed its bright fountains, showed its rueful wastes,
Its shoals[1] and headlands; and a tower he raised
Refulgent,[2] where eternal breakers roll,
For all to see, but no man to approach.

((1846) Walter Savage Landor (1775–1864),[3] 'Shakespeare')

1. shallows. 2. brilliant, radiant. 3. author of *Imaginary Conversations* (1824–53), a series of dialogues between historical figures, and a vast body of occasional verse; admired by Browning and Ezra Pound.

153 Shakespeare's 'negative capability'

Several things dove-tailed in my mind, and at once it struck me what quality went to form a man of achievement, especially in literature, and which Shakespeare possessed so enormously; I mean *Negative Capability* – that is, when a man is capable of being in uncertainties, mysteries, doubts, without any irritable reaching after fact and reason. Coleridge, for instance, would let go by a fine isolated verisimilitude[1] caught from the Penetralium[2] of mystery, from being incapable of remaining content with half-knowledge. This pursued through volumes would perhaps take us no further than this: that with a great poet, the sense of beauty overcomes every other consideration, or rather obliterates all consideration.

((wr. 1817) John Keats (1795–1821), from a letter to George and Thomas Keats, 21 December)

1. likeness. 2. innermost shrine.

154 On Sitting Down to Read *King Lear* Once Again

O golden-tongued Romance, with sérene lute!
   Fair plumèd Siren,[1] Queen of far-away!
   Leave melodising on this wintry day,
Shut up thine olden pages, and be mute.
Adieu! For, once again, the fierce dispute
   Betwixt damnation and impassioned clay[2]
   Must I burn through; once more humbly assay[3]
The bitter-sweet of this Shakespearian fruit.
Chief poet, and ye clouds of Albion,[4]
   Begetters of our deep eternal theme!
When through the old oak forest I am gone,[5]

Let me not wander in a barren dream,
But when I am consumèd in the fire,
Give me new phoenix-wings[6] to fly at my desire.
            ((wr. 1818; pub. 1838) John Keats (1795–1821))

1. Romance is imagined as a temptress. 2. human life (in Gen. 2:7, man is formed by God from clay). 3. test. 4. England. 5. i.e. when I have finished reading *King Lear*. 6. the phoenix was a mythical Arabian bird which was alleged to burn itself on a funeral pyre and then to rise, with renewed vigour, from its own ashes; Keats hopes that his searing experience of reading *King Lear* will lead to a renewed outburst of his own creativity.

155 *Shakespeare's comprehensive humanity*

The soul of Man is larger than the sky,
Deeper than ocean, or the abysmal dark
Of the unfathomed centre. Like that Ark[1]
Which in its sacred hold uplifted high,
O'er the drowned hills, the human family,
And stock reserved of every living kind,
So, in the compass of the single mind,
The seeds and pregnant forms in essence lie
That make all worlds. Great poet, 'twas thy art
To know thyself, and in thyself to be
Whate'er Love, Hate, Ambition, Destiny,
Or the firm, fatal purpose of the heart,
Can make of Man. Yet thou wert still the same,
Serene of thought, unhurt by thy own flame.
            ((1833) Hartley Coleridge (1796–1849),[2] 'To Shakespeare')

1. i.e. Noah's. 2. see 93 n.4.

156 *Shakespeare's supremacy*

Others abide our question;[1] thou art free.
We ask and ask; thou smilest and art still,
Out-topping knowledge.[2] For the loftiest hill,
Who to the stars uncrowns his majesty,

Planting his steadfast footsteps in the sea,
Making the heaven of heavens his dwelling-place,
Spares but[3] the cloudy border of his base
To the foiled searching of mortality;[4]

And thou, who didst the stars and sunbeams know,
Self-schooled, self-scanned;[5] self-honoured, self-secure,
Didst tread on earth unguessed at. Better so!

All pains the immortal spirit must endure,
All weakness which impairs, all griefs which bow,
Find their sole speech in that victorious brow.
            ((wr. 1844; pub. 1849) Matthew Arnold (1822–88), 'Shakespeare')

1. wait long enough for us to be able to derive answers to our probing questioning of them. 2. exceeding our comprehension. 3. only leaves. 4. the baffled questioning of ordinary mortals. 5. the object of your own scrutiny.

157 *Shakespeare beyond praise*

Not if men's tongues and angels' all in one
  Spake, might the word be said that might speak thee.
  Streams, winds, woods, flowers, fields, mountains, yea, the sea,
What power is in them all to praise the sun?
His praise is this: he can be praised of none.
  Man, woman, child, praise God for him; but he
  Exults not to be worshipped, but to be.
He is; and, being, beholds his work well done.
All joy, all glory, all sorrow, all strength, all mirth,
Are his; without him, day were night on earth.
  Time knows not his from time's own period.
All lutes, all harps, all viols, all flutes, all lyres
Fall dumb before him ere one string suspires.[1]
  All stars are angels; but the sun is God.
      ((1882) Algernon Charles Swinburne (1837–1909),[2] 'Shakespeare',
            from 'Sonnets on the English Dramatic Poets')

1. breathes forth sound. 2. see 123 n.4.

The 'metaphysical' poets

158 *The dangers of 'conceits'*

Some to conceit[1] alone their taste confine,
And glittering thoughts struck out at every line;
Pleased with a work where nothing's just or fit;
One glaring chaos and wild heap of wit.
Poets, like painters, thus, unskilled to trace
The naked nature and the living grace,
With gold and jewels cover every part,
And hide with ornaments their want of art.
True wit is Nature[2] to advantage[3] dressed;[4]
What oft was thought,[5] but ne'er so well expressed;
Something whose truth convinced at sight we find,
That gives us back the image of our mind.[6]
As shades more sweetly recommend the light,
So modest plainness sets off sprightly wit.
For works may have more wit than does 'em good,
As bodies perish through excess of blood.
      ((wr. 1709; pub. 1711) Alexander Pope (1688–1744), from *An*
            Essay on Criticism)

1. far-fetched metaphors and similes. 2. see 23 n.1. 3. in a way that reveals her true beauties. 4. (i) presented (with the hint that Nature will be better 'dressed' the more naked she seems) (ii) arranged (as in a garden). 5. lurking in people's minds in a dim and inchoate form. 6. that produces in the reader a spark of recognition.

159 Characteristics of the 'metaphysical' poets

The most heterogeneous ideas are yoked by violence together. Nature and art are ransacked for illustrations, comparisons, and allusions. Their learning instructs and their subtlety surprises; but the reader commonly thinks his improvement dearly bought, and, though he sometimes admires, is seldom pleased.

From this account of their compositions, it will be readily inferred that they were not successful in representing or moving the affections. As they were wholly employed on something unexpected and surprising, they had no regard to that uniformity of sentiment[1] which enables us to conceive and to excite the pains and the pleasure of other minds. They never inquired what, on any occasion, they should have said or done, but wrote rather as beholders than partakers of human nature; as beings looking upon good and evil, impassive and at leisure; as Epicurean[2] deities, making remarks on the actions of men, and the vicissitudes[3] of life, without interest[4] and without emotion. Their courtship was void of fondness, and their lamentation of sorrow. Their wish was only to say what they hoped had been never said before.

Nor was the sublime more within their reach than the pathetic;[5] for they never attempted that comprehension[6] and expanse of thought which at once fills the whole mind, and of which the first effect is sudden astonishment, and the second rational admiration. Sublimity is produced by aggregation,[7] and littleness by dispersion.[8] Great thoughts are always general,[9] and consist in positions not limited by exceptions, and in descriptions not descending to minuteness.[10] It is with great propriety that subtlety, which in its original import means exility[11] of particles, is taken in its metaphorical meaning for nicety[12] of distinction. Those writers who lay on the watch for novelty could have little hope of greatness; for great things cannot have escaped former observation. Their attempts were always analytic. They broke every image into fragments, and could no more represent, by their slender conceits and laboured particularities, the prospects[13] of nature, or the scenes of life, than he who dissects a sunbeam with a prism can exhibit the wide effulgence[14] of a summer noon.

((1779) Samuel Johnson (1709–84), from 'Cowley' in *Lives of the Poets*)

1. those feelings common (at least potentially) to all human beings. 2. the Greek philosopher Epicurus (341–270 BC) taught that the gods live happily in space, caring nothing for our world or any other. 3. changing circumstances, fortunes. 4. concern, involvement. 5. capacity to display, and to induce in the reader, sympathetic involvement. 6. inclusiveness. 7. encompassing many details or perceptions in a single view. 8. breaking down potentially large thoughts into numerous disparate details. 9. comprehensive (not 'generalised'). 10. insignificant, and therefore distracting, detail. 11. minuteness. 12. exactness, precision. 13. views, scenes. 14. splendid radiance.

John Donne (1572–1631)

160 To John Donne [1]

    Donne, the delight of Phoebus[1] and each Muse,
      Who, to thy one, all other brains refuse;[2]
    Whose every work of thy most early[3] wit
      Came forth example, and remains so yet;
    Longer a-knowing[4] than most wits do live,
      And which no affection praise enough can give!
    To it[5] thy language, letters, arts, best life,
      Which might with half mankind maintain a strife.[6]
    All which I meant to praise, and yet[7] I would;
      But leave, because I cannot as I should!

                    ((1616) Ben Jonson (1572–1637))

1. Apollo (see 19 n.1). 2. refuse to inspire all other poets' brains, because they are inspiring yours. 3. fully developed at an early age; in his *Conversations* with Drummond of Hawthornden, Jonson expressed the view that Donne had 'written all his best pieces ere he was 25 years old'. 4. practising his art. 5. as well as your wit. 6. rival. 7. still.

161 To John Donne [2]

    Who shall doubt, Donne, whe'er[1] I a poet be,
      When I dare send my epigrams to thee?
    That so alone canst judge, so alone dost make,[2]
      And in thy censures,[3] evenly, dost take
    As free simplicity to disavow[4]
      As thou has best authority to allow.
    Read all I send; and if I find but one
      Marked by thy hand, and with the better stone,[5]
    My title's sealed. Those that for claps do write,
      Let puisnees',[6] porters', players' praise delight,
    And, till they burst, their backs, like asses', load;
      A man should seek great glory, and not broad.

                    ((1616) Ben Jonson (1572–1637))

1. whether. 2. who write so supremely well. 3. criticisms. 4. are as straightforward about disapproving of. 5. it was a Roman custom to reckon happy days or events with white ('better') stones, and unhappy days with black ones. 6. novices'.

162 To Lucy, Countess of Bedford, with Mr Donne's Satires

    Lucy,[1] you brightness of our sphere, who are
      Life of the Muses' day, their morning star![2]
    If works (not the authors) their own grace[3] should look,[4]
      Whose poems would not wish to be your book?
    But these, desired by you, the maker's ends
      Crown with their own. Rare poems ask rare friends.
    Yet satires (since the most of mankind be

Their unavoided[5] subject) fewest see;
    For none e'er took that pleasure in sin's sense,
But, when they heard it taxed,[6] took more offence.
    They, then, that, living where the matter's bred,[7]
Dare for these poems yet both ask and read,[8]
    And like them too, must needfully, though few,
Be of the best; and 'mongst those, best are you.
    Lucy, you brightness of our sphere, who are
The Muses' evening, as their morning, star.
                ((1616) Ben Jonson (1572–1637))

1. Lucy, Countess of Bedford (?1581–1627) was the patroness of Drayton (see 85 n.3) and Daniel (see 4 n.2), as well as of Jonson and Donne; Jonson plays on the derivation of her name from the Latin *lux, lucis* ('light'). 2. Lucifer (the planet Venus). 3. good fortune. 4. seek. 5. inevitable. 6. criticised. 7. in the society being pilloried in the satires. 8. dare both to ask for and to read these poems.

163 Donne's life and works

He that would write an epitaph for thee,
    And do it well, must first begin to be
Such as thou wert; for none can truly know
    Thy worth, thy life, but he that hath lived so.
He must have wit to spare, and to hurl down,
    Enough to keep[1] the gallants of the town;
He must have learning plenty, both the laws
    Civil and common, to judge any cause;[2]
Divinity great store, above the rest,[3]
    Not of the last edition,[4] but the best.
He must have language, travel,[5] all the arts,
    Judgement to use, or else he wants thy parts;
He must have friends the highest, able to do,
    Such as Maecenas[6] and Augustus too.
He must have such a sickness, such a death,
    Or else his vain descriptions come beneath.[7]
Who then shall write an epitaph for thee,
    He must be dead first; let it alone for me.
            ((1633) Richard Corbet (1582–1635),[8] 'An Epitaph on
                                Dr Donne, Dean of Paul's')

1. maintain, sustain; Donne's early years were spent among the 'wits' and 'gallants' of Elizabethan London, and his early poems were probably written for circulation in such a milieu. 2. Donne was a student of law at Lincoln's Inn in the early 1590s. 3. Donne was ordained deacon and priest in 1615, and elected Dean of St Paul's in 1621. 4. probably a reference to Puritan innovations in Anglican practices, not subscribed to by Donne. 5. Donne travelled abroad extensively, probably before attending Lincoln's Inn, and again in 1605, and certainly as a gentleman-adventurer in the 1590s and with Sir Robert Drury in 1611-12.
6. Gaius Maecenas (d. 8 BC), trusted counsellor to the emperor Augustus, and patron to the Roman poets Virgil, Horace, and Propertius; Donne counted several of the most powerful of the Jacobean aristocracy, as well as James I himself, among his patrons and supporters.
7. Donne described the after-effects of death with a bizarre luridness in his sermon *Death's Duel* (1631), and in the same year posed for a drawing of himself in his funeral shroud.
8. chaplain to James I, and later Bishop of Oxford, then Norwich; as a poet, Corbet is best known for his ballad 'The Fairies' Farewell' (beginning 'Farewell, rewards and fairies,...'); he may have met Donne at the gatherings of wits at the Mermaid Tavern in London during 1612.

164 Praising Donne

Having delivered now what praises are,[1]
It rests that I should to the world declare
Thy praises, Donne, whom I so loved alive,[2]
That with my witty Carew[3] I should strive
To celebrate thee dead, did I not need
A language by itself, which should exceed
All those which are in use; for while I take
Those common words which men may even rake
From dunghill-wits, I find them so defiled,
Slubbered[4] and false, as if they had exiled
Truth and propriety, such as do tell
So little other things, they hardly spell[5]
Their proper meaning, and therefore unfit
To blazon forth thy merits, or thy wit.
   Nor will it serve that thou didst so refine
Matter with words, that both did seem divine
When thy breath uttered them, for, thou being gone,
They straight did follow thee; let therefore none
Hope to find out an idiom and sense
Equal to thee and to thy eminence,
Unless our gracious King give words their bound,
Call in false titles,[6] which each-where are found
In prose and verse, and as bad coin and light[7]
Suppress them and their values, till the right
Take place and do appear, and then in lieu
Of those forged attributes stamp[8] some anew,
Which, being current, and by all allowed,
In epitaphs and tombs might be avowed[9]
More then their 'scutcheons.[10]

((wr. ?1631–2; pub. 1665) Edward, Lord Herbert of Cherbury
(1582–1648),[11] from 'Elegy for Dr Donne')

1. the first part of the poem has defined, in general terms, the conditions under which praise is most properly expressed. 2. Donne and Herbert were friends, Donne having addressed a poem to Herbert while the latter was serving with an English force which was helping the Prince of Orange to besiege Juliers in 1610. 3. see 165. 4. (i) soiled, dirty (ii) careless, hasty. 5. denote. 6. invalid claims (with a pun on 'titles', meaning the 'names' of documents, books, etc.). 7. below the legal weight (probably because 'clipped'). 8. mint. 9. acknowledged, heeded. 10. crests (on the tombs). 11. elder brother of George Herbert; diplomat, philosopher, historian, and deist; author of a frank and informative autobiography, *The Life of Lord Herbert, Written by Himself* (pub. 1765).

165 An Elegy upon the Death of Dr Donne, Dean of Paul's

Can we not force from widowed poetry,
Now thou art dead,[1] great Donne, one elegy
To crown thy hearse? Why yet dare we not trust,
Though with unkneaded dough-baked prose, thy dust,
Such as the unscissored[2] churchman, from the flower
Of fading rhetoric, short-lived as his hour,
Dry as the sand that measures it,[3] should lay
Upon thy ashes on the funeral day?

Have we no voice, no tune? Didst thou dispense
Through all our language both the words and sense?
'Tis a sad truth. The pulpit may her plain
And sober Christian precepts still retain;
Doctrines it may, and wholesome uses, frame,
Grave homilies and lectures; but the flame
Of thy brave[4] soul, that shot such heat and light
As burnt our earth, and made our darkness bright,
Committed holy rapes upon our will,
Did through the eye the melting heart distil,
And the deep knowledge of dark truths so teach
As sense might judge what fancy could not reach,[5]
Must be desired[6] forever. So the fire
That fills with spirit and heat the Delphic choir,[7]
Which, kindled first by thy Promethean[8] breath,
Glowed here awhile, lies quenched now in thy death.

   The Muses' garden, with pedantic weeds
O'erspread, was purged by thee; the lazy seeds
Of servile imitation thrown away,
And fresh invention planted; thou didst pay
The debts of our penurious bankrupt age –
Licentious thefts, that make poetic rage[9]
A mimic[10] fury, when our souls must be
Possessed, or with Anacreon's ecstasy,
Or Pindar's,[11] not their own. The subtle cheat
Of sly exchanges,[12] and the juggling feat
Of two-edged words,[13] or whatsoever wrong
By ours was done the Greek or Latin tongue,
Thou hast redeemed, and opened us a mine
Of rich and pregnant fancy;[14] drawn a line
Of masculine[15] expression, which had good
Old Orpheus[16] seen, or all the ancient brood
Our superstitious fools admire, and hold
Their lead more precious than thy burnished gold,
Thou hadst been their exchequer,[17] and no more
They each in other's dust had raked for ore.

   Thou shalt yield no precédence, but of time,
And the blind fate of language, whose tuned chime[18]
More charms the outward sense; yet thou mayst claim
From so great disadvantage greater fame,
Since to the awe of thy imperious wit
Our stubborn language bends, made only fit
With her tough thick-ribbed hoops to gird about[19]
Thy giant fancy, which had proved too stout
For their soft melting phrases. As in time
They had the start, so did they cull the prime
Buds of invention many a hundred year,
And left the rifled fields, besides the fear
To touch their harvest; yet from those bare lands
Of what is purely thine, thy only hands
(And that thy smallest work[20]) have gleanèd more
Than all those times and tongues could reap before.

But thou are gone, and thy strict laws will be
Too hard for libertines[21] in poetry.
They will repeal[22] the goodly exiled train
Of gods and goddesses, which in thy just reign
Were banished nobler poems; now, with these,
The silenced tales o'the *Metamorphoses*
Shall stuff their lines, and swell the windy page,
Till verse, refined by thee in this last age,
Turn ballad-rhyme, or those old idols be
Adored again with new apostasy.[23]

   O pardon me, that break with untuned[24] verse
The reverend silence that attends thy hearse,
Whose awful[25] solemn murmurs were to thee,
More than these faint lines, a loud elegy,
That did proclaim in a dumb eloquence
The death of all the arts; whose influence,
Grown feeble, in these panting numbers[26] lies
Gasping short-winded accents,[27] and so dies.
So doth the swiftly-turning wheel not stand
In the instant we withdraw the moving hand,
But some small time maintain a faint, weak course,
By virtue of the first impulsive force;
And so, whilst I cast on thy funeral pile
Thy crown of bays,[28] oh, let it crack[29] awhile,
And spit disdain, till the devouring flashes
Suck all the moisture up, then turn to ashes.

   I will not draw the envy, to engross[30]
All thy perfections, or weep all our loss;
Those are too numerous[31] for an elegy,
And this too great to be expressed by me.
Though every pen should share a distinct part,
Yet art thou theme enough to tire[32] all art;
Let others carve the rest; it shall suffice
I on thy tomb this epitaph incise :
   Here lies a king, that ruled as he thought fit
   The universal monarchy of wit;
   Here lie two flamens,[33] and both those the best;
   Apollo's first, at last the true God's priest.

((1633) Thomas Carew (?1595–1640)[34])

1. Donne died on 31 March 1631. 2. with uncut hair (?through grief). 3. hourglasses were used by preachers to measure the duration of their sermon. 4. magnificent, excellent. 5. so that people could clearly understand things which are normally too obscure even for imagination to reach. 6. lacked, missed. 7. poets (see 127 n.4). 8. in Greek myth, the Titan Prometheus stole fire from heaven for the benefit of mankind; Donne is imagined as having done something analogous for the benefit of his fellow-poets. 9. inspiration. 10. imitative, derivative. 11. the light verses on the pleasures of drink and love attributed to the Greek poet Anacreon (6th century BC) were much imitated in the Renaissance; for Pindar, see 94 n.3. 12. ?plagiarisms. 13. perhaps a reference to the habit, common in Renaissance poetry, of using English words in ways that require knowledge of their Latin or Greek derivations. 14. imagining. 15. a reference to the 'strong lines' of Donne's verse which his followers admired for their daring playing-off of speech rhythms against the expected metrical pattern. 16. see 12 n.10. 17. source of currency. 18. regular rhymed verse. 19. the conceit perhaps refers to the hooping of barrels with metal bands, perhaps to the whalebone hoops which

women wore beneath their skirts; if the latter, the conceit would be taking up, playfully, the earlier reference to Donne's 'masculine' expression: the tough intractability of the English language was a suitable undergarment for (was fit to 'gird about') Donne's imagination; only such an 'imperious wit' as his could subject such a stubborn garment to adequate control. 20. the bulk of Donne's sermons far exceeds that of his poetical works. 21. undisciplined practitioners. 22. recall; mythological subjects from the *Metamorphoses* of the Roman poet Ovid (Publius Ovidius Naso, 43 BC–AD 17 – see 181 n.1) had been particularly popular with the poets and dramatists who were writing in Donne's youth and early manhood. 23. a second abandonment of Christian principles, because (i) the Ovidian tales are of pagan gods, and (ii) because they are regarded with idolatrous reverence. 24. unharmonious, limping. 25. awe-struck. 26. verses. 27. stressed syllables. 28. laurels. 29. crackle (in the flames). 30. catalogue in legal fullness. 31. (i) many (ii) poetical. 32. (i) weary (ii) dress, attire. 33. in Roman religion, the priests of specific deities; here the gods of poetry and of the Christian religion. 34. ambassador, courtier, and friend of Ben Jonson and Suckling (see 173 n.5); author of the court masque *Coelum Britannicum* (1634) and of shorter poems which combine the influences of Donne and Ben Jonson, as well as of various continental poets.

166 Donne's hallowing of passion

Passion's excess for thee we need not fear,
Since first by thee our passions hallowed[1] were;
Thou mad'st our sorrows, which before had been
Only for the success,[2] sorrows for sin;
We owe thee all those tears, now thou art dead,
Which we shed not, which for ourselves we shed.
Nor didst thou only consecrate our tears,
Give a religious tincture[3] to our fears,
But even our joys had learned an innocence;
Thou didst from gladness separate offence;[4]
All minds at once sucked grace from thee, as where,
The curse revoked, the nations had one ear.[5]
Pious dissector! thy one hour did treat
The thousand mazes of the heart's deceit;
Thou didst pursue our loved and subtle sin
Through all the foldings we had wrapped it in,
And in thine own large mind finding the way
By which ourselves we from ourselves convey,[6]
Didst in us, narrow models, know the same
Angles, though darker, in our meaner frame.
((1635) Sidney Godolphin (1610–43),[7] from 'Elegy on John Donne')

1. made holy (by Donne's sermons and religious verse). 2. the result of our deeds. 3. colouring. 4. wickedness. 5. as at the Last Judgement, when the curse of Eden will be finally revoked for Man (see Rev. 22). 6. conceal. 7. acquainted with Jonson, and a member of the circle of scholars and writers who met at Great Tew, the house near Oxford of Lucius Cary, Viscount Falkland (1610–43); killed while fighting on the royalist side in the Civil War.

167 On Donne's Poetry

With Donne, whose Muse on dromedary[1] trots,
Wreath iron pokers into true-love knots;
Rhyme's sturdy cripple, fancy's maze and clew,[2]
Wit's forge and fire-blast, meaning's press and screw.
((wr. ?1818; pub. 1836) Samuel Taylor Coleridge (1772–1834))

1. camel trained for riding. 2. ball of string by means of which one finds one's way out of a maze.

168 Donne and the 'metaphysicals'

Brief was the reign of pure poetic truth;
A race of thinkers next, with rhymes uncouth,
And fancies fashioned in laborious brains,
Made verses heavy as o'erloaded wains.[1]
Love was their theme, but love that dwelt in stones,[2]
Or charmed the stars in their concentric zones;[3]
Love that did erst[4] the nuptial bond conclude
'Twixt immaterial form and matter rude;
Love that was riddled, sphered,[5] transacted, spelt,
Sublimed,[6] projected,[7] everything but felt.
Or if in age, in orders,[8] or the cholic,
They damned all loving as a heathen frolic,
They changed their topic, but in style the same,
Adored their maker as they wooed their dame.
Thus Donne, not first, but greatest of the line,
Of stubborn thoughts a garland thought to twine;
To his fair maid brought cabalistic[9] posies,
And sung quaint ditties of metempsychosis;[10]
'Twists iron poker into true love-knots',[11]
Coining hard words, not found in polyglots.[12]

((1851) Hartley Coleridge (1796–1849),[13] 'Donne')

1. waggons. 2. see, for example, Donne's 'Nocturnal Upon St Lucy's Day', 33–4. 3. a reference to the Elizabethan belief (classically derived, see 14 n.1) that the sun, planets, and fixed stars were set in transparent concentric spheres orbiting round the earth; the spheres are frequently alluded to in the poetry of Donne and his admirers; see, for example, 'Love's Growth', St.2. 4. at the beginning of time. 5. set among the spheres, idealised. 6. transformed by chemical process into a vapour (a metaphor of a type frequently used in Donne's poetry). 7. planned, calculated. 8. when they had become priests (as did Donne, and later his admirers George Herbert and Richard Crashaw). 9. esoteric, obscure. 10. *Metempsychosis* ['The Transmigration of the Soul'] is the subtitle of *The Progress of the Soul*, Donne's notoriously obscure satirical poem (wr. 1601) which charts the progress of the soul of Heresy from the Garden of Eden. 11. an allusion to 167. 12. books written in several languages. 13. see 93 n.4.

Ben Jonson (1572–1637)

169 On *The New Inn*:[1] Ode, To Himself

Come leave the lothèd stage,
And the more loathsome age,
Where Pride and Impudence, in faction knit,
 Usurp the chair of Wit;
Indicting and arraigning every day
 Something they call a play.
Let their fastidious, vain
Commission[2] of the brain
Run on and rage, sweat, censure, and condemn;
They were not made for thee, less thou for them.

Say that thou pour'st them wheat,

And they will acorns eat;
'Twere simple fury[3] still[4] thyself to waste
    On such as have no taste;
To offer them a surfeit of pure bread
    Whose appetites are dead.
    No, give them grains[5] their fill,
    Husks, draff[6] to drink and swill;
If they love lees, and leave the lusty wine,
Envy them not; their palate's with the swine.

    No doubt some mouldy tale
    Like *Pericles*,[7] and stale
As the shrieve's crusts,[8] and nasty as his fish;
    Scraps out of every dish,
Thrown forth, and raked into the common tub,[9]
    May keep up the play-club;[10]
    There sweepings do as well
    As the best-ordered meal;[11]
For who the relish of these guests will fit
Needs set them but the alms-basket of wit.

    And much good do't you then;
    Brave plush and velvet men[12]
Can feed on orts;[13] and safe in your stage-clothes[14]
    Dare quit, upon your oaths,
The stagers and the stage-wrights too, your peers,[15]
    Of larding your large ears
    With their foul comic socks,[16]
    Wrought upon twenty blocks;[17]
Which, if they're torn and turned and patched enough,
The gamesters[18] share your guilt,[19] and you their stuff.[20]

    Leave[21] things so prostitute,
    And take the Alcaic[22] lute,
Or thine own Horace, or Anacreon's[23] lyre;
    Warm thee by Pindar's[24] fire;
And though thy nerves[25] be shrunk, and blood be cold,
    Ere years have made thee old,
    Strike that disdainful heat
    Throughout, to their defeat;
As curious[26] fools, and envious of thy strain,
May, blushing, swear no palsy's in thy brain.[27]

    But when they hear thee sing
    The glories of thy King,
His zeal to God, and his just awe o'er men,[28]
    They may, blood-shaken, then
Feel such a flesh-quake to possess their powers,
    As they shall cry, 'Like ours
    In sound of peace or wars
    No harp e'er hit the stars,[29]
In tuning forth the acts of his sweet reign,
And raising Charles's chariot 'bove his wain.'[30]

                    ((1631) Ben Jonson (1572–1637))

1. this poem expresses Jonson's indignation at the 'vulgar censure' of his play *The New Inn* (1629) 'by some malicious spectators'; it provoked several replies (see, for example, 171), some of which mimicked Jonson's form and metre. 2. perhaps an allusion to the Court of High Commission, a judicial committee established in the reign of Elizabeth 1 to investigate ecclesiastical cases, and abolished in 1641. 3. pure madness. 4. constantly. 5. malt left over after brewing. 6. dregs. 7. the play, partly by Shakespeare, first published in 1609; it draws on the story of Apollonius of Tyre, of which there had been several previous tellings in English. 8. sheriff's (i.e. prison) food. 9. where left-overs were collected from feasts in the City and at Court, for distribution to the poor. 10. the coterie of contemporaries who set themselves up in judgement on new plays. 11. in an earlier version of the poem, Jonson had here referred, abusively, to his former servant Richard Brome, whose play *The Love-Sick Maid* had been extremely successful in the same year that *The New Inn* had failed. 12. the richly dressed members of the audience. 13. scraps. 14. finery worn to attend plays; actors often wore the cast-off clothes of the theatre-goers. 15. the actors and playwrights, the 'peers' (equals in stupidity) of the audience, use the excuse of the audience's 'oaths' ((i) legal affidavits (ii) boistrous row) to absolve ('quit') themselves of the charge of having stuffed the audience's ears with their nonsense. 16. see 12 n.1. 17. (i) moulds on which 'socks' were made (ii) blockheads. 18. actors. 19. with a pun on 'gilt' (gilded finery). 20. (i) clothes (ii) nonsense. 21. Jonson now returns to addressing himself. 22. Alcaeus (b. *c.*620 BC) was a Greek lyric poet imitated in Latin by Horace (for whom see 20 n.1, 31 n.1), whom Jonson regarded as one of his own principal models (Jonson cast himself as Horace in his play *Poetaster* [pub. 1602]). 23. see 165 n.11; the 'Anacreontics' were frequently associated with the *Odes* of Horace; Jonson, along with many other renaissance poets, wrote verse in the 'Anacreontic' style. 24. see 94 n.3. 25. muscles. 26. hard-to-please. 27. Jonson had suffered a paralytic stroke in 1628. 28. the awe in which men hold the King. 29. Horace (*Odes*, I.i.35–6) had claimed that if his lyric poetry was praised, his head would 'touch the stars'. 30. 'Charles's Wain' is the constellation, The Great Bear; Jonson puns on 'wane'; Charles 1 had succeeded to the throne in 1625.

170 An Ode for Ben Jonson

    Ah Ben!
  Say how, or when,
  Shall we thy guests
  Meet at those lyric feasts,
    Made at The Sun,
The Dog, The Triple Tun?[1]
  Where we such clusters[2] had
As made us nobly wild, not mad;
  And yet each verse of thine
Outdid the meat, outdid the frolic wine.

    My Ben,
  Or[3] come again,
  Or send to us
Thy wit's great over-plus;
    But teach us yet
Wisely to husband it;[4]
  Lest we that talent[5] spend,
And having once brought to an end
  That precious stock, the store
Of such a wit the world should have no more.
        (wr. ?1637; pub. 1648) Robert Herrick (1591–1674)[6]

1. three London inns where Ben Jonson and his admirers, the 'Sons of Ben' (who included Herrick) met regularly. 2. meetings, gatherings. 3. either. 4. Jonson was renowned for the craftsmanship and economy of his art. 5. (i) literary skill (ii) precious coin. 6. one of the 'Cavalier' poets; a clergyman and disciple of Jonson, the author of *Hesperides* (1648), a collection of secular poems, many of them short lyrics, and *Noble Numbers* (also 1648), a volume of religious verse; Herrick's poetry was neglected for some time after his death, but many of his poems were printed in the influential Victorian anthology, Palgrave's *Golden Treasury* (in the compilation of which Tennyson played a significant part), and his work was highly praised by Swinburne (on whom see 123 n.4).

171 To Ben Jonson, Upon Occasion of his Ode of Defiance Annexed to his Play of *The New Inn*[1]

'Tis true, dear Ben, thy just, chastising hand
Hath fixed upon the sotted[2] age a brand,
To their swollen pride and empty scribbling due;
It can nor judge nor write; and yet 'tis true
Thy comic Muse, from the exalted line
Touched by thy *Alchemist*, doth since decline
From that her zenith, and foretells a red
And blushing evening, when she goes to bed;[3]
Yet such as shall outshine the glimmering light
With which all stars shall gild the following night.
Nor think it much (since all thy eaglets may
Endure the sunny trial) if we say
This hath the stronger wing, or that doth shine
Tricked up in fairer plumes, since all are thine.[4]
Who hath his flock of cackling geese compared
With thy tuned choir of swans?[5] Or else who dared
To call thy births deformed? But if thou bind
By city-custom, or by gavelkind,[6]
In equal shares thy love on all thy race,
We may distinguish of their sex and place;[7]
Though one hand form them, and though one brain strike
Souls into all, they are not all alike.
Why should the follies, then, of this dull age
Draw from thy pen such an immodest rage
As seems to blast thy (else immortal) bays,[8]
When thine own tongue proclaims thy itch of[9] praise?
Such thirst will argue drought. No, let be hurled
Upon thy works[10] by the detracting world
What malice can suggest; let the rout[11] say,
The running sands that, ere thou make a play,
Count the slow minutes, might a Goodwin[12] frame,
To swallow, when thou hast done, thy shipwrecked name.
Let them the dear expense of oil upbraid,
Sucked by thy watchful lamp, that hath betrayed
To theft the blood of martyred authors, spilt
Into thy ink, whilst thou grow'st pale with guilt.[13]
Repine not at[14] the taper's thrifty waste
That sleeks[15] thy terser poems; nor is haste
Praise, but excuse; and if thou overcome
A knotty writer, bring the booty home;

> Nor think it theft, if the rich spoils so torn
> From conquered authors be as trophies worn.[16]
> Let others glut[17] on the extorted praise
> Of vulgar breath; trust thou to after-days;
> Thy laboured works[18] shall live, when Time devours
> The abortive offspring of their hasty hours.
> Thou art not of their rank; the quarrel lies
> Within thine own verge;[19] then let this suffice:
> The wiser world doth greater thee confess
> Than all men else, than thyself only less.
>
> ((wr. c.1631; pub. 1640) Thomas Carew (?1595–1640)[20])

1. see 169. 2. stupid. 3. with the exception of *Bartholomew Fair* (1614), Jonson's plays after *The Alchemist* (1610) have generally been regarded as representing a decline in his powers; Dryden called the last four published plays (which include *The New Inn*) Jonson's 'dotages'. 4. an allusion to the proverb, 'Only the eagle can gaze at the sun'; even Jonson's weaker plays pass this test, being able to gaze on the sun-like genius of their maker. 5. alluding (i) to the old fable that swans sing just before their death (ii) to the myth that Apollo, god of poetry and music, became a swan. 6. by 'city-custom' (the legal practice adopted in London) a citizen's estate was divided equally among wife, children, and executors; 'gavelkind' was the system applied in Kent, whereby an intestate citizen's property was divided equally among his sons. 7. rank. 8. laurels. 9. desire for. 10. Jonson had been pilloried for his alleged presumption in calling the handsome folio collection of plays and poems which he published in 1616 his *Works*; plays, at that date, were generally thought of as ephemera, not worthy of collection in omnibus form; see also 173 n.2. 11. rabble. 12. the Goodwin Sands (in the English Channel off Ramsgate) posed a threat to shipping; Carew advises Jonson to ignore those who rebuke him for spending a long time on his plays (such a long time that the sand in Jonson's hour-glass forms a sandbank); in Carew's view, Jonson is more likely to have his reputation wrecked by hasty writing than by lengthy planning. 13. Jonson was famous for his creative adaptations (his enemies called them plagiarisms) from the work of earlier writers. 14. do not begrudge. 15. polishes, works over. 16. compare Dryden's remarks (176) on Jonson's 'thefts'. 17. feed themselves. 18. the works on which Jonson has worked hardest. 19. jurisdiction, domain. 20. see 165 n.34.

172 *Ben Jonson and mankind*

> Mirror of poets! mirror of our age!
> Which, her whole face beholding on thy stage,
> Pleased, and displeased, with her own faults, endures
> A remedy like those whom music cures.
> Thou hast alone those various inclinations
> Which Nature gives to ages, sexes, nations,
> So tracèd with thy all-resembling pen,
> That whate'er custom has imposed on men,
> Or ill-got habit (which deforms them so,
> That scarce a brother can his brother know)
> Is represented to the wondering eyes
> Of all that see, or read, thy comedies.
> Whoever in those glasses[1] looks, may find
> The spots returned, or graces, of his mind;
> And by the help of so divine an art,
> At leisure view, and dress, his nobler part.
> Narcissus,[2] cozened by that flattering well,
> Which nothing could but of his beauty tell,

Had here, discovering the deformed estate
Of his fond mind, preserved himself with hate.
But virtue too, as well as vice, is clad
In flesh and blood so well, that Plato had
Beheld what his high fancy once embraced:
Virtue with colours, speech, and motion graced.[3]
The sundry postures of thy copious Muse
Who would express, a thousand tongues must use;
Whose fate's no less peculiar[4] than thy art;
For as thou couldst all characters impart,
So none could render thine, which still escapes,
Like Proteus,[5] in variety of shapes;
Who was nor this, nor that, but all we find,
And all we can imagine, in mankind.
((1638) Edmund Waller (1606–87),[6] 'Upon Ben Jonson')

1. mirrors. 2. the handsome youth of Greek myth who fell in love with his own reflection. 3. an allusion to Plato's decription (*Republic*, II.378c–e) of those (for Plato) ideal poets who depict only virtuous conduct in their works, and who thus provide perfect instruction for the young. 4. individual, distinctive. 5. see 55 n.1. 6. see 26 n.10.

173 *Apollo judges Jonson*[1]

The first that broke silence was good old Ben,
Prepared before with Canary wine,
And he told them plainly he deserved the bays,
For his were called 'works', where others' were but 'plays'.[2]
                                           And
Bid them remember how he had purged the stage
Of errors that had lasted many an age;
And he hopes they did not think *The Silent Woman*,
The Fox,[3] and *The Alchemist* out-done by no man.

Apollo stopped him there, and bade him not go on,
'Twas merit, he said, and not presumption,
Must carry it; at which Ben turned about,
And in great choler offered to go out;
                                           But
Those that were there thought it not fit
To discontent so ancient a wit;
And therefore Apollo called him back again,
And made him mine host of his own New Inn.[4]
((wr. ?1637; pub. 1646) Sir John Suckling (1609–41),[5] from 'The Wits' ['A Sessions of the Poets'])

1. the poem depicts a mock-trial, at which Apollo has the task of presenting his laurel to the most deserving contemporary poet. 2. see 171 n.10; an anonymous contemporary epigram ran: 'Pray tell me, Ben, where does the mystery lurk?/What others call a play, you call a work'; a friend of Jonson quipped back: 'The author's friend thus for the author says:/Ben's plays are works, when others' works are plays'. 3. i.e. *Volpone*. 4. punning on the title of Jonson's unsuccessful play (see 169 n.1). 5. court poet and royalist activist in the 1630s and 1640s; fled to France in 1641 and probably committed suicide on the continent; his poetry was particularly praised by Dr Johnson for its 'gaiety'.

174 On Ben Jonson

The Muses' fairest light in no dark time;
The wonder of a learnèd age; the line
Which none can pass; the most proportioned wit
To Nature;[1] the best judge of what was fit;
The deepest, plainest, highest, clearest, pen;
The voice most echoed by consenting men;
The soul which answered best to all well said
By others, and which most requital[2] made;
Tuned to the highest key of ancient Rome,
Returning all her music with his own;
In whom, with Nature, study claimed a part,
And yet who to himself owed all his art;
   Here lies Ben Jonson. Every age will look
With sorrow here, with wonder on his book.
                                       ((1638) Sidney Godolphin (1610–43)[3])

1. the imagination best fitted to the Nature which was its subject. 2. repayment; the reference is to Jonson's creative adaptation of others' words and thoughts (see also 171 n.13), and particularly to his use in his own work of such Roman poets as Catullus, Horace, Martial, and Juvenal. 3. see 166 n.7.

175 *Jonson's art*

Where shall we find a Muse like thine, that can
So well present, and show man unto man,
That each one finds his twin, and thinks thy art
Extends not to the gestures, but the heart?
Where one so showing life to life, that we
Think thou taught'st custom, and not custom thee?
Manners, that were themes to thy scenes, still flow
In the same stream, and are their comments now;
These times thus living o'er thy models, we
Think them not so much wit, as prophecy;
And though we know the character, may swear
A Sibyl's[1] finger hath been busy there.
Things common thou speak'st proper, which, though known
For public, stamped by thee grow thence thine own;
Thy thoughts so ordered, so expressed, that we
Conclude that thou didst not discourse, but see;
Language so mastered, that thy numerous feet,
Laden with genuine words, do always meet[2]
Each in his art; nothing unfit doth fall,
Showing the poet, like the wise man, all.
Thine equal skill thus wresting[3] nothing, made
Thy pen seem not so much to write, as trade.[4]
          ((1638) William Cartwright (1611–43),[5] from 'In the Memory of
                                      the Most Worthy Benjamin Jonson')

1. the Sibyls were prophetess-priestesses who revealed the oracles of Apollo; Jonson has so accurately captured the 'manners' (patterns of behaviour) of his day that he seems to have predicted actualities rather than to have invented fictions. 2. Jonson's versification is equally polished in every line. 3. distorting awkwardly. 4. walk, step naturally. 5. one of the 'Sons

of Ben' (see 170 n.1); this poem, along with 172 and 174, was included in *Jonsonus Virbius* (1638), a collection of elegies on Jonson by admirers and disciples.

176 *Jonson's judiciousness*

He was a most severe judge of himself as well as others. One cannot say he wanted[1] wit, but rather that he was frugal of it. In his works you find little to retrench or alter. Wit, and language, and humour also, in some measure, we had before him; but something of art was wanting to the drama till he came. He managed his strength to more advantage than any who preceded him. You seldom find him making love in any of his scenes, or endeavouring to move the passions. His genius was too sullen and saturnine[2] to do it gracefully, especially when he knew he came after those who had performed both to such an height. Humour[3] was his proper sphere, and in that he delighted most to represent mechanic[4] people. He was deeply conversant in the ancients, both Greek and Latin, and he borrowed boldly from them. ... But he has done his robberies so openly that one may see he fears not to be taxed[5] by any law. He invades authors like a monarch, and what would be theft in other poets is only victory in him.[6]

((1668) John Dryden (1631–1700), from *Of Dramatic Poesy: an Essay*)

1. lacked. 2. gloomy. 3. the presentation of people's characters and dispositions. 4. working-class. 5. charged. 6. compare Carew's remarks on Jonson's creative borrowings in 171.

177 *Jonson and comedy*

You, then, that would the comic laurels wear,
To study Nature be your only care;
Whoe'er knows Man, and by a curious[1] art
Discerns the hidden secrets of the heart;
He who observes and naturally can paint
The jealous fool, the fawning sycophant,
A sober wit, an enterprising ass,
A humorous Otter,[2] or a Hudibras,[3]
May safely in these noble lists engage,
And make 'em act and speak upon the stage.
Strive to be natural in all you write,
And paint with colours that may please the sight.
Nature in various figures does abound,
And in each mind are different humours[4] found;
A glance, a touch, discovers to the wise,
But every man has not discerning eyes. ...
Your actors must by reason be controlled;
Let young men speak like young, old men like old;
Observe the town, and study well the court,
For thither various characters resort;
Thus 'twas great Jonson[5] purchased his renown,
And in his art had borne away the crown;
If, less desirous of the people's praise,

>   He had not with low farce debased his plays,
>   Mixing dull buffoonery with wit refined,
>   And Harlequin[6] with noble Terence[7] joined.
>   When in *The Fox* I see the tortoise hissed,[8]
>   I lose the author of *The Alchemist*.
>   ((1683) Sir William Soames (c.1645–86)[9] and John Dryden
>   (1631–1700), from their translation of Boileau's
>   *L'Art poétique*, Canto III)

1. searching. 2. a henpecked husband in Jonson's *Epicoene, or The Silent Woman* (acted 1609–10; pub. 1616). 3. the eponymous hero of Samuel Butler's satirical poem (1662–80), a quixotic Presbyterian knight-errant. 4. moods, tempers, states of feeling. 5. Jonson is substituted in this English translation for Molière in Boileau's original; the publisher Jacob Tonson noted in 1708 that it was Dryden who had been responsible for making English substitutions for the French authors named by Boileau. 6. one of the stock characters in the traditional Italian theatre, the Commedia dell'Arte. 7. see 125 n.24. 8. the reference is to the farcical scene in Jonson's *Volpone* in which the foolish Sir Politic Would-Be hides himself in a giant tortoiseshell. 9. Sheriff of Suffolk, 1672–3; created baronet, 1685.

178 *Jonson and the passions*

>   Plain Humour,[1] shown with her whole various face,
>   Not masked with any antic[2] dress,
>   Nor screwed in forced, ridiculous grimace
>   (The gaping rabble's dull delight,
>   And more the actor's than the poet's wit),
>   Such did she enter on thy stage,
>   And such was represented to the wondering age;
>   Well wast thou skilled[3] and read in Humankind,
>   In every wild fantastic passion of his mind,
>   Didst into all his hidden inclinations dive,
>   What each from Nature does receive,
>   Or age, or sex, or quality,[4] or country give;
>   What Custom, too, that mighty sorceress,
>   Whose powerful witchcraft does transform
>   Enchanted Man to several monstrous images,
>   Makes this an odd and freakish monkey turn,
>   And that a grave and solemn ass appear,
>   And all a thousand beastly shapes of folly wear;
>   Whate'er caprice or whimsy leads awry
>   Perverted and seduced mortality,
>   Or does incline, and bias it
>   From what's discreet, and wise, and right, and good, and fit;
>   All in thy faithful glass were so expressed,
>   As if they were reflections of thy breast,
>   As if they had been stamped on thy own mind,
>   And thou the universal vast idea of mankind.
>   ((wr. 1678; pub. 1683) John Oldham (1653–83),[5] from 'Upon the
>   Works of Ben Jonson')

1. temperamental disposition. 2. bizarre, eccentric. 3. knowledgeable, insightful. 4. social rank. 5. author of *Satires upon the Jesuits* (1681) and of translations and imitations of classical and French poetry (Juvenal, Horace, Boileau, etc.); Oldham died young, and was commemorated by Dryden in a famous elegy (see 253).

179 *Jonson's studious art*

Then Jonson came, instructed from the school
To please in method and invent by rule;[1]
His studious patience and laborious art
By regular approach essayed[2] the heart;
Cold approbation gave the lingering bays,[3]
For those who durst not censure, scarce could praise.
A mortal born, he met the general doom,
But left, like Egypt's kings, a lasting tomb.[4]
  ((1747) Samuel Johnson (1709–84), from 'Prologue Spoken by Mr
    Garrick at the Opening of the Theatre in Drury Lane')

1. the reference is to Jonson's unashamed admiration for, and studious emulation of, the principles and practice of classical drama. 2. examined the composition of. 3. a reference to the attacks received by Jonson in his lifetime (see, for example, 169, 171 and ns.). 4. the Pharaohs were thought to have been buried in the pyramids; Jonson's 'lasting tomb' is his works.

180 *Jonson on Parnassus*

Broad-based, broad-fronted, bounteous, multiform,
 With many a valley impleached[1] with ivy and vine,
 Wherein the springs of all the streams run wine,
And many a crag full-faced against the storm,
The mountain where thy Muse's feet made warm
 Those lawns that revelled with her dance divine
 Shines yet with fire as it was wont to shine
From tossing torches round the dance aswarm.

Nor less, high-stationed on the grey grave heights,
 High-thoughted seers with heaven's heart-kindling lights
  Hold converse; and the herd of meaner things
Knows or by fiery scourge or fiery shaft
When wrath on thy broad brows has risen, and laughed,
 Darkening thy soul with shadow of thundrous wings.
  ((1882) Algernon Charles Swinburne (1837–1909),[2] 'Ben Jonson',
    from 'Sonnets on the English Dramatic Poets')

1. entwined. 2. see 123 n.4.

George Sandys (1578–1644)

181 *Sandys's Ovid*

Then dainty Sandys,[1] that hath to English done
Smooth-sliding Ovid,[2] and hath made him run
With so much sweetness and unusual grace,
As though the neatness of the English pace
Should tell the jetting[3] Latin that it came
But slowly after, as though stiff and lame.
  ((1627) Michael Drayton (1563–1631)[4], from 'To ... Henry
    Reynolds, Esquire, Of Poets and Poesy')

1. Sandys was a member of the Great Tew circle (see 166 n.7); his translation of Ovid's great mythological poem, the *Metamorphoses* (first complete edition, 1626; revised with an elaborate allegorical prose commentary, 1632) replaced Arthur Golding's version in fourteeners (1567; the version known by Shakespeare), and was reprinted throughout the 17th century; Sandys's translation played an important part in establishing heroic couplets as the standard poetic form for narrative verse in the later 17th and 18th centuries. 2. Ovid was renowned for the smoothness and elegance of his versification. 3. boastful, proud. 4. see 85 n.3.

182 To my Worthy Friend, Master George Sandys, on his Translation of the Psalms[1]

I press not to the choir,[2] nor dare I greet
The holy place with my unhallowed feet;[3]
My unwashed Muse pollutes not things divine,
Nor mingles her profaner notes with thine;
Here humbly at the porch[4] she listening stays,
And with glad ears sucks in thy sacred lays.
So dévout penitents of old were wont,
Some without door and some beneath the font,
To stand and hear the Church's liturgies,
Yet not assist the solemn exercise.
Sufficeth her that she a lay-place[5] gain,
To trim thy vestments, or but bear thy train;
Though nor in tune nor wing she reach thy lark,[6]
Her lyric feet may dance before the Ark.[7]
Who knows but that her wandering eyes, that run
Now hunting glow-worms,[8] may adore the sun?[9]
A pure flame may, shot by Almighty Power
Into my breast, the earthy flame devour;
My eyes in penitential dew may steep
That brine which they for sensual love did weep;
So, though 'gainst Nature's course, fire may be quenched
With fire, and water be with water drenched.
Perhaps my restless soul, tired with pursuit
Of mortal beauty, seeking without fruit
Contentment there, which hath not, when enjoyed,
Quenched all her thirst, nor satisfied, though cloyed,
Weary of her vain search below, above
In the first fair[10] may find the immortal love.
Prompted by thy example, then, no more
In moulds of clay will I my God adore,
But tear those idols from my heart, and write
What his blest Spirit, not fond love, shall indite.
Then I no more shall court the verdant bay,[11]
But the dry leafless trunk on Golgotha,[12]
And rather strive to gain from thence one thorn,
Than all the flourishing wreaths by laureates worn.

((1638) Thomas Carew (?1595–1640)[13])

1. Sandys's *Paraphrase Upon the Divine Psalms* had first appeared in 1636; Carew's poem was prefixed to the second edition. 2. (i) the part of a church nearest the sanctuary (ii) 'quire': a gathering of sheets of paper in a book; Carew's conceits liken features of church architecture to the structure and contents of Sandys's book. 3. the 'feet' are also the poetic 'feet' (metrical

units) of Carew's verse. 4. (i) church entrance (ii) the 'preliminaries' (prefatory material) to Sandys's volume. 5. a place appropriate to a layman. 6. the lark sings when flying heavenwards. 7. sacred chest containing the tables of the law, and placed in the holiest place of the Jewish tabernacle. 8. the phantasms of secular (particularly amatory) subject-matter. 9. sun/son (i.e. Christ); Carew may, one day, be worthy to write religious verse. 10. God. 11. the laurel awarded to the triumphant poet. 12. the cross on which Christ died. 13. see 165 n.34.

George Herbert (1593–1633)

183 Herbert's 'The Temple'

What Church[1] is this? Christ's Church. Who builds it?
Mr George Herbert. Who assisted it?
Many assisted; who, I may not say,
So much contention might arise that way.
If I say Grace[2] gave all, Wit[3] straight doth thwart,[4]
And says, 'All that is there is mine.' But Art
Denies and says, 'There's nothing there but's mine;'
Nor can I easily the right define.
Divide; say Grace the matter gave, and Wit
Did polish it, Art measured, and made fit
Each several piece, and framed it all together.
No, by no means; this may not please them neither.
None's well contented with a part alone,
When each doth challenge all to be his own;
The matter, the expressions, and the measures,[5]
Are equally Art's, Wit's, and Grace's treasures.
Then he that would impartially discuss
This doubtful question, must answer thus:
In building of this temple, Mr Herbert
Is equally all Grace, all Wit, all Art.
   Roman and Grecian Muses all give way;
   One English poem darkens all your day.
      ((1640) Christopher Harvey (1597–1663),[6] from *The Synagogue*)

1. Herbert's *The Temple* (1633) contains nearly all his surviving poems; an introductory poem, 'The Church Porch', and two quatrains, 'Superliminare' ['The Threshold'], precede the main collection of poems, which is sub-titled 'The Church'. 2. (i) God's supernatural and freely given assistance (ii) elegance. 3. imagination. 4. contradict. 5. metres. 6. friend of Izaak Walton (the biographer of Donne and Herbert and author of *The Compleat Angler* [1653]); *The Synagogue*, a collection of poems in imitation of Herbert, was appended anonymously to the 1640 edition of *The Temple*, and was subsequently reprinted with most of the later editions of Herbert's volume.

184 On Mr George Herbert's Book Entitled The Temple of Sacred Poems, Sent to a Gentlewoman

Know you, fair, on what you look;
Divinest love lies in this book,
Expecting fire from your eyes,
To kindle this his sacrifice.

When your hands untie these strings,
Think you've an angel by the wings;
One that gladly will be nigh,
To wait upon each morning sigh;
To flutter in the balmy air
Of your well-perfumèd prayer.
These white plumes of his he'll lend you,
Which every day to heaven will send you,
To take acquaintance of the sphere,[1]
And all the smooth-faced kindred there.
    And, though Herbert's name do owe[2]
    These devotions, fairest, know
    That while I lay them on the shrine
    Of your white hand, they are mine.
                ((1646) Richard Crashaw (?1612–49)[3]

1. the vault of heaven. 2. possess. 3. author of *Steps to the Temple* (1646), a collection of ornate religious poems which are indebted to continental baroque poetry and mysticism; Crashaw was converted to Roman Catholicism *c.*1645.

Edmund Waller (1606–87)

185 To Poet Edmund Waller, Occasioned for his Writing a Panegyric on Oliver Cromwell[1]

From whence, vile poet, didst thou glean thy wit,
And words for such a vicious poem fit?
Where couldst thou paper find was not too white,
Or ink, that could be black enough to write?
What servile devil tempted thee to be
A flatterer of thine own slavery?
To kiss thy bondage, and extol the deed
At once that made thy Prince[2] and country bleed?
I wonder much thy false heart did not dread
And shame to write what all men blush to read;
Thus with a base ingratitude to rear
Trophies unto thy master's murderer?
    Who called thee coward, Waller, much mistook
The characters of thy pedantic look;[3]
Thou hast at once abused thyself and us;
He's stout that dares flatter a tyrant thus.
    Put up thy pen and ink, muzzle thy Muse,
Adulterate hag, fit for a common stews,[4]
No good man's library; writ thou hast
Treason in rhyme, has all thy works defaced;
Such is thy fault, that when I think to find
A punishment of the severest kind
For thy offence, my malice cannot name
A greater, than once to commit the same.
    Where was thy reason, then, when thou began
To write against the sense of God and man?

Within thy guilty breast despair took place;
Thou wouldst despairing die in spite of grace.
At once thou art judge and malefactor shown;
Each sentence in thy poem is thine own.
  Then what thou hast pronounced, go execute;
Hang up thy self, and say I bade thee do it;
Fear not thy memory; that cannot die;
This panegyric is thy elegy;
Which shall be, when or wheresoever read,
A living poem to upbraid thee dead.
           ((wr. ?1655; pub. 1689) Charles Cotton (1630–87)[5])

1. Waller, who had been a staunch royalist before the Civil War, and was to enjoy court favour after the Restoration, published 'A Panegyric to My Lord Protector' in 1655. 2. Charles 1, executed in 1649. 3. in John Riley's portrait of Waller (now in the National Portrait Gallery), the poet has a dry, solemn demeanour. 4. brothel. 5. Cotton, a staunch royalist, was a friend of Richard Lovelace (see 230), and wrote a continuation of Izaak Walton's *The Compleat Angler* (1676); he also translated Montaigne (1685–6), and wrote burlesques of Virgil (1664) and Lucian (1665).

186 *Waller and English verse*

Waller came last,[1] but was the first whose art
Just weight and measure did to verse impart;
That of a well-placed word could teach the force,
And showed for poetry a nobler course.
His happy genius did our tongue refine,
And easy words with pleasing numbers join;
His verses to good method did apply,
And changed harsh discord[2] to soft harmony.
All owned his laws, which, long approved and tried,
To present authors now may be a guide.
Tread boldly in his steps, secure from fear,
And be, like him, in your expressions clear.
           ((1683) Sir William Soames (c.1645–86)[3] and John Dryden
           (1631–1700), from their translation of Boileau's *L'Art
           poétique*, Canto 1)

1. the extract is part of a 'procession' of poets; Waller is substituted for Boileau's François de Malherbe (1555–1628). 2. the kind of crabbed cacophony which, late 17th- and 18th-century poets felt, had characterised much Jacobean couplet verse. 3. see 177 n.9.

187 *Waller and panegyric*

Waller, by nature for the bays[1] designed,
With force and fire and fancy[2] unconfined,
In panegyrics[3] does excel mankind.
He best can turn, enforce, and soften things
To praise great conquerors, or to flatter kings.
           ((wr. 1675–6; pub. 1680) John Wilmot, Earl of Rochester (1647–
                                80), from 'An Allusion to Horace')

1. poetic laurels. 2. imagination. 3. as well as writing in praise of Cromwell (see 185), Waller wrote panegyrics on both Charles I and II.

Sir Richard Fanshawe (1608–66)

188 *Fanshawe*[1] *and translation*

That servile path thou nobly dost decline
Of tracing word by word and line by line.
Those are the laboured births of slavish brains;
Not the effects of poetry, but pains;
Cheap, vulgar arts, whose narrowness affords
No flight for thoughts, but poorly sticks at words.
A new and nobler way thou dost pursue
To make translations and translators too.
They but preserve the ashes, thou the flame;
True to his sense, but truer to his fame;
Fording his current, where thou find'st it low,
Let'st in thine own to make it rise and flow;
Wisely restoring whatsoever grace
It lost by change of times, or tongues, or place;
Nor fettered to his numbers and his times,[2]
Betray'st his music to unhappy rhymes;
Nor are the nerves[3] of his compacted strength
Stretched and dissolved into unsinewed length;
Yet after all, lest we should think it thine,
Thy spirit to his circle dost confine.
New names, new dressings, and the modern cast,
Some scenes, some persons altered, had outfaced[4]
The world it were thy work; for we have known
Some thanked and praised for what was less their own.
That master's hand which to the life can trace
The airs, the lines, and features of a face,
May with a free and bolder stroke express
A varied posture or a flattering dress;
He could have made those like, who made the rest,
But that he knew his own design was best.

((wr. ?1643–4; pub. 1648) Sir John Denham (1615–69),[5] from 'To Sir Richard Fanshawe, Upon his Translation of *Pastor Fido*')

1. Fanshawe, a royalist poet, translated from Horace, Virgil and Camoëns (see 47 n.4), as well as making a version (the subject of the present poem) of the popular pastoral play, *Il Pastor Fido* ['The Faithful Shepherd'] by Giovanni Battista Guarini (1538-1612). 2. Fanshawe has made no attempt to preserve the metrical scheme of his original. 3. muscles. 4. boasted to. 5. royalist poet, in exile during the Interregnum; translated episodes from Books II and IV of Virgil's *Aeneid*; Denham's best known poem is the topographical reflection, *Cooper's Hill* (see 221).

John Milton (1608–74)

189 Milton's epic inspiration

(i)

Of Man's first disobedience, and the fruit
Of that forbidden tree[1] whose mortal taste
Brought death into the world, and all our woe,
With loss of Eden, till one greater Man[2]
Restore us, and regain the blissful seat,
Sing heavenly Muse,[3] that on the secret top
Of Oreb, or of Sinai, did inspire
That shepherd,[4] who first taught the chosen seed,[5]
In the beginning how the heavens and earth
Rose out of chaos; or if Sion[6] hill
Delight thee more, and Siloa's brook[7] that flowed
Fast by the oracle of God; I thence
Invoke thy aid to my adventurous song,
That with no middle flight intends to soar
Above the Aonian mount,[8] while it pursues
Things unattempted yet in prose or rhyme.[9]
And chiefly thou, O Spirit,[10] that dost prefer
Before all temples the upright heart and pure,
Instruct me, for thou know'st; thou from the first
Wast present, and with mighty wings outspread
Dove-like sat'st brooding on the vast abyss
And mad'st it pregnant. What in me is dark
Illumine, what is low raise and support;
That to the height of this great argument[11]
I may assert[12] eternal providence,
And justify[13] the ways of God to men.

(ii)

Descend from heaven, Urania,[14] by that name
If rightly thou art called, whose voice divine
Following, above the Olympian hill[15] I soar,
Above the flight of Pegaséan[16] wing.
The meaning, not the name,[17] I call; for thou
Nor of the Muses nine, nor on the top
Of old Olympus dwell'st, but heavenly born,
Before the hills appeared or fountain flowed,
Thou with eternal Wisdom didst converse,[18]
Wisdom thy sister, and with her didst play
In presence of the almighty Father, pleased
With thy celestial song. Up led by thee
Into the heaven of heavens I have presumed,
An earthly guest, and drawn empyreal air,[19]
Thy tempering;[20] with like safety guided down
Return me to my native element;[21]
Lest from this flying steed unreined (as once
Bellerophon,[22] though from a lower clime),

Dismounted on the Aleian field I fall
Erroneous[23] there to wander and forlorn.
Half yet remains unsung, but narrower bound
Within the visible diurnal sphere;[24]
Standing on earth, not rapt[25] above the pole,[26]
More safe I sing with mortal voice, unchanged
To hoarse or mute, though fallen on evil days,
On evil days though fallen and evil tongues;
In darkness, and with dangers compassed round,
And solitude;[27] yet not alone, while thou
Visit'st my slumbers nightly, or when morn
Purples the east; still govern thou my song,
Urania, and fit audience find, though few.

(iii)

No more of talk where God or angel guest
With Man, as with his friend, familiarly used
To sit indulgent, and with him partake
Rural repast,[28] permitting him the while
Venial[29] discourse unblamed; I now must change
Those notes to tragic;[30] foul distrust, and breach
Disloyal on the part of Man, revolt,
And disobedience; on the part of heaven,
Now alienated, distance and distaste,
Anger and just rebuke, and judgement given,
That brought into this world a world of woe,
Sin and her shadow Death, and Misery,
Death's harbinger;[31] sad task, yet argument[32]
Not less but more heroic than the wrath
Of stern Achilles on his foe pursued
Thrice fugitive about Troy wall;[33] or rage
Of Turnus for Lavinia disespoused,
Or Neptune's ire, or Juno's, that so long
Perplexed the Greek and Cytherea's son;[34]
If answerable[35] style I can obtain
Of my celestal patroness,[36] who deigns
Her nightly visitation unimplored,
And díctates to me slumbering, or inspires
Easy my unpremeditated verse;
Since first this subject for heroic song
Pleased me long choosing, and beginning late;[37]
Not sedulous[38] by nature to indite
Wars, hitherto the only argument[39]
Heroic deemed, chief mastery[40] to dissect[41]
With long and tedious havoc fabled knights
In battles feigned; the better fortitude
Of patience and heroic martyrdom
Unsung; or to describe races and games,[42]
Or tilting furniture,[43] emblazoned shields,
Impresses[44] quaint, caparisons[45] and steeds;
Bases[46] and tinsel trappings, gorgeous knights
At joust and tournament; then marshalled feast

Served up in hall with sewers, and seneschals;[47]
The skill of artifice or office mean,[48]
Not that which justly gives heroic name
To person or to poem. Me of these[49]
Nor skilled nor studious, higher argument
Remains, sufficient of itself to raise
That name,[50] unless an age too late, or cold
Climate,[51] or years damp my intended wing
Depressed, and much they may, if all be mine,
Not hers who brings it nightly to my ear.
((1667) John Milton (1608-74), from *Paradise Lost*, Bks. I, VII, IX)

1. the Tree of Knowledge; Adam's and Eve's eating of its forbidden fruit causes their expulsion from the Garden of Eden, and brings mortality into the world for the first time. 2. Christ, the 'second Adam' whose redeeming love counteracts the effects of Adam's and Eve's sin at the Fall. 3. Urania (see n.17). 4. Moses, who received divine inspiration and instruction on Mount Horeb (Exod. 3) and Mount Sinai (Exod. 19); Moses was believed to have been the author of the early books of the Old Testament, on which Milton drew largely in *Paradise Lost*. 5. the Israelites. 6. in Jerusalem; King David's residence and a place of sacred song, oracle, and ritual for the Jews. 7. a spring flowing by the Temple in Jerusalem (a Christian counterpart to the springs haunted by the Muses of the pagan poets). 8. Helicon (see 11 n.5). 9. verse. 10. the Holy Spirit, like Urania an aspect of divine inspiration. 11. story, subject. 12. maintain the cause of, champion. 13. demonstrate poetically the justice of, provide spiritual understanding of. 14. see n.17. 15. Mount Olympus, home of the classical gods, and a resort of the Muses. 16. see 11 n.6. 17. 'Urania' means 'the heavenly one'; Milton invokes heavenly power, not the classical personage named Urania (the Muse of astronomy). 18. live in company with. 19. the air of the the 'first region' of heaven, thought to be too fine for mortal lungs. 20. tempered, and thus made suitable for a mortal, by Urania. 21. earth. 22. Bellerophon attempted to ascend to heaven on Pegasus but was thrown to the ground for his presumption; he landed on the Aleian plain. 23. (i) wandering (ii) straying. 24. the second half of *Paradise Lost* is set, for the most part, on earth; from earth, the universe appears to revolve with a 'diurnal' (daily) motion. 25. enraptured. 26. the highest point of the universe. 27. Milton is writing as a member of the defeated parliamentary party after the Restoration; he was blind, poor, and (as a prominent apologist for the regicide) politically a *persona non grata*; he had been imprisoned for several months during 1660. 28. Bks. V-VIII of *Paradise Lost* relate how the archangel Raphael was sent by God to discourse with Adam and Eve (who receive him hospitably), and to warn Adam of the threat posed to their happiness by Satan; in Bk.VIII Adam had related how, after his creation, he conversed freely with God. 29. allowable; Raphael had allowed Adam to interrogate him about the creation, the angels' revolt, and the heavenly motions; God had welcomed Adam's request for a companion with whom he could share the delights of Eden. 30. Milton is about to tell of the Fall, and of God's judgement on fallen Man. 31. in Bk. X of *Paradise Lost*, Sin and Death build a bridge from hell to earth, bringing mortality to the world for the first time. 32. story, material. 33. see Homer's *Iliad*, Bk. XXII. 34. Virgil's *Aeneid* had told of Juno's hostility to Aeneas, the son of Cytherea (Venus), and of Aeneas' betrothal to the princess Lavinia (who had previously been promised in marriage to Turnus, King of the Rutuli); Homer's *Odyssey* had told of the wanderings, after the fall of Troy, of Odysseus ('the Greek'), imposed by the hostility of the sea god Neptune. 35. appropriate, suitable. 36. Urania (see n.17). 37. Milton had begun planning a poetic work on the Fall in the early 1640s. 38. diligent, assiduous. 39. subject matter. 40. art, skill. 41. classical and renaissance epic poets had given lengthy and detailed descriptions of wounds inflicted in battle. 42. as in *Iliad*, Bk. XXIII (the funeral games for Hector) and *Aeneid*, Bk. V (games in honour of Aeneas' father, Anchises). 43. equipment; Milton here refers to the knightly epics of Spenser and the Italians, Boiardo, Ariosto (author of *Orlando Furioso* [1532]), and Tasso (see 60 n.6). 44. devices on shields. 45. richly ornamented cloths, spread over the saddles or harnesses of horses. 46. cloth housings of horses. 47. the 'marshal' organised the seating at knightly banquets; the 'sewers' arranged and served the meals; the 'seneschal' was the household

steward. 48. the province of mechanical artifice and of an agency less dignified than epic poetry. 49. the details of knightly etiquette, etc. 50. of epic. 51. (i) of location (England) (ii) of age.

190 On Mr Milton's *Paradise Lost*

When I beheld the poet blind, yet bold,
In slender book his vast design unfold,
Messiah crowned, God's reconciled decree,
Rebelling angels, the forbidden tree,
Heaven, hell, earth, chaos, all; the argument[1]
Held me a while, misdoubting[2] his intent,
That he would ruin (for I saw him strong)
The sacred truths to fable and old song
(So Samson groped the temple's posts in spite[3]),
The world o'erwhelming to revenge his sight.

    Yet as I read, soon growing less severe,
I liked his project,[4] the success did fear;
Through that wide field how he his way should find,
O'er which lame Faith leads Understanding blind;
Lest he perplexed the things he would explain,
And what was easy he should render vain.

    Or if a work so infinite he spanned,
Jealous I was that some less skilful hand[5]
(Such as disquiet[6] always what is well,
And by ill-imitating would excel)
Might hence presume the whole creation's day
To change in scenes, and show it in a play.

    Pardon me, mighty poet, nor despise
My causeless, yet not impious, surmise.
But I am now convinced that none will dare
Within thy labours to pretend a share.
Thou hast not missed one thought that could be fit,
And all that was improper dost omit;
So that no room is here for writers left,
But to detect[7] their ignorance or theft.

    That majesty which through thy work doth reign,
Draws the devout, deterring the profane,
And things divine thou treat'st of in such state
As them preserves, and thee, inviolate.
At once delight and horror on us seize,
Thou sing'st with so much gravity and ease;
And above human flight dost soar aloft[8]
With plume so strong, so equal, and so soft.
The bird named from that Paradise you sing
So never flags, but always keeps on wing.

    Where couldst thou words of such a compass[9] find?
Whence furnish such a vast expense of mind?
Just heaven thee, like Tiresias,[10] to requite,
Rewards with prophecy thy loss of sight.

    Well mightst thou scorn thy readers to allure
With tinkling rhyme, of thine own sense secure;
While the town-Bays[11] writes all the while and spells,

And, like a pack-horse, tires without his bells.
Their fancies like our bushy points[12] appear;
The poets tag them, we for fashion wear.
I too, transported by the mode,[13] offend,
And while I meant to 'praise' thee must 'commend'.[14]
Thy verse created, like thy theme, sublime,
In number, weight, and measure,[15] needs not rhyme.

((1674) Andrew Marvell (1621–78))

1. from the fourth issue of the first edition of *Paradise Lost* onwards, the text of the poem was prefaced by 'The Argument', a prose summary of the plot of the whole epic, printed continuously, not distributed through the several books of the poem, as in later editions. 2. being apprehensive about. 3. Milton's tragedy *Samson Agonistes*, which tells of the blind Samson's destruction of the Philistines' temple, had appeared in 1671. 4. plan, mental conception. 5. John Dryden was given permission by Milton to make an 'opera' out of *Paradise Lost*, (*The State of Innocence*, licensed in 1674 but not published till 1677); Milton, Marvell, and Dryden had all worked together, in the mid-1650s, in the same office of the Cromwellian administration. 6. trouble. 7. expose. 8. echoing Milton's own claim (*Paradise Lost*, I.13–14). 9. range, scope, inclusiveness. 10. a Theban, stricken with blindness by Hera, but rewarded by Zeus, by way of compensation, with long life and the gift of prophecy; Milton had become totally blind by the early 1650s, his condition having been exacerbated by his tireless propagandising for the parliamentary cause. 11. Dryden had been satirised as 'Mr Bays' in the popular burlesque play, *The Rehearsal* (1672); in 1668, Milton added to the remaining copies of the first edition of *Paradise Lost* a short essay, 'The Verse', in which he defended his decision to write his poem in blank, rather than rhymed, verse, which he scornfully described as 'the invention of a barbarous age'; Dryden's dramatic adaptation of the poem (see n.5) was rhymed. 12. tasselled cords used for fastening hose. 13. the fashion of writing in rhyme. 14. because 'commend' is required as a rhyme-word for 'offend'. 15. metrical patterning.

191 Epigram on Milton

Three poets,[1] in three distant ages born,
Greece, Italy, and England did adorn.
The first in loftiness of thought surpassed,
The next in majesty; in both the last.
The force of Nature could no further go;
To make a third, she joined the former two.

((1688) John Dryden (1631–1700))

1. Homer, Virgil, and Milton.

192 *Milton's war in heaven*[1]

Have we forgot how Raphael's numerous prose[2]
Led our exalted souls through heavenly camps,
And marked the ground where proud apostate thrones[3]
Defied Jehovah? Here, 'twixt host and host
(A narrow but a dreadful interval),
Portentous sight! before the cloudy van[4]
Satan with vast and haughty strides advanced,
Came towering, armed in adamant[5] and gold.
There bellowing engines,[6] with their fiery tubes,
Dispersed etherial forms, and down they fell
By thousands, angels on archangels rolled;

Recovered, to the hills they ran, they flew,
Which, with their ponderous load, rocks, waters, woods,
From their firm seats torn by the shaggy tops,
They bore like shields before them through the air,
Till, more incensed, they hurled them at their foes.
All was confusion; heaven's foundations shook,
Threatening no less than universal wreck;
For Michael's arm main promontories flung,
And over-pressed whole legions weak with sin;
For they blasphemed and struggled as they lay,
Till the great ensign of Messiah blazed,
And, armed with vengeance, God's victorious Son
(Effulgence of eternal Deity),
Grasping ten thousand thunders in his hand,
Drove the old original rebels headlong down,
And sent them flaming to the vast abyss.
   ((1685) Wentworth Dillon, Earl of Roscommon (?1633–85),[7]
     from *An Essay on Translated Verse* (2nd edn))

1. narrated in Bk. VI of *Paradise Lost*. 2. blank verse, the form imitated in this passage; Roscommon added the passage in the second edition of his *Essay*; the rest of his poem is in rhymed couplets; the story of the angels' revolt against God is told to Adam and Eve by the archangel Raphael. 3. renegade angels; 'thrones' are the third order or rank of angels. 4. the foremost division of his troops. 5. see 137 n.5. 6. artillery. 7. see 20 n.7.

193 *Milton's sublime majesty*

But Milton next, with high and haughty stalks,
Unfettered[1] in majestic numbers[2] walks.
No vulgar hero can his Muse engage;
Nor earth's wide scene confine his hallowed rage.[3]
See! see! he upward springs, and, towering high,
Spurns the dull province of mortality;
Shakes heaven's eternal throne with dire alarms,
And sets the almighty Thunderer in arms.
Whate'er his pen describes I more than see,
Whilst every verse, arrayed in majesty,
Bold and sublime, my whole attention draws,
And seems above the critics' nicer[4] laws.
How are you struck with terror and delight,
When angel with archangel copes in fight![5]
When great Messiah's outspread banner shines,
How does the chariot rattle in his lines!
What sound of brazen wheels, what thunder scare
And stun the reader with the din of war!
With fear my spirits and my blood retire,
To see the seraphs sunk in clouds of fire;
But when, with eager steps, from hence I rise,
And view the first gay scenes of Paradise,[6]
What tongue, what words of rapture can express
A vision so profuse of pleasantness!
  ((1694) Joseph Addison (1672–1719),[7] from 'An Account of the
      Greatest English Poets')

1. because unconstrained by rhyme (see 190 n.11). 2. imposing verse. 3. inspired frenzy. 4. stricter, more pedantic. 5. in Bk. VI of *Paradise Lost.* 6. in Bks. IV-V. 7. best known today as an essayist; through his magazine, *The Spectator* (1711–12, 1714), Addison acted as an arbiter of social, literary, and moral taste in early 18th-century England.

194 *Adam and Eve in Eden*

There is scarce a speech of Adam or Eve in the whole poem wherein the sentiments and allusions are not taken from this, their delightful habitation. The reader, during their whole course of action, always finds himself in the walks of Paradise. In short, as the critics have remarked that in those poems wherein shepherds are actors, the thoughts ought always to take a tincture from the woods, fields, and rivers; so we may observe that our first parents seldom lose sight of their happy station in anything they speak or do; and, if the reader will give me leave to use the expression, that their thoughts are always 'paradisiacal'.

((1712) Joseph Addison (1672–1719),[1] from *The Spectator*, No. 321)

1. see 193 n.7; this and the following extract are from a series of *Spectator* papers (Nos. 267, 273, 279, 285, 291, 297, 303, 309, 315, 321, 327, 333, 339, 345, 351, 357, 363, 369) which together provide a comprehensive critique of *Paradise Lost.*

195 *Books VI and VII of 'Paradise Lost'*

The Seventh Book ... is an instance of that sublime which is not mixed and worked up with passion. The author appears in a kind of composed and sedate majesty; and, though the sentiments do not give so great an emotion as those in the former book, they abound with as magnificent ideas. The Sixth Book, like a troubled ocean, represents greatness in confusion; the Seventh affects the imagination like the ocean in a calm, and fills the mind of the reader, without producing in it anything like tumult or agitation.

((1712) Joseph Addison (1672–1719),[1] from *The Spectator*, No. 339)

1. see 193 n.7.

196 *Milton's daring*

> Give me the Muse whose generous[1] force,
>   Impatient of the reins,
> Pursues an unattempted course,
> Breaks all the critic's iron chains,
> And bears to Paradise the raptured mind.
>
>   There Milton dwells; the mortal sung
>   Themes not presumed by mortal tongue;
>   New terrors, or new glories, shine
> In every page, and flying scenes divine
> Surprise the wondering sense, and draw our souls along.
>   Behold his Muse, sent out to explore
> The unapparent[2] deep where waves of chaos roar,

And realms of night unknown before.
   She traced a glorious path unknown,
Through fields of heavenly war, and seraphs overthrown,
   Where his adventurous genius led;

Sovereign, she framed a model of her own,
   Nor thanked the living nor the dead.
The noble hater of degenerate rhyme[3]
Shook off the chains, and built his verse sublime;
A monument too high for coupled souls to climb.
   He mourned the garden lost below;
   (Earth is the scene for tuneful woe!)
   Now bliss beats high in all his veins;
   Now the lost Eden he regains,
Keeps his own air, and triumphs in unrivalled strains.

Immortal bard! thus thy own Raphael[4] sings,
   And knows no rule but native fire;
All heaven sits silent while to his sovereign strings
   He talks unutterable things;
With graces infinite his untaught fingers rove
   Across the golden lyre;
   From every note devotion springs;
   Rapture, and harmony, and love,
O'erspread the listening choir.
   ((1706) Isaac Watts (1674–1748),[5] from 'The Adventurous Muse'
                       in *Horae Lyricae*, Bk. II)

1. well-bred (the metaphor is from horse-rearing). 2. obscure. 3. see 190 n.11. 4. see 189 ns 28–9. 5. Nonconformist minister and theologian; his works include a versified version of the Psalms (1719), a number of famous hymns (e.g. 'Our God, our help in ages past', 'When I survey the wondrous cross') and moral songs for children, some of which were parodied by Lewis Carroll in the 'Alice' books.

197 *Milton's faults*

Milton's strong pinion[1] now[2] not heaven can bound,
Now serpent-like in prose he sweeps the ground;
In quibbles, angel and archangel join,
And God the Father turns a school-divine.[3]
Not that I'd lop the beauties from his book,
Like slashing Bentley[4] with his desperate hook.
   ((1737) Alexander Pope (1688–1744), from 'The First Epistle of
              the Second Book of Horace Imitated: To Augustus')

1. wing; the reference is to the 'flights' of Milton's imagination. 2. sometimes. 3. an expert in the formal procedures of theological discourse (the 'schoolmen' were the academic theologians of medieval Europe); the reference is to those passages in *Paradise Lost* where God expounds the theological basis of his actions. 4. Richard Bentley (1662–1742), the celebrated classical scholar, had published an edition of *Paradise Lost* (1732) in which he had suggested hundreds of emendations to Milton's text, on the supposition that Milton's original intentions had been perverted by an incompetent amanuensis.

198 Milton's godlike mind

His was the treasure of two thousand years,
Seldom indulged to man, a godlike mind,
Unlimited and various as his theme;
Astonishing as chaos, as the bloom
Of blowing Eden fair, soft as the talk
Of our grand parents, and as heaven sublime.
((1727) James Thomson (1700–48), from 'Summer'[1] in *The Seasons*)

1. Thomson's poem, one of the most popular of the 18th century, was published serially, and underwent many textual changes between 1726 and 1746; this passage is taken from the early (1727–38) text of 'Summer'.

199 Milton's appetite of greatness

The appearances of nature and the occurrences of life did not satiate his appetite of greatness. To paint things as they are requires a minute attention, and employs the memory rather than the fancy.[1] Milton's delight was to sport in the wide regions of possibility; reality was a scene too narrow for his mind. He sent his faculties out upon discovery, into worlds where only imagination can travel, and delighted to form new modes of existence, and furnish sentiment[2] and action to superior beings, to trace the counsels of hell, or accompany the choirs of heaven.
((1779) Samuel Johnson (1709–84), from 'Milton' in *Lives of the Poets*)

1. imagination. 2. feeling.

200 The purity and greatness of Milton's narration

In Milton, every line breathes sanctity of thought and purity of manners,[1] except when the train of the narration requires the introduction of the rebellious spirits; and even they are compelled to acknowledge their subjection to God, in such a manner as excites reverence and confirms piety.

Of human beings there are but two; but those two are the parents of mankind, venerable before their fall for dignity and innocence, and amiable[2] after it for repentance and submission. In their first state, their affection is tender without weakness, and their piety sublime without presumption. When they have sinned, they show how discord begins in mutual frailty, and how it ought to cease in mutual forbearance; how confidence of the divine favour is forfeited by sin, and how hope of pardon may be obtained by penitence and prayer. A state of innocence we can only conceive, if indeed in our present misery it be possible to conceive it; but the sentiments and worship proper to a fallen and offending being we have all to learn, as we have all to practise.

The poet, whatever be done, is always great. Our progenitors, in their first state, conversed with angels; even when folly and sin had degraded them, they had not in their humiliation 'the port of mean suitors',[3] and they rise again to reverential regard[4] when we find that their prayers were heard.

((1779) Samuel Johnson (1709–84), from 'Milton' in *Lives of the Poets*)

1. modes of behaviour. 2. lovely, pleasing. 3. *Paradise Lost*, XI.8. 4. respect (on the reader's part).

201 *The sublimity of 'Paradise Lost'*

The characteristic quality of his poem is sublimity.[1] He sometimes descends to the elegant; but his element is the great. He can occasionally invest himself with grace; but his natural port[2] is gigantic loftiness. He can please when pleasure is required; but it is his peculiar power to astonish.[3]

((1779) Samuel Johnson (1709–84), from 'Milton' in *Lives of the Poets*)

1. for Johnson's definition of 'the Sublime', see 159. 2. manner. 3. 'to confound with some sudden passion, as with fear or wonder; to amaze; to surprise; to stun' (Johnson, *Dictionary*).

202 *Milton's Adam and Eve*

To Adam and to Eve are given, during their innocence, such sentiments as innocence can generate and utter. Their love is pure benevolence and mutual veneration; their repasts are without luxury,[1] and their diligence without toil.[2] Their addresses to their Maker have little more than the voice of admiration and gratitude. Fruition[3] left them nothing to ask, and innocence left them nothing to fear.

But with guilt enter distrust and discord, mutual accusation and stubborn self-defence; they regard each other with alienated minds, and dread their Creator as the avenger of their transgression. At last they seek shelter in his mercy, soften to repentance, and melt in supplication.

((1779) Samuel Johnson (1709–84), from 'Milton' in *Lives of the Poets*)

1. gluttony. 2. onerous labour. 3. 'pleasure given by possession or use' (Johnson, *Dictionary*).

203 *Milton's adventurousness*

> Nor second[1] he, that rode sublime[2]
> Upon the seraph-wings of Ecstasy,
> The secrets of the abyss to spy.
> He passed the flaming bounds of place and time;[3]
> The living throne, the sapphire-blaze,[4]
> Where angels tremble while they gaze,
> He saw; but blasted with excess of light,[5]
> Closed his eyes in endless night.

((wr. 1751–4; pub. 1757) Thomas Gray (1716–71), from 'The Progress of Poesy: a Pindaric Ode')

1. after Shakespeare. 2. (i) lofty (ii) aloft. 3. Gray here praises Milton by drawing on the same passage of Lucretius alluded to by Pope, when praising Homer, in the the Preface to his *Iliad* (see 27 n.4). 4. Gray draws on the apocalyptic description of God in Ezekiel 1:20–8, on which Milton had himself drawn in *Paradise Lost*, VI.750–9. 5. see *Paradise Lost*, III.380.

204 Milton's abode[1]

High on some cliff, to heaven up-piled,
Of rude access,[2] of prospect wild,
Where, tangled round the jealous steep,[3]
Strange shades o'erbrow the vallies deep,
And holy genii[4] guard the rock,
Its glooms[5] embrown, its springs unlock,
While, on its rich ambitious[6] head,
An Eden, like his own, lies spread;
I view that oak, the fancied glades among,
By which as Milton lay,[7] his evening ear,
From many a cloud that dropped ethereal dew,
Nigh sphered in heaven its[8] native strains could hear,
On which that ancient trump[9] he reached was hung;
   Thither oft his glory greeting,
   From Waller's myrtle shades retreating,[10]
With many a vow from Hope's aspiring tongue,
My trembling feet his guiding steps pursue;
   In vain; such bliss to one alone
   Of all the sons of soul was known;
And Heaven and Fancy,[11] kindred powers,
Have now o'erturned the inspiring bowers,[12]
Or curtained close such scene from every future view.
   ((1746) William Collins (1721–59),[13] from 'Ode on the Poetical Character')

1. in this passage, Collins draws on Milton's own descriptions of Eden (in *Paradise Lost*, Bk. IV) to evoke a sense of the remote purity of Milton's poetic imagination. 2. rough and difficult to gain entrance to. 3. the cliff's steepness 'jealously' protects the summit from intrusion. 4. protective spirits. 5. darkness, shade. 6. (i) towering (ii) aspiring. 7. Collins recalls Milton's 'Il Penseroso', 59–60. 8. i.e. heaven's. 9. the 'trumpet', on which Milton 'played' the imposing 'tunes' of his verse, is imagined as hanging from the oak tree. 10. Collins refers to his own (unsuccessful) attempts to emulate Milton rather than the line of courtly and amatory verse represented by Waller (see 185–7); the 'myrtle' was sacred to Venus, and thus denotes love. 11. imagination. 12. as Sir Guyon destroyed the Bower of Bliss in Spenser's *Fairy Queen* (II.xii.83). 13. see 144 n.8.

205 Milton and Memory

   Rise, hallowed Milton! rise, and say
   How, at thy gloomy close of day,[1]
How, when 'depressed by age, beset by wrongs',
When 'fallen on evil days and evil tongues',[2]
   When Darkness, brooding on thy sight,
   Exiled the sovereign lamp of light,[3]
Say, what could then one cheering hope diffuse?
What friends were thine, save Memory and the Muse?
   Hence the rich spoils thy studious youth
   Caught from the stores of ancient truth;
Hence all thy classic wanderings could explore,
When rapture led thee to the Latian shore;[4]
   Each scene that Tiber's bank supplied,
   Each grace that played on Arno's side,

The tepid gales through Tuscan glades that fly,
The blue serene that spreads Hesperia's[5] sky,
  Were still thine own; thy ample mind
  Each charm received, retained, combined.
And thence 'the nightly visitant'[6] that came
To touch thy bosom with her sacred flame,
  Recalled the long-lost beams of grace,
  That whilom[7] shot from Nature's face,
When God, in Eden, o'er her youthful breast
Spread, with his own right hand, perfection's gorgeous vest.[8]
      ((1756) William Mason (1725–97),[9] from 'Ode to Memory')

1. at the end of his life, when writing *Paradise Lost*. 2. see 189 (ii). 3. see 190 n.10. 4. in the late 1630s, Milton had travelled abroad, particularly in Italy, where he had studied classical antiquities in Rome and visited Galileo at his villa near Florence. 5. Italy's. 6. Milton's Muse (see 189). 7. formerly, once. 8. garment, clothing. 9. friend and correspondent of Thomas Gray and Horace Walpole; edited Gray's works and wrote his biography; Mason was a leading enthusiast for the Picturesque and primitivism (the cult of the 'noble savage').

206 *Milton's pious genius*

    Philosophy, baptised[1]
In the pure fountain of eternal love,
Has eyes indeed; and, viewing all she sees
As meant to indicate a God to man,
Gives him his praise, and forfeits not her own.
Learning has borne such fruit in other days
On all her branches; Piety has found
Friends in the friends of science, and true prayer
Has flowed from lips wet with Castalian dews.[2]
Such was thy wisdom, Newton,[3] childlike sage!
Sagacious reader of the works of God,
And in his word sagacious. Such too thine,
Milton, whose genius had angelic wings,
And fed on manna.[4]
    ((1785) William Cowper (1731–1800), from *The Task*, Bk. III)

1. i.e. *if* it is thus baptised. 2. those of poets; Castalia is a spring on Mt. Parnassus, home of the Muses. 3. see 30 n.5. 4. the miraculous food supplied by God to the children of Israel during their wanderings in the wilderness.

207 *A vision of Milton*

Apart, and on a sacred hill retired,
Beyond all mortal inspiration fired,
The mighty Milton sits; an host around
Of listening angels guard the holy ground;
Amazed, they see a human form aspire
To grasp with daring hand a seraph's lyre;
Inly irradiate with celestial beams,
Attempt those high, those soul-subduing themes
(Which humbler denizens of heaven decline),
And celebrate, with sanctity divine,

The starry field from warring angels won,
And God triumphant in his victor Son.[1]
Nor less the wonder, and the sweet delight,
His milder scenes and softer notes excite,
When, at his bidding, Eden's blooming grove
Breathes the rich sweets of innocence and love.
With such pure joy as our forefather knew
When Raphael, heavenly guest, first met his view,
And our glad sire, within his blissful bower,
Drank the pure converse of the etherial power;[2]
Round the blest bard his raptured audience throng,
And feel their souls imparadised in song.
((1782) William Hayley (1745–1820),[3] from *An Essay on Epic Poetry*, Ep. III)

1. see *Paradise Lost*, Bk. VI. 2. see 189 ns 28–9. 3. prolific and popular poet at the turn of the 18th century; friend and biographer of Cowper and a friend of Southey; Hayley was offered (but declined) the office of Poet Laureate in 1790.

208 *Milton and England*[1]

Milton! thou shouldst be living at this hour;
England hath need of thee; she is a fen
Of stagnant waters; altar, sword, and pen,
Fireside, the heroic wealth of hall and bower,
Have forfeited their ancient English dower
Of inward happiness. We are selfish men;
Oh raise us up! return to us again,
And give us manners, virtue, freedom, power.
Thy soul was like a star, and dwelt apart;
Thou had'st a voice whose sound was like the sea;[2]
Pure as the naked heavens, majestic, free,
So didst thou travel on life's common way
In cheerful godliness; and yet thy heart
The lowliest duties on herself did lay.
((wr. 1802; pub. 1807) William Wordsworth (1770–1850), 'London, 1802')

1. one of a series of poems written after Wordsworth's return from France, when he was struck 'with the vanity and parade of our own country ... as contrasted with the quiet, and I may say the desolation, that the Revolution has produced in France' (from Wordsworth's notes dictated to Isabella Fenwick, 1843). 2. In *The Prelude* (1850 text, III.283–302), Wordsworth remembered drinking, as an undergraduate, in Milton's former rooms at Christ's College, Cambridge, and conjured images of the 'soul awful' of the aged Milton, 'uttering odious truth,/Darkness before, and danger's voice behind' and of the young student Milton's 'Angelical, keen eye, courageous look,/And conscious step of purity and pride'.

209 *Milton's Satan*

In its utmost abstraction and consequent state of reprobation, the will becomes satanic pride and rebellious self-idolatry in the relations of the spirit to itself, and remorseless despotism relatively to others; the more hopeless as the more obdurate by its subjugation of sensual impulses, by its superiority to toil and pain and pleasure; in short, by the fearful resolve to find in itself alone the one absolute motive of action, under which all other motives from within and from without must be either subordinated or crushed. This is the character which Milton has so philosophically as well as sublimely embodied in the Satan of his *Paradise Lost*. Alas! too often has it been embodied in real life. Too often has it given a dark and savage grandeur to the historic page. And wherever it has appeared, under whatever circumstances of time and country, the same ingredients have gone to its composition; and it has been identified by the same attributes: hope in which there is no cheerfulness; steadfastness within and immovable resolve, with outward restlessness and whirling activity; violence with guile; temerity with cunning; and, as the result of all, interminableness of object with perfect indifference of means. These are the qualities that have constituted the commanding genius; these are the marks that have characterised the masters of mischief, the liberticides and mighty hunters of mankind, from Nimrod[1] to Bonaparte.[2]

((1816) Samuel Taylor Coleridge (1772–1834), from *The Statesman's Manual*)

1. the first monarch, the 'mighty hunter' of Gen. 10:9. 2. Napoleon.

210 *The love of Milton's Adam and Eve*

The love of Adam and Eve in Paradise is of the highest merit – not phantomatic,[1] and yet removed from everything degrading. It is the sentiment of one rational being towards another, made tender by a specific difference in that which is essentially the same in both; it is a union of opposites, a giving and receiving mutually of the permanent in either, a completion of each in the other.

((wr. 1819; pub. 1836) Samuel Taylor Coleridge (1772–1834), from a lecture on 'Milton and the *Paradise Lost*' (published in *Literary Remains*))

1. insubstantially spiritual.

211 *Milton in his poetry*

In the *Paradise Lost*, indeed in every one of his poems, it is Milton himself whom you see; his Satan, his Adam, his Raphael, almost his Eve, are all John Milton; and it is a sense of this intense egotism that gives me the greatest pleasure in reading Milton's works. The egotism of such a man is a revelation of spirit.

((wr. 1833; pub. 1835) Samuel Taylor Coleridge (1772–1834), from *Table Talk*)

212 *Milton the tyrant-hater*

If, fallen in evil days on evil tongues,[1]
   Milton appealed to the avenger, Time,
If Time, the avenger, execrates his wrongs,
   And makes the word 'Miltonic' mean 'sublime',
He[2] deigned not to belie his soul in song,

Nor turn his very talent to a crime;
He did not loathe the sire to laud the son,³
But closed the tyrant-hater he begun.

Think'st thou, could he – the blind old man – arise,
  Like Samuel from the grave,⁴ to freeze once more
The blood of monarchs with his prophecies,
  Or be alive again, again all hoar
With time and trials, and those helpless eyes,
  And heartless daughters,⁵ worn, and pale, and poor;
Would *He* adore a sultan? *he* obey
The intellectual eunuch Castlereagh?⁶

((1819) George Gordon, Lord Byron (1788–1824), from *Don Juan*,
Canto I, Dedication)

1. see 189 (ii). 2. unlike the 'Lake Poets' (Wordsworth, Southey, *et al.*) who, Byron has alleged, have compromised their artistic integrity by accepting favours from the corrupt and reactionary political establishment of the day. 3. unlike many of his contemporaries, Milton did not write in praise of Charles II at the Restoration. 4. in 1 Sam. 28:13–14 the witch of Endor conjures up the spirit of Samuel for Saul. 5. 'Milton's two elder daughters are said to have robbed him of his books, besides cheating and plaguing him in the economy of his house' (Byron's note, 1833). 6. Robert Stewart, Viscount Castlereagh (1769–1822), Foreign Secretary, 1812–22, and one of Byron's political *bêtes noires*.

213 *A lament for Milton*

Most musical of mourners, weep again!
Lament anew, Urania!¹ He died,
Who was the sire of an immortal strain,
Blind, old, and lonely, when his country's pride,²
The priest, the slave, and the liberticide,
Trampled and mocked with many a lothèd rite
Of lust and blood; he went, unterrified,
Into the gulf of death; but his clear sprite
Yet reigns o'er earth; the third³ among the sons of light.

((1821) Percy Bysshe Shelley (1792–1822), from *Adonais*⁴)

1. see 189 n.17. 2. grammatically the object of 'trampled and mocked'. 3. Shelley regarded Milton as the third great epic poet, after Homer and Dante. 4, Shelley voiced similar sentiments to those expressed in this passage in the fragment 'Milton's Spirit' (wr. 1820; pub. 1870), where he wrote that 'from [Milton's] touch sweet thunder flowed, and shook/All human things built in contempt of Man'.

214 *Milton's Satan as moral being*

Milton's Devil as a moral being is as far superior to his God, as one who perseveres in some purpose which he has conceived to be excellent in spite of adversity and torture, is to one who, in the cold security of undoubted triumph, inflicts the most horrible revenge upon his enemy, not from any mistaken notion of inducing him to repent of a perseverance in enmity, but with the alleged design of exasperating him to deserve new torments. Milton has so far violated the popular creed (if this shall be judged to be a violation) as to have alleged no superiority of moral virtue to his God over his Devil. And this bold neglect of a direct moral purpose is the most decisive proof of the supremacy of Milton's genius.[1] He mingled, as it were, the elements of human nature as colours upon a single palette, and arranged them in the composition of his great picture according to the laws of epic truth, that is, according to the laws of that principle by which a series of actions of the external universe and of intelligent and ethical beings is calculated to excite the sympathy of succeeding generations of mankind.

((wr. 1821; pub. 1840) Percy Bysshe Shelley (1792–1822), from *A Defence of Poetry*)

---

1. Shelley's sentiment here is in some ways similar to that of William Blake who had declared, in *The Marriage of Heaven and Hell* (c.1790–3), that Milton 'was a true poet, and of the Devil's party without knowing it'.

215 *Milton and his critics*

Though faction's scorn[1] at first did shun
With coldness thy inspirèd song,
Though clouds of malice passed thy sun,
   They could not hide it long;
Its brightness soon exhaled away
Dank night, and gained eternal day.

The critics' wrath did darkly frown
Upon thy Muse's mighty lay;
But blasts that break the blossom down
   Do only stir the bay;
And thine shall flourish, green and long,
With the eternity of song.

Thy genius saw, in quiet mood,
Gilt fashion's follies pass thee by,
And, like the monarch of the wood,
   Towered o'er it to the sky,
Where thou couldst sing of other spheres,
And feel the fame of future years.

Though bitter sneers and stinging scorns
Did throng the Muse's dangerous way,
Thy powers were past such little thorns,
   They gave thee no dismay;
The scoffer's insult passed thee by,
Thou smil'st and mad'st him no reply.

((1826) John Clare (1793–1864), from 'To John Milton, from his Honoured Friend, William Davenant'[2])

---

1. see 189 n.27. 2. part of a series of poems written in the manner of other poets; here the style imitated is that of Sir William Davenant (1606–68), court poet to Charles I and later playwright under the restored Charles II; in 1650, Davenant was captured by the parliamentary forces, and it was said that he escaped death only through Milton's intervention.

JOHN MILTON (1608-74)

216 Milton: Alcaics[1]

O mighty-mouthed inventor of harmonies,
O skilled to sing of time or eternity,
   God-gifted organ-voice of England,
      Milton, a name to resound for ages;
Whose Titan angels, Gabriel, Abdiel,
Starred[2] from Jehovah's gorgeous armouries,
   Tower, as the deep-domed empyrëan[3]
      Rings to the roar of an angel onset;
Me[4] rather all that bowery loneliness,
The brooks of Eden mazily[5] murmuring,
   And bloom profuse and cedar arches
      Charm, as a wanderer out in ocean,
Where some refulgent[6] sunset of India
Streams o'er a rich ambrosial[7] ocean isle,
   And crimson-hued the stately palm-woods
      Whisper in odorous heights of even.[8]

((1863) Alfred, Lord Tennyson (1809-92))

1. the poem's metre imitates (as far as is possible in English) the four line stanza-form thought to have been invented by the Greek poet Alcaeus (see 169 n.22). 2. adorned; Tennyson refers to the war in heaven (*Paradise Lost*, Bk. VI). 3. the highest heavens. 4. grammatically the object of 'charm'. 5. in their wandering course. 6. radiant, gleaming. 7. divinely fragrant. 8. evening.

217 *Milton's epic style and Homer's*

Milton charges himself so full with thought, imagination, knowledge, that his style will hardly contain them. He is too full-stored to show us in much detail one conception, one piece of knowledge; he just shows it to us in a pregnant, allusive way, and then he presses on to another; and all this fullness, this pressure, this condensation, this self-constraint, enters into his movement, and makes it what it is: noble, but difficult and austere. Homer is quite different. He says a thing, and says it to the end, and then begins another; while Milton is trying to press a thousand things into one. So that, whereas, in reading Milton, you never lose the sense of laborious and condensed fullness, in reading Homer you never lose the sense of flowing and abounding ease. With Milton, line runs into line, and all is straitly[1] bound together. With Homer, line runs off from line, and all hurries away onward.

((1861) Matthew Arnold (1822-88), from *On Translating Homer*, Lecture III)

1. strictly, rigorously.

Richard Crashaw (?1612–49)

218 On the Death of Mr Crashaw[1]

Poet and saint! to thee alone are given
The two most sacred names of earth and heaven:
The hard and rarest union which can be
Next that of Godhead with humanity.
Long did the Muses banished slaves abide,
And built vain pyramids to mortal pride;[2]
Like Moses, thou (though spells and charms withstand)
Hast brought them nobly home back to their Holy Land.
　　Ah, wretched we, poets of earth! but thou
Wert, living, the same poet which thou art now.
Whilst angels sing to thee their airs divine,
And joy in an applause so great as thine.
Equal society with them to hold,
Thou needst not make new songs, but say the old.
And they, kind spirits, shall all rejoice to see
How little less than they exalted man may be.
Still the old heathen gods in numbers[3] dwell,
The heavenliest thing on earth still keeps up hell.
Nor have we yet quite purged the Christian land;
Still idols here, like calves at Bethel, stand.[4]
And though Pan's death long since all oracles broke,
Yet still in rhyme the fiend Apollo spoke;
Nay, with the worst of heathen dotage we,
Vain men, the monster Woman deify;[5]
Find stars, and tie our fates there in a face,
And Paradise in them by whom we lost it,[6] place.
What different faults corrupt our Muses thus?
Wanton as girls, as old wives fabulous![7]
　　Thy spotless Muse, like Mary, did contain
The boundless Godhead; she[8] did well disdain
That her eternal verse employed should be
On a less subject than eternity;
And for a sacred mistress scorned to take
But her, whom God himself scorned not his spouse to make.
It, in a kind, her miracle did do;
A fruitful mother was, and virgin too.
　　How well, blest swan, did Fate contrive thy death,
And made thee render up thy tuneful breath
In thy great mistress' arms! thou most divine
And richest offering of Loreto's shine!
Where like some holy sacrifice to expire,
A fever burns thee, and Love lights the fire.[9]
Angels, they say, brought the famed chapel there,
And bore the sacred load in triumph through the air.[10]
'Tis surer much they brought thee there, and they,
And thou, their charge, went singing all the way.
　　Pardon, my mother Church,[11] if I consent
That angels led him when from thee he went,[12]
For even in error sure no danger is

When joined with so much piety as his.
Ah, mighty God, with shame I speak it, and grief,
Ah, that our greatest faults were in belief!
And our weak reason were even weaker yet,
Rather than thus our wills too strong for it.
His faith, perhaps, in some nice tenets might
Be wrong; his life, I'm sure, was in the right.
And I myself a Catholic will be,
So far, at least, great saint, to pray to thee.
   Hail, bard triumphant! and some care bestow
On us, the poets militant below!
Opposed by our old enemy, adverse Chance,
Attacked by Envy, and by Ignorance,
Enchained by Beauty, tortured by Desires,
Exposed by Tyrant-Love to savage beasts and fires.
Thou from low earth in nobler flames didst rise,
And, like Elijah, mount alive the skies.[13]
Elisha-like (but with a wish much less,
More fit thy greatness, and my littleness)
Lo, here I beg – I whom thou once didst prove
So humble to esteem, so good to love –
Not that thy spirit might on me doubled be,
I ask but half thy mighty spirit for me.
And when my Muse soars with so strong a wing,
'Twill learn of things divine, and first of thee to sing.
                        ((1656) Abraham Cowley (1618–67))

1. on Crashaw, see 184 n.3; Cowley and Crashaw were contemporaries at Cambridge in the 1630s, and both spent time in Paris during the Interregnum; Crashaw joined the Roman Catholic Church around 1645, and in 1649 became a canon at the cathedral of the Santa Casa at Loreto in Italy. 2. like the children of Israel during their sojourn in Egypt. 3. poetry. 4. a reference to the two golden calves set up at Bethel and Dan by the sinful King Jeroboam, and worshipped by the children of Irael (1 Kgs. 12). 5. the death of Pan, the Greek god of flocks and shepherds, was supposed to have coincided with the birth of Christ, when the oracles of pagan antiquity were also supposed to have ceased; Cowley suggests, however, that Apollo continued his activities by inspiring amatory poetry. 6. by Eve's eating the fruit of the Tree of Knowledge. 7. given to narrating fantastic stories. 8. Crashaw's Muse, which devoted itself to sacred rather than amatory subjects, and thus is imagined as having given birth, like Mary, in a virginal state. 9. Crashaw died of a fever shortly after taking up his post at Loreto. 10. the Santa Casa (see n.1) was the reputed home of the Virgin Mary at Nazareth, which was said to have been miraculously transported to Fiume in Dalmatia in 1291, thence to Recanati in 1294, and finally to Loreto. 11. the Church of England. 12. when Crashaw became a Roman Catholic. 13. the prophet Elijah ascended by a whirlwind into Heaven (2 Kgs. 2:11); his successor Elisha had asked that a 'double portion' of Elijah's spirit might be 'upon' him (ibid., 2:9).

Samuel Butler (1612–80)

219 *Virtues and faults of 'Hudibras'*[1]

What burlesque could, was by that genius done;
Yet faults it has, impossible to shun;
The unchanging strain for want of grandeur cloys,
And gives too oft the horse-laugh mirth of boys;

> The short-legged verse and double-jingling sound
> So quick surprise us, that our heads run round;[2]
> Yet in this work peculiar life presides,
> And wit, for all the world to glean besides.
>> ((1730) Walter Harte (1709–74),[3] from 'An Essay on Satire,
>> Particularly on *The Dunciad*')

1. see 177 n.3. 2. *Hudibras* is written throughout in octosyllabic couplets which often deploy deliberately absurd rhymes. 3. see 31 n.8.

220 *The verse of 'Hudibras'*

> Peace to Swift's faults! his wit hath made them pass,
> Unmatched by all, save matchless *Hudibras*!
> Whose author is perhaps the first we meet,
> Who from our couplet lopped two final feet;[1]
> Nor less in merit than the longer line,[2]
> This measure moves a favourite of the Nine,[3]
> Though at first view eight feet may seem in vain
> Formed, save in ode,[4] to bear a serious strain.
>> ((1809) George Gordon, Lord Byron (1788–1824), from *Hints
>> from Horace*)

1. see 219 n.2; much of Swift's occasional verse is written in octosyllabics. 2. the heroic (iambic pentameter) couplet. 3. the Muses. 4. otosyllabic lines are sometimes used, along with lines in other metres, in odes (see, for example, Dryden's *Alexander's Feast*).

Sir John Denham (1615–69)

221 *The River Thames and Denham's verse*[1]

> O could I flow like thee, and make thy stream
> My great example, as it is my theme!
> Though deep, yet clear, though gentle, yet not dull,
> Strong without rage,[2] without o'er-flowing full.
>> ((1655)[3] Sir John Denham (1615–69),[4] from *Cooper's Hill*)

1. these lines, from Denham's famous poem describing and reflecting upon the landscape around the poet's house near the Thames at Egham, were praised by Dryden and Johnson, and became something of a *locus classicus* for displaying the potential of the heroic couplet for 'smoothness' and 'sweetness'. 2. vehemence, violence. 3. Denham's poem was first published in 1642, but substantially revised in subsequent editions. 4. see 188 n.5.

Abraham Cowley (1618–67)

222 *Cowley's covenant with his Muse*

> Me from the womb the midwife Muse did take;
> She cut my navel,[1] washed me, and mine head
>> With her own hands she fashionèd;
> She did a covenant[2] with me make,
> And circumcised my tender soul, and thus she spake:

'Thou of my Church shalt be;
 Hate and renounce,' said she,
'Wealth, honour, pleasures, all the world, for me.
Thou neither great at Court, nor in the war,
Nor at the Exchange[3] shalt be, nor at the wrangling Bar.[4]
Content thyself with the small, barren praise
 That neglected verse does raise.'
 She spake, and all my years to come
 Took their unlucky doom.[5]
Their several ways of life let others choose,
 Their several pleasures let them use;
But I was born for love, and for a Muse.

 With Fate what boots it to contend!
 Such I began, such am, and so must end.
 The star that did my being frame
 Was but a lambent[6] flame,
 And some small light it did dispense,
 But neither heat[7] nor influence.[8]
No matter, Cowley, let proud Fortune see
That thou canst her despise no less than she does thee.
 Let all her gifts the portion be
 Of Folly, Lust, and Flattery,
 Fraud, Extortion, Calumny,
 Murder, Infidelity,
 Rebellion and Hypocrisy.
 Do thou nor grieve nor blush to be
 As all the inspirèd tuneful men,
And all thy great forefathers were from Homer down to Ben.[9]
 ((1656) Abraham Cowley (1618–67),[10] from 'Destiny')

1. umbilical cord. 2. the engagement with God entered into by believers at baptism, or on being received into the Church. 3. the building where merchants met for the transaction of business. 4. the lawcourts. 5. fate, destiny. 6. one that plays gently on material without burning it. 7. (i) passion (ii) vigour. 8. (i) power bestowed by Fate (ii) influence in the world. 9. Ben Jonson. 10. see 15 n.19.

223 *Cowley and Virgil*

 His English stream so pure did flow,
 As all that saw and tasted know.
 But for his Latin vein,[1] so clear,
 Strong, full, and high it doth appear,
 That, were immortal Virgil here,
 Him for his judge he would not fear;
 Of that great portraiture, so true
 A copy pencil never drew.
 My Muse her song had ended here,
 But both their genii straight appear;
 Joy and Amazement her did strike;
 Two twins she never saw so like.
 'Twas taught by wise Pythagoras[2]
 One soul might through more bodies pass;
 Seeing such transmigration here,

She thought it not a fable there.
Such a resemblance of all parts,
Life, death, age, fortune, nature, arts,
Then lights her torch at theirs, to tell
And show the world this parallel.
Fixed and contémplative their looks,
Still turning over Nature's books;
Their works chaste, moral, and divine,
Where profit and delight combine;
They gilding dirt, in noble verse
Rustic philosophy rehearse;[3]
When heroes, gods, or god-like kings
They praise[4] on their exalted wings,
To the celestial orbs they climb,
And with the harmonious spheres keep time.
Nor did their actions fall behind
Their words, but with like candour shined.
Each drew fair characters, yet none
Of these they feigned excels their own.
Both by two generous princes[5] loved,
Who knew, and judged what they approved;
Yet, having each the same desire,
Both from the busy throng retire;[6]
Their bodies to their minds resigned,
Cared not to propagate their kind;[7]
Yet though both fell before their hour,
Time on their offspring hath no power,
Nor fire,[8] nor Fate their bays shall blast,
Nor Death's dark veil their day o'ercast.

((1667) Sir John Denham (1615–69),[9] from 'On Mr Abraham Cowley, his Death and Burial amongst the Ancient Poets')

1. Cowley's Latin poem *Plantarum Libri Duo* ['Of Plants, In Two Books'] was published in 1662. 2. the Greek philosopher (b. c.580 BC) who taught the doctrine of 'metempsychosis' (transmigration of souls). 3. Virgil's *Georgics* deals with the lives of farmers; Cowley frequently treated rural subjects, not least in his last work, the *Essays*. 4. Cowley treated heroic actions in his epic *The Davideis* (1656); he flattered Charles II in a fulsome Ode. 5. Augustus and Charles II; Cowley was in fact disappointed by his failure to gain preferment after the Restoration. 6. Cowley retired to a sequestered retreat at Chertsey in 1665; Virgil was said to have been planning to spend his last years in the private study of philosophy. 7. both Cowley and Virgil were bachelors. 8. Virgil is alleged to have requested on his death bed that the *Aeneid* be burnt. 9. see 188 n.5.

224 Cowley's 'Miscellanies' and 'Pindaric Odes'

Your Miscellanies[1] do appear
Just such another glorious indigested heap
As the first mass was, where
All heavens and stars enclosèd were,
Before they each one to their place did leap;
Before God, the great censor,[2] them bestowed,
According to their ranks, in several tribes abroad;[3]

> Whilst yet sun and moon
> Were in perpetual conjunction;[4]
> Whilst all the stars were but one milky way,
>   And in natural embraces lay.
> Whilst yet none of the lamps of heaven might
> Call this their own, and that another's light.
>   So glorious a lump as thine,
> Which chemistry may separate, but not refine;[5]
>   So mixed, so pure, so united does it shine,
> A chain of sand, of which each link is all divine. ...
>
>   Thy high Pindarics[6] soar
> So high, where never any wing till now could get;
>   And yet thy wit
> Doth seem so great as those that do fly lower.
>   Thou stand'st on Pindar's back;
> And therefore thou a higher flight dost take;
> Only thou art the eagle, he the wren;
>   Thou hast brought him from the dust,
>   And made him live again.
> Pindar has left his barbarous Greece, and thinks it just
>   To be led by thee to the English shore;
> An honour to him; Alexander[7] did no more,
> Nor scarce so much, when he did save his house before,
>   When his word did assuage
>   A warlike army's violent rage;
>   Thou hast given to his name,
> Than that great conqueror saved him from, a brighter flame.
> He only left some walls where Pindar's name might stay,
>   Which with time and age decay;
>   But thou hast made him once again to live;
>   Thou didst to him new life and breathing give.
>   And, as in the last resurrection,
> Thou hast made him rise more glorious, and put on
> More majesty; a greater soul is given to him by you,
> Than ever he in happy Thebes or Greece could show.
>   ((1656) Thomas Sprat (1635–1713),[8] from 'Upon the Poems of
>   the English Ovid, Anacreon, Pindar, and Virgil, Abraham
>   Cowley, in Imitation of his own Pindaric Odes')

1. Cowley's *Miscellanies* form the first part of his collected *Works* (1656), and include the 'Ode; Of Wit' (see 17), 'The Chronicle' (see 227), the poem on Crashaw (see 218), and the *Anacreontics* (see 165 n.11, and 169 n.23). 2. organiser, judge (particularly of moral matters). 3. scattered around. 4. in the same position when viewed from earth. 5. free from any impurities. 6. Cowley's *Pindaric Odes* (a section of the 1656 *Works*), the style of which was purportedly based on that of Pindar (see 94 n.3); Pindar's 'soaring' style led him to be nicknamed 'the Theban eagle'. 7. an allusion to the story of Alexander the Great's capture of Thebes, Pindar's native city; Alexander razed the city to the ground, but ordered that Pindar's house be spared. 8. friend and biographer of Cowley, Bishop of Rochester and Dean of Westminster; Sprat is often cited (on the strength of a passage, taken out of context, from his *History of the Royal Society* [1667]) as an unqualified advocate of the plain, prosaic way of writing associated with the New Science, but in this poem, as elsewhere, he appears as an imitator of Cowley at his most fancifully exuberant.

225 Cowley's wit

Great Cowley then,[1] a mighty genius, wrote,
O'er-run with wit, and lavish of his thought;
His turns[2] too closely on the reader press;
He more had pleased us, had he pleased us less.
One glittering thought no sooner strikes our eyes
With silent wonder, but new wonders rise.
As in the Milky Way a shining white
O'erflows the heavens with one continued light;
That not a single star can show his rays,
Whilst jointly all promote the common blaze.
Pardon, great poet, that I dare to name
The unnumbered beauties of thy verse with blame;
Thy fault is only wit in its excess;
But wit like thine in any shape will please.
What Muse but thine can equal hints inspire,
And fit the deep-mouthed Pindar[3] to thy lyre;
Pindar, whom others in a laboured strain,
And forced expression, imitate in vain?
Well-pleased in thee he soars with new delight,
And plays in more unbounded verse,[4] and takes a nobler flight.
   Blest man! whose spotless life and charming lays
Employed the tuneful prelate in thy praise;[5]
Blest man! who now shall be for ever known,
In Sprat's successful labours and thy own.

((1694) Joseph Addison (1672–1719),[6] from 'An Account of the Greatest English Poets')

1. after Spenser, in Addison's catalogue. 2. stylistic embellishments, particularly those involving the repetition of words in slightly different meanings (as with 'pleased' in Addison's own next line). 3. see 94 n.3 and 224. 4. Cowley's *Pindaric Odes* were celebrated for the experimental freedom of their irregular stanza forms. 5. Addison refers to Sprat's poem (see 224). 6. see 193 n.7.

226 Cowley's wit and morality

Who now reads Cowley?[1] if he pleases yet,[2]
His moral pleases, not his pointed wit;
Forgot his epic, nay Pindaric art,[3]
But still I love the language of his heart.[4]

((1737) Alexander Pope (1688–1744), from 'The First Epistle of the Second Book of Horace Imitated: To Augustus')

1. Pope himself, in fact, read Cowley attentively from boyhood onwards, and frequently echoes the earlier poet's work in his own verse. 2. still. 3. Pope refers to Cowley's epic *The Davideis* (see 223 n.4) and to his *Pindaric Odes* (see 224, 225). 4. The reference here seems to be to the moral and autobiographical writing in Cowley's last volume, the *Essays* (1668).

227 'The Chronicle' and Cowley's mind

'The Chronicle'[1] is a composition unrivalled and alone; such gaiety of fancy, such facility of expression, such varied similitude, such a succession of images, and such a dance of words, it is vain to expect except from

Cowley. His strength always appears in his agility; his volatility[2] is not the flutter of a light, but the bound of an elastic[3] mind. His levity[4] never leaves his learning behind it; the moralist, the politician, and the critic, mingle their influence even in this airy frolic of genius. To such a performance Suckling[5] could have brought the gaiety but not the knowledge, Dryden could have supplied the knowledge, but not the gaiety.

((1779) Samuel Johnson (1709–84), from 'Cowley' in *Lives of the Poets*)

1. Cowley's ballad is based on a series of fanciful analogies between the narrator's love-affairs and the recent political history of England. 2. 'mutability of mind; airiness; liveliness' (Johnson, *Dictionary*). 3. springy. 4. gaiety. 5. see 173 n.5.

228 *Ingenious Cowley*

Thee too,[1] enamoured of the life I loved,[2]
Pathetic[3] in its praise, in its pursuit
Determined, and possessing it at last[4]
With transports such as favoured lovers feel,
I studied, prized, and wished that I had known,
Ingenious Cowley! and, though now reclaimed
By modern lights[5] from an erroneous taste,
I cannot but lament thy splendid wit,
Entangled in the cobwebs of the schools,[6]
I still revere thee, courtly though retired;
Though stretched at ease in Chertsey's silent bowers,[7]
Not unemployed; and finding rich amends
For a lost world in solitude and verse.

((1785) William Cowper (1731–1800), from *The Task*, Bk. IV)

1. Cowper has been discussing Milton. 2. Cowper has been reflecting on his love of a life of rural retirement. 3. moving, affecting. 4. see 223 n.6. 5. sources of illumination, authorities; many critics of Cowper's day had animadverted on the (to them) poor taste of Cowley's fanciful ingenuity. 6. see 197 n.3. 7. see 223 n.6; it was at Chertsey that Cowley had composed his *Essays* (see 15 n.19, 226 n.4).

229 *Cowley's extravagance*

Dispenser of wide-wasting woe,
Creation's laws you overthrow.
Mankind in your fierce flames you burn
And drown in their own tears by turn.
Deluged had been the world in vain,
Your fire soon dried its clothes again.

((1853) Walter Savage Landor (1775–1864),[1] 'Cowley's Style')

1. see 152 n.3; Landor imitates the conceits of Cowley's own poetry in his reflections on that poetry.

Richard Lovelace (1618–57)

230 To his Noble Friend, Mr Lovelace,[1] upon his Poems

Sir,
Our[2] times are much degenerate from those
Which your sweet Muse, which your fair fortune chose,
And as complexions alter with the climes,
Our wits have drawn the infection of our times.
That candid age no other way could tell
To be ingenious, but by speaking well.
Who best could praise had then the greatest praise,
'Twas more esteemed to give than wear the bays;[3]
Modest ambition studied only then
To honour not herself but worthy men..
These virtues now are banished out of town,
Our civil wars have lost the civic crown.[4]
He highest builds who with most art destroys,
And against others' fame his own employs.
I see the envious caterpillar sit
On the fair blossom of each growing wit.

   The air's already tainted with the swarms
Of insects which against you rise in arms;
Word-peckers, paper-rats, book-scorpions,
Of wit corrupted the unfashioned sons.
The barbèd censurers[5] begin to look
Like the grim cónsistory[6] on thy book,
And on each line cast a reforming eye,
Severer than the young presbýtery.
Till when in vain they have thee all perused,
You shall, for being faultless, be accused.
Some, reading your *Lucasta*, will allege
You wronged in her the House's privilege;[7]
Some that you under sequestration are,
Because you writ when going to the war,[8]
And one the book prohibits, because Kent
Their first petition by the author sent.[9]

   But when the beauteous ladies came to know
That their dear Lovelace was endangered so –
Lovelace that thawed the most congealèd breast,
He who loved best[10] and them defended best,
Whose hand so rudely grasps the steely brand,
Whose hand so gently melts the lady's hand –
They all in mutiny, thou yet undressed,
Sallied,[11] and would in his defence contest.
And one, the loveliest that was yet e'er seen,
Thinking that I too of the rout[12] had been,
Mine eyes invaded with a female spite
(She knew what pain 'twould be to lose that sight).
'O no, mistake not,' I replied, 'for I
In your defence, or in his cause, would die.'
But he, secure of glory and of time,

Above their envy, or mine aid, doth climb.
Him valiantest men and fairest nymphs approve;
His book in them finds judgement, with you love.

((1649) Andrew Marvell (1621–78)[13])

1. court poet in the reign of Charles I; imprisoned by Parliament during the Interregnum, and financially ruined by his outlays for the royalist cause; Marvell's poem was one of the commendatory verses prefixed to the first edition of Lovelace's *Lucasta*. 2. Marvell was only three years younger than Lovelace, but addresses him as a member of an earlier, pre-war culture. 3. laurels honouring a successful poet. 4. the garland of oak leaves given to a man who had saved the life of a fellow-citizen in battle. 5. those who enforced the Printing Ordinance of 1643 which ensured that all books had to be licensed. 6. Court of Presbyters; the Scots had attempted to pressurise Parliament into establishing a Presbyterian form of church government in England, and a Presbytery had been established in 1643. 7. usurped the parliamentary privilege of free speech (by having his lovers claim, in the first song of *Lucasta*, to 'speak like spirits unconfined'). 8. Lovelace is said to have prepared his volume for the press while in prison ('under sequestration'); the second song in *Lucasta* is the famous 'To Lucasta, Going to the Wars'. 9. Lovelace had been imprisoned in 1642 for presenting to Parliament a Kentish petition that the King's rights be restored. 10. Lovelace is said to have been greatly adored by the females of his acquaintance. 11. came forth. 12. of the mob attacking Lovelace. 13. Marvell himself receives no author entry in this anthology because poetic responses to him focused almost exclusively on his career as a politician rather than as a poet.

Poets of the later 17th and early 18th centuries

231 *The wits of the Stuart Court*

But for the wits of either Charles's days,
The mob of gentlemen who wrote with ease;
Sprat,[1] Carew,[2] Sedley,[3] and a hundred more
(Like twinkling stars the miscellánies[4] o'er),
One simile, that solitary shines
In the dry desert of a thousand lines,
Or lengthened thought that gleams through many a page,
Has sanctified whole poems for an age.

((1737) Alexander Pope (1688–1744), from 'The First Epistle of the Second Book of Horace Imitated: To Augustus')

1. see 224 n.8. 2. see 165 n.34. 3. see 239 n.1. 4. many poems by 'the mob of gentlemen' were included in the various collections of 'miscellany poems' published at the end of the 17th and the beginning of the 18th centuries, particularly the six-volume collection by Dryden's publisher, Jacob Tonson.

232 *'Correctness' and the English poets*

We conquered France,[1] but felt our captive's charms;
Her arts victorious triumphed o'er our arms;
Britain to soft refinements less a foe,
Wit grew polite, and numbers[2] learned to flow.
Waller[3] was smooth, but Dryden taught to join
The varying verse, the full resounding line,
The long majestic march, and energy divine.
Though still some traces of our rustic vein

And splay-foot verse[4] remained, and will remain.
Late, very late, correctness grew our care,
When the tired nation breathed from civil war.
Exact Racine, and Corneille's[5] noble fire,
Showed us that France had something to admire.
Not but the tragic spirit was our own,
And full in Shakespeare, fair in Otway[6] shone;
But Otway failed to polish or refine,
And fluent Shakespeare scarce effaced[7] a line.
Even copious Dryden wanted, or forgot,
The last and greatest art: the art to blot.[8]

((1737) Alexander Pope (1688–1744), from 'The First Epistle of the Second Book of Horace Imitated: To Augustus')

1. the reference is to Henry V's conquest of France in the 15th century. 2. versification. 3. see 185–7 and ns. 4. see 186 n.2. 5. Jean Racine (1639–99) and Pierre Corneille (1606-84), the two greatest tragic dramatists of 17th-century France, the former famous for his ability to fuse intense passion with limpid elegance, the latter for the sounding rhetoric of his noble dramatic personages. 6. Thomas Otway (1652-85), Restoration tragedian, best known for *Venice Preserved* (1682); Otway made an adaptation of Racine's *Bérénice* in 1676. 7. crossed out; compare Ben Jonson's comments in 126. 8. delete.

233 *Tragedy after the Restoration*

Then, crushed by rules,[1] and weakened as refined,
For years the power of tragedy declined;
From bard to bard, the frigid caution crept,
Till Declamation[2] roared, while Passion slept.
Yet still did Virtue deign the stage to tread,
Philosophy remained, though Nature fled.[3]
But forced at length her ancient reign to quit,
She saw great Faustus[4] lay the ghost of wit;
Exulting Folly hailed the joyful day,
And Pantomime and Song confirmed her sway.

((1747) Samuel Johnson (1709–84), from 'Prologue Spoken by Mr Garrick at the Opening of the Theatre in Drury Lane')

1. the pseudo-Aristotelian doctrines, popular in the late 17th and early 18th centuries, which stated that dramas must observe the three Unities: of place (the action must be restricted to a single location), of time (the action represented should be of equivalent duration to the representation itself), and of action (the action should have the singleness of a living organism); Johnson exposed the fallacies on which such doctrines rest (when rigidly and dogmatically applied) in the Preface to his edition of Shakespeare. 2. frigid rhetoric. 3. tragedies like Addison's popular *Cato* (1713), though lacking in dramatic life (Johnson called *Cato* 'rather a poem in dialogue than a drama'), contained lofty moral and philosophical sentiments. 4. the Faust legend was a popular subject in the 18th century for farcical 'afterpieces' to serious dramas.

234 *Restoration poetry and its aftermath*

When Cromwell fought for power, and while he reigned
The proud protector[1] of the power he gained,
Religion harsh, intolerant, austere,
Parent of manners[2] like herself severe,
Drew a rough copy of the Christian face,
Without the smile, the sweetness, or the grace;

The dark and sullen humour³ of the time
  Judged every effort of the Muse a crime;
  Verse in the finest mould of fancy⁴ cast
  Was lumber in an age so void of taste;
  But when the second Charles assumed the sway,
  And arts revived beneath a softer day,
  Then, like a bow long forced into a curve,
  The mind, released from too constrained a nerve,⁵
  Flew to its first position with a spring
  That made the vaulted roofs of pleasure ring.
  His Court, the dissolute and hateful school
  Of wantonness, where vice was taught by rule,
  Swarmed with a scribbling herd, as deep inlaid
  With brutal lust as ever Circe⁶ made.
  From these a long succession, in the rage
  Of rank obscenity, debauched their age;
  Nor ceased till, ever anxious to redress
  The abuses of her sacred charge, the press,⁷
  The Muse instructed a well-nurtured train
  Of abler votaries to cleanse the stain,
  And claim the palm for purity of song,
  That lewdness had usurped and worn so long.
  Then decent pleasantry and sterling sense,
  That neither gave nor would endure offence,
  Whipped out of sight, with satire just and keen,
  The puppy pack that had defiled the scene.
          ((1782) William Cowper (1731–1800), from 'Table Talk')

1. Oliver Cromwell became Lord Protector of England in 1653. 2. modes of behaviour. 3. mood. 4. imagination. 5. too taut a bowstring. 6. the reference is to the 'court wits' of the Restoration (Rochester, Sedley, Etherege, and others), gentlemen-poets whose work (see 239) was notorious for its licentious obscenity; Circe was the enchantress in Homer's *Odyssey* who turned Odysseus' companions into swine. 7. printed literature.

235 *Pope and his predecessors*

  Time was, ere yet in these degenerate days¹
  Ignoble themes obtained mistaken praise,
  When sense and wit with poesy allied,
  No fabled graces, flourished side by side;
  From the same fount their inspiration drew,
  And, reared by taste, bloomed fairer as they grew.
  Then, in this happy isle, a Pope's pure strain
  Sought the rapt soul to charm, nor sought in vain;
  A polished nation's praise aspired to claim,
  And raised the people's, as the poet's fame.
  Like him great Dryden poured the tide of song,
  In stream less smooth, indeed, yet doubly strong.
        ((1809) George Gordon, Lord Byron (1788–1824), from *English
                                          Bards and Scotch Reviewers*)

1. Byron's poem denounces those whom he sees as the poetasters and hack critics of his own day, indicting their work as a sad falling-off after the achievement of Dryden and Pope.

236 *The couplet poets*

                A schism
Nurtured by foppery and barbarism
Made great Apollo blush for this his land.
Men were thought wise who could not understand
His glories; with a puling infant's force
They swayed about upon a rocking horse[1]
And thought it Pegasus.[2] Ah, dismal-souled!
The winds of heaven blew, the ocean rolled
Its gathering waves; ye felt it not. The blue
Bared its eternal bosom, and the dew
Of summer nights collected still to make
The morning precious. Beauty was awake!
Why were ye not awake? But ye were dead
To things ye knew not of; were closely wed
To musty laws lined out with wretched rule
And compass vile, so that ye taught a school
Of dolts to smooth, inlay, and clip, and fit,
Till, like the certain wands of Jacob's wit,
Their verses tallied.[3] Easy was the task;
A thousand handicraftsmen wore the mask
Of Poesy. Ill-fated, impious race
That blasphemed the bright lyrist[4] to his face,
And did not know it! No, they went about,
Holding a poor, decrepit standard out,
Marked with most flimsy mottoes, and in large
The name of one Boileau![5]
        ((1817) John Keats (1795–1821), from 'Sleep and Poetry')

1. the heroic couplet. 2. see 11 n.6. 3. Keats alludes to the story of Jacob's deceiving of Laban (see Gen. 30), in order to obtain a better flock; the 'wands' are the semi-peeled wooden rods with which Jacob induced the female animals to bring forth parti-coloured offspring which, by the terms of his agreement with Laban, he was entitled to keep. 4. Apollo. 5. Nicolas Boileau-Despréaux (1636–1711), French poet and critic, whose poem *L'Art poétique* (1674) was widely admired in late 17th- and 18th-century England, but which later came to be disliked as a repository of procrustean 'neoclassical' doctrine.

John Dryden (1631–1700)

237 *Dryden and the lure of the theatre*

      O gracious God, how far have we
Profaned thy heavenly gift of poesy,
Made prostitute and profligate the Muse,
Debased to each obscene and impious use,
Whose harmony was first ordained above
For tongues of angels, and for hymns of love!
O wretched we! Why were we hurried down
   This lubric[1] and adulterate age –
   Nay added fat pollutions of our own –
To increase the steaming ordures of the stage?
      ((1686) John Dryden (1631–1700), from 'To ... Anne Killigrew')

1. lascivious, wanton.

238 Dryden and love poetry

Old as I am,[1] for ladies' love unfit,
The power of beauty I remember yet,
Which once inflamed my soul, and still inspires my wit.
If love be folly, the severe divine[2]
Has felt that folly, though he censures mine;
Pollutes the pleasures of a chaste embrace,
Acts what I write, and propagates in grace,
With riotous excess, a priestly race. ...
   What needs he paraphrase on what we mean?
We were at worst but wanton; he's obscene.
I, nor my fellows nor myself excuse;
But love's the subject of the comic Muse;
Nor can we write without it, nor would you
A tale of only dry instruction view;
Nor love is always of a vicious[3] kind,
But oft to virtuous acts inflames the mind;
Awakes the sleepy vigour of the soul,
And, brushing o'er, adds motion to the pool.
Love, studious how to please, improves our parts
With polished manners, and adorns with arts.
Love first invented verse, and formed the rhyme,
The motion measured, harmonised the chime;
To liberal[4] acts enlarged the narrow-souled,
Softened the fierce, and made the coward bold;
The world when waste, he peopled with increase,
And warring nations reconciled in peace.
   ((1700) John Dryden (1631–1700), from 'Cymon and Iphigenia'
                                 in *Fables Ancient and Modern*)

1. Dryden was 68 at the time; the *Fables* contains a number of poems (mostly translated and adapted from Chaucer, Ovid and Homer) which treat the subject of love. 2. Jeremy Collier (1650–1726), a clergyman who, in his *Short View of the ... English Stage* (1698), had attacked Dryden's plays, and those of his contemporaries, for their immorality; Dryden suggests that the specificity of Collier's recall of the material he is censuring betrays the cleric's secret relish of that which he purports to deplore. 3. morally wicked, corrupting. 4. beneficent, generous.

239 Dryden the would-be rake

Sedley[1] has that prevailing, gentle art,
That can with a resistless charm impart
The loosest wishes to the chastest heart;
Raise such a conflict, kindle such a fire,
Betwixt declining virtue and desire,
Till the poor vanquished maid dissolves away
In dreams all night, in sighs and tears all day.
   Dryden in vain tried this nice[2] way of wit,
For he to be a tearing blade thought fit.
But when he would be sharp, he still was blunt;

To frisk his frolic fancy, he'd cry 'Cunt!'
Would give the ladies a dry bawdy bob,³
And thus he got the name of Poet Squab.⁴
But, to be just, 'twill to his praise be found,
His excellencies more than faults abound;
Nor dare I from his sacred temples tear
That laurel⁵ which he best deserves to wear.
   But does not Dryden find even Jonson dull,
Fletcher and Beaumont uncorrect, and full
Of lewd lines, as he calls 'em; Shakespeare's style
Stiff and affected⁶ – to his own the while
Allowing all the justness that his pride
So arrogantly had to these denied?
And may not I have leave impartially
To search and censure Dryden's works, and try
If those gross faults his choice pen does commit
Proceed from want of judgement, or of wit?
Or if his lumpish⁷ fancy⁸ does refuse
Spirit and grace to his loose, slattern⁹ Muse?
         ((wr. 1675–6; pub. 1680) John Wilmot, Earl of Rochester
                  (1647–80), from 'An Allusion to Horace')

1. Sir Charles Sedley (?1639–1701), Restoration courtier and poet, notorious for his profligacy; the author of elegantly seductive lyrics. 2. delicate, refined. 3. coition without omission. 4. a 'squab' is an inexperienced person. 5. Dryden had been created Poet Laureate in 1668. 6. in his *Defence of the Epilogue* (1672), Dryden had remarked on the linguistic faults of Fletcher and Shakespeare; for his strictures on Shakespeare, see also 128. 7. gross. 8. imagination. 9. sluttish, slovenly.

240 *On 'Absalom and Achitophel'*

Take it as earnest of a faith renewed,¹
Your theme is vast, your verse divinely good;
Where, though the Nine² their beauteous strokes repeat,
   And the turned lines on golden anvils beat,
It looks as if they struck them at a heat.³
So all serenely great, so just, refined,
Like angels' love to human seed inclined,
It starts a giant, and exalts the kind.
'Tis spirit seen, whose fiery atoms roll
So brightly fierce, each syllable's a soul.
'Tis miniature of Man, but he's all heart;
'Tis what the world would be, but wants the art;
To whom even the fanatics⁴ altars raise,
Bow in their own despite, and grin your praise;
As if a Milton from the dead arose,
Filed off the rust, and the right party⁵ chose.
         ((1681) Nathaniel Lee (?1649–92),⁶ from 'To the Unknown Author⁷
                              of *Absalom and Achitophel*')

1. as a pledge of my renewed confidence in the Court; immediately before writing this poem,

Lee had been writing work of a republican tendency; *Absalom* had, apparently, persuaded him to rejoin the royalist camp. 2. the Muses. 3. at one blow, without prolonged labour. 4. those hostile to Charles II (who would not be expected to admire Dryden's royalist satire). 5. the royalists. 6. playwright and collaborator with Dryden on *Oedipus* and *The Duke of Guise* (1682). 7. *Absalom* was published anonymously, but Dryden's authorship was an open secret.

241 *Dryden and the theatre*

Our King returned, and banished peace restored,
The Muse ran mad to see her exiled lord;
On the cracked stage the bedlam heroes roared,[1]
And scarce could speak one reasonable word;
Dryden himself, to please a frantic[2] age,
Was forced to let his judgement stoop to rage;[3]
To a wild audience he conformed his voice,
Complied to custom, but not erred through choice.
Deem then the people's, not the writer's, sin
Almanzor's rage, and rants of Maximin;[4]
That fury spent, in each elaborate piece
He vies for fame with ancient Rome and Greece.

((1701) George Granville, Lord Lansdowne (1667–1735),[5] from 'An Essay upon Unnatural Flights in Poetry')

1. a reference to the 'heroic plays' popular at the Restoration, which featured swaggering larger-than-life heroes and were written in a flamboyantly elevated style. 2. mad, outrageous. 3. madness, extravagance. 4. Almanzor and Maximin are characters in two of Dryden's heroic plays, *The Conquest of Granada* (1672) and *Tyrannic Love* (1670); Dryden's later work is largely in the form of translations from Greek and Roman poetry. 5. poet and statesman; author of commendatory verses to Dryden's *Virgil* (1697) and the dedicatee of Pope's *Windsor Forest* (1713).

242 *Dryden in old age*

As years advance, the abated soul, in most,
Sinks to low ebb, in second childhood lost;
And spoiling Age, dishonouring our kind,
Robs all the treasures of the wasted mind;
With hovering clouds obscures the muffled sight,
And dim suffusion of enduring night;
But the rich fervour of his rising rage[1]
Prevailed o'er all the infirmities of age,
And, unimpaired by injuries of Time,
Enjoyed the bloom of a perpetual prime.[2]
His fire not less, he more correctly writ,
With ripened judgement, and digested wit;
When the luxuriant ardour of his youth
Succeeding years had tamed to better growth,
And seemed to break the body's crust away,
To give the expanded mind more room to play;
Which, in its evening, opened on the sight
Surprising beams of full meridian[3] light;
As thrifty of its splendour it had been,

And all its lustre had reserved till then.
So the descending sun, which hid his ray
In mists before, diminishing the day,
Breaks radiant out upon the dazzled eye,
And in a blaze of glory leaves the sky.
((wr. 1706; pub. 1721) Jabez Hughes (?1685–1731),[4] from
'Upon Reading Mr Dryden's *Fables*')

1. inspiration. 2. dawn, morning. 3. noontide. 4. civil servant, translator, and younger brother of John Hughes (1677–1720), poet, translator, and editor of Spenser.

243 *Dryden's creative Muse*

In his vast miscellaneous works we find
What charms at once and edifies the mind;
His pregnant Muse has in the offspring shown
What's rare for use or beauty to be known;
In monumental, everlasting verse,
Epitomised he grasped the universe.
No power but his could tune a British lyre
To sweeter notes than any Tuscan[1] choir,
Teutonic words to animate and raise
Strong, shining, musical as Attic lays;[2]
Rude matter indisposed[3] he formed polite,[4]
His Muse seemed rather to create than write.
((1700) Anon.,[5] from 'To the Memory of Mr Dryden')

1. Italian. 2. Greek poems. 3. disorganised. 4. made elegant. 5. Dryden's 18th-century editor, Edmund Malone, suggested that this poem might be by Captain Gibbons, the son of Dryden's physician.

244 *Dryden's 'Alexander's Feast'*

Hear how Timotheus'[1] varied lays surprise,
And bid alternate passions fall and rise!
While at each change the son of Libyan Jove[2]
Now burns with glory, and then melts with love;
Now his fierce eyes with sparkling fury glow,
Now sighs steal out, and tears begin to flow;
Persians and Greeks like turns of nature found,
And the world's victor stood subdued by sound!
The power of music all our hearts allow,
And what Timotheus was, is Dryden now.
((wr. 1709; pub. 1711) Alexander Pope (1688–1744), from *An
Essay on Criticism*[3])

1. in Dryden's poem, Timotheus, court musician to Alexander the Great, is entertaining his master, as Alexander celebrates his victory over the Persians; such is the affective power of his song that he can conjure up whatever mood he wishes in his auditors. 2. Alexander was said to have been proclaimed the son of Zeus by an oracle in Libya. 3. for Pope on Dryden, see also 232.

245 Envy against Dryden

Pride, Malice, Folly, against Dryden rose,
In various shapes of parsons,[1] critics, beaux;[2]
But sense survived when merry jests were past,
For rising merit will buoy up at last.
Might he return, and bless once more our eyes,
New Blackmores[3] and new Milbournes[4] must arise;
Nay should great Homer lift his awful[5] head,
Zoilus[6] again would start up from the dead.
Envy will merit, as its shade[7] pursue;
But, like a shadow, proves the substance true;
For envied wit, like Sol[8] eclipsed, makes known
The opposing body's grossness, not its own.
When first that sun too powerful beams displays,
It draws up vapours which obscure its rays;
But even those clouds at last adorn its way,
Reflect new glories, and augment the day.

((wr. 1709; pub. 1711) Alexander Pope (1688–1744), from *An Essay on Criticism*)

1. e.g. Collier (see 238 n.2). 2. e.g. Rochester (see 239). 3. Sir Richard Blackmore (see 31 n.7) had attacked Dryden as 'an old, revolted, unbelieving bard' in his *Prince Arthur* (1695). 4. Luke Milbourne (1649–1720), a clergyman, had attacked Dryden's translation of Virgil in a series of Notes on the volume (1698). 5. awe-inspiring. 6. a 4th century BC Greek rhetorician who had vilified Homer, and whose name thus became proverbial for a carping critic. 7. shadow. 8. the sun.

246 Dryden as satirist

In Albion[1] then, with equal lustre bright,
Great Dryden rose, and steered by Nature's light.
Two glimmering orbs[2] he just observed from far,
The ocean wide, and dubious either star.
Donne teemed with wit, but all was maimed and bruised,
The periods endless, and the sense confused;[3]
Oldham[4] rushed on, impetuous and sublime,
But lame in language, harmony, and rhyme;
These, with new graces, vigorous Nature joined
In one, and centred them in Dryden's mind.
How full thy verse! Thy meaning how severe!
How dark[5] thy theme! Yet made exactly clear.
Not mortal is thy accent, nor thy rage,
Yet mercy softens, or contracts, each page.
Dread bard! instruct us to revere thy rules,
And hate, like thee, all rebels, and all fools.

((1730) Walter Harte (1709–74), from 'An Essay on Satire, Particularly on *The Dunciad*')

1. England. 2. celestial bodies. 3. see 186 n.2. 4. see 253 n.1. 5. disguised; Dryden's major satires are cast in the oblique forms of allegory and mock-heroic.

247 Dryden compared with Pope

Dryden knew more of Man in his general[1] nature, and Pope in his local manners.[2] The notions of Dryden were formed by comprehensive speculation, and those of Pope by minute attention. There is more dignity in the knowledge of Dryden and more certainty in that of Pope. ...

Of genius – that power which constitutes a poet; that quality without which judgement is cold and knowledge is inert; that energy which collects, combines, amplifies, and animates – the superiority must, with some hesitation, be allowed to Dryden. It is not to be inferred that of this poetical vigour Pope had only a little, because Dryden had more; for every other writer since Milton must give place to Pope; and even of Dryden it must be said that, if he has brighter paragraphs, he has not better poems. Dryden's performances were always hasty, either excited by some external occasion, or extorted by domestic necessity; he composed without consideration, and published without correction. What his mind could supply at call, or gather in one excursion, was all that he sought, and all that he gave. The dilatory caution of Pope[3] enabled him to condense his sentiments, to multiply his images, and to accumulate all that study might produce or chance might supply. If the flights of Dryden therefore are higher, Pope continues longer on the wing. If of Dryden's fire the blaze is brighter, of Pope's the heat is more regular and constant. Dryden often surpasses expectation, and Pope never falls below it. Dryden is read with frequent astonishment, and Pope with perpetual delight.

((1781) Samuel Johnson (1709–84), from 'Pope' in *Lives of the Poets*)

1. fundamental, universal. 2. conduct in specific circumstances. 3. Pope was a constant and assiduous reviser of his works, both before and after their first publication.

248 Dryden's couplet verse and odes

> Behold, where Dryden's less presumptuous[1] car,[2]
> Wide o'er the fields of glory, bear
> Two coursers[3] of etherial race,
> With necks in thunder clothed, and long-resounding pace.
>
>   Hark, his hands the lyre explore![4]
> Bright-eyed Fancy[5] hovering o'er
> Scatters from her pictured urn
> Thoughts that breathe and words that burn.
> But ah! 'tis heard no more –

((wr. 1751–4; pub. 1757) Thomas Gray (1716–71), from 'The Progress of Poesy: a Pindaric Ode')

1. than Milton's. 2. chariot. 3. horses; the reference is also to the paired lines of Dryden's couplet verse; this passage, Gray wrote in a note, was 'meant to express the stately march and sounding energy of Dryden's rhymes'. 4. Gray refers to Dryden's odes, particularly the two odes on St Cecilia's Day (1687, 1697). 5. imagination.

249 *Dryden's thought*

Chatting on deck was Dryden too,
The Bacon[1] of the rhyming crew;
None ever crossed our mystic sea
More richly stored with thought than he;
Though never tender nor sublime,
He struggles with, and conquers, Time.
((1834) Walter Savage Landor (1775–1864),[2] from 'To Wordsworth')

1. Sir Francis Bacon (1561–1626), philosopher, essayist, natural scientist, and politician.
2. see 152 n.3.

250 *Dryden's power in the couplet*

Dryden is all power, and he knows it. He soars at ease, he sails at ease, he swoops at ease, and he trusses[1] at ease. ... Dryden alone moves unfettered in the fettering couplet, alone of those who have submitted to the fetters. For those who write distichs,[2] running them into one another, head over heels, till you do not know where to look after the rhyme – these do not wear their fetters, and with an all-mastering grace dance to the chime, but they break them and caper about, the fragments clanking dismally and strangely about their heels. Turn from the clumsy clowns to Glorious John[3] – sinewy, flexible, well-knit, agile, stately-stepping, gracefully-bending, stern, stalwart – or sitting his horse, 'erect and fair', in careering, and carrying his steel-headed lance of true stuff, level and steady to its aim, and impetuous as a thunderbolt.
((1845) 'Christopher North' (John Wilson) (1785–1854),[3] from *North's Specimens of the British Critics*)

1. seizes his prey (a falconry term, like the other verbs in the sentence). 2. rhyming couplets. 3. Claud Halcro's designation of Dryden in Sir Walter Scott's *The Pirate* (1821). 3. see 55 n.2.

Thomas Shadwell (?1642–92)

251 *Flecknoe celebrates Shadwell's talents*[1]

This is thy province, this thy wondrous way,
New humours to invent for each new play;[2]
This is that boasted bias of thy mind,[3]
By which one way, to dullness, 'tis inclined;
Which makes thy writings lean on one side still,
And, in all changes, that way bends thy will.
Nor let thy mountain belly make pretence
Of likeness;[4] thine's a tympany[5] of sense.
A tun[6] of man in thy large bulk is writ,
But sure thou'rt but a kilderkin[7] of wit.
Like mine, thy gentle numbers feebly creep;
Thy tragic Muse gives smiles, thy comic sleep.
With whate'er gall thou sett'st thyself to write,

Thy inoffensive satires never bite.
In thy felonious heart though venom lies,
It does but touch thy Irish pen[8] and dies.
Thy genius calls thee not to purchase fame
In keen iambics,[9] but mild anagram.[10]
Leave writing plays, and choose for thy command
Some peaceful province in acrostic[11] land.
There thou mayst wings display and altars[12] raise,
And torture one poor word ten thousand ways.
Or if thou wouldst thy different talents[13] suit,
Set thy own songs, and sing them to thy lute.

((wr. 1676; pub. 1682) John Dryden (1631–1700), from *Mac Flecknoe*)

1. Thomas Shadwell was a minor poet and dramatist (Poet Laureate, 1689) with whom Dryden had been engaged in literary disputes since the late 1660s; Dryden had been particularly outraged by Shadwell's grotesque portrayal of himself as the literary heir of Ben Jonson; in *Mac Flecknoe*, Dryden imagines, in mock-heroic manner, the handing over of the kingdom of Non-sense to Shadwell by Richard Flecknoe (d. ?1678), a minor poet who had been previously pilloried by Marvell, and who had also presented himself as a disciple of Jonson. 2. an allusion to Shadwell's Dedication to *The Virtuoso* (1676); Shadwell had boasted that he had presented four 'entirely new' humours (distinct types of psychological disposition) in his play. 3. in the Epilogue to *The Humourists* (1671), Shadwell had described a 'humour' as 'a bias of the mind/By which with violence 'tis one way inclined'. 4. to Ben Jonson; in his poem 'My Picture Left in Scotland', Jonson had referred, humorously, to his own 'mountain belly'. 5. swelling. 6. large wine cask. 7. quarter-tun. 8. neither Flecknoe nor Shadwell were in fact Irish, but the joke generated the title of Dryden's poem ('Mac' being Irish for 'son of'). 9. biting satire. 10. verbal trifling. 11. see 17 n.10. 12. as in George Herbert's poems 'Easter Wings' and 'The Altar', where the shape of the printed poem on the page imitates its subject. 13. in the Preface to his *Psyche* (1675), Shadwell had boasted of his musical expertise.

John Wilmot, Earl of Rochester (1647–80)

252 *Rochester's aristocratic credo*

Should I be troubled when the purblind knight,[1]
Who squints more in his judgement than his sight,
Picks silly faults, and censures what I write;
Or when the poor-fed poets of the town
For scraps and coach-room[2] cry my verses down?
I loathe the rabble; 'tis enough for me
If Sedley,[3] Shadwell,[4] Shepherd,[5] Wycherley,[6]
Godolphin,[7] Butler,[8] Buckhurst,[9] Buckingham,[10]
And some few more whom I omit to name,
Approve my sense; I count their censure fame.

((wr. 1675–6; pub. 1680) John Wilmot, Earl of Rochester (1647–80), from 'An Allusion to Horace')

1. Sir Car Scroope (1649–80), minor poet and court wit; often mocked by his contemporaries for his poor eyesight. 2. the opportunity to ride in a superior's coach. 3. see 239 n.1. 4. see 251. 5. Sir Fleetwood Shepherd (1634–98), another court wit and minor poet. 6. William

Wycherley (1641–1715), dramatist; author of *The Country Wife* (1675). 7. Sidney Godolphin (1645–1712), statesman; nephew of the author of 166 and 174. 8. see 219–220. 9. Charles Sackville, Lord Buckhurst and later Earl of Dorset (1638–1706), court wit and patron of Dryden. 10. George Villiers, Duke of Buckingham (1628–87), courtier; pilloried by Dryden as 'Zimri' in *Absalom and Achitophel*.

John Oldham (1653–83)

253 To the Memory of Mr Oldham[1]

Farewell, too little, and too lately known,
Whom I began to think and call my own;
For sure our souls were near allied, and thine
Cast in the same poetic mould with mine.
One common note on either lyre did strike,
And knaves and fools we both abhorred alike.
To the same goal did both our studies drive;
The last set out, the soonest did arrive.
Thus Nisus fell upon the slippery place,
While his young friend performed and won the race.[2]
O early ripe! to thy abundant store
What could advancing age have added more?
It might (what Nature never gives the young)
Have taught the numbers[3] of thy native tongue.
But satire needs not those, and wit will shine
Through the harsh cadence of a rugged line;[4]
A noble error, and but seldom made,
When poets are by too much force betrayed.
Thy generous fruits, though gathered ere their prime,
Still showed a quickness;[5] and maturing time
But mellows what we write to the dull sweets of rhyme.
Once more, hail and farewell; farewell, thou young,
But ah too short, Marcellus[6] of our tongue;
Thy brows with ivy, and with laurels bound;
But Fate and gloomy Night encompass thee around.

((1684) John Dryden (1631–1700))

1. a talented poet who died at the age of 30; his *Satires upon the Jesuits* preceded Dryden's *Absalom and Achitophel*, and his creative translations from Horace, Juvenal, and Boileau (1678–83) were the first substantial essays after the Restoration in a mode of writing which was to be taken up and enriched by Dryden and Pope; nothing is known of his relations with Dryden. 2. In Bk. V of Virgil's *Aeneid*, two friends, Nisus and Euryalus, run together in a foot race; Nisus, the older man, is on the point of winning the race when he slips and falls; he trips the next runner, thereby enabling his friend Euryalus to win. 3. harmonious versification. 4. Oldham's *Satires upon the Jesuits* (1681) were renowned for their metrical 'roughness', cultivated deliberately as appropriate to the satirist's 'harsh' task. 5. sharpness, pungency. 6. the nephew and adopted son of Augustus, who was expected to succeed him as Emperor, but who died in 23 BC.

Anne Finch, Countess of Winchilsea (1661–1720)

254 *Anne Finch's[1] verse*

Her style in rhyme is often admirable: chaste, tender, and vigorous, and entirely free from sparkle, antithesis, and that overculture which reminds one, by its broad glare, its stiffness and heaviness, of the double daisies of the garden, compared with their modest and sensitive kindred of the fields.

((wr. 1830) William Wordsworth (1770–1850), from a letter to Alexander Dyce, 10 May)

1. friend of Pope, Swift, Gay and Rowe; her *Miscellany Poems* appeared in 1713.

Jonathan Swift (1667–1745)

255 *Swift's satire*[1]

Perhaps I may allow the Dean
Had too much satire in his vein.
And seemed determined not to starve it,
Because no age could more deserve it.
Yet malice never was his aim;
He lashed the vice, but spared the name.
No individual could resent,
Where thousands equally were meant.
His satire points at no defect,
But what all mortals may correct;
For he abhorred that senseless tribe
Who call it humour when they jibe;
He spared a hump or crooked nose,
Whose owners set not up for beaux.
True, genuine dullness[2] moved his pity,
Unless it offered to be witty.
Those who their ignorance confessed,
He ne'er offended with a jest;
But laughed to hear an idiot quote
A verse from Horace, learnt by rote.

((1739) Jonathan Swift (1667–1745), from 'Verses on the Death of Dr Swift')

1. the imagined speaker is one of a club assembled at the Rose Tavern, Drury Lane, whose conversation turns to the character of the late Dean Swift. 2. stupidity, as opposed to wilful obtuseness or vapid pretentiousness.

Thomas Parnell (1679–1718)

256 Parnell's[1] moral Muse

This tomb, inscribed to gentle Parnell's name,
May speak our gratitude, but not his fame.
What heart but feels his sweetly moral lay,
That leads to Truth through Pleasure's flowery way?
Celestial themes confessed his tuneful aid;[2]
And heaven, that lent him genius, was repaid.
Needless to him the tribute we bestow,
The transitory breath of fame below;
More lasting rapture from his works shall rise,
While converts thank their poet in the skies.
((1776) Oliver Goldsmith (?1730–74), 'Epitaph on Thomas Parnell')

1. see 21 n.2; Goldsmith wrote a Life of Parnell for the 1770 edition of the latter's poems.
2. Parnell was a clergyman, and his works contain several poems on religious subjects, including the lengthy work 'The Gift of Poetry', inspired, wrote Parnell, by 'a zeal the Maker's praise to show'.

Edward Young (1683–1765)

257 On Reading Dr Young's Satires, Called *The Universal Passion*, by which he means Pride[1]

If there be truth in what you sing;
Such godlike virtues in the King;
A minister[2] so filled with zeal,
And wisdom for the common weal;
If he who in the chair presides[3]
So steadily the Senate guides;
If others, whom you make your theme,
Are seconds in this glorious scheme;
If every peer whom you commend
To worth and learning be a friend;
If this be truth, as you attest,
What land was ever half so blessed?
No falsehood now among the great,
And tradesmen now no longer cheat;
Now on the bench fair Justice shines;
Her scale to neither side inclines.
Now Pride and Cruelty are flown,
And Mercy here exalts her throne;
For such is good example's power,
It does its office every hour,
Where governors are good and wise;
Or else the truest maxim lies;
For, so we find, all ancient sages
Decree that *ad exemplum regis*,[4]

Through all the realm his virtues run,
Ripening and kindling like the sun.
If this be true, then how much more,
When you have named at least a score
Of courtiers, each in their degree,
If possible, as good as he.
   Or, take it in a different view,
I ask, if what you say be true,
If you affirm the present age
Deserves your satire's keenest rage;
If that same *Universal Passion*
With every vice[5] hath filled the nation;
If virtue[6] dares not venture down,
But just a step below the Crown;
If clergymen, to show their wit,
Prize classics more than holy writ;
If bankrupts, when they are undone,
Into the Senate House can run,
And sell their votes at such a rate,
As will retrieve a lost estate;
If law be such a partial whore
To spare the rich, and plague the poor;
If these be of all crimes the worst,
What land was ever half so cursed?
         ((wr. ?1726; pub. 1733) Jonathan Swift (1667–1745))

1. see 22 n.7; Young was broadly an ally of the Tory opposition circle centring on Pope and Swift, but also maintained polite relations with the ruling Hanoverian/Whig establishment. 2. Swift refers particularly to Young's Seventh Satire, which was dedicated to the politician Sir Robert Walpole (1676–1745), whom Swift and his circle detested as a corrupt manipulator. 3. Spencer Compton, Speaker of the House of Commons, 1715–27, the addressee of Young's Fourth Satire. 4. following the example of the King. 5. (i) wickedness (ii) Whig politics. 6. (i) goodness (ii) Tory opposition.

258 *Young's 'Night Thoughts'*

In his *Night Thoughts*[1] he has exhibited a very wide display of original poetry, variegated with deep reflections and striking allusions, a wilderness of thought, in which the fertility of fancy scatters flowers of every hue and of every odour. This is one of the few poems in which blank verse could not be changed for rhyme but with disadvantage. The wild diffusion of the sentiments, and the digressive sallies[2] of imagination, would have been compressed and restrained by confinement to rhyme. The excellence of this work is not exactness, but copiousness;[3] particular lines are not to be regarded; the power is in the whole, and in the whole there is a magnificence like that ascribed to Chinese plantation, the magnificence of vast extent and endless diversity.
         ((1781) Samuel Johnson (1708–84), from 'Young' in *Lives of the Poets*)

1. see 22 n.7. 2. flights. 3. 'exuberance of style' (Johnson, *Dictionary*).

Alexander Pope (1688–1744)

259 *The milieu of Pope the satirist*

Fortesque:[1] Alas, young man! your days can ne'er be long;
In flower of age you perish for a song!
Plums[2] and directors, Shylock and his wife,[3]
Will club their testers[4] now, to take your life!
Pope: What? armed for Virtue when I point the pen,
Brand the bold front[5] of shameless, guilty men,
Dash the proud gamester in his gilded car,[6]
Bare the mean heart that lurks beneath a star;[7]
Can there be wanting to defend her cause,
Lights of the Church, or guardians of the laws?
Could pensioned Boileau lash in honest strain
Flatterers and bigots even in Louis' reign?[8]
Could Laureate Dryden pimp and friar[9] engage,
Yet neither Charles nor James be in a rage?
And I not strip the gilding off a knave,
Unplaced, unpensioned, no man's heir or slave?[10]
I will, or perish in the generous cause.
Hear this, and tremble! you, who 'scape the laws.
Yes, while I live, no rich or noble knave
Shall walk the world, in credit, to his grave.
To Virtue only and her friends, a friend,
The world beside may murmur, or commend.
Know, all the distant din that world can keep
Rolls o'er my grotto,[11] and but sooths my sleep.
There my retreat the best companions grace,
Chiefs out of war, and statesmen out of place.
There St John[12] mingles with my friendly bowl,
The feast of reason and the flow of soul;
And he whose lightning pierced the Iberian lines,[13]
Now forms my quincunx,[14] and now ranks my vines,
Or tames the genius of the stubborn plain
Almost as quickly as he conquered Spain.
   Envy must own, I live among the great,
No pimp of pleasure, and no spy of state;
With eyes that pry not, tongue that ne'er repeats,
Fond to spread friendships, but to cover heats,[15]
To help who want, to forward who excel;
This, all who know me, know; who love me, tell;
And who unknown defame me, let them be
Scribblers or peers, alike are mob to me.

((1733) Alexander Pope (1688–1744), from 'The First Satire of the Second Book of Horace Imitated')

---

1. William Fortesque (1687–1749), prominent lawyer and (though a member of the Court Party) friend of Pope, is imagined as cross-questioning the poet on his career as a satirist. 2. bribes (a 'plum' is slang for £100,000). 3. Edward (1681–1761) and Lady Mary (1689–1762) Wortley Montague, butts of Pope's satire; Montague was renowned for his meanness. 4. sixpences. 5. forehead. 6. chariot (i.e. coach). 7. part of the insignia of knighthood. 8. Boileau (see 236 n.5) had attacked flatterers and bigots in his *Satires* and in *Le Lutrin*, but

had, in fact, himself flattered Louis XIV in fulsome terms. 9. in the person of Friar Dominic in *The Spanish Friar* (1681); James II had, in fact, banned Dryden's play for its anti-Catholic sentiments. 10. as a Catholic, Pope could not hold a place (an official state post); he twice refused a pension; he owed his independence in large part to the success of his *Homer*, which made him a fortune of *c.* £10,000. 11. an ornamental underground passage built by Pope in the grounds of his house at Twickenham. 12. Henry St John, Viscount Bolingbroke (1678–1751), Tory statesman, philosopher, former friend of Dryden, and intimate of Pope. 13. Charles Mordaunt, Earl of Peterborough (1658–1735); Pope refers to his military triumphs in Spain in 1705. 14. arrangement of five trees; during his retirement, Mordaunt indulged his passion for landscape gardening, an interest which he shared with Pope. 15. conceal fits of anger.

260 *Pope's friends and critics*

Why did I write? What sin to me unknown
Dipped me in ink – my parents' or my own?
As yet a child, nor yet a fool to fame,
I lisped in numbers, for the numbers came.[1]
I left no calling for this idle trade,
No duty broke, no father disobeyed.
The Muse but served to ease some friend, not wife,
To help me through this long disease, my life,[2]
To second, Arbuthnot,[3] thy art and care,
And teach the being you preserved, to bear.

But why then publish? Granville[4] the polite,
And knowing Walsh[5] would tell me I could write;
Well-natured Garth[6] inflamed with early praise,
And Congreve[7] loved, and Swift endured, my lays.
The courtly Talbot,[8] Somers,[9] Sheffield[10] read,
Even mitred Rochester[11] would nod the head,
And St John's[12] self (great Dryden's friends before)
With open arms received one poet more.
Happy my studies, when by these approved!
Happier their author, when by these beloved!
From these the world will judge of men and books,
Not from the Burnets,[13] Oldmixons,[14] and Cooks.[15]

Soft were my numbers; who could take offence
While pure description held the place of sense?[16]
Like gentle Fanny's[17] was my flowery theme:
A painted mistress, or a purling stream.
Yet then did Gildon[18] draw his venal quill;
I wished the man a dinner, and sat still;
Yet then did Dennis[19] rave in furious fret;
I never answered; I was not in debt;
If want provoked, or madness made them print,
I waged no war with Bedlam[20] or the Mint.[21]

Did some more sober critic come abroad?
If wrong, I smiled; if right, I kissed the rod.
Pains, reading, study, are their just pretence,[22]
And all they want[23] is spirit, taste, and sense.
Commas and points[24] they set exactly right,
And 'twere a sin to rob them of their mite.[25]

> Yet ne'er one sprig of laurel graced these ribalds,[26]
> From slashing Bentley[27] down to piddling[28] Tibbalds.[29]
> Each wight[30] who reads not, and but scans[31] and spells,
> Each word-catcher that lives on syllables,
> Even such small critics some regard may claim,
> Preserved in Milton's or in Shakespeare's name.[32]
> Pretty, in amber to observe the forms
> Of hairs, or straws, or dirt, or grubs, or worms!
> The things, we know, are neither rich nor rare,
> But wonder how the devil they got there?
> ((wr. 1731–4; pub. 1735) Alexander Pope (1688–1744), from 'An Epistle to Dr Arbuthnot')

1. Pope's fancy – that his earliest prattle was in the form of verse – imitates that of Ovid (*Tristia*, IV.x.21–6). 2. Pope suffered from a wasting disease (a form of spinal tuberculosis) which curved his spine, stunted his growth, and, in later years, gave him severe pain. 3. John Arbuthnot (1667–1735), addressee of this poem, was physician to Queen Anne, and a close friend of Swift and Pope, with whom he had been associated (during 1714) in the 'Scriblerus Club', a literary group dedicated to ridiculing false taste and pedantry. 4. see 241 n.5. 5. William Walsh (1663–1708), poet, critic, and one of Pope's earliest friends; Dryden had called him 'the best critic of our nation'. 6. Sir Samuel Garth (1661–1719), physician to George I, and author of the mock-heroic poem *The Dispensary* (1699); Garth had been an intimate of Dryden's and had encouraged the young Pope in the writing of his *Pastorals*. 7. William Congreve (1670–1729), dedicatee of Pope's *Iliad*, is now best remembered as the author of the comedy, *The Way of the World* (1700); Dryden had written a warm commendatory poem to Congreve's *The Double Dealer* (1694), and Congreve had supplied a memorable encomium on Dryden in the Dedication to his edition of Dryden's *Dramatic Works* (1717). 8. Charles Talbot, Duke of Shrewsbury (1660–1718), reluctant politician and ambassador, who had corresponded with Dryden about his *Virgil* (to which he had been a subscriber), and who prompted Pope to 'versify' Donne's *Satires*. 9. John, Baron Somers (1651–1716), prominent Whig politician; Somers had contributed to Dryden's *Plutarch* (1684) and had subscribed to his *Aeneid* (1697); he encouraged Pope in the writing of his *Pastorals*. 10. John Sheffield, Earl of Mulgrave, Duke of Buckingham and Normanby (1648–1721); Pope edited his poetical works (1723); Sheffield had been the dedicatee of Dryden's *Aureng-Zebe* (1676). 11. Francis Atterbury (1662–1732), Bishop of Rochester; member of the Scriblerus Club (see n.3); he had translated Dryden's *Absalom and Achitophel* into Latin in 1682. 12. see 259 n.12. 13. Thomas Burnet (1694–1753), a lawyer, had written against Pope's *Homer*, and was later attacked by Pope in Bk. III of *The Dunciad*. 14. John Oldmixon (1673–1742), Whig hack writer who had pirated three of Pope's poems, and attacked Pope in his *Arts of Logic and Rhetoric* (1728). 15. Thomas Cooke (1703–56), minor translator and author of various attacks on Pope. 16. Pope refers to his early descriptive verse in the *Pastorals* (1709) and *Windsor Forest* (1713). 17. Lord Hervey (1696–1743), attacked as 'Sporus' later in the 'Epistle to Arbuthnot'; here pilloried as the archetypal insipid amateur gentleman-poet. 18. Charles Gildon (1665–1724), miscellaneous hack writer who has attacked Pope in 1714 as an 'easy versifier' with too great an opinion of himself. 19. John Dennis (1657–1734), poet, dramatist, and critic, had been offended by a slighting reference in Pope's *Essay on Criticism* and was subsequently involved in a long-standing feud with the poet; in *The Narrative of Dr Robert Norris* (1717), Pope represented Dennis's intemperance as downright lunacy. 20. the hospital of St Mary of Bethlehem, a lunatic asylum. 21. a sanctuary for debtor-poets in Southwark. 22. what they can justly claim. 23. lack. 24. full stops. 25. minute value. 26. brutal wretches. 27. see 197 n.4; for Pope, the erudite classical scholar and Master of Trinity College, Cambridge was the archetype of the acrimonious and literal-minded pedant. 28. nit-picking. 29. the scholar and dramatist, Lewis Theobald (1688–1744) had attacked Pope's edition of Shakespeare in his own *Shakespeare Restored* (1726). 30. person. 31. counts the metrical units of verse. 32. For Bentley's edition of *Paradise Lost*, see 197 n.4; Theobald's edition of Shakespeare had appeared in 1733–4.

261 *The satirist's motives*

Pope: Ask you what provocation I have had?
The strong antipathy of good to bad.
When truth or virtue an affront endures,
The affront is mine, my friend, and should be yours.
Mine, as a foe professed to false pretence,
Who thinks a coxcomb's honour like his sense;
Mine, as a friend to every worthy mind;
And mine as man, who feel for all mankind.
Friend: You're strangely proud.
                      Pope: So proud, I am no slave;
So impudent, I own myself no knave;
So odd, my country's ruin makes me grave.
Yes, I am proud; I must be proud to see
Men not afraid of God, afraid of me;
Safe from the Bar, the Pulpit, and the Throne,
Yet touched and shamed by ridicule alone.
  O sacred weapon, left for truth's defence!
Sole dread of folly, vice, and insolence!
To all but heaven-directed hands denied,
The Muse may give thee, but the gods must guide.
Reverent I touch thee, but with honest zeal
To rouse the watchmen of the public weal;
To virtue's work provoke the tardy Hall,[1]
And goad the prelate slumbering in his stall.
    ((1738) Alexander Pope (1688–1744), from 'Epilogue to the Satires: Dialogue II')

1. Westminster Hall, which formerly housed the High Court of Justice; Pope's ambition is to stir the Law and the Church to support the cause of true Justice.

262 *Pope's independence*

Hail, happy Pope, whose generous mind,
Detesting all the statesman kind,
Contemning courts, at courts unseen,
Refused the visits of a queen![1]
A soul with every virtue fraught[2]
By sages, priests, or poets taught;
Whose filial piety excels
Whatever Grecian story tells;
A genius for all stations fit,
Whose meanest[3] talent is his wit;
His heart too great, though fortune little,
To lick a rascal statesman's spittle;
Appealing to the nation's taste,
Above the reach of want is placed;
By Homer dead was taught to thrive,
Which Homer never could alive;[4]
And sits aloft on Pindus'[5] head,
Despising slaves that cringe for bread.
    ((1730) Jonathan Swift (1667–1745), from 'A Libel on the Reverend Dr Delany')

1. alluding to a (probably erroneous) story that Pope had once left his house to avoid a visit from Queen Caroline, wife of George II. 2. filled. 3. smallest. 4. see 259 n.10. 5. a mountain home of the Muses.

263 'The Rape of the Lock'

How flame the glories of Belinda's hair,
Made by thy Muse the envy of the fair!
Less shone the tresses Egypt's princess wore,
Which sweet Callimachus so sung before.[1]
Here courtly trifles set the world at odds,
Belles war with beaux, and whims descend for gods.
The new machines in names of ridicule
Mock the grave frenzy of the chemic fool;[2]
But know, ye fair, a point concealed with art,
The sylphs and gnomes are but a woman's heart;
The graces stand in sight; a satyr train
Peep o'er their heads, and laugh behind the scene.
((1717) Thomas Parnell (1679–1718),[3] from 'To Mr Pope')

1. the Hellenistic poet Callimachus (c.305–c.240 BC) wrote 'The Lock of Berenice', in which, as in Pope's poem, a lock of the heroine's hair is transformed into a constellation. 2. the sylphs and gnomes, the 'machines' (intervening supernatural personages) of *The Rape of the Lock* partly parody the spirits who appear in the pseudo-scientific ('chemic') teachings of the Rosicrucians, an arcane magical society. 3. see 21 n.2; Parnell was a member of the Scriblerus Club (see 260 n.3) and contributed an introductory essay to Pope's translation of the *Iliad*.

264 Pope's early verse

When Pope's harmonious Muse with pleasure roves
Amidst the plains, the murmuring streams, and groves,[1]
Attentive Echo, pleased to hear his songs,
Through the glad shade each warbling note prolongs;
His various numbers[2] charm our ravished ears,
His steady judgement far out-shoots his years,
And early in the youth the god appears.
((1712) John Gay (1685–1732),[3] from 'On a Miscellany of Poems')

1. as in the *Pastorals* and *Windsor Forest*. 2. varied versification. 3. poet and dramatist, best known for *The Beggar's Opera* (1728); a member of the Scriblerus Club (see 260 n.3).

265 Pope's 'Iliad'

'Tis true what famed Pythagoras[1] maintained,
That souls departed in new bodies reigned;
We most approve the doctrine since we see
The soul of god-like Homer breathe in thee.
Old Ennius first, then Virgil felt her fires,[2]
But now a British poet she inspires.
   To you, O Pope, the lineal right extends,
To you the hereditary Muse descends.
At a vast distance we of Homer heard,

Till you brought in and naturalised the bard;
Bade him our English rights and freedom claim,
His voice, his habit, and his air the same.
Now in the mighty stranger we rejoice,
And Britain thanks thee with a public voice.
  See, too, the poet, a majestic shade,
Lifts up in awful[3] pomp his laureled head,
To thank his súccessor, who sets him free
From the vile hands of Hobbes and Ogilby;
Who vexed his venerable ashes more
Than his ungrateful Greece the living bard before.[4]
  While Homer's thoughts in thy bold lines are shown,
Though worlds contend, we claim him for our own;
Our blooming boys proud Ilion's[5] fate bewail;
Our lisping babes repeat the dreadful tale;
Even in their slumbers they pursue the theme,
Start, and enjoy a sight in every dream.
By turns the chief and bard their souls inflame,
And every little bosom beats for fame.
Thus shall they learn (as future times will see)
From him to conquer, or to write from thee.
  ((1727) Christopher Pitt (1699–1748),[6] from 'To Mr Pope, on his Translation of Homer's *Iliad*')

1. see 223 n.2. 2. the epic poem *Annales* by the Roman poet Quintus Ennius (239–169 BC) had opened with a dream vision in which Homer appeared to Ennius and hailed him as his reincarnation; Virgil's *Aeneid* is copiously indebted to the Homeric epics. 3. awe-inspiring. 4. the philosopher Thomas Hobbes (1588–1679) and the printer, cartographer, and royalist propagandist, John Ogilby (1600–76), had both made inept translations of Homer; ancient traditions maintained that Homer was blind and poor. 5. Troy's. 6. clergyman and poet, author of a translation of Virgil's *Aeneid* which was admired (albeit less than Dryden's version) by Samuel Johnson.

266 *Pope and the dunces*

Above all flattery, all thirst of gain,
And mortal but in sickness and in pain,[1]
Thou taught'st old Satire nobler fruits to bear,
And checked her licence with a moral care;
Thou gav'st the thought new beauties not its own,
And touched the verse with graces yet unknown;
Each lawless branch thy level eye surveyed,
And still corrected Nature as she strayed;
Warmed Boileau's[2] sense with Britain's genuine fire,
And added softness to Tassoni's[3] lyre.
  Yet mark the hideous nonsense of the age,
And thou thyself the subject of its rage.
So, in old times, round godlike Scaeva[4] ran
Rome's dastard sons, a million and a man.
  The exalted merits of the wise and good
Are seen far off and rarely understood.
The world's a father to a dunce unknown,
And much he thrives, for, Dullness,[5] he's thy own.

No hackney brethren e'er condemned him twice;
He fear no enemies but dust and mice.
    If Pope but writes, the devil, Legion, raves,
And meagre critics mutter in their caves;
(Such critics of necessity consume
All wit, as hangmen ravished maids at Rome.)
Names he a scribbler? all the world's in arms;
Augusta, Granta, Rhedecyna[6] swarms;
The guilty reader fancies what he fears,
And every Midas trembles for his ears.[7]
    See all such malice, obloquy,[8] and spite,
Expire ere morn, the mushroom of a night.
Transient as vapours glimmering through the glades,
Half-formed and idle as the dreams of maids.
Vain as the sick man's vow, or young man's sigh,
Third-nights of bards,[9] or Henley's sophistry.[10]
    These ever hate the poet's sacred line;
These hate whate'er is glorious or divine.
From one eternal fountain beauty springs,
The energy of wit and truth of things.
That source is God; from him they downwards tend,
Flow round, yet in their native centre end.
Hence rules, and truth, and order, dunces strike;
Of arts, and virtues, enemies alike.
            ((1730) Walter Harte (1709–74), from 'An Essay on Satire,
                                    Particularly on *The Dunciad*')

1. see 260 n.2. 2. see 236 n.5, 259 n.8. 3. Alessandro Tassoni (1565–1635), Italian poet whose mock-heroic *La Secchia Rapita* ['The Rape of the Bucket'] (1624) provided a partial precedent for Pope's *Rape of the Lock*. 4. Scaeva was a brave soldier in Caesar's army who rallied his leader's troops in battle against Pompey; they revered him as a living embodiment of Virtus ['Valour']. 5. the fictional goddess of Pope's *Dunciad*, enemy of human intelligence and creativity in all its forms, and patroness of the hack, the modish, and the pedantic. 6. Augusta was an ancient name for London; the river Granta (or Cam) flows by the backs of several Cambridge colleges (including Bentley's Trinity – see 260 n.27); Rhedecyna is a Latinism derived from the Welsh name for Oxford (Rhydychen); Pope had attacked both university academicism and London literary hackery in *The Dunciad*. 7. alluding to the story of Midas who was given a pair of ass's ears by Apollo, only his barber being privy to the secret. 8. slander. 9. see 29 n.4. 10. John 'Orator' Henley (1692–1756), an eccentric London preacher, renowned for his pompous and wayward rhetoric.

267 *Pope's genius*

Of his intellectual character, the constituent and fundamental principle was good sense, a prompt and intuitive perception of consonance[1] and propriety. He saw immediately, of his own conceptions, what was to be chosen, and what to be rejected; and, in the works of others, what was to be shunned, and what was to be copied.

But good sense alone is a sedate and quiescent[2] quality, which manages its possessions well, but does not increase them; it collects few materials for its own operations, and preserves safety, but never gains supremacy. Pope had likewise genius; a mind active, ambitious, and adventurous, always investigating, always aspiring; in its widest searches still longing to go forward, in its highest flights still wishing to be higher; always imagining something greater than it knows, always endeavouring more than it can do.

((1781) Samuel Johnson (1709–84), from 'Pope' in *Lives of the Poets*)

1. consistency. 2. static.

268 *Pope's finesse*

Then Pope, as harmony itself exact,
In verse well disciplined, complete, compact,
Gave virtue and morality a grace
That, quite eclipsing Pleasure's painted face,
Levied a tax of wonder and applause
Even on the fools that trampled on their laws.
But he (his musical finesse was such,
So nice[1] his ear, so delicate his touch)
Made poetry a mere mechanic art,
And every warbler has his tune by heart.

((1782) William Cowper (1731–1800), from 'Table Talk')

1. discriminating.

269 *Pope's satires ineffective?*[1]

Our Pope, they say, once entertained the whim
Who feared not God should be afraid of him;[2]
But grant they feared him, was it further said
That he reformed the hearts he made afraid?
Did Chartres[3] mend? Ward,[4] Waters,[5] and a score
Of flagrant felons, with his floggings sore?
Was Cibber[6] silenced? No; with vigour blessed,
And brazen front, half earnest, half in jest,
He dared the bard to battle, and was seen
In all his glory matched with Pope and spleen;
Himself he stripped, the harder blow to hit,
Then boldly matched his ribaldry with wit;[7]
The poet's conquest truth and time proclaim,
But yet the battle hurt his peace and fame.

((1812) George Crabbe (1754–1832), from 'The Patron' in *Tales*)

1. this extract forms part of a letter in which a father warns his son (an aspiring poet) against entertaining too high hopes of his new profession. 2. see 261. 3. Francis Chartres, or Charteris (1675–1732), a notorious debauchee, gambler, and agent of Walpole. 4. John Ward (d. 1755), an MP expelled for forgery. 5. Peter Walter (?1664–1745), MP for Bridport, who amassed a vast personal fortune by sharp financial dealing. 6. Colley Cibber (1671–1757), actor, playwright, and eventually Poet Laureate, the anti-hero of Pope's revised *Dunciad* (1743). 7. the 1743 *Dunciad* was partly provoked by 'A Letter from Mr Cibber to Mr Pope' (1742), in which Cibber had maligned the poet; Cibber replied to Pope's poem in 'Another Occasional Letter' (1744).

270 Pope's poetry the book of life

Neither time, nor distance, nor grief, nor age can ever diminish my veneration for him, who is the great moral poet of all times, of all climes, of all feelings, and of all stages of existence. The delight of my boyhood, the study of my manhood, perhaps (if allowed to me to attain it), he may be the consolation of my age. His poetry is the book of life. Without canting, and yet without neglecting religion, he has assembled all that a good and great man can gather together of moral wisdom clothed in consummate beauty. Sir William Temple[1] observes that of all the numbers of mankind that live within the compass of a thousand years, for one man that is born capable of making a great poet, there may be a thousand born capable of making as great generals and ministers of state as any in story. Here is a statesman's opinion of poetry; it is honourable to him, and to the art. Such a 'poet of a thousand years' was Pope. A thousand years will roll away before such another can be hoped for in our literature. But it can *want* them – he himself is a literature.

((1821) George Gordon, Lord Byron (1788–1824), from 'Observations upon "Observations": a Second Letter to John Murray, Esq., on the Revd W.L. Bowles's Strictures on the Life and Writings of Pope')

1. Sir William Temple (1628–99), diplomat, statesman, and patron of Swift.

271 Pope and his commentators

From mortal gratitude, decide, my Pope,
Have wits immortal more to fear or hope?
Wits toil and travail round the plant of fame,
Their works its garden, and its growth their aim;
Then commentators, in unwieldy dance,
Break down the barriers of the trim pleasance,[1]
Pursue the poet, like Acteon's[2] hounds,
Beyond the fences of his garden grounds,
Rend from the singing robes each borrowed gem,
Rend from the laurelled brows the diadem,
And if one rag of character they spare,
Comes the biographer, and strips it bare!
   Such, Pope, has been thy fortune, such thy doom.
Swift the ghouls gathered at the poet's tomb,
With dust of notes to clog each lordly line,
Warburton, Warton, Croker, Bowles[3] combine!
Collecting cackle, Johnson condescends
To interview the drudges of your friends.[4]
Thus though your Courthope holds your merits high,
And still proclaims your poems poetry,[5]
Biographers, un-Boswell-like, have sneered,[6]
And dunces edit him whom dunces feared!

((1886) Andrew Lang (1844–1912),[7] from 'Epistle to Mr Alexander Pope' in *Letters to Dead Authors*)

1. ornamental garden. 2. the hunter Acteon was changed into a stag by Artemis, then hunted and torn to pieces by his own hounds. 3. the main editors and annotators of Pope's works in

the 18th and early 19th centuries; J.W. Croker's work was incorporated in the standard Victorian edition of Pope by W. Elwin and W.J. Courthope (1871–89). 4. in his 'Life of Pope', Samuel Johnson drew frequently on the testimony of Pope's friends and acquaintances. 5. as Johnson had done in his 'Life' ('If Pope is not a poet, where is poetry to be found?'). 6. Pope's biographers had not treated the poet with the sympathy and affection lavished on Samuel Johnson by James Boswell (1740–95) in his famous *Life of Johnson* (1791). 7. prolific poet, Greek scholar, folklorist, historian, novelist, and critic, particularly renowned for his translation (with S.H. Butcher) of Homer, and for his collections of fairy tales, each one named after a different colour.

John Dyer (1699–1757)

272 To the Poet, John Dyer

Bard of *The Fleece*,[1] whose skilful genius made
That work a living landscape fair and bright,
Nor hallowed less with musical delight
Than those soft scenes through which thy childhood strayed,
Those southern tracts of Cambria,[2] 'deep embayed
With green hills fenced, with ocean's murmur lulled';[3]
Though hasty Fame hath many a chaplet[4] culled
For worthless brows, while in the pensive shade
Of cold neglect she leaves thy head ungraced,
Yet pure and powerful minds, hearts meek and still,
A grateful few, shall love thy modest lay,
Long as the shepherd's bleating flock shall stray
O'er naked Snowdon's wide aërial waste;[5]
Long as the thrush shall pipe on Grongar Hill![6]
((wr. ?1807–11; pub. 1815) William Wordsworth (1770–1850))

1. Dyer's poem *The Fleece* (1757) concerns the wool trade, and mingles practical information with landscape description. 2. Dyer spent his early years as an itinerant artist in South Wales before being ordained. 3. quoted, with slight changes, from *The Fleece*, III.437–8. 4. ceremonial wreath. 5. echoing *The Fleece*, I.92–5. 6. Dyer's *Grongar Hill* (1726) describes the landscapes around the river Towy, near Llangathen, Dyfed.

James Thomson (1700–48)

273 *Thomson's integrity*

Through all thy various *Winter*,[1] full are found
Magnificence of thought, and pomp of sound,
Clear depth of sense, expression's heightening grace,
And goodness, eminent in power, and place!
For this, the wise, the knowing few, commend
With zealous joy, for thou art Virtue's friend;
Even Age, and Truth severe, in reading thee,
That heaven inspires the Muse, convinced agree. ...
Thou, careless of the statesman's smile or frown,
Tread that straight way that leads to fair renown.
By Virtue guided, and by Glory fired,

And, by reluctant Envy slow admired,
Dare to do well, and in thy boundless mind
Embrace the general welfare of thy kind;
Enrich them with the treasures of thy thought,
What heaven approves, and what the Muse has taught.
Where thy power fails, unable to go on,
Ambitious, greatly *will* the good undone.
So shall thy name, through ages, brightening shine,
And distant praise, from worth unborn, be thine;
So shalt thou, happy, merit heaven's regard,
And find a glorious, though a late, reward!

((1726) David Mallet (?1705–65),[2] from 'To Mr Thomson, on his Publishing the Second Edition of his Poem called *Winter*')

1. the first to be composed of Thomson's *The Seasons* (on which, see 198 n.1). 2. see 132 n.3.

274 Thomson and nature

(i)

His descriptions of extended scenes and general effects bring before us the whole magnificence of nature, whether pleasing or dreadful. The gaiety of spring, the splendour of summer, the tranquillity of autumn, and the horror of winter, take in their turns possession of the mind. The poet leads us through the appearances of things as they are successively varied by the vicissitudes[1] of the year, and imparts to us so much of his own enthusiasm, that our thoughts expand with his imagery, and kindle with his sentiments. Nor is the naturalist without his part in the entertainment; for he is assisted to recollect and to combine, to arrange his discoveries, and to amplify the sphere of his contemplation.

(ii)

He thinks in a peculiar train, and he thinks always as a man of genius; he looks round on nature and on life with the eye which Nature bestows only on a poet; the eye that distinguishes, in everything presented to its view, whatever there is on which imagination can delight to be detained, and with a mind that at once comprehends the vast and attends to the minute. The reader of *The Seasons* wonders that he never saw before what Thomson shows him, and that he never yet has felt what Thomson impresses.

((1781) Samuel Johnson (1709–84), from 'Thomson' in *Lives of the Poets*)

1. changes.

275 Ode Occasioned by the Death of Mr Thomson

In yonder grave a druid[1] lies,
 Where slowly winds the stealing wave![2]
The year's best sweets shall duteous[3] rise
 To deck its poet's sylvan grave!

In yon deep bed of whispering reeds
   His airy harp[4] shall now be laid,
That he, whose heart in sorrow bleeds,
   May love through life the soothing shade.

Then maids and youths shall linger here,
   And while its[5] sounds at distance swell,
Shall sadly seem in Pity's ear
   To hear the woodland pilgrim's knell.

Remembrance oft shall haunt the shore
   When Thames in summer wreaths is dressed,
And oft suspend the dashing oar
   To bid his gentle spirit rest!

And oft as Ease and Health retire
   To breezy lawn, or forest deep,
The friend shall view yon whitening spire,
   And 'mid the varied landscape weep.

But thou, who own'st that earthy bed,
   Ah! what will every dirge avail?
Or tears, which Love and Pity shed,
   That mourn beneath the gliding sail?

Yet lives there one, whose heedless eye
   Shall scorn thy pale shrine glimmering near?
With him, sweet bard, may Fancy die
   And Joy desert the blooming year.

But thou, lorn[6] stream, whose sullen tide
   No sedge-crowned sisters[7] now attend,
Now waft me from the green hill's side,
   Whose cold turf hides the buried friend!

And see, the fairy vallies fade,
   Dun[8] night has veiled the solemn view!
Yet once again, dear parted shade,
   Meek Nature's child, again adieu!

The genial[9] meads assigned to bless
   Thy life, shall mourn thy early doom;
Their hinds[10] and shepherd-girls shall dress
   With simple hands thy rural tomb.

Long, long, thy stone, and pointed[11] clay
   Shall melt the musing Briton's eyes.
'O vales, and wild woods,' shall he say,
   'In yonder grave your druid lies!'

                        ((1749) William Collins (1721–59)[12])

1. alluding (i) to Thomson's powers as a nature poet and (ii) to his assertion and defence of ancient British liberty, in *The Seasons*. 2. Thomson died at Richmond, and was buried in its

parish church, near the Thames. 3. because Thomson had celebrated them in *The Seasons*. 4. the Aeolian harp (which resonates when placed in a current of air), referred to by Thomson in *The Castle of Indolence* (1748). 5. the harp's. 6. deserted. 7. the Naiads or river-nymphs, who, since Thomson's death, no longer inhabit the Thames. 8. dark. 9. life-propagating. 10. rustics. 11. pointed out to passers-by; the reference may, alternatively, be to the shape of Thomson's imagined monument. 12. see 144 n.8.

Poets of the mid-18th century

276 *The Muses' desertion*

Whether on Ida's[1] shady brow,
  Or in the chambers of the East,
The chambers of the sun, that now
  From ancient melody have ceased;

Whether in heaven ye wander fair,
  Or the green corners of the earth,
Or the blue regions of the air,
  Where the melodious winds have birth;

Whether on crystal rocks ye rove,
  Beneath the bosom of the sea,
Wandering in many a coral grove,
  Fair Nine,[2] forsaking poetry!

How have you left the ancient love
  That bards of old enjoyed in you!
The languid strings do scarcely move!
  The sound is forced, the notes are few![3]
((wr. ?1769–77; pub. 1783) William Blake (1757–1827), 'To the Muses')

1. a mountain in Phrygia, renowned in Greek myth. 2. the Muses. 3. this poem records Blake's disappointment with the poetry of the generations immediately preceding his own, but, like the whole volume from which it comes (*Poetical Sketches*), shows the unmistakable influence of mid-18th-century poetic idiom and diction.

Samuel Johnson (1709–84)

277 Epitaph on Dr Johnson

Here Johnson lies, a sage, by all allowed,
Whom to have bred may well make England proud;
Whose prose was eloquence by wisdom taught,
The graceful vehicle of virtuous thought;
Whose verse may claim – grave, masculine, and strong –
Superior praise to the mere poet's song;

Who many a noble gift from heaven possessed,
And faith at last, alone worth all the rest.
Oh man immortal by a double prize:
By fame on earth, by glory in the skies!
((1785) William Cowper (1731–1800))

William Shenstone (1714–63)

278 *Shenstone, poet of peace*

Nor, Shenstone,[1] thou
Shalt pass without thy meed,[2] thou son of peace!
Who knew'st, perchance, to harmonise thy shades
Still softer than thy song; yet was that song
Nor rude, nor inharmonious, when attuned
To pastoral plaint, or tale of slighted love.
((1771) William Mason (1725–97),[3] from *The English Garden*, Bk. I)

1. essayist and landscape-gardener, as well as poet; Shenstone specialised in rural subjects.
2. reward, due recognition. 3. see 205 n.9.

Thomas Gray (1716–71)

279 *Gray's poetic aspirations*

Oh lyre divine, what daring spirit
Wakes thee now? Though he inherit
Nor the pride nor ample pinion
That the Theban eagle[1] bear,
Sailing with supreme dominion
Through the azure deep of air;
Yet oft before his infant eyes would run
Such forms as glitter in the Muse's ray
With orient[2] hues, unborrowed of the sun;
Yet shall he mount, and keep his distant way
Beyond the limits of a vulgar fate,
Beneath the good how far – but far above the great.
((wr. 1751–4; pub. 1757) Thomas Gray (1716–71), from 'The Progess of Poesy: a Pindaric Ode')

1. Pindar (see 94 n.3). 2. bright.

280 *Gray's 'Odes' and 'Elegy Written in a Country Churchyard'*

These odes are marked by glittering accumulations of ungraceful ornaments; they strike, rather than please; the images are magnified by affectation; the language is laboured into harshness. The mind of the writer seems to work with unnatural violence: 'Double, double, toil and trouble.'[1] He has a kind of strutting dignity, and is tall by walking on tiptoe. His art and his struggle are too visible, and there is too little appearance of ease and Nature. ...

In the character of his 'Elegy' I rejoice to concur with the common reader; for by the common sense of readers uncorrupted with literary prejudices, after all the refinements of subtlety and the dogmatism of learning, must be finally decided all claim to poetical honours. The 'Churchyard' abounds with images which find a mirror in every mind, and with sentiments to which every bosom returns an echo. The four stanzas beginning 'Yet even these bones ...' are to me original; I have never seen the notions in any other place; yet he that reads them here persuades himself that he has always felt them. Had Gray written often thus, it had been vain to blame, and useless to praise him.

((1781) Samuel Johnson (1709–84), from 'Gray' in *Lives of the Poets*)

1. *Macbeth*, IV.i.10–11.

281 *Gray and nature*

Closed is that curious[1] ear by Death's cold hand
That marked each error of my careless strain
With kind severity;[2] to whom my Muse
Still loved to whisper what she meant to sing
In louder accent; to whose taste supreme
She first and last appealed, nor wished for praise,
Save when his smile was herald to her fame.
Yes, thou art gone; yet Friendship's faltering tongue
Invokes thee still; and still by Fancy soothed,
Fain would she hope her Gray attends the call.
Why then, alas, in this my favourite haunt
Place I the urn, the bust, the sculptured lyre,
Or fix this votive tablet, fair inscribed
With numbers worthy thee, for they are thine?
Why, if thou hear'st me still, these symbols sad
Of fond memorial? Ah, my pensive soul!
He hears me not, nor ever more shall hear
The theme his candour, not his taste, approved.
   Oft, smiling as in scorn, oft would he cry,
'Why waste thy numbers on a trivial art
That ill can mimic even the humblest charms
Of all-majestic Nature?' At the word
His eye would glisten, and his accents glow
With all the poet's frenzy: 'Sovereign queen,
Behold and tremble, while thou view'st her state
Throned on the heights of Skiddaw![3] Call thy art
To build her such a throne; that art will feel
How vain her best pretensions. Trace her march
Amid the purple crags of Borrowdale.[4]
And try like those to pile thy range of rock
In rude tumultuous chaos. See, she mounts
Her Naiad car,[5] and down Lodore's dread cliff
Falls many a fathom, like the headlong Bard
My fabling fancy plunged in Conway's flood,[6]
Yet not like him to sink in endless night;

For, on its boiling bosom, still she guides
Her buoyant shell, and leads the wave along;
Or spreads it broad, a river or a lake,
As suits her pleasure; will thy boldest song
E'er brace the sinews of enérvate art
To such dread daring? Will it even direct
Her hand to emulate those softer charms
That deck the banks of Dove,[7] or call to birth
The bare romantic crags and copses green
That sidelong grace her circuit, whence the rills,
Bright in their crystal purity, descend
To meet their sparkling queen? Around each fount
The hawthorns crowd, and knit their blossomed sprays
To keep their sources sacred. Here, even here,
Thy art, each active sinew stretched in vain,
Would perish in its pride. Far rather thou
Confess her scanty power, correct, control,
Tell her how far, nor farther, she may go;
And rein with Reason's curb fantastic Taste.'

((wr. 1771; pub. 1779) William Mason (1725–97),[8] from *The English Garden*, Bk. III)

1. inquisitive, searching. 2. Gray and Mason were friends at Cambridge, and Gray had helped his young admirer in his earlier attempts at verse; in his *Memoirs* of Gray (1775), Mason published Gray's journal of a tour of the Lake District in 1769. 3. a mountain in the Lake District, north of Keswick. 4. the valley of the Derwent in Cumbria. 5. chariot drawn by river nymphs. 6. Gray's ode, 'The Bard' (1757) ends with the hero's suicide by leaping into the 'roaring tide' of Conway from a high cliff; the Lodore Falls are in the Lake District. 7. a river in Cumbria. 8. see 205 n.9.

282 Gray's soothing verse

Not that her blooms are marked with beauty's hue,
My rustic Muse her votive chaplet[1] brings;
Unseen, unheard, O Gray, to thee she sings!
While slowly pacing through the churchyard dew,
At curfew time, beneath the dark green yew,
Thy pensive genius strikes the moral strings;[2]
Or borne sublime on Inspiration's wings,
Hears Cambria's bards devote[3] the dreadful clew[4]
Of Edward's race, with murders foul defiled;[5]
Can aught my pipe to reach thine ear essay?[6]
No, bard divine! For many a care beguiled
By the sweet magic of thy soothing lay,
For many a raptured thought, and vision wild,
To thee this strain of gratitude I pay.

((1777) Thomas Warton (1728–90),[7] 'Sonnet 6: To Mr Gray')

1. wreath presented as an offering. 2. alluding to Gray's 'Elegy Written in a Country Churchyard'. 3. denounce. 4. maze. 5. the hero of Gray's 'The Bard' (1757) denounces Edward I and the Plantagenet kings for having suppressed and slaughtered the bards of Wales. 6. attempt. 7. see 105 n.7.

Mark Akenside (1721–1770)

283 *Akenside's[1] imagery*

His images are displayed with such luxuriance of expression that they are hidden, like Butler's moon, by a 'veil of light';[2] they are forms fantastically lost under superfluity of dress. ... The words are multiplied till the sense is hardly perceived; attention deserts the mind, and settles in the ear. The reader wanders through the gay diffusion, sometimes amazed, and sometimes delighted; but, after many turnings in the flowery labyrinth, comes out as he went in. He remarked[3] little, and laid hold on nothing.

((1781) Samuel Johnson (1709–84), from 'Akenside' in *Lives of the Poets*)

1. see 36 n.3.   2. see Samuel Butler, *Hudibras*, Pt. 2, Canto 1, 905–8.   3. noted.

William Collins (1721–59)

284 Remembrance of Collins,[1] Composed upon the Thames near Richmond

Glide gently, thus for ever glide,
O Thames, that other bards may see
As lovely visions by thy side
As now, fair river, come to me.
O glide, fair stream, for ever so,
Thy quiet soul on all bestowing,
Till all our minds for ever flow
As thy deep waters now are flowing.

Vain thought! Yet be as now thou art,
That in thy waters may be seen
The image of a poet's heart,
How bright, how solemn, how serene!
Such as did once the poet bless,
Who, murmuring here a later ditty,
Could find no refuge from distress
But in the milder grief of pity.[2]

Now let us, as we float along,
For *him* suspend the dashing oar;
And pray that never child of song
May know that poet's sorrows more.
How calm! how still! the only sound,
The dripping of the oar suspended!
The evening darkness gathers round
By virtue's holiest powers attended.

((1798) William Wordsworth (1770–1850))

1. see 144 n.8.   2. alluding to Collins's Ode on Thomson (see 275).

Christopher Smart (1722–71)

285 *Smart's 'Song to David'*

Smart,[1] solely of such songmen,[2] pierced the screen
'Twixt thing and word, lit language straight from soul,–
Left no fine film-flake on the naked coal
Live from the censer shapely or uncouth,
Fire-suffused through and through, one blaze of truth
Undeadened by a lie, ...
No matter if the marvel came to pass
The way folk judged – if power too long suppressed
Broke loose and maddened, as the vulgar guessed,
Or simply brain-disorder (doctors said)
A turmoil of the particles disturbed
Brain's workaday performance in your head,
Spurred spirit to wild action health had curbed;
And so verse issued in a cataract
Whence prose, before and after, unperturbed
Was wont to wend its way. Concede the fact
That here a poet was who always could –
Never before did – never after would –
Achieve the feat; how were such fact explained?

Was it that when, by rarest chance, there fell
Disguise from Nature, so that Truth remained
Naked, and whoso saw for once could tell
Us others of her majesty and might
In large, her lovelinesses infinite
In little, – straight you used the power wherewith
Sense, penetrating as through rind to pith
Each object, thoroughly revealed might view
And comprehend the old things thus made new,
So that while eye saw, soul to tongue could trust
Thing which struck word out, and once more adjust
Real vision to right language, till heaven's vault
Pompous[3] with sunset, storm-stirred sea's assault
On the swilled rock-ridge, earth's embosomed brood
Of tree and flower and weed, with all the life
That flies or swims or crawls, in peace or strife,
Above, below, – each had its note and name
For Man to know by, – Man who, now – the same
As erst[4] in Eden, needs that all he sees
Be named him ere he note by what degrees
Of strength and beauty to its end design
Ever thus operates – (your thought and mine,
No matter for the many dissident) –
So did you sing your Song, so truth found vent
In words for once with you?

((1887) Robert Browning (1812–89), from 'With Christopher Smart' in *Parleyings with Certain People of Importance in their Day*)

1. Smart was troubled by fits of madness throughout life, and published *A Song to David* in

1763, after a spell of confinement in an asylum; one contemporary report alleges that Smart inscribed the poem with a key on the wainscot of his cell, having been denied pen and paper; Browning contrasts the ecstatic inspiration of the *Song* with the (to him) routine competence of Smart's other poetry; Smart's *Song* has been admired by several other English poets, including Edmund Blunden (see 357 n.6). 2. the lyric poets between Milton and Keats. 3. full of pomp. 4. formerly.

Thomas Warton (1728–90)

86 *Warton's[1] novelty*

Wheresoe'er I turn my view,
All is strange, yet nothing new;
Endless labour all along,
Endless labour to be wrong;
Phrase that Time has flung away,
Uncouth words in disarray;
Tricked in antique ruff and bonnet,
Ode, and Elegy, and Sonnet.

((1777) Samuel Johnson (1709–84), 'Lines on Thomas Warton's Poems')

1. see 105 n.7; Johnson pillories what he sees as Warton's pedantic antiquarianism, and his artificial attempts to revive earlier verse forms.

William Cowper (1731–1800)

287 *Cowper's mild warmth*

Tenderest of tender hearts, of spirits pure
The purest! Such, O Cowper, such wert thou,
But such are not the happiest; thou wert not,
Till borne where all those hearts and spirits rest.[1]
Young was I, when from Latin lore and Greek
I played the truant for thy sweeter *Task*,[2]
Nor since that hour hath aught our Muses held
Before me seemed so precious; in one hour,
I saw the poet and the sage unite,
More grave than man, more versatile than boy!
Spenser shed over me his sunny dreams;
Chaucer far more enchanted me; the force
Of Milton was for boyhood too austere,
Yet often did I steal a glance at Eve;
Fitter for after-years was Shakespeare's world,
Its distant light had not come down to mine.
Thy milder beams with wholesome temperate warmth
Filled the small chamber of my quiet breast.
I would become as like thee as I could;
First rose the wish and then the half-belief,
Founded like other half- and whole-beliefs
On sand and chaff! 'We must be like,' said I,

'I loved my hare before I heard of his.³'
'Twas very true; I loved him, though he stamped
Sometimes in anger, often moodily.
I am the better for it. Still I love
God's unperverted creatures, one and all –
I dare not call them brute, lest they retort.
And here is one who looks into my face,
Waving his curly plumes upon his back,
And bids me promise faithfully, no hare
Of thine need fear him when they meet above.
((1853) Walter Savage Landor (1775–1864),⁴ 'Cowper')

1. Cowper suffered from acute religious melancholia and an overwhelming sense of his own sin; his feelings are recorded in a prose *Memoir* (wr. *c.*1767; pub. 1816). 2. Cowper's six-book blank-verse poem, *The Task* (1785) encompasses autobiography, natural description, and moral reflection. 3. a famous passage in Bk. III of *The Task* evokes Cowper's feelings for his pet hare. 4. see 152 n.3.

288 *Cowper and the countryside*

Cowper, the poet of the fields,
    Who found the Muse on common ground;
The homesteads that each cottage shields
    He loved, and made them classic ground.

The lonely house, the rural walk,
    He sang so musically true,
E'en now they share the people's talk
    Who love the poet Cowper too.

Who has not read the 'Winter Storm'¹
    And does not feel the fallen snow,
And woodmen keeping noses warm
    With pipes, wherever forests grow?...

The 'Winter's Walk' and 'Summer's Noon' -
    We meet together by the fire,
And think the walks are o'er too soon,
    When books are read, and we retire.

Who travels o'er those sweet fields now,
    And brings not Cowper to his mind?
Birds sing his name in every bough,
    Nature repeats it in the wind.

And every place the poet trod
    And every place the poet sung,
Are like the Holy Land of God
    In every mouth, on every tongue.
((wr. before 1856; pub. 1935) John Clare (1793–1864), 'Cowper')

1. Bk. IV of *The Task* contains a depiction of a fall of snow at evening.

289 Cowper's soul

Sweet are thy strains, celestial bard;
   And oft, in childhood's years,
I've read them o'er and o'er again,
   With floods of silent tears.

The language of my inmost heart
   I traced in every line;
My sins, *my* sorrows, hopes, and fears,
   Were there – and only mine.

All for myself the sigh would swell,
   The tear of anguish start;
I little knew what wilder woe
   Had filled the poet's heart.

I did not know the nights of gloom,
   The days of misery;
The long, long years of dark despair,
   That crushed and tortured thee.[1]

But they are gone; from earth at length
   Thy gentle soul is passed,
And in the bosom of its God
   Has found its home at last.

It must be so, if God is love,
   And answers fervent prayer;
Then surely thou shalt dwell on high,
   And I may meet thee there.

Is He the source of every good,
   The spring of purity?
Then in thine hours of deepest woe,
   Thy God was still with thee.

How else, when every hope was fled,
   Couldst thou so fondly cling
To holy things and holy men?[2]
   And how so sweetly sing

Of things that God alone could teach?
   And whence that purity,
That hatred of all sinful ways,
   That gentle charity?

Are *these* the symptoms of a heart
   Of heavenly grace bereft,
For ever banished from its God,
   To Satan's fury left?

> Yet, should thy darkest fears be true,
> If heaven be so severe,
> That such a soul as thine is lost –
> Oh, how shall *I* appear?
> ((wr. 1842; pub. 1846) Anne Brontë (1820–49),³ 'To Cowper')

1. see 287 n.1. 2. Cowper was greatly influenced and helped by the Evangelical minister and former slave trader, John Newton, with whom he wrote his *Olney Hymns* (1779). 3. sister of Charlotte and Emily Brontë, and author of the novels *Agnes Grey* (1847) and *The Tenant of Wildfell Hall* (1848); Cowper was admired by a number of women writers of the generations following his own, including Jane Austen, and Elizabeth Barrett Browning, whose poem 'Cowper's Grave', like Anne Brontë's 'To Cowper', makes reference to Cowper's melancholy and religious anguish.

Charles Churchill (1732–64)

290 *Churchill's negligence*

> Contemporaries all surpassed, see one,
> Short his career, indeed, but ably run:
> Churchill,¹ himself unconscious of his powers,
> In penury consumed his idle hours,
> And, like a scattered seed at random sown,
> Was left to spring by vigour of his own.
> Lifted at length, by dignity of thought
> And dint of genius, to an affluent lot,
> He laid his head in Luxury's soft lap,
> And took, too often, there his easy nap.
> If brighter beams than all he threw not forth,
> 'Twas negligence in him, not want of worth.
> Surly and slovenly, and bold and coarse,
> Too proud for art, and trusting in mere force,
> Spendthrift alike of money and of wit,
> Always at speed, and never drawing bit,
> He struck the lyre in such a careless mood,
> And so disdained the rules he understood,
> The laurel seemed to wait on his command;
> He snatched it rudely from the Muses' hand.
> ((1782) William Cowper (1731–1800), from 'Table Talk')

1. Charles Churchill was a school friend of Cowper's; after an early manhood in poverty, he scored a success with his satirical poems on actors, *The Rosciad* and *The Apology* (both 1761); his later verse is mainly in the form of vehemently abusive personal and political satire; Churchill was a close friend and associate of the politician and journalist, John Wilkes (1727–96).

Thomas Chatterton (1752–70)

291 *Chatterton's promise, and tragic end*

 Elate of heart and confident of fame,
From vales where Avon sports, the minstrel came,[1]
  Gay as the poet hastes along
  He meditates the future song,
How Ælla battled with his country's foes,[2]
  And, whilst fancy in the air
  Paints him many a vision fair,
His eyes dance rapture and his bosom glows.
With generous joy he views the ideal gold;
  He listens to many a widow's prayers,
  And many an orphan's thanks he hears;
   He soothes to peace the care-worn breast,
   He bids the debtor's eyes know rest,
   And liberty and bliss behold;
And now he punishes the heart of steel,
And her own rod he makes Oppression feel.[3]

Fated to heave sad disappointment's sigh,
To feel the hope now raised, and now depressed,
To feel the burnings of an injured breast,
  From all thy fate's deep sorrow keen
  In vain, O youth, I turn the affrighted eye;
  For powerful fancy ever nigh
The hateful picture forces on my sight.
  There, death of every dear delight,
  Frowns Poverty of giant mien!
In vain I seek the charms of youthful grace,
Thy sunken eye, thy haggard cheeks it shows,
The quick emotions struggling in the face
  Faint index of thy mental throes,
When each strong passion spurned control,
And not a friend was nigh to calm thy stormy soul.
   ((wr. 1790; pub. 1893) Samuel Taylor Coleridge (1772–1834),
       from 'Monody on the Death of Chatterton')

1. Chatterton was born in Bristol (near the river Avon); he was the author of pseudo-medieval poems (attributed to an apocryphal 15th century Bristol poet, Thomas Rowley), which were published posthumously in 1777; Chatterton went to London in 1770 to seek his literary fortune, but was soon reduced to poverty and despair, and committed suicide, by taking arsenic, at the age of 17; for the ensuing generations, Chatterton's life became a symbol of the suffering and neglected genius, at odds with his society; in his 'Resolution and Independence' (wr. 1802; pub. 1807), Wordsworth referred to Chatterton as 'the marvellous boy,/The sleepless soul that perished in his pride'; a famous picture of 'The Death of Chatterton' (1856) by Henry Wallis hangs in the Tate Gallery. 2. Ælla was the most famous of Chatterton's fictional creations, a Saxon hero at the time of the Danish invasions of Britain. 3. Chatterton's last works were topical poems, championing the cause of 'Wilkes and Liberty'.

292 To Chatterton

O Chatterton, how very sad thy fate![1]
   Dear child of sorrow, son of misery!
   How soon the film of death obscured that eye,
Whence genius wildly flashed, and high debate.
How soon that voice, majestic and elate,
   Melted in dying murmurs! Oh, how nigh
   Was night to thy fair morning! Thou didst die
A half-blown floweret which cold blasts amate.[2]
But this is past; thou art among the stars
   Of highest heaven; to the rolling spheres
Thou sweetly singest; naught thy hymning mars,
   Above the ingrate[3] world and human fears,
On earth the good man base detraction bars
   From thy fair name, and waters it with tears.

((wr. 1815; pub. 1848) John Keats (1795–1821))

1. see 291 n.1. 2. destroy (Keats here imitates Chatterton's antique diction). 3. unfriendly, ungrateful.

George Crabbe (1754–1832)

293 *Crabbe's dissatisfaction with pastoral*[1]

Fled are those times, when, in harmonious strains,
The rustic poet praised his native plains;
No shepherds now, in smooth, alternate[2] verse,
Their country's beauty, or their nymphs', rehearse;
Yet still for these we frame the tender strain,
Still in our lays fond Corydons[3] complain,
And shepherds' boys their amorous pains reveal,
The only pains, alas, they never feel!
   On Mincio's[4] banks, in Caesar's bounteous reign,
If Tityrus[5] found the Golden Age again,
Must sleepy bards the flattering dream prolong,
Mechanic echoes of the Mantuan[6] song?
From truth and nature shall we widely stray,
Where Virgil, not where Fancy,[7] leads the way?
   Yes, thus the Muses sing of happy swains,
Because the Muses never knew their pains;
They boast their peasants' pipes; but peasants now
Resign their pipes and plod behind the plough;
And few, amid the rural tribe, have time
To number syllables, and play with rhyme;
Save honest Duck,[8] what son of verse could share
The poet's rapture and the peasant's care?
Or the great labours of the field degrade,
With the new peril of a poorer trade?

((1783) George Crabbe (1754–1832), from *The Village*, Bk. I)

1. Crabbe's poems in *The Village* (1783), *The Parish Register* (1807), *The Borough* (1810), *Tales* (1812), and *Tales of the Hall* (1819), depict the grim realities of late 18th- and early 19th-century

village life, rather than adopting the idealising conventions of Golden Age pastoral. 2. pastoral poetry often contains dialogues in which two interlocutors discourse in one-line exchanges. 3. the shepherd in Virgil's second Eclogue (and hence a stock name for pastoral shepherds). 4. a river referred to in Virgil's Seventh Eclogue. 5. a shepherd in the *Eclogues*. 6. Mantua was Virgil's birthplace. 7. Imagination. 8. Stephen Duck (1705-56), poet and farm labourer, whose poem *The Thresher's Labour* (1730) depicts the realities of rural toil, albeit often in the language of conventional pastoral.

294 *Crabbe's realism*

> The year revolves, and I again explore
> The simple annals of my parish poor;
> What infant members in my flock[1] appear,
> What pairs I blessed in the departed year;
> And who, of old or young, or nymphs or swains,
> Are lost to life, its pleasures and its pains.
>   No Muse I ask, before my view to bring
> The humble actions of the swains I sing:
> How passed the youthful, how the old their days;
> Who sank in sloth, and who aspired to praise;
> Their tempers, manners, morals, customs, arts,
> What parts[2] they had, and how they employed their parts;
> By what elated, soothed, seduced, depressed,
> Full well I know; these records give the rest.
>   ((1807) George Crabbe (1754–1832), from *The Parish Register*, Pt. I)

1. from 1789 to 1814 Crabbe held the living of Muston, Leicestershire; he was absent, living in Suffolk, from 1792 to 1805. 2. faculties, accomplishments.

295 *Crabbe and nature*

> There be who say, in these enlightened days,
> That splendid lies are all the poet's praise;
> That strained Invention, ever on the wing,
> Alone impels the modern bard to sing;
> 'Tis true that all who rhyme, nay, all who write,
> Shrink from that fatal word to genius: trite;
> Yet Truth sometimes will lend her noblest fires,
> And decorate the verse herself inspires;
> This fact in Virtue's name let Crabbe attest;
> Though Nature's sternest painter, yet the best.
>   ((1809) George Gordon, Lord Byron (1788–1824), from *English Bards and Scotch Reviewers*)

296 *Crabbe and the human heart*

> We still have bards who, with aspiring head,
> Rise o'er the crazed, the dying, and the dead.
> For instance, there's old Crabbe – though some may deem
> He shows small taste in choosing of a theme;
> None but a bard his own true lines can tell;
> He chooses right who executes it well.

>And Crabbe has done it well; although his verse
>Be somewhat rude, 'tis pregnant, strong, and terse;
>And he has feeling; I who never weep,
>And o'er a Werther's[1] woes am apt to sleep,
>Even I, though somewhat rude, can feel for woe
>Such as I've known, or such as I may know;
>Even I can feel at tales of love or strife,
>Stamped, as are his, with traits of real life,
>He knows the human heart (which, by the way,
>Is more than some psychologists can say).
>He knows it well; and draws with faithful pen
>Nor Corsairs,[2] Pedlars, Waggoners,[3] but men.
>And then his background – how the figures glow
>With all the mimic art of Gerald Dow,[4]
>Each in itself a picture – while the soul
>Of one great moral breathes throughout the whole.
>>((1820) Charles Hughes Terrot (1790–1872),[5] from 'Common Sense: a Poem')

1. the sensitive, melancholy eponymous hero of Goethe's novel (1774), which enjoyed a great vogue in the late 18th century throughout Europe. 2. referring to Byron's early romantic tale, *The Corsair* (1814), the hero of which is a dashing and mysterious pirate chief. 3. referring to the rustic heroes of Wordsworth's *The Excursion* (1814) and *The Waggoner* (1819). 4. Gerrit Dou (1613–75), Dutch painter, renowned for his precision and accuracy in depicting scenes of everyday life. 5. Bishop of Edinburgh, 1841–62; Terrot's poems were written in his early years, his later life being devoted to theology and mathematics.

297 Crabbe and Wordsworth

>Give Crabbe, dear Helen,[1] on your shelf,
>A place by Wordsworth's mightier self;
>In token that your taste, self-wrought
>From mines of independent thought,
>And shaped by no exclusive rule
>Of whim or fashion, sect or school,
>Can honour genius, whatsoe'er
>The garb it chance or choose to wear.
>
>Nor deem, dear Helen, unallied
>The bards we station side by side;
>Different their harps – to each his own;
>But both are true and pure of tone.
>Brethren, methinks, in times like ours
>Of misused gifts, perverted powers;
>Brethren are they, whose kindred song
>Nor hides the right, nor gilds the wrong.
>>((wr. 1837; pub. 1864) Winthrop Mackworth Praed (1802–39),[2] 'To Helen, with Crabbe's Poems: a Birthday Present')

1. Praed's wife. 2. barrister, Member of Parliament, and occasional poet; author of *vers de société*, light satire, and magazine verse, collected after his death in *Poems* (1864).

William Blake (1757-1827)

298 *Blake, imagination, and vision*[1]

Fun I love, but too much fun is of all things the most loathsome. Mirth is better than fun, and happiness is better than mirth. I feel that a man may be happy in this world. And I know that this world is a word of imagination and vision. I see everything I paint in this world, but everybody does not see alike. To the eyes of a miser, a guinea is far more beautiful than the sun, and a bag worn with the use of money has more beautiful proportions than a vine filled with grapes. The tree which moves some to tears of joy is in the eyes of others only a green thing which stands in the way. Some see nature all ridicule and deformity, and by these I shall not regulate my proportions; and some scarce see nature at all. But to the eyes of the man of imagination, nature is imagination itself. As a man is, so he sees. As the eye is formed, such are its powers. You certainly mistake when you say that the visions of fancy are not to be found in this world. To me, this world is all one continued vision of fancy or imagination, and I feel flattered when I am told so. ... I am happy to find a great majority of fellow mortals who can elucidate my visions; and particularly they have been elucidated by children, who have taken a greater delight in contemplating my pictures that I even hoped. Neither youth nor childhood is folly or incapacity. Some children are fools, and so are some old men. But there is a vast majority on the side of imagination or spiritual sensation.

((wr. 1799) William Blake (1757–1827), from a letter to Revd Dr John Trussler, 23 August)

1. though this passage refers primarily to Blake's paintings and engravings, it is also illuminating about his poetical work, most of which was engraved with accompanying, often integral, illustrations and illuminations.

299 William Blake (To Frederick Shields, on his Sketch of Blake's Work-room and Death-room, 3 Fountain Court, Strand)

This is the place. Even here the dauntless soul,
   The unflinching hand, wrought on; till in that nook,
   As on that very bed, his life partook
New birth, and passed. Yon river's dusky shoal,
Whereto the close-built coiling lanes unroll,
   Faced his work-window, whence his eyes would stare,
   Thought-wandering, unto nought that met them there,
But to the unfettered irreversible goal.

This cupboard, Holy of Holies, held the cloud
   Of his soul writ and limned;[1] this other one,
His true wife's charge, full oft to their abode
   Yielded for daily bread the martyr's stone,[2]
   Ere yet their food might be that bread alone,
The words now home-speech of the mouth of God.

((1881) Dante Gabriel Rossetti (1828–82)[3]

1. painted, depicted (referring to Blake's double career as poet and painter/engraver). 2. Blake's last years were spent in increasing poverty and neglect. 3. the 'Pre-Raphaelite' painter and poet owned the sketch book and commonplace book used by Blake sporadically between c.1793 and 1818; his brother, William Michael Rossetti (1829–1919), was responsible for an important early edition of Blake's poems (1874).

300 *Blake's solitariness*

He came to the desert of London town
   Grey miles long;
He wandered up and he wandered down,
   Singing a quiet song.

He came to the desert of London town,
   Mirk[1] miles broad;
He wandered up and he wandered down,
   Ever alone with God.

There were thousands and thousands of human kind
   In this desert of brick and stone;
But some were deaf and some were blind,
   And he was there alone.

At length the good hour came; he died
   As he had lived, alone;
He was not missed from the desert wide,
   Perhaps he was found at the Throne.

((1866) James Thomson ('B.V.') (1834–82),[2] 'William Blake')

1. obscure, dark. 2. see 73 n.3.

301 *Blake, reason, and the passions*

The reason, and by the reason he meant deductions from the observations of the senses, binds us to mortality because it binds us to the senses, and divides us from each other by showing us our clashing interests; but imagination divides us from mortality by the immortality of beauty, and binds us to each other by opening the secret doors of all hearts. He cried again and again that everything that lives is holy,[1] and that nothing is unholy except things that do not live – lethargies, and cruelties, and timidities, and that denial of imagination which is the root they grew from in old times. Passions, because most living, are most holy – and this was a scandalous paradox in his time – and man shall enter eternity borne upon their wings.

((1897) William Butler Yeats (1865–1939), from 'William Blake and the Imagination')

1. Yeats alludes to the last line of Blake's 'Song of Liberty' in *The Marriage of Heaven and Hell* (c.1790–3).

302 *Blake and the future*

There have been men who loved the future like a mistress, and the future mixed her breath into their breath and shook her hair about them, and hid them from the understanding of their times. William Blake was one of these men, and if he spoke confusedly and obscurely it was because he spoke of things for whose speaking he could find no models in the world he knew. He announced the religion of art, of which no man dreamed in the world he knew; and he understood it more perfectly than the thousands of subtle spirits who have received its baptism in the world we know, because in the beginning of important things – in the beginning of love, in the beginning of the day, in the beginning of any work – there is a moment when we understand more perfectly than we understand again until all is finished.

((1897) William Butler Yeats (1865–1939), from 'William Blake and the Imagination')

303 *Blake's visions*

Self-educated WILLIAM BLAKE
Who threw his spectre in the lake,
Broke off relations in a curse
With the Newtonian Universe.[1]
But even as a child would pet
The tigers VOLTAIRE[2] never met,
Took walks with them through Lambeth, and
Spoke to Isaiah in the Strand,[3]
And heard inside each mortal thing
Its holy emanation sing.

((1940) Wystan Hugh Auden (1907–73), from 'New Year Letter, Jan. 1, 1940')

1. Blake anathematised Newton (see 30 n.5) as the definer of a mathematical, material universe with no place for spirit or the imagination. 2. French philosopher and champion of free thought (1694–1778), admired by Blake as a chastiser of hypocrisy, but suspected as a materialist; one of Blake's most famous poems is 'The Tiger'. 3. Blake claimed to have spoken directly with the prophet Isaiah.

The Regency and 'Lake' Poets

304 *The Regency poets process before Apollo*

But now[1] came the men of right visiting claims;
I forget in what order, but here are the names:
There was Campbell,[2] for Hope and fine war-songs renowned,
With a wail underneath them of tenderer sound;
And Rogers[3] who followed, as Memory should;
And Scott, full of Scotland's old minstrelling mood
(The god overwhelmed him with thanks for his novels[4]);
Then Crabbe,[5] asking questions concerning Greek hovels;
And Byron, with eager indifference; and Moore,[6]

With admiring glad eyes that came leaping before;
And Southey,[7] with dust from the books on his shelf;
And Wordsworth, whose porcelain was taken for delf,
And Coleridge, whose poetry's poetry's self.[8]

((1811; rev. 1860) James Henry Leigh Hunt (1784–1859),[9] from 'The Feast of the Poets')

1. Hunt's poem imagines the poets of his day attending on Apollo in an inn. 2. Thomas Campbell (1777–1844), best known for *The Pleasures of Hope* (1799) and his war songs 'The Battle of the Baltic' and 'Ye Mariners of England'. 3. Samuel Rogers (1765–1855), highly successful poet, art collector, and friend of Wordsworth and Scott; praised by Byron (see 305); Rogers made his reputation with *The Pleasures of Memory* (1792). 4. Scott's poems date from the earlier part of his career; his 'Waverley' novels, which showed his talents to better advantage, appeared between 1814 and 1831; in 1802–3 Scott published *Minstrelsy of the Scottish Border*, a collection of the old ballads. 5. see 293–7 and ns. 6. Thomas Moore (1779–1852), Irish poet and friend of Byron, most famous for his *Irish Melodies* and the oriental tales, *Lalla Rookh* (1817). 7. see 110 n.5. 8. Hunt's poem was substantially revised after its first appearance in 1811; the present text is based on that of the last edition (1860); in 1811, the account of Wordsworth and Coleridge had been far less complimentary. 9. literary editor and essayist; friend of Byron and Moore, and lifelong supporter of Keats; attacked with Keats as an example of the 'Cockney' school of poets.

305 *The Lake Poets: a sceptic's view*

You gentlemen, by dint of long seclusion
   From better company, have kept your own
At Keswick,[1] and, through still-continued fusion
   Of one another's minds, at last have grown
To deem as a most logical conclusion,
   That Poesy has wreaths for you alone;
There is a narrowness in such a notion,
Which makes me wish you'd change your lakes for ocean.

I would not imitate the petty thought,
   Nor coin my self-love to so base a vice,
For all the glory your conversion brought,
   Since gold alone should not have been its price.
You have your salary; was't for that you wrought?
   And Wordsworth has his place in the Excise.[2]
You're shabby fellows, true, but poets still,
And duly seated on the immortal hill.

Your bays may hide the baldness of your brows,
   Perhaps some virtuous blushes; let them go!
To you I envy neither fruit nor boughs,
   And for the fame you would engross[3] below,
The field is universal, and allows
   Scope to all such as feel the inherent glow;
Scott,[4] Rogers,[5] Campbell,[6] Moore,[7] and Crabbe[8] will try
'Gainst you the question with posterity.[9]

((1819) George Gordon, Lord Byron (1788–1824), from *Don Juan*, Canto 1, Dedication)

1. in the Lake District; the home of Southey (see 110 n.5) from 1809 to 1843; Wordsworth, Coleridge and Lamb also stayed at Keswick. 2. Southey became Poet Laureate in 1813;

Wordsworth was given the sinecure post of Distributor of Stamps for the County of Westmorland in the same year. 3. monopolise. 4. see 304 n.4 and 327. 5. see 304 n.3. 6. see 304 n.2. 7. see 304 n.6. 8. see 293–7. 9. later in Canto 1 of *Don Juan*, Byron included in his set of 'poetical commandments' the following instructions: 'Thou shalt believe in Milton, Dryden, Pope;/ Thou shalt not set up Wordsworth, Coleridge, Southey;/ Because the first is crazed beyond all hope,/ The second drunk, the third so quaint and mouthey'.

William Wordsworth (1770–1850)

306 *Wordsworth and the feelings of human nature*

You[1] have given me praise for having reflected faithfully in my poems the feelings of human nature. I would fain hope that I have done so. But a great poet ought to do more than this; he ought, to a certain degree, to rectify men's feelings, to give them new compositions of feeling, to render their feelings more sane, pure, and permanent; in short, more consonant to Nature, that is, to eternal Nature, and the great moving spirit of things. He ought to travel before men occasionally as well as at their sides.

((wr. 1802) William Wordsworth (1770–1850), from a letter to John Wilson, dated 7 June)

1. Wordsworth is replying to a letter from the young John Wilson (see 55 n.2), who had written to him, praising *Lyrical Ballads*.

307 *Wordsworth and his muse*

On Man, on Nature, and on human life,
Musing in solitude, I oft perceive
Fair trains of imagery before me rise,
Accompanied by feelings of delight
Pure, or with no unpleasing sadness mixed;
And I am conscious of affecting thoughts
And dear remembrances, whose presence soothes
Or elevates the mind, intent to weigh
The good and evil of our mortal state.
   To these emotions, whencesoe'er they come,
Whether from breath of outward circumstance,
Or from the soul (an impulse to herself),
I would give utterance in numerous[1] verse.
Of truth, of grandeur, beauty, love, and hope,
And melancholy fear subdued by faith;
Of blessed consolations in distress;
Of moral strength, and intellectual power;
Of joy in widest commonalty spread;
Of the individual mind, that keeps her own
Inviolate retirement, subject there
To conscience only, and the law supreme
Of that intelligence which governs all,
I sing; 'fit audience let me find though few!'[2]
   So prayed, more gaining than he asked, the bard

In holiest mood. Urania,[3] I shall need
Thy guidance, or a greater Muse, if such
Descend to earth or dwell in highest heaven!
For I must tread on shadowy ground, must sink
Deep, and, aloft ascending, breathe in worlds
To which the heaven of heavens is but a veil.
All strength, all terror, single or in bands,
That ever was put forth in personal form,
Jehovah with his thunder, and the choir
Of shouting angels, and the empyreal[4] thrones –
I pass them unalarmed. Not chaos,[5] not
The darkest pit of lowest Erebus,[6]
Nor aught of blinder vacancy, scooped out
By help of dreams, can breed such fear and awe
As fall upon us often when we look
Into our minds, into the mind of Man,
My haunt, and the main region of my song.
   Beauty – a living presence of the earth,
Surpassing the most fair ideal forms
Which craft of delicate spirits hath composed
From earth's materials – waits upon my steps;
Pitches her tents before me as I move,
An hourly neighbour. Paradise, and groves
Elysian,[7] Fortunate Fields[8] – like those of old
Sought in the Atlantic main – why should they be
A history only of departed things,
Or a mere fiction of what never was?
For the discerning intellect of Man,
When wedded to this goodly universe
In love and holy passion, shall find these
A simple produce of the common day.
   I, long before the blissful hour arrives,
Would chant in lonely peace, the spousal verse
Of this great consummation; and, by words
Which speak of nothing more than what we are,
Would I arouse the sensual from their sleep
Of death, and win the vacant and the vain
To noble raptures; while my voice proclaims
How exquisitely the individual mind
(And the progressive powers perhaps no less
Of the whole species) to the external world
Is fitted; and how exquisitely too –
Theme this but little heard of among men –
The external world is fitted to the mind;
And the creation (by no lower name
Can it be called) which they with blended might
Accomplish; this is our high argument.[9]
   Such grateful[10] haunts foregoing, if I oft
Must turn elsewhere, to travel near the tribes
And fellowships of men, and see ill sights
Of madding passions mutually inflamed;
Must hear humanity in fields and groves

Pipe solitary anguish; or must hang
Brooding above the fierce confederate storm
Of sorrow, barricadoed evermore
Within the walls of cities – may these sounds
Have their authentic comment; that even these
Hearing, I be not downcast or forlorn!
Descend, prophetic spirit! that inspir'st
The human soul of universal earth,
Dreaming on things to come; and dost possess
A metropolitan[11] temple in the hearts
Of mighty poets. Upon me bestow
A gift of genuine insight, that my song
With star-like virtue in its place may shine,
Shedding benignant influence, and secure,
Itself, from all malevolent effect
Of those mutations that extend their sway
Throughout the nether sphere! And if with this
I mix more lowly matter; with the thing
Contémplated, describe the mind and man
Contémplating; and who, and what he was;
The transitory being that beheld
This vision; when, and where, and how he lived;
Be not this labour useless. If such theme
May sort[12] with highest objects, then, dread power –
Whose gracious favour is the primal source
Of all illumination – may my life
Express the image of a better time,
More wise desires, and simpler manners; nurse
My heart in genuine freedom; all pure thoughts
Be with me; so shall thy unfailing love
Guide, and support, and cheer me to the end!

((wr. ?1798; pub. 1814) William Wordsworth (1770–1850), from *The Recluse*, quoted 'as a kind of prospectus of the design and scope of the whole poem' in Preface to *The Excursion*[13])

1. in a regular metre, harmonious, musical (compare *Paradise Lost*, V.150). 2. alluding to Milton's invocation to *Paradise Lost*, Bk. VII (see 189 [ii]); Wordsworth explicitly compares and contrasts his epic ambitions with those of Milton. 3. see 189 n.17. 4. of highest heaven (see *Paradise Lost*, II.430); for 'thrones', see 192 n.3. 5. the formless void between heaven and hell, visited by Satan in *Paradise Lost*, Bk. II. 6. hell (see *Paradise Lost*, II.883). 7. see 12 n.11. 8. the Isles of the Blest, anciently thought to lie beyond the Pillars of Hercules (Straits of Gibraltar), in the Atlantic. 9. see 189 n.11. 10. pleasing. 11. a temple which, figuratively, both befits a capital city and a bishop. 12. accord. 13. in the late 1790s, Wordsworth was planning a vast three-part philosophical poem, to be entitled *The Recluse*; *The Prelude* was designed as the introduction to this project; the second part was published separately as the nine-book *Excursion* in 1814.

308 To William Wordsworth, Composed on the Night after his Recitation of a Poem on the Growth of an Individual Mind

Friend of the wise, and teacher of the good!
Into my heart have I received that lay[1]
More than historic, that prophetic lay

Wherein (high theme by thee first sung aright)
Of the foundations and the building up
Of a human spirit thou hast dared to tell
What may be told, to the understanding mind
Revealable; and what within the mind
By vital breathings secret as the soul
Of vernal growth, oft quickens in the heart
Thoughts all too deep for words!
                        Theme hard as high,
Of smiles spontaneous, and mysterious fears[2]
(The first-born they of Reason, and twin-birth),
Of tides obedient to external force,
And currents self-determined, as might seem,
Or by some inner power; of moments awful,[3]
Now in thy inner life, and now abroad,
When power streamed from thee, and thy soul received
The light reflected, as a light bestowed –
Of fancies fair, and milder hours of youth,
Hyblean[4] murmurs of poetic thought
Industrious in its joy, in vales and glens,
Native or outland, lakes and famous hills!
Or on the lonely high-road, when the stars
Were rising; or by secret mountain streams,
The guides and the companions of thy way!
   Of more than fancy, of the social sense
Distending wide, and man beloved as man,
Where France in all her towns lay víbrating
Like some becalmèd bark beneath the burst
Of heaven's immediate thunder, when no cloud
Is visible, or shadow on the main.
For thou wert there,[5] thine own brows garlanded,
Amid the tremor of a realm aglow
Amid a mighty nation jubilant,
When from the general heart of humankind
Hope sprang forth like a full-born deity!
Of that dear Hope afflicted and struck down,
So summoned homeward, thenceforth calm and sure
From the dread watch-tower of Man's absolute self,
With light unwaning on her eyes, to look
Far on – herself a glory to behold,
The angel of the vision![6] Then (last strain)
Of duty, chosen laws controlling choice,
Action and joy! – An Orphic[7] song indeed,
A song divine of high and passionate thoughts
To their own music chanted!
                        O great bard!
Ere yet that last strain dying awed the air,
With steadfast eye I viewed thee in the choir
Of ever-enduring men. The truly great
Have all one age, and from one visible space
Shed influence! They, both in power and act,
Are permanent, and time is not with them,

Save as it worketh for them, they in it.
Nor less a sacred roll than those of old,
And to be placed, as they, with gradual fame
Among the archives of mankind, thy work
Makes audible a linkèd lay of truth,
Of truth profound a sweet continuous lay,
Not learnt, but native, her own natural notes!
Ah, as I listened with a heart forlorn,
The pulses of my being beat anew;
And even as life returns upon the drowned,
Life's joy rekindling roused a throng of pains,
Keen pangs of love, awakening as a babe
Turbulent, with an outcry in the heart;
And fears self-willed, that shunned the eye of hope;
And hope that scarce would know itself from fear;
Sense of past youth, and manhood come in vain,
And genius given, and knowledge won in vain;
And all which I had culled in wood-walks wild,[8]
And all which patient toil had reared, and all
Commune with thee had opened out – but flowers
Strewed on my corse, and borne upon my bier,
In the same coffin, for the self-same grave!

   That way no more! and ill beseems it me,
Who came a welcomer in herald's guise,
Singing of glory, and futurity,
To wander back on such unhealthful road,
Plucking the poisons of self-harm! And ill
Such intertwine beseems triumphal wreaths
Strewed before thy advancing!
                      Nor do thou,
Sage bard, impair the memory of that hour
Of thy communion with my nobler mind
By pity or grief, already felt too long!
Nor let my words import more blame than needs.
The tumult rose and ceased; for peace is nigh
Where wisdom's voice has found a listening heart.
Amid the howl of more than wintry storms,
The halcyon[9] hears the voice of vernal hours
Already on the wing.
                    Eve following eve,
Dear tranquil time, when the sweet sense of home
Is sweetest! moments for their own sake hailed,
And more desired, more precious for thy song,
In silence listening, like a dévout child,
My soul lay passive, by thy various strain
Driven as in surges now beneath the stars,
With momentary stars of my own birth,
Fair constellated foam,[10] still darting off
Into the darkness; now a tranquil sea,
Outspread and bright, yet swelling to the moon.

   And when – O friend, my comforter and guide,
Strong in thyself, and powerful to give strength! –

Thy long-sustainèd song finally closed,
And thy deep voice had ceased – yet thou thyself
Wert still before my eyes, and round us both
That happy vision of belovèd faces –
Scarce conscious, and yet conscious of its close
I sat, my being blended in one thought
(Thought was it? or aspiration? or resolve?),
Absorbed, yet hanging still upon the sound;
And when I rose, I found myself in prayer.
((wr. 1807; pub. 1817) Samuel Taylor Coleridge (1772–1834))

1. *The Prelude* (first complete version, wr. 1805), which is addressed to Coleridge, and which Wordsworth read aloud to him over two weeks in 1806; Wordsworth did not publish *The Prelude* until 1850, and asked Coleridge not to publish this poem; Coleridge, however, did so, but under the title 'To a Gentleman'; the poem was revised after Coleridge's quarrel with Wordsworth in 1810. 2. charted in *The Prelude*, Bks. I-II. 3. awesome, awe-inspiring. 4. honeyed, mellifluous (Hybla in ancient Sicily was renowned for its honey). 5. alluding to Wordsworth's accounts of his stay in France and of the French Revolution (*Prelude*, Bks. IX-X). 6. probably an allusion to 'the great vision of the guarded mount', when St Michael was said to have appeared to the monks at St Michael's Mount, Cornwall (see Milton, 'Lycidas', 161). 7. oracular, prophetic, befitting Orpheus (on whom, see 12 n.10). 8. in his walks with Wordsworth when he was living in Somerset (1796–8). 9. a mythological bird, able to calm the sea and nest upon it. 10. foam which darts off from a moving vessel's side like a small constellation of stars.

309 *'Lyrical Ballads'*[1]

It was agreed that my endeavours should be directed to persons and characters supernatural, or at least romantic; yet so as to transfer from our inward nature a human interest and a semblance of truth sufficient to procure for these shadows of imagination that willing suspension of disbelief for the moment, which constitutes poetic faith. Mr Wordsworth, on the other hand, was to propose to himself as his object, to give the charm of novelty to things of every day, and to excite a feeling analogous to the supernatural, by awakening the mind's attention to the lethargy of custom, and directing it to the loveliness and the wonders of the world before us; an inexhaustible treasure, but for which, in consequence of the film of familiarity and selfish solicitude,[2] we have eyes, yet see not, ears that hear not, and hearts that neither feel nor understand.

((1817) Samuel Taylor Coleridge (1772–1834), from *Biographia Literaria*, Ch. 14)

1. the celebrated collection of poems by Wordsworth and Coleridge, first published in 1798, and including 'The Ancient Mariner' (by Coleridge) and 'The Thorn', 'The Idiot Boy' and 'Tintern Abbey' (by Wordsworth); the volume was expanded, and its famous Preface added, in the editions of 1800 and 1802. 2. over-preoccupation with our own parochial anxieties and concerns.

310 *Wordsworth's freshness with the familiar*

To find no contradiction in the union of old and new; to contemplate the Ancient of Days[1] and all his works with feelings as fresh as if all had then sprang forth at the first creative fiat,[2] characterises the mind that feels the riddle of the world, and may help to unravel it. To carry on the feelings of childhood into the powers of manhood; to combine the child's sense of wonder and novelty with the appearances which every day, for perhaps forty years, had rendered familiar,

> With sun and moon and stars throughout the year,
> And man and woman,[3]

this is the character and privilege of genius, and one of the marks which distinguish genius from talents. And therefore is it the prime merit of genius and its most unequivocal mode of manifestation, so to represent familiar objects as to awaken in the minds of others a kindred feeling concerning them, and that freshness of sensation which is the constant accompaniment of mental, no less than of bodily, convalescence. Who has not a thousand times seen snow fall on water? Who has not watched it with a new feeling, from the time that he has read Burns's comparison of sensual pleasure

> To snow that falls upon a river
> A moment white, then gone forever![4]

In poems, equally as in philosophic disquisitions, genius produces the strongest impressions of novelty, while it rescues the most admitted truths from the impotence caused by the very circumstance of their universal admission. Truths of all others the most awful and mysterious, yet being at the same time of universal interest are too often considered as *so* true that they lose all the life and efficiency of truth, and lie bedridden in the dormitory of the soul, side by side with the most despised and exploded errors.

((1817) Samuel Taylor Coleridge (1772–1834), from *Biographia Literaria*, Ch. 4[6])

1. God. 2. the act of divine creation. 3. quoted from Milton, Sonnet 22 ('To Mr. Cyriack Skinner, Upon his Blindness'). 4. quoted from 'Tam O'Shanter'. 5. effectiveness, power. 6. this whole passage is quoted in *Biographia Literaria* from Coleridge's own earlier periodical, *The Friend* (1809–10).

311 The unique strengths of Wordsworth's genius

(i)

Wordsworth, where he is indeed Wordsworth, may be mimicked by copyists, he may be plundered by plagiarists; but he cannot be imitated, except by those who are not born to be imitators. For without his depth of feeling and his imaginative power, his sense would want its vital warmth and peculiarity; and without his strong sense, his mysticism would become sickly – mere fog and dimness!

(ii)

... a correspondent weight and sanity of the thoughts and sentiments, won, not from books, but from the poet's own meditative observation. They are fresh, and have the dew upon them. His Muse, at least when in her strength of wing, and when she hovers aloft in her proper element,

> Makes audible a linkèd lay of truth,
> Of truth profound a sweet continuous lay,
> Not learnt, but native, her own natural notes![1]

(iii)

... the perfect truth of nature in his images and descriptions, as taken immediately from nature, and proving a long and genial intimacy with the very spirit which gives the physiognomic[2] expression to all the works of nature. Like a green field reflected in a calm and perfectly transparent lake, the image is distinguished from the reality only by its greater softness and lustre. Like the moisture or the polish on a pebble, genius neither distorts nor false-colours its objects; but, on the contrary, brings out many a vein and many a tint, which escapes the eye of common observation, thus raising to the rank of gems what had been often kicked away by the hurrying foot of the traveller on the dusty high road of custom.

(iv)

... a meditative pathos, a union of deep and subtle thought with sensibility; a sympathy with man as man; the sympathy indeed of a contemplator, rather than a fellow-sufferer or co-mate ... but of a contemplator from whose view no difference of rank conceals the sameness of the nature; no injuries of wind, or weather, or toil, or even of ignorance, wholly disguise the human face divine. The superscription and the image of the Creator still remain legible to *him* under the dark lines, with which guilt or calamity had cancelled or cross-barred it. Here the man and the poet lose and find themselves in each other, the one as glorified, the latter as substantiated. In this mild and philosophic pathos, Wordsworth appears to me without a compeer.

(v)

... the gift of imagination in the highest and strictest sense of the word. In the play of fancy,[3] Wordsworth, to my feelings, is not always graceful, and sometimes recondite. The likeness is occasionally too strange, or demands too peculiar a point of view, or is such as appears the creature of pre-determined research, rather than spontaneous presentation. Indeed his fancy seldom displays itself as mere and unmodified fancy. But in imaginative power, he stands nearest of all modern writers to Shakespeare and Milton; and yet in a kind perfectly unborrowed and his own. To employ his own words, which are at once an instance and an illustration, he does indeed to all thoughts and to all objects

> add the gleam,
> The light that never was, on sea or land,
> The consecration, and the poet's dream.[4]

((1817) Samuel Taylor Coleridge (1772–1834), from *Biographia Literaria*, Ch. 22)

1. quoted from 308. 2. facial. 3. as defined by Coleridge, an inferior faculty which merely orders existing images into new combinations rather than, like the imagination, 'dissolv[ing], diffus[ing], dissipat[ing], in order to re-create'. 4. from Wordsworth's 'Stanzas Suggested by a Picture of Peele Castle'.

312 Wordsworth and human nature

To their question, 'Why did you choose such a character, or a character from such a rank of life?', the poet might in my opinion fairly retort, 'Why, with the conception of my character, did you make wilful choice of mean or ludicrous associations not furnished by me, but supplied from your own sickly and fastidious feelings?' How was it, indeed, probable that such arguments could have any weight with an author whose plan, whose guiding principle and main object it was to attack and subdue that state of association which leads us to place the chief value on those things on which man differs from man, and to forget or disregard the high dignities which belong to human nature, the sense and the feeling which *may* be, and *ought* to be, found in *all* ranks? The feelings with which, as Christians, we contemplate a mixed congregation rising or kneeling before their common maker, Mr Wordsworth would have us entertain at *all* times, as men, and as readers; and by the excitement of this lofty, yet prideless impartiality in *poetry*, he might hope to have encouraged its continuance in *real life*. The praise of good men be his!

((1817) Samuel Taylor Coleridge (1772–1834), from *Biographia Literaria*, Ch. 22)

313 The simple Wordsworth

Next comes the dull disciple of thy[1] school,
That mild apostate[2] from poetic rule,
The simple Wordsworth, framer of a lay
As soft as evening in his favourite May,
Who warns his friend 'to shake off toil and trouble,
And quit his books, for fear of growing double';[3]
Who, both by precept and example, shows
That prose is verse, and verse is merely prose;
Convincing all, by demonstration plain,
Poetic souls delight in prose insane;
And Christmas stories tortured into rhyme
Contain the essence of the true sublime.
Thus, when he tells the tale of Betty Foy,
The idiot mother of 'an idiot boy';[4]
A moon-struck, silly lad, who lost his way,
And, like his bard, confounded night with day;
So close on each pathetic part he dwells,
And each adventure so sublimely tells,
That all who view the 'idiot in his glory'
Conceive the bard the hero of the story.

((1809) George Gordon, Lord Byron (1788–1824), from *English Bards and Scotch Reviewers*)

1. Byron has been discussing Southey. 2. deserter, renegade. 3. see 'The Tables Turned', in *Lyrical Ballads*. 4. see 'The Idiot Boy', in *Lyrical Ballads*.

314 *Don Juan, Wordsworth, and Coleridge*

Young Juan[1] wandered by the glassy brooks,
    Thinking unutterable things; he threw
Himself at length within the leafy nooks
    Where the wild branch of the cork forest grew;
There poets find materials for their books,
    And every now and then we read them through,
So that their plan and prosody are eligible,
Unless, like Wordsworth, they prove unintelligible.

He, Juan (and not Wordsworth), so pursued
    His self-communion with his own high soul,
Until his mighty heart, in its great mood,
    Had mitigated part, though not the whole
Of its disease; he did the best he could
    With things not very subject to control,
And turned, without perceiving his condition,
Like Coleridge, into a metaphysician.[2]
    ((1819) George Gordon, Lord Byron (1788–1824), from *Don Juan*,
    Canto I)

1. the hero of Byron's poem, a young gentleman of Seville, given, in certain moods, to romantic reverie. 2. an allusion to Coleridge's interest in German philosophy and aesthetics.

315 *Wordsworth's lakeland verse*

We learn from Horace, Homer sometimes sleeps;[1]
    We feel without him Wordsworth sometimes wakes,
To show with what complacency he creeps
    With his dear *Waggoners* about his lakes.[2]
He wishes for 'a boat' to sail the deeps.
    Of ocean? No, of air. And then he makes
Another outcry for 'a little boat'[3]
And drivels seas to set it well afloat.

If he must fain sweep o'er the etherial plain,
    And Pegasus[4] runs restive in his 'waggon',
Could he not beg the loan of Charles's Wain?[5]
    Or pray Medea for a single dragon?[6]
Or if too classic for his vulgar brain,
    He feared his neck to venture such a nag on,
And he must needs mount nearer to the moon,
Could not the blockhead ask for a balloon?

'Pedlars' and 'boats' and 'waggons'! Oh ye shades
    Of Pope and Dryden, are we come to this?
That trash of such sort not alone evades

> Contempt, but from the bathos' vast abyss
> Floats scum-like uppermost, and these Jack Cades[7]
> Of sense and song above your graves may hiss.
> The 'little boatman' and his 'Peter Bell'
> Can sneer at him who drew Achitophel![8]
>> ((1821) George Gordon, Lord Byron (1788–1824), from *Don Juan*, Canto III)

1. see Horace, *Ars Poetica*, 1.359. 2. Wordsworth's *The Waggoner* was published in May 1819. 3. Byron alludes to the opening lines of Wordsworth's *Peter Bell* (wr. 1798; pub. 1819). 4. see 11 n.6. 5. the constellation, The Great Bear (with a play on wain = waggon). 6. in Euripides' *Medea*, the heroine flees in a chariot drawn by dragons. 7. vulgar rebels (Jack Cade led a rebellion of commoners against Henry VI in 1450). 8. Wordsworth had criticised Dryden (author of *Absalom and Achitophel*) and Pope in the 'Essay Supplementary to the Preface' in his *Poems* (1815).

316 *Wordsworth as poet of nature*

> Poet of Nature, thou hast wept to know
> That things depart which never may return:
> Childhood and youth, friendship and love's first glow,
> Have fled like sweet dreams, leaving thee to mourn.[1]
> These common woes I feel. One loss is mine
> Which thou too feel'st, yet I alone deplore.
> Thou wert as a lone star, whose light did shine
> On some frail bark[2] in winter's midnight roar;
> Thou hast like to a rock-built refuge stood
> Above the blind and battling multitude;
> In honoured poverty thy voice did weave
> Songs consecrate to truth and liberty;
> Deserting these,[3] thou leavest me to grieve,
> Thus having been, that thou shouldst cease to be.
>> ((1816) Percy Bysshe Shelley (1792–1822), 'To Wordsworth')

1. Shelley alludes to Wordsworth's 'Ode: Intimations of Immortality'. 2. boat. 3. Shelley laments (as he also does in the 'Verses Written on Receiving a Celandine in a Letter from England', written in the same year) what he sees as Wordsworth's abandonment of his earlier radical principles (see 305 n.2).

317 *Wordsworth's mind*

> All things that Peter[1] saw and felt
>   Had a peculiar aspect to him;
> And when they came within the belt
> Of his own nature, seemed to melt,
>   Like cloud to cloud, into him.
>
> And so the outward world uniting
>   To that within him, he became
> Considerably uninviting
> To those who, meditation slighting,
>   Were moulded in a different frame.

And he scorned them, and they scorned him;
    And he scorned all they did; and they
  Did all that men of their own trim
  Are wont to do to please their whim,
    Drinking, lying, swearing, play. ...

  He had a mind which was somehow
    At once circumference and centre
  Of all he might or feel or know;
  Nothing went ever out, although
    Something did ever enter.

  He had as much imagination
    As a pint pot; he never could
  Fancy another situation,
  From which to dart his contemplation,
    Than that wherein he stood.

  Yet his was individual mind,
    And new-created all he saw
  In a new manner, and refined
  Those new creations, and combined
    Them, by a master-spirit's law.

  Thus – though unimaginative –
    An apprehension clear, intense,
  Of his mind's work, had made alive
  The things it wrought on; I believe
    Wakening a sort of thought in sense.

  But from the first 'twas Peter's drift
    To be a kind of moral eunuch,
  He touched the hem of Nature's shift,
  Felt faint – and never dared uplift
    The closest, all-concealing tunic.
         ((wr. 1819; pub. 1839) Percy Bysshe Shelley (1792–1822),
                                        from *Peter Bell the Third*)

1. Wordsworth is satirically identified with the hero of his own *Peter Bell* (1819), which had already been parodied by John Hamilton Reynolds (1796–1852) in *Peter Bell: a Lyrical Ballad*.

318 *Wordsworth's egotism*

For the sake of a few fine imaginative or domestic passages, are we to be bullied into a certain philosophy engendered in the whims of an egotist?[1] Every man has his speculations, but every man does not brood and peacock over them till he makes a false coinage and deceives himself. Many a man can travel to the very bourne of heaven, and yet want confidence to put down his half-seeing. Sancho[2] will invent a journey heavenward as well as anybody. We hate poetry that has a palpable design upon us, and, if we do not agree, seems to put its hand in its breeches' pocket. Poetry should be great and unobtrusive, a thing which enters into one's soul, and does not startle it or amaze it with itself, but with its subject. How beautiful are the retired flowers! How would they lose their beauty were they to throng into the highway, crying out, 'Admire me; I am a violet! Dote on me; I am a primrose!'

((wr. 1818) John Keats (1795–1821), from a letter to J.H.Reynolds, 5 February)

1. Keats is replying to the imagined proposition 'that Wordsworth, etc., should have their due from us'. 2. Sancho Panza, Don Quixote's earthy peasant squire in Cervantes's novel.

319 Keats and Wordsworth's explorative genius

I will return to Wordsworth – whether or no he has an extended vision or a circumscribed grandeur; whether he is an eagle in his nest, or on the wing. And to be more explicit, and to show you how tall I stand by the giant, I will put down a simile of human life as far as I now perceive it; that is, to the point to which I say we both arrived at ... I compare human life to a large mansion of many apartments, two of which I can only describe, the doors of the rest being as yet shut upon me.

The first we step into we call the infant or thoughtless chamber, in which we remain as long as we do not think. We remain there a long while and – notwithstanding the doors of the second chamber remain wide open – showing a bright appearance, we care not to hasten to it, but are at length imperceptibly impelled by the awakening of this thinking principle within us.

We no sooner get into the second chamber, which I shall call the chamber of maiden-thought, than we become intoxicated with the light and the atmosphere; we see nothing but pleasant wonders, and think of delaying there for ever in delight. However, among the effects this breathing is father of is that tremendous one of sharpening one's vision into the heart and nature of Man; of convincing one's nerves that the world is full of misery and heartbreak, pain, sickness, and oppression, whereby this chamber of maiden-thought becomes gradually darkened, and at the same time on all sides of it many doors are set open – but all dark, all leading to dark passages. We see not the balance of good and evil. We are in a mist. *We* are now in that state; we feel 'the burden of the mystery'. To this point was Wordsworth come, as far as I can conceive, when he wrote 'Tintern Abbey',[1] and it seems to me that his genius is explorative of those dark passages. Now if we live, and go on thinking, we too shall explore them. He is a genius, and superior to us, in so far as he can, more than we, make discoveries, and shed a light in them.

((wr. 1818) John Keats (1795–1821), from a letter to J.H. Reynolds, 3 May)

1. from which Keats's earlier quotation is taken.

320 To William Wordsworth

Yes, mighty poet, we have read thy lines,
And felt our hearts the better for the reading.
A friendly spirit, from thy soul proceeding,
Unites our souls; the light from thee that shines
Like the first break of morn, dissolves, combines
All creatures with a living flood of beauty.

For thou hast proved that purest joy is duty,
And love a fondling, that the trunk entwines
Of sternest fortitude. Oh, what must be
Thy glory here, and what the huge reward
In that blest region of thy poesy?
For long as man exists, immortal bard,
Friends, husbands, wives, in sadness or in glee,
Shall love each other more for loving thee.
((wr. 1839; pub. 1851) Hartley Coleridge (1796–1849)[1]

1. see 93 n.4.

321 To William Wordsworth on his Seventy-Fifth Birthday

Happy the year, the month, that finds alive
A worthy man in health at seventy-five.
Were he a man no further known than loved,
And but for unremembered deeds approved,
A gracious boon it were from God to earth
To leave that good man by his humble hearth.
But if the man be one whose virtuous youth,
Loving all Nature, was in love with truth;
And, with the fervour of religious duty,
Sought in all shapes the very form of beauty,
Feeling the current of the tuneful strain,
Joy in his heart, and light upon his brain,
Knew that the gift was given, and not in vain;
Whose careful manhood never spared to prune
What the rash growth of youth put forth too soon;[1]
Too wise to be ashamed to grow more wise;
Culling the truth from specious fallacies;
Then may the world rejoice to find alive
So good, so great a man, at seventy-five.
((wr. 1845; pub. 1851) Hartley Coleridge (1796–1849)[2]

1. referring to Wordsworth's habit of continually revising and reshaping his poems. 2. see 93 n.4.

322 *Unread Wordsworth*

He lived amidst the untrodden ways
  To Rydal Lake[1] that lead;
A bard whom there were none to praise,
  And very few to read.

Behind a cloud his mystic sense,
  Deep hidden, who can spy?
Bright as the night when not a star
  Is shining in the sky.

Unread his works; his 'Milk White Doe'[2]
  With dust is dark and dim;
It's still in Longman's shop – and oh!
  The difference to him![3]
((1869) Hartley Coleridge (1796–1849),[4] 'He lived amidst ...')

1. from 1813, Wordsworth lived at Rydal Mount near Grasmere. 2. Wordsworth's *The White Doe of Rylstone* was published as an expensive quarto by Longman in 1815; Wordsworth had completed the poem in 1801, but, partly due to the hostile reception of his *Poems* (1807), he had been reluctant to publish it; on publication, *The White Doe* was hostilely reviewed and sold slowly. 3. an allusion to the last line of Wordsworth's 'Lucy' poem, 'She dwelt among the untrodden ways'. 4. see 93 n.4.

323 On a Portrait of Wordsworth by B.R. Haydon[1]

Wordsworth upon Helvellyn! Let the cloud
Ebb audibly along the mountain-wind,
Then break against the rock, and show behind
The lowland valleys floating up to crowd
The sense with beauty. He with forehead bowed
And humble-lidded eyes, as one inclined
Before the sovereign thought of his own mind,
And very meek with inspirations proud,
Takes here his rightful place as poet-priest
By the high altar, singing prayer and prayer
To the higher heavens. A noble vision free
Our Haydon's hand has flung out from the mist;
No portrait this, with academic[2] air!
This is the poet and his poetry.

((1844) Elizabeth Barrett Browning (1806–61)[3])

1. Benjamin Robert Haydon (1786–1846) had been himself the subject of a sonnet by Wordsworth; his portrait of 1842 depicts the poet musing, with head bowed and arms folded, on the summit of the mountain Helvellyn in the Lake District. 2. of the kind associated with the routine items exhibited at the Royal Academy. 3. see 67 n.1.

324 *Wordsworth's healing power*

And Wordsworth! Ah, pale ghosts, rejoice!
For never has such soothing voice
Been to your shadowy world conveyed,
Since erst, at morn, some wandering shade
Heard the clear song of Orpheus come
Through Hades, and the mournful gloom.[1]
Wordsworth has gone from us – and ye,
Ah, may ye feel his voice as we!
He too upon a wintry clime
Had fallen – on this iron time
Of doubts, disputes, distractions, fears.
He found us when the age had bound
Our souls in its benumbing round;
He spoke, and loosed our heart in tears.
He laid us as we lay at birth
On the cool flowery lap of earth;
Smiles broke from us, and we had ease;
The hills were round us, and the breeze
Went o'er the sun-lit fields again;
Our foreheads felt the wind and rain.

Our youth returned; for there was shed
On spirits that had long been dead,
Spirits dried up and closely furled,
The freshness of the early world.

Ah! since dark days still bring to light
Man's prudence and Man's fiery might,
Time may restore us in his course
Goethe's[2] sage mind and Byron's force;
But where will Europe's latter hour
Again find Wordsworth's healing power?
Others will teach us how to dare,
And against fear our breast to steel;
Others will strengthen us to bear –
But who, ah! who, will make us feel?
The cloud of mortal destiny,
Others will front it fearlessly –
But who, like him, will put it by?

Keep fresh the grass upon his grave
O Rotha,[3] with thy living wave!
Sing him thy best! for few or none
Hears thy voice right, now he is gone.[4]
((1850) Matthew Arnold (1822–88), from 'Memorial Verses, April 1850')

1. see 12 ns. 10 and 12. 2. Johann Wolfgang von Goethe (1749–1832), the great German writer, had been Arnold's subject earlier in the poem. 3. the river flowing by Grasmere churchyard in Cumbria where Wordsworth is buried. 4. in his 'Stanzas in Memory of the Author of "Obermann", November 1849', Arnold had written of Wordsworth in a more critical manner, commenting that 'Wordsworth's eyes avert their ken/From half of human fate'.

325 *The shock-wave of Wordsworth's 'Immortality Ode'*

There have been in all history a few, a very few, men whom common repute, even where it did not trust them, has treated as having had something happen to them that does not happen to other men – as having *seen something*, whatever that really was. Plato is the most famous of these. Or, to put it as it seems to me I must somewhere have written to you or to somebody, human nature in these men saw something, got a shock – wavers in opinion, looking back, whether there was anything in it or no – but is in a tremble ever since. Now what Wordsworthians mean is ... that in Wordsworth, when he wrote that Ode, human nature got another of those shocks, and the tremble from it is spreading. This opinion I do strongly share; I am, ever since I knew the Ode, in that tremble. You know what happened to crazy Blake, himself a most poetically electrical subject, both active and passive, at his first hearing: when the reader came to 'the pansy at my feet',[1] he fell into a hysterical excitement. Now commonsense forbid we should take on like these unstrung hys-

terical creatures! Still, it was a proof of the power of the shock.
    ((wr. 1886) Gerard Manley Hopkins (1844–89), from a letter to R.W. Dixon, 23 October)

1. 'Ode: Intimations of Immortality', l.54.

326 Wordsworth's two voices

Two voices are there; one is of the deep;
It learns the storm-cloud's thunderous melody,
Now roars, now murmurs with the changing sea,
Now bird-like pipes, now closes soft in sleep;
And one is of an old, half-witted sheep
Which bleats articulate monotony,
And indicates that two and one are three,
That grass is green, lakes damp, and mountains steep;
And, Wordsworth, both are thine. At certain times,
Forth from the heart of thy melodious rhymes
The form and pressure of high thoughts will burst;
At other times – good Lord! I'd rather be
Quite unacquainted with the A B C
Than write such hopeless rubbish as thy worst!
    ((1891) James Kenneth Stephen (1859–92),[1] 'A Sonnet on Wordsworth')

1. educated at Eton and King's College, Cambridge; author of light verse collected in *Lapsus Calami* and *Quo Musa Tendis* (1891).

Sir Walter Scott (1771–1832)

327 Scott's poetic romances

Thus Lays of Minstrels[1] – may they be the last! –
On half-strung harps whine mournful to the blast,
While mountain spirits prate to river sprites,
That dames may listen to the sound at nights;
And goblin brats, of Gilpin Horner's[2] brood,
Decoy young border-nobles through the wood,
And skip at every step, Lord knows how high,
And frighten foolish babes, the Lord knows why;
While high-born ladies in their magic cell,
Forbidding knights to read who cannot spell,
Despatch a courier to a wizard's grave,[3]
And fight with honest men to shield a knave.
    Next view in state, proud prancing on his roan,
The golden-crested, haughty Marmion,[4]
Now forging scrolls, now foremost in the fight,
Not quite a felon, yet but half a knight,
The gibbet or the field prepared to grace;
A mighty mixture of the great and base.
And thinkst thou, Scott, by vain conceit perchance,

On public taste to foist thy stale romance,
Though Murray with his Miller may combine[5]
To yield thy Muse just half-a-crown per line?
No! when the sons of song descend to trade,
Their bays are sear,[6] their former laurels fade.
Let such forego the poet's sacred name,
Who rack their brains for lucre, not for fame;
Still for stern Mammon may they toil in vain,
And sadly gaze on gold they cannot gain!
Such be their meed,[7] such still the just reward
Of prostituted Muse and hireling bard!
For this we spurn Apollo's venal son,
And bid 'a long good night to Marmion'.[8]
  These are the themes that claim our plaudits[9] now;
These are the bards to whom the Muse must bow;
While Milton, Dryden, Pope, alike forgot,
Resign their hallowed bays to Walter Scott.
  ((1809) George Gordon, Lord Byron (1788–1824), from *English Bards and Scotch Reviewers*)

1. Scott's *The Lay of the Last Minstrel* (1805) is a verse romance, the narrator of which is an ancient bard, the last of his race. 2. goblin prankster and page to Lord Cranstoun in Scott's poem; Horner lures away the little son of the Lady of Branksome Hall. 3. In Scott's story, the Lady commissions Sir William Deloraine to recover from the tomb of a wizard a magic book which will help her in her vengeance against the slayer of her husband. 4. Scott's *Marmion*, a tale of the early 16th century in six cantos, was published in 1808; its eponymous hero, a favourite of Henry VIII, is a compound of nobility and villainy. 5. John Murray (1778–1843), Byron's own publisher, who combined with William Miller of Albemarle Street to publish *Marmion*. 6. withered, dried up. 7. reward. 8. see *Marmion*, Canto VI, St. 28. 9. approval.

Samuel Taylor Coleridge (1772–1834)

328 *Coleridge's mind a life unto itself*

I have thought
Of thee, thy learning, gorgeous eloquence,
And all the strength and plumage of thy youth,
Thy subtle speculations,[1] toils abstruse
Among the schoolmen,[2] and Platonic forms[3]
Of wild ideal pageantry, shaped out
From things well-matched or ill, and words for things,
The self-created sustenance of a mind
Debarred from Nature's living images,
Compelled to be a life unto herself,
And unrelentingly possessed by thirst
Of greatness, love, and beauty.[4]
  ((wr. 1805; pub. 1850) William Wordsworth (1770–1850), from *The Prelude*, Bk. VI)

1. see 314 n.2. 2. see 197 n.3. 3. see 17 n.14. 4. this extract comes from one of several passages on Coleridge in *The Prelude*; on the relations between the two poets at this time, see 308 n.1; in his 'Extempore Effusion upon the Death of James Hogg' (1835), Wordsworth described Coleridge as 'The rapt one, of the godlike forehead,/The heaven-eyed creature'.

329 *Coleridge's obscurity*

Shall gentle Coleridge pass unnoticed here,
To turgid ode and tumid[1] stanza dear?
Though themes of innocence amuse him best,
Yet still Obscurity's a welcome guest.
If Inspiration should her aid refuse
To him who takes a pixy for a Muse,
Yet none in lofty numbers can surpass
The bard who soars to elegise an ass.[2]
So well the subject suits his noble mind,
He brays the laureate of the long-eared kind.
((1809) George Gordon, Lord Byron (1788–1824), from
English Bards and Scotch Reviewers)

1. inflated, bombastic. 2. Coleridge's 'Songs of the Pixies' were first published in 1796; his 'To a Young Ass' had first appeared in 1794.

330 *Coleridge and poetry*

He was a mighty poet – and
   A subtle-souled psychologist;
All things he seemed to understand,
Of old or new, of sea or land –
   But his own mind – which was a mist.

This was a man who might have turned
   Hell into heaven – and so in gladness
A heaven unto himself have earned;
But he in shadows undiscerned
   Trusted – and damned himself to madness.

He spoke of poetry, and how
   'Divine it was – a light – a love –
A spirit which like wind doth blow
As it listeth, to and fro;[1]
   A dew rained down from God above;

A power which comes and goes like dream,
   And which none can ever trace –
Heaven's light on earth – truth's brightest beam.'
And when he ceased, there lay the gleam
   Of those words upon his face.
((wr. 1819; pub. 1839) Percy Bysshe Shelley (1792–1822), from
Peter Bell the Third)

1. see John 3:8.

331 *Coleridge's mind*

You will see Coleridge, he who sits obscure
In the exceeding lustre, and the pure
Intense irradiation of a mind
Which, with its own internal lightning blind,

Flags wearily through darkness and despair –
A cloud-encircled meteor of the air,
A hooded eagle¹ among blinking owls.
((wr. 1820; pub. 1824) Percy Bysshe Shelley (1792–1822),
from 'Letter to Maria Gisborne')

1. eagles are traditionally supposed to be able to look directly into the sun; Coleridge, Shelley suggests, is blinded by his own sun-like radiance.

Robert Southey (1774–1843)

332 *An epitaph for Southey*

Ye vales and hills¹ whose beauty hither drew
The poet's steps, and fixed him here, on you
His eyes have closed! and ye, loved books, no more
Shall Southey feed upon your precious lore,
To works that ne'er shall forfeit their renown,
Adding immortal labours of his own –
Whether he traced historic truth, with zeal
For the State's guidance, or the Church's weal,²
Or fancy, disciplined by studious art,
Informed his pen, or wisdom of the heart,
Or judgements sanctioned in the patriot's mind
By reverence for the rights of all mankind.³
Wide were his aims, yet in no human breast
Could private feelings meet for holier rest.
His joys, his griefs, have vanished like a cloud
From Skiddaw's⁴ top; but he to heaven was vowed
Through his industrious life, and Christian faith
Calmed in his soul the fear of change and death.
((wr. 1843; pub. 1845) William Wordsworth (1770–1850),
'Inscription for a Monument in Crosthwaite Church,⁵ in
the Vale of Keswick')

1. around Keswick, where Southey lived from 1802 until his death on 21 March 1843. 2. Southey's voluminous works include a life of Nelson (1813), a history of Brazil (1810–19), a history of the Peninsular War (1823–32), and *The Book of the Church* (1824). 3. Southey's early work displays a revolutionary and humanitarian fervour on which writers of the younger generation felt he had reneged in later life (similar charges were levelled at Wordsworth; see 305 n.2; 316 n.3). 4. see 281 n.3. 5. the site of Southey's grave.

333 *Southey defends himself*¹

He said – (I only give the heads) – he said,
  He meant no harm in scribbling; 'twas his way
Upon all topics; 'twas, besides, his bread,
  Of which he buttered both sides; 'twould delay
Too long the assembly (he was pleased to dread),
  And take up rather more time than a day
To name his works – he would but cite a few:
'Wat Tyler', 'Rhymes on Blenheim', 'Waterloo'.

He had written praises of a regicide;[2]
  He had written praises of all kings whatever;
He had written for republics far and wide,
  And then against them bitterer than ever;
For pantisocracy[3] he once had cried
  Aloud, a scheme less moral than 'twas clever;
Then grew a hearty anti-jacobin[4] –
Had turned his coat – and would have turned his skin.

He had sung against all battles, and again
  In their high praise and glory; he had called
Reviewing 'the ungentle craft',[5] and then
  Become as base a critic as e'er crawled –
Fed, paid, and pampered by the very men
  By whom his Muse and morals had been mauled;
He had written much blank verse, and blanker prose,
And more of both than anybody knows.
    ((1822) George Gordon, Lord Byron (1788–1824), from *The Vision of Judgement*)

1. Byron had included a lengthy attack on 'the ballad-monger Southey' in his *English Bards and Scotch Reviewers* (1809); this had concentrated on Southey's early narrative poems, *Joan of Arc* (1796), *Thalaba* (1801), and *Madoc* (1805), which Byron had stigmatised as dull, far-fetched, and prolix ('Oh Southey, Southey, cease thy varied song!/ A bard may chant too often and too long!'); in the Preface to his hexameter poem *A Vision of Judgement* (1821), Southey launched a virulent attack on Byron's poems as 'monstrous combinations of horrors and mockery, lewdness and impiety'; Byron took his revenge in *The Vision of Judgement*, by satirising Southey, along with the whole era of George III to which, as Poet Laureate, Southey had lent his endorsement; in this passage, Southey defends his achievements before a tribunal of the angels. 2. in his early poem on Henry Martin, one of those who had condemned Charles I. 3. in 1794–5 Southey and Coleridge had planned to set up a utopian community on the banks of the Susquehanna in North America. 4. an opponent of French revolutionary ideas; a Tory magazine called *The Anti-Jacobin* had appeared in 1797–8. 5. in his *Remains of Henry Kirke White* (1808).

James Henry Leigh Hunt (1784–1859)

334 Written on the Day that Mr Leigh Hunt left Prison[1]

What though, for showing truth to flattered state,
  Kind Hunt was shut in prison, yet has he,
  In his immortal spirit, been as free
As the sky-searching lark, and as elate.
Minion of grandeur, think you he did wait?
  Think you he naught but prison walls did see,
  Till, so unwilling, thou unturn'dst the key?
Ah, no! Far happier, nobler, was his fate.
In Spenser's halls he strayed, and bowers fair,
  Culling enchanted flowers; and he flew
With daring Milton through the fields of air;[2]
  To regions of his own his genius true

Took happy flights. Who shall his fame impair
When thou art dead and all thy wretched crew?
((wr. 1815; pub. 1817) John Keats (1795–1821))

1. Hunt (see 304 n.9) had been imprisoned in 1813 for a libellous article on the Prince Regent in his liberal journal *The Examiner*, which he continued to edit in prison; he was later responsible for publishing Keats and Shelley in its pages. 2. Hunt had expressed his admiration for Spenser and Milton in his 'The Feast of the Poets' (see 304 and 335).

The post-Wordsworth generation

335 *Later diners at Apollo's table*

'Twas in eighteen eleven those bards[1] came to dine;
I now add a word in eighteen fifty-nine.
For divers times more did those nine laurelled brothers
Receive invitations to dine with new others.
As Thurlow,[2] to wit, with his old poet-strain,
Whose crotchets that way hurt a really fine vein;
And Keats, the god's own young historian of gods;
With Shelley, diviner still, planning abodes
For earth to enjoy with surpassers of Plato;[3]
And Landor,[4] whom two Latin poets sent bay to
(Catullus and Ovid); with Procter,[5] whose songs
Have made such sweet air of life's raptures and wrongs,
Besides setting free the true tongue of the stage
For Landor to join in full many a page,
And Shelley at Rome with so lofty a rage.[6]
Tom Hood,[7] too, was feasted, strange glad and sad brain,
Whose mirth, you may notice, turns all upon pain.
His puns are such breeders of puns, in and in,
Our laughter becomes a like manifold din;
Yet a right poet also was Hood, and could vary
His jokes with deep fancies of centaur and fairy;[8]
And aye on his fame will a tear be attending,
Who wrote the starved song,[9] with its burden[10] unending.
((1860) James Henry Leigh Hunt (1784–1859), from 'The Feast of the Poets' (revised edition))

1. see 304. 2. Edward Thurlow (1781–1829), a now-forgotten minor poet whose *Poems on Several Occasions* appeared in 1813. 3. Plato's theory of forms (see 17 n.14) was a pervasive influence on Shelley's thought. 4. see 152 n.3. 5. Bryan Waller Procter (1787–1874), friend of Hunt, Lamb, Hazlitt, and Dickens; wrote under the pseudonym of 'Barry Cornwall'; his tragedy *Mirandola* was produced at the Covent Garden Theatre in 1821. 6. Landor's plays include the trilogy *Andrea of Hungary, Giovanna of Naples*, and *Fra Rupert* (1839–40); Shelley published *The Cenci* and wrote *Prometheus Unbound* while in Rome in 1819. 7. see 66 n.2. 8. Hood's poems include 'The Plea of the Midsummer Fairies'. 9. 'The Song of the Shirt' (see 66 n.2). 10. refrain.

George Gordon, Lord Byron (1788–1824)

336 *Byron in 'Childe Harold'*

He who, grown agèd in this world of woe,
In deeds, not years, piercing the depths of life,
So that no wonder waits him; nor below
Can love or sorrow, fame, ambition, strife,
Cut to his heart again with the keen knife
Of silent, sharp endurance; he can tell
Why thought seeks refuge in lone caves, yet rife
With airy images, and shapes which dwell
Still unimpaired, though old, in the soul's haunted cell.

'Tis to create, and in creating live
A being more intense, that we endow
With form our fancy, gaining as we give
The life we image, even as I do now.
What am I? Nothing; but not so art thou,
Soul of my thought! with whom I traverse earth,
Invisible but gazing, as I glow
Mixed with thy spirit, blended with thy birth,
And feeling still with thee in my crushed feelings' dearth.

Yet must I think less wildly; I *have* thought
Too long and darkly, till my brain became
In its own eddy boiling and o'erwrought,
A whirling gulf of fantasy and flame;
And thus, untaught in youth my heart to tame,
My springs of life were poisoned. 'Tis too late!
Yet am I changed; though still enough the same
In strength to bear what time cannot abate,
And feed on bitter fruits without accusing Fate.

((1816) George Gordon, Lord Byron (1788–1824), from *Childe Harold*, Canto III[1])

---

1. Byron's poem describes the foreign wanderings of its eponymous hero (a thinly disguised persona for Byron himself), who has abandoned a life of hedonism at home; Canto III, in which Childe Harold wanders in Belgium, by the Rhine, and in the Alps, is Byron's attempt to scrutinise the after-effects of the collapse of his marriage to Annabella Milbanke.

337 *Byron's improvisatory verse in 'Don Juan'*

I perch upon a humbler promontory,
   Amidst life's infinite variety;
With no great care for what is nicknamed glory,
   But speculating as I cast mine eye
On what may suit or may not suit my story,
   And never straining hard to versify,
I rattle on exactly as I'd talk
With anybody in a ride or walk.

I don't know that there may be much ability
   Shown in this sort of desultory rhyme;
But there's a conversational facility,
   Which may round off an hour upon a time.
Of this I'm sure at least, there's no servility
   In mine irregularity of chime,
Which rings what's uppermost of new or hoary
Just as I feel the 'improvisatore'.[1]

((1824) George Gordon, Lord Byron (1788–1824), from *Don Juan*, Canto XV)

1. an Italian extempore speaker of verse.

338 *A lament for Byron*

                    He is now at rest;
And praise and blame fall on his ear alike,
Now dull in death. Yes, Byron, thou art gone,
Gone like a star that through the firmament
Shot and was lost, in its eccentric course
Dazzling, perplexing. Yet thy heart, methinks,
Was generous, noble – noble in its scorn
Of all things low or little; nothing there
Sordid or servile. If imagined wrongs
Pursued thee, urging thee sometimes to do
Things long regretted, oft, as many know,
None more than I, thy gratitude would build
On slight foundations; and, if in thy life
Not happy, in thy death thou surely wert,
Thy wish accomplished; dying in the land
Where thy young mind had caught etherial fire,
Dying in Greece, and in a cause so glorious![1]
   They in thy train – ah, little did they think,
As round we went, that they so soon should sit
Mourning beside thee, while a nation mourned,
Changing her festal for her funeral song;
That they so soon should hear the minute-gun,[2]
As morning gleamed on what remained of thee,
Roll o'er the sea, the mountains, numbering
Thy years of joy and sorrow.
                        Thou art gone;
And he who would assail thee in thy grave,
Oh, let him pause! For who among us all,
Tried as thou wert – even from thine earliest years,
When wandering, yet unspoilt, a highland-boy[3] –
Tried as thou wert, and with thy soul of flame;
Pleasure, while yet the down was on thy cheek,
Uplifting, pressing, and to lips like thine,
Her charmèd cup – ah, who among us all
Could say he had not erred as much, and more?

((1830) Samuel Rogers (1763–1855),[4] from *Italy*)

1. Byron died while fighting for Greek independence from the Turks, a cause which he had held dear since his youth. 2. gun fired at intervals of a minute, used to signify mourning. 3. Byron's mother was Scottish, and his early days were spent in Aberdeen. 4. see 304 n.3.

339 Byron's daring energy

Not for thy crabbed state-creed,[1] wayward wight,[2]
Thy noble lineage, nor thy virtues high,
(God bless the mark!) do I this homage plight;
No – 'tis thy bold and native energy;
Thy soul that dares each bound to overfly,
Ranging through Nature on erratic wing;
These do I honour, and would fondly try
With thee a wild aërial[3] strain to sing;
Then O! round Shepherd's[4] head thy charmèd mantle fling.
((1815) James Hogg (1770–1835), 'To the Right Honourable Lord Byron' in *Pilgrims of the Sun*)

1. liberal politics (Hogg was a Tory). 2. man. 3. light as air, elevated. 4. Hogg was known as 'The Ettrick Shepherd', after his birthplace and original occupation; his poetical gifts were first discovered by Sir Walter Scott; he later became a friend of Byron, Wordsworth, Southey, and John Murray (see 327 n.5), and edited *Blackwood's Edinburgh Magazine* with John Wilson (see 55 n.2).

340 Sonnet to Byron[1]

If I esteemed you less, envy would kill
Pleasure, and leave to wonder and despair
The ministration of the thoughts that fill
The mind which, like a worm whose life may share
A portion of the unapproachable,
Marks your creations' rise as fast and fair
As perfect worlds at the Creator's will.
But such is my regard, that nor your power
To soar above the heights where others climb,
Nor fame, that shadow of the unborn hour
Cast from the envious future on the time,
Move one regret for his unhonoured name
Who dares these words; the worm beneath the sod
May lift itself in homage of the god.
((wr. ?1821; pub. 1832) Percy Bysshe Shelley (1792–1822))

1. in Shelley's MS, the sonnet is prefaced by the words, 'I am afraid these verses will not please you, but...'; Shelley had part-dramatised Byron as Count Maddalo in his *Julian and Maddalo: A Conversation* (wr. 1818).

341 On Byron's death

A splendid sun hath set! When shall our eyes
Behold a morn so beautiful arise
As that which gave his mighty genius birth,
And all-eclipsed the lesser lights on earth!
His first young burst of twilight did declare

Beyond that haze a sun was rising there;
As when the morn, to usher in the day,
Speeds from the East in sober garb of grey;
At first, till warming into wild delight,
She casts her mantle off and shines in light.
The labour of small minds an age may dream,
And be but shadows on time's running stream;
While genius, in an hour, makes what shall be,
The next, a portion of eternity.
((1835) John Clare (1793–1864),[1] 'Lord Byron')

1. Clare was a long-standing admirer of Byron; two of the most ambitious poems of his asylum years are entitled 'Childe Harold' and 'Don Juan', in which Byronic characters are adopted as personae for Clare himself.

342 Byron's plaintive melody

Byron, how sweetly sad thy melody,
   Attuning still the soul to tenderness,
   As if soft Pity, with unusual stress,
Had touched her plaintive lute, and thou, being by,
Hadst caught the tones, nor suffered them to die.
   O'ershading sorrow doth not make thee less
   Delightful; thou thy griefs dost dress
With a bright halo, shining beamily;
As when a cloud a golden moon doth veil,
   Its sides are tinged with a resplendent glow,
Through the dark robe oft amber rays prevail,
   And like fair veins in sable marble flow.
Still warble, dying swan; still tell the tale,
   The enchanting tale, the tale of pleasing woe.[1]
((wr. 1814; pub. 1848) John Keats (1795–1821), 'To Lord Byron')

1. Keats is here thinking of the early Byron of the oriental tales (1813–14); later, in *The Fall of Hyperion*, Bk. I (wr. 1819), Keats was to refer more critically (with Byron in mind) to 'large self-worshippers/ And careless hectorers in proud, bad verse'.

343 The impact of Byron

When Byron's eyes were shut in death,
We bowed our head and held our breath.
He taught us little; but our soul
Had *felt* him like the thunder's roll.
With shivering heart the strife we saw
Of passion with eternal law;
And yet with reverential awe,
We watched the fount of fiery life
Which served for that Titanic[1] strife.
((1850) Matthew Arnold (1822–88), from 'Memorial Verses, April 1850')

1. like the rebel-giants of Greek myth.

344 *Byron as natural force*

What a spendthrift, one is tempted to cry, is Nature! With what prodigality, in the march of generations, she employs human power, content to gather almost always little result from it, sometimes none! Look at Byron, that Byron whom the present generation of Englishmen are forgetting; Byron, the greatest natural force, the greatest elementary power, I cannot but think, which has appeared in our literature since Shakespeare. And what became of this wonderful production of Nature? He shattered himself, he inevitably shattered himself to pieces, against the huge, black, cloud-topped, interminable precipice of British Philistinism. But Byron, it may be said, was eminent only by his genius, only by his inborn force and fire; he had not the intellectual equipment of a supreme modern poet; except for his genius, he was an ordinary nineteenth-century English gentleman, with little culture and with no ideas.

((1865) Matthew Arnold (1822–88), from 'Heinrich Heine' in *Essays in Criticism: First Series*)

345 *Byron, sixty years on*

The fashion changes! Maidens do not wear,
   As once they wore, in necklaces and lockets,
A curl ambrosial of Lord Byron's hair;
   Don Juan is not always in our pockets –
Nay, a new writer's readers do not care
   Much for your verse, but are inclined to mock its
Manners and morals. Ay, and most young ladies
To yours prefer the 'Epic' called 'of Hades'![1]

I do not blame them; I'm inclined to think
   That with the reigning taste 'tis vain to quarrel;
And Burns might teach his votaries to drink,
   And Byron never meant to make them moral.
You yet have lovers true, who will not shrink
   From lauding you and giving you the laurel;
The Germans too, those men of blood and iron,
Of all our poets chiefly swear by Byron.

Farewell, thou Titan[2] fairer than the gods!
   Farewell, farewell, thou swift and lively spirit,
Thou splendid warrior with the world at odds,
   Unpraised, unpraisable, beyond thy merit;
Chased, like Orestes,[3] by the Furies' rods,
   Like him at length thy peace dost thou inherit;
Beholding whom, men think how fairer far
Than all the steadfast stars the wandering star.

((1886) Andrew Lang (1844–1912),[4] from 'To Lord Byron', in *Letters to Dead Authors*)

1. Sir Lewis Morris's (1833–1907) *Epic of Hades* (1876–7), a series of monologues spoken by mythological characters as the poet tours the Underworld. 2. see 343 n.1. 3. who avenged his mother Clytemnestra's murder of his father, Agamemnon, and was constantly pursued by the Furies. 4. see 271 n.7.

Percy Bysshe Shelley (1792–1822)

346 *The West Wind and Shelley's inspiration*

    Make me thy lyre, even as the forest is;
    What if my leaves are falling like its own!
    The tumult of thy mighty harmonies

    Will take from both a deep, autumnal tone,
    Sweet though in sadness. Be thou, spirit fierce,
    My spirit! Be thou me, impetuous one!

    Drive my dead thoughts[1] over the universe
    Like withered leaves to quicken a new birth!
    And, by the incantation of this verse,

    Scatter, as from an unextinguished hearth,
    Ashes and sparks, my words among mankind!
    Be through my lips to unawakened earth

    The trumpet of a prophecy! O Wind,
    If winter comes, can spring be far behind?
    ((1820) Percy Bysshe Shelley (1792–1822), from 'Ode to the West Wind')

1. Shelley's unsuccessful poems which had not inspired the radical mood in their readers which their author had hoped for.

347 Lines Written ... on a Blank Leaf of 'Prometheus Unbound'

    Write it in gold – a spirit of the sun,
    An intellect ablaze with heavenly thoughts,
    A soul with all the dews of pathos shining,
    Odorous with love, and sweet to silent woe
    With the dark glories of concéntrate song,
    Was sphered in mortal earth. Angelic sounds
    Alive with panting thoughts sunned the dim world.
    The bright creations of an human heart
    Wrought magic in the bosoms of mankind.
    A flooding summer burst on poetry;
    Of which the crowning sun, the night of beauty,
    The dancing showers, the birds whose anthems wild,
    Note after note, unbind the enchanted leaves
    Of breaking buds, eve, and the flow of dawn,
    Were centred and condensed in his one name,
    As in a providence – and that was SHELLEY.
        ((wr. 1822; pub. 1851) Thomas Lovell Beddoes (1803–49)[1])

1. author of *Death's Jest-Book* (1850), a play in the Elizabethan/Jacobean manner; much of Beddoes's work shows a taste for macabre and grotesque subjects.

348 Shelley's divine eloquence

Holy and mighty poet of the spirit
That broods and breathes along the universe![1]
In the least portion of whose starry verse
Is the great breath the spherèd heavens inherit;
No human song is eloquent as thine;
For, by a reasoning instinct all divine,
Thou feel'st the soul of things; and thereof singing,
With all the madness of a skylark,[2] springing
From earth to heaven, the intenseness of thy strain,
Like the lark's music all around us ringing,
Laps us in God's own heart, and we regain
Our primal life ethereal! Men profane
Blaspheme thee; I have heard thee 'dreamer' styled;
I've mused upon their wakefulness – and smiled.
((1835) Thomas Wade (1805–75),[3] 'Shelley')

1. alluding to Shelley's 'Ode to the West Wind' (see 346). 2. alluding to Shelley's 'To a Skylark'. 3. author of plays in the 1820s; his first mature volume of verse was published in 1835, and showed strong Shelleyan influence; he continued to write pamphlet and magazine verse till the 1870s.

349 Shelley, sun-treader

Sun-treader,[1] life and light be thine for ever!
Thou art gone from us; years go by, and spring
Gladdens, and the young earth is beautiful,
Yet thy songs come not; other bards arise,
But none like thee; they stand, thy majesties,
Like mighty works which tell some spirit there
Hath sat regardless of neglect and scorn,
Till, its long task completed, it hath risen
And left us, never to return, and all
Rush in to peer and praise when all in vain.
   The air seems bright with thy past presence yet,
But thou art still for me as thou hast been
When I have stood with thee as on a throne,
With all thy dim creations gathered round
Like mountains, and I felt of mould like them,
And with them creatures of my own were mixed,
Like things half-lived, catching and giving life.
But thou art still for me who have adored,
Though single, panting but to hear thy name
Which I believed a spell to me alone,
Scarce deeming thou wast as a star to men!
As one should worship long a sacred spring
Scarce worth a moth's flitting, which long grasses cross,
And one small tree embowers droopingly –
Joying to see some wandering insect won
To live in its few rushes, or some locust
To pasture on its boughs, or some wild bird
Stoop for its freshness from the trackless air;

And then should find it but the fountain-head,
Long lost, of some great river washing towns
And towers, and seeing old woods which will live
But by its banks untrod of human foot,
Which, when the great sun sinks, lie quivering
In light as some thing lieth half of life
Before God's foot, waiting a wondrous change;
Then girt with rocks which seek to turn or stay
Its course in vain, for it does ever spread
Like a sea's arm as it goes rolling on,
Being the pulse of some great country – so
Wast thou to me, and art thou to the world!
  And I, perchance, half feel a strange regret
That I am not what I have been to thee;[2]
Like a girl one has silently loved long
In her first loneliness in some retreat,
When, late emerged, all gaze and glow to view
Her fresh eyes and soft hair and lips which bloom
Like a mountain berry; doubtless it is sweet
To see her thus adored, but there have been
Moments when all the world was in our praise,
Sweeter than any pride of after-hours.
  Yet, sun-treader, all hail! From my heart's heart
I bid thee hail! E'en in my wildest dreams,
I proudly feel I would have thrown to dust
The wreaths of fame which seemed o'erhanging me,
To see thee for a moment as thou art.
          ((1833) Robert Browning (1812–89), from *Pauline*)

1. Browning's poem is cast in the form of a confession, made to Pauline; one of its earliest readers, John Stuart Mill, assumed, as many have done since, that the speaker of the confession was a persona of the (at that date anonymous) author; Browning was powerfully affected by his first reading of Shelley's works in 1826. 2. Browning's youthful enthusiasm for Shelley had abated somewhat in the mean time.

350 *Shelley, the real and the ideal*

The *Remains*[1] – produced within a period of ten years, and at a season of life when other men of at all comparable genius have hardly done more than prepare the eye for future sight and the tongue for speech – present us with the complete enginery of a poet, as signal in the excellence of its several adaptitudes[2] as transcendent in the combination of effects – examples, in fact, of the whole poet's function of beholding with an understanding keenness the universe, Nature, and Man, in their actual state of perfection-in-imperfection; of the whole poet's virtue of being untempted by the manifold partial developments of beauty and good on every side, into leaving them the ultimates he found them, – induced by the facility of the gratification of his own sense of those qualities, or by the pleasure of acquiescence in the shortcomings of his predecessors in art, and the pain of disturbing their conventionalisms; the whole poet's virtue, I repeat, of looking higher than any manifestation yet made of both beauty and good, in order to suggest from the utmost actual realisation of the one, a corresponding capability in the other, and out of the calm, purity, and energy of Nature, to reconstitute and store up for the forthcoming stage of Man's being, a gift in repayment of that former gift, in which Man's own thought and passion had been lavished by the poet on the else-incompleted magnificence of the sunrise, the else-uninterpreted mystery of the lake – so drawing out, lifting up, and assimilating this ideal of a future man, thus descried as possible, to the present reality of the poet's soul already arrived at the higher state of development, and still aspirant to elevate and extend itself in conformity with its still-improving perceptions of, no longer the eventual human, but the actual divine.

In conjunction with which noble and rare powers, came the subordinate power of delivering these attained results to the world in an embodiment of verse more closely answering to, and indicative of, the process of the informing spirit (failing, as it occasionally does, in art, only to succeed in highest art) – with a diction more adequate to the task in its natural and acquired richness, its material colour and spiritual transparency; the whole being moved by, and suffused with, a music at once of the soul and the sense, expressive both of an external might of sincere passion and an internal fitness and consonancy – than can be attributed to any other writer whose record is among us. Such was the spheric poetic faculty of Shelley, as its own self-sufficing central light, radiating equally through immaturity and accomplishment, through many fragments and occasional completion, reveals it to a competent judgement.

((1852) Robert Browning (1812–89), from 'An Essay on Percy Bysshe Shelley' [Introductory Essay]')

1. Mary Shelley's collected edition of Shelley's poems had appeared in 1839; her edition of Shelley's essays, letters, and translations was published in 1840. 2. adaptednesses, special aptitudes.

351 Percy Bysshe Shelley: Inscription for the Couch, Still Preserved, on which he Passed the Last Night of his Life

'Twixt those twin worlds – the world of sleep, which gave
  No dream to warn; the tidal world of death,
  Which the earth's sea, as the earth, replenisheth –
Shelley, Song's orient sun, to breast the wave,
Rose from this couch that morn.[1] Ah! did he brave
  Only the sea? or did man's deed of hell
  Engulf his bark 'mid mists impenetrable?
No eye discerned, nor any power might save.

When that mist cleared, O Shelley! what dread veil
  Was rent for thee, to whom far-darkling Truth
  Reigned sovereign guide through thy brief ageless youth?
Was the truth *thy* truth, Shelley? Hush! All hail,
Past doubt, thou gav'st it; and in Truth's bright sphere
Art first of praisers, being most praisèd here.

((1881) Dante Gabriel Rossetti (1828–82)[2])

1. Shelley was drowned in a storm in the Bay of Lerici in August 1822. 2. see 299 n.3.

352 Shelley's musicality

Compared with that of most others, his language is as a river to a canal – a river ever flowing 'at its own sweet will', and whose music is the unpurposed result of its flowing. So subtly sweet and rich are the tones, so wonderfully are developed the perfect cadences, that the meaning of the words of the singing is lost and dissolved in the overwhelming rapture of the impression. I have often fancied, while reading them, that his words were really transparent, or that they throbbed with living lustres. Meaning is therein firm and distinct, but 'scarce visible through extreme loveliness';[1] so that the mind is often dazzled from perception of the surpassing grandeur and power of his creations. I doubt not that Apollo was mightier than Hercules,[2] though his divine strength was veiled in the splendour of his symmetry and beauty more divine.

But when we have allowed that a man is pre-eminently a singer, the question naturally follows, What is the matter of his song? Does his royal robe of verse envelop a real king of men, or one who is intrinsically a slave? And here may fitly be adduced Wordsworth's remark, that the style is less the *dress* than the *incarnation* of the thought.[3] Noble features have been informed by ignoble natures, and beautiful language has expressed thoughts impure and passions hateful; great hearts have pulsed in unsightly bodies, and grand ideas have found but crabbed utterance; yet still it is true that generally the countenance is a legible index to the spirit, and the style to the thought.

((1860) James Thomson ('B.V.') (1834–82),[4] from 'Shelley')

1. Shelley, *Epipsychidion*, l.104. 2. the fabulously strong demi-god of antiquity. 3. see 43.
4. see 73 n.3.

353 The voice of Shelley, incarnate seraph[1]

   A voice of right amidst a world gone wrong,
     A voice of hope amidst a world's despair,
   A voice instinct with such melodious song
     As hardly until then had thrilled the air
     Of this gross underworld wherein we fare
   With heavenly inspirations, too divine
   For souls besotted with earth's sensual wine.

   All powers and virtues that ennoble men –
     The hero's courage and the martyr's truth,
   The saint's white purity, the prophet's ken,[2]
     The high unworldliness of ardent youth,
     The poet's rapture, the apostle's ruth –
   Informed the song; whose theme all themes above
   Was still the sole supremacy of love.

   The peals of thunder echoing through the sky,
     The moaning and the surging roar of seas,
   The rushing of the storm's stern harmony,
     The subtlest whispers of the summer breeze,
     The notes of singing birds, the hum of bees,

All sounds of nature, sweet and wild and strong,
Commingled in the flowing of the song;

Which flowing mirrored all the universe,
  With sunsets flushing down the golden lines,
And mountains towering in the lofty verse,
  And landscapes with their olives and their vines
  Spread out beneath a sun which ever shines,
With moonlit seas and pure star-spangled skies,
The world a poem, and earth Paradise.

But ever and anon in its swift sweetness
  The voice was heard to lisp and hesitate,
Or quiver absently from its completeness,
  As one in foreign realms who must translate
  Old thoughts into new language. Ah, how great
The difference between our rugged tongue
And that in which its hymns before were sung!

A glorious voice of glorious inspiration;
  A voice of rapid rapture so intense
That in its musical intoxication
  The truth, arrayed with such an affluence
  Of Beauty, half-escaped the ravished sense;
A sun scarce visible in its own shine,
A god forgotten in his gorgeous shrine.

A voice divinely sweet, a voice no less
  Divinely sad; for all the maddening jar
Of all the wide world's sin and wretchedness
  Swelled round its music, as when round a star
  Black storm-clouds gather and its white light mar;
Pure music is pure bliss in heaven alone;
Earth's air transmutes it to melodious moan.
  ((wr. 1861; pub. 1884) James Thomson ('B.V.') (1834–82),[3] from 'Shelley')

1. Thomson's poem tells of an angel who is sent to earth to sing, incarnated as Shelley.
2. foreknowledge. 3. see 73 n.3.

354 Shelley's 'Lines Written among the Euganean Hills'

It is a rhapsody of thought and feeling coloured by contact with nature, but not born of the contact; and such as it is all Shelley's work is, even when most vague and vast in its elemental scope of labour and of aim. A soul as great as the world lays hold on the things of the world; on all life of plants, and beasts, and men; on all likeness of time, and death, and good things and evil. His aim is rather to render the effect of a thing than a thing itself; the soul and spirit of life rather than the living form; the growth rather than the thing grown.

((1869) Algernon Charles Swinburne (1837–1909),[1] from 'Notes on the Text of Shelley')

1. see 123 n.4.

355 Shelley's heart

O heart of hearts, the chalice of Love's fire,
  Hid round with flowers and all the bounty of bloom;
  O wonderful and perfect heart, for whom
The lyrist Liberty made life a lyre;
O heavenly heart, at whose most dear desire
  Dead Love, living and singing, cleft his tomb,
  And with him risen and regent in death's room
All day thy choral pulses rang full choir;
O heart whose beating blood was running song,
  O sole thing sweeter than thine own songs were,
    Help us for thy free love's sake to be free,
True for thy truth's sake, for thy strength's sake strong,
  Till very Liberty make clean and fair
    The nursing earth as the sepulchral sea.[1]
      ((wr. 1869; pub. 1871) Algernon Charles Swinburne (1837–
      1909),[2] 'Cor Cordium' ['The Heart of Hearts'])

1. see 351 n.1. 2. see 123 n.4.

John Clare (1793–1864)

356 Clare's Rural Muse[1]

  Muse of the fields, oft have I said farewell
To thee, my boon companion, loved so long,
And hung thy sweet harp in the bushy dell,
For abler hands to wake an abler song.
Much did I fear my homage did thee wrong;
Yet, loath to leave, as oft I turned again;
And to its wires mine idle hands would cling,
Torturing it into song. It may be vain;
  Yet still I try, ere Fancy droops her wing,
And hopeless Silence comes to numb its every string.

  Muse of the pasture brooks, on thy calm sea
Of poesy I've sailed; and though the will
To speed were greater than my prowess be,
I've ventured with much fear of usage ill,
Yet more of joy. Though timid be my skill,
As not to dare the depths of mightier streams,
Yet rocks abide in shallow ways, and I
Have much of fear to mingle with my dreams.
  Yet, lovely Muse, I still believe thee by,
And think I see thee smile, and so forget I sigh.

Muse of the cottage hearth, oft did I tell
My hopes to thee, nor feared to plead in vain;
But felt around my heart thy witching spell,
That bade me as thy worshipper remain;
I did, and worship on; Oh! once again
Smile on my offerings, and so keep them green;
Bedeck my fancies like the clouds of even,
Mingling all hues which thou from heaven dost glean.
To me a portion of thy power be given,
If theme so mean as mine may merit aught of heaven.

For thee in youth I culled the simple flower,
That on thy bosom gained a sweeter hue,
And took thy hand along life's sunny hour,
Meeting the sweetest joys that ever grew;
More friends were needless, and my foes were few.
Though freedom then be deemed as rudeness now,
And what once won thy praise now meets disdain,
Yet the last wreath I braided for thy brow
Thy smiles did so commend, it made me vain
To weave another one, and hope for praise again.[2]

With thee the spirit of departed years
Wakes that sweet voice that time hath rendered dumb,
And freshens, like to spring, loves, hopes and fears
That in my bosom found an early home,
Wooing the heart to ecstasy. I come
To thee, when sick of care, of joy bereft,
Seeking the pleasures that are found in bloom;
And happy hopes, that time hath only left
Around the haunts where thou didst erst sojourn!
Then smile, sweet cherubim, and welcome my return.

With thee the raptures of life's early day
Appear, and all that pleased me when a boy.
Though pains and cares have torn the best away,
And winters crept between us to destroy,
Do thou commend, the recompense is joy;
The tempest of the heart shall soon be calm;
Though sterner Truth against my dreams rebel,
Hope feels success; and all my spirits warm
To strike with happier mood thy simple shell
And seize thy mantle's hem – Oh! say not fare-thee-well.

((1835) John Clare (1793–1864), from 'To the Rural Muse')

1. this poem acted as a Preface to Clare's third published volume of verse, *The Rural Muse* (1835). 2. see 357 ns. 1–2.

357 The Death Mask of John Clare

Kind was the hand that at the last
   This mortal likeness drew,
And more than kindness took the cast –
   'Twas prophecy, come true.

Doubt surely questioned, why record
   This old forgotten face?
But after-time with love's reward
   Has blessed the act of grace.

So, Clare, your rich, sweet, serious gaze
   Meets me through sixty years,
Now sets my wonderment ablaze,
   Now fascinates my tears.

I think when young you blushed among
   The gay town's curious eyes;[1]
How tripped the truth from beauty's tongue,
   'A noble in disguise!'

God's noble, slave of earth, upraised
   To bright conception's song,
And by the world down dashed and dazed,[2]
   How held you out so long?

For even the raven's young, you said,
   Are answered when they cry,
But when your children wanted bread,
   At length the stony sky

Seemed all one frown! the tired mind groaned
   Defeat day after day,
And purpose to the dust dethroned
   In riddles mocked the play.

Then from loved fields, from wife, from child,
   You helplessly were haled;
Where the thronged mad high heaven reviled
   Was freedom's friend enjailed.

Twenty dim years you lived where some
   Gnash ivy from the wall,
And others shrieking, others dumb
   With their dark dæmons brawl.[3]

Still welcomed you the bee and bird
   In morning's crystal dew,
Still garlanded with spring-like word
   Spring's 'gold yminted new'.

A thrall, you reached the allotted span,[4]
  Your countenance wore no sign
Of your Bastille,[5] you looked the Man,
  Serene and night divine.

Came death; the boundary wall was cleft,
  Green pastures mile on mile
Gleamed flowers your childhood knew, you left
  Your prison with a smile.

((1925) Edmund Blunden (1896–1974)[6]

1. the title page of Clare's first published volume, *Poems Descriptive of Rural Life and Scenery* (1820), described its author as 'John Clare, a Northamptonshire Peasant'; the volume sold well, and Clare was for a short while something of a celebrity, visiting many prominent literary figures in London in the early 1820s. 2. Clare tried in later volumes to please his publishers by writing in a potentially popular manner, but his later work was neglected, and sold badly; he had to take on labouring work to support his wife and children. 3. Clare was confined from 1842 to 1864 in Northampton Asylum, where he continued to write. 4. Clare died at the age of 70. 5. the Asylum. 6. best known for his poetry, and for *Undertones of War* (1928), a memoir of his experiences in the First World War, Blunden was also a literary scholar, editing some of Clare's MS poems, and writing studies of Hardy and Shelley.

John Keats (1795–1821)

358 *'Endymion' as prentice-work*

In *Endymion* I have most likely but moved into the go-cart[1] from the leading-strings.[2] In poetry I have a few axioms, and you will see how far I am from their centre. First, I think poetry should surprise by a fine excess and not by singularity; it should strike the reader as a wording of his own highest thoughts, and appear almost a remembrance. Second, its touches of beauty should never be half way, thereby making the reader breathless instead of content; the rise, the progress, the setting of imagery should like the sun come natural to him, shine over him, and set soberly, although in magnificence leaving him in the luxury of twilight. But it is easier to think what poetry should be, than to write it, and this leads me on to another axiom: that if poetry comes not as naturally as the leaves to a tree, it had better not come at all. However it may be with me, I cannot help looking into new countries with 'O for a Muse of fire to ascend!'[3] If *Endymion* serves me as a pioneer, perhaps I ought to be content. I have great reason to be content, for I thank God I can read and perhaps understand Shakespeare to his depths, and I have, I am sure, many friends who, if I fail, will attribute any change in my life and temper to humbleness rather than to pride – to a cowering under the wings of great poets, rather than to a bitterness that I am not appreciated.

((wr. 1818) John Keats (1795–1821), from a letter to John Taylor, 27 February)

1. framework on castors to enable a child to learn to walk. 2. reins. 3. the opening words of Shakespeare's *Henry V*.

359 Keats's free poetic soul

Fair and free soul of poesy, O Keats!
Oh, how my temples throb, my heart-blood beats,
   At every image, every word of thine!
Thy bosom, pierced by Envy,[1] drops to rest;
Nor hearest thou the friendlier voice, nor seest
   The sun of fancy climb along thy line.

But under it, although a viperous brood
That stung an Orpheus[2] (in a clime more rude
   Than Rhodope and Haemus[3] frown upon)
Still writhes and hisses, and peers out for more
Whose buoyant blood they leave concreted gore,
   Thy flowers root deep, and split the creviced stone.

Ill may I speculate on scenes to come,
Yet I would dream to meet thee at our home
   With Spenser's quiet, Chaucer's livelier ghost,
Cognate[4] to thine – not higher, and less fair -
And Madeline and Isabella[5] there
   Shall say, 'Without thee half our loves were lost.'
               ((1828) Walter Savage Landor (1775–1864),[6] 'Keats')

1. referring to the infamously hostile reviews of Keats's *Endymion* (1818). 2. see 12 n.10. 3. mountains in northern Greece. 4. members of the same family. 5. heroines, respectively, of Keats's 'The Eve of St Agnes' and 'Isabella'. 6. see 152 n.3.

360 Keats and nature

   He is made one with Nature; there is heard
His voice in all her music, from the moan
Of thunder, to the song of night's sweet bird;
He is a presence to be felt and known
In darkness and in light, from herb and stone,
Spreading itself where'er that Power may move
Which has withdrawn his being to its own;
Which wields the world with never-wearied love,
Sustains it from beneath, and kindles it above.

He is a portion of the loveliness
Which once he made more lovely; he doth bear
His part, while the one Spirit's plastic[1] stress
Sweeps though the dull, dense world, compelling there,
All new successions to the forms they wear;
Torturing the unwilling dross that checks its flight
To its own likeness, as each mass may bear;
And bursting in its beauty and its might
From trees and beasts and men into the heaven's light.
           ((1821) Percy Bysshe Shelley (1792–1822), from *Adonais*)

1. moulding, forming.

361 To the Memory of John Keats

Thy worldly hopes and fears have passed away;
  No more its trifling[1] thou shalt feel or see;
Thy hopes are ripening in a brighter day,
  While these left buds[2] thy monument shall be.
When Rancour's aims have passed in naught away,
  Enlarging specks discerned in more than thee,
And beauties 'minishing which few display[3] –
  When these are past, true child of Poesy,
Thou shalt survive. Ah, while a being dwells,
  With soul, in Nature's joys, to warm like thine,
With eye to view her fascinating spells,
  And dream entrancèd o'er each form divine,
Thy worth, enthusiast shall be cherished here,
Thy name with him shall linger, and be dear.

                        ((1821) John Clare (1793–1864))

1. see 359 n.1. 2. Keats's poems. 3. Keats's critics have focused on his faults, wishing to withhold praise from those beauties which his works (unlike those of most writers) display.

362 Sonnet Written in Keats's *Endymion*

  I saw pale Dian,[1] sitting by the brink
    Of silver falls, the overflow of fountains
  From cloudy steeps; and I grew sad to think
    Endymion's foot was silent on those mountains,
  And he but a hushed name, that Silence keeps
    In dear remembrance – lonely, and forlorn,
  Singing it to herself until she weeps
    Tears that perchance still glisten in the morn;
  And as I mused, in dull imaginings,
    There came a flash of garments, and I knew
  The awful Muse by her harmonious wings,
    Charming the air to music as she flew.
  Anon there rose an echo through the vale
  Gave back Endymion in a dream-like tale.

                        ((1823) Thomas Hood (1799–1845)[2])

1. Diana, the moon goddess, who, as Cynthia or Phoebe, falls in love with the eponymous hero of Keats's poem. 2. see 66 n.2; Keats was a notable influence on Hood's early poetry.

363 *Keats's early death*[1]

  By Keats's soul, the man who never stepped
  In gradual progress like another man,
  But, turning grandly on his central self,
  Ensphered himself in twenty perfect years,
  And died, not young (the life of a long life
  Distilled to a mere drop, falling like a tear
  Upon the world's cold cheek to make it burn
  For ever); by that strong excepted soul,
  I count it strange and hard to understand
  That nearly all young poets should write old,

That Pope was sexagenary at sixteen,
And beardless Byron academical,[2]
And so with others. It may be perhaps
Such have not settled long and deep enough
In trance, to attain to clairvoyance – and still
The memory mixes with the vision, spoils,
And works it turbid.

((1856) Elizabeth Barrett Browning (1806–61),
from *Aurora Leigh*, Bk. I[3])

1. Aurora (see 67 n.1) is speaking. 2. learned. 3. see 67 n.1.

364 *Pang-dowered Keats*

The weltering[1] London ways where children weep
   And girls whom none call maidens laugh – strange road
   Miring his outward steps, who inly trode
The bright Castalian[2] brink and Latmos'[3] steep: –
Even such his life's cross-paths; till deathly deep
   He toiled through sands of Lethe;[4] and long pain,
   Weary with labour spurned and love found vain,
In dead Rome's sheltering shadow wrapped his sleep.[5]

O pang-dowered poet, whose reverberant lips
   And heart-strung lyre awoke the moon's eclipse;
   Thou whom the daisies glory in growing o'er –
Their fragrance clings around thy name, not writ
But rumoured in water,[6] while the fame of it
   Along time's flood goes echoing evermore.

((1881) Dante Gabriel Rossetti (1828–82),[7] 'John Keats')

1. winding. 2. Castalia is a spring on Mt. Parnassus (see 11 n.7). 3. the mountain scene of Keats's *Endymion*. 4. the river of oblivion in the classical underworld, referred to at the beginning of Keats's 'Ode on Melancholy'. 5. Rossetti refers to Keats's tuberculosis, to his ill-treatment at the hands of the reviewers (see 359 n.1), to his unfulfilled love for Fanny Brawne, and to his death in Rome (23 February 1821). 6. alluding to Keats's dying wish that on his tomb should be inscribed the words 'Here lies one whose name was writ in water.' 7. see 299 n.3.

365 On Keats, 18 January, 1849 (Eve of St Agnes)

A garden in a garden; a green spot
   Where all is green; most fitting slumber-place
   For the strong man grown weary of a race
Soon over. Unto him a goodly lot
Hath fallen in fertile ground; there thorns are not,
   But his own daisies; silence, full of grace,
   Surely hath shed a quiet on his face;
His earth is but sweet leaves that fall and rot.
What was his record of himself, ere he
   Went from us? 'Here lies one whose name was writ
   In water.'[1] While the chilly shadows flit
Of sweet St Agnes' Eve,[2] while basil springs –

His name, in every humble heart that sings,
Shall be a fountain of love, verily.³
                    ((1849) Christina Rossetti (1830–94)⁴)

1. see 364 n.6. 2. the setting for Keats's story of Madeline and Porphyro (*The Eve of St Agnes*). 3. in Keats's 'Isabella', the heroine places her dead lover's severed head in a pot of basil, which she cherishes as a macabre memorial of her love. 4. sister of Dante Gabriel Rossetti (see 299 n.3), and authoress of a wide variety of poetry, from the children's 'Goblin Market' (1862) to religious verse.

366 Keats's happiness?

*Hic.*¹ Yet surely there are men who have made their art
Out of no tragic war, lovers of life,
Impulsive men that look for happiness
And sing when they have found it.

Ille.   No, not sing,
For those that love the world serve it in action.
Grow rich, popular and full of influence,
And should they paint or write, still it is action:
The struggle of the fly in marmalade.
The rhetorician would deceive his neighbours,
The sentimentalist himself; while art
Is but a vision of reality.
What portion in the world can the artist have
Who has awakened from the common dream
But dissipation and despair?

Hic.   And yet
No one denies to Keats love of the world;
Remember his deliberate happiness.

Ille. His art is happy, but who knows his mind?
I see a schoolboy when I think of him,
With face and nose pressed to a sweet-shop window,
For certainly he sank into his grave
His senses and his heart unsatisfied,
And made – being poor, ailing and ignorant,
Shut out from all the luxury of the world,
The coarse-bred son of a livery-stable keeper –²
Luxuriant song.
                    ((wr. 1915; pub. 1919) William Butler Yeats (1865–1939),
                    from 'Ego Dominus Tuus' ['I am thy master']³ in
                    The Wild Swans at Coole)

1. Yeats's poem, on the nature of art and the creative power, is cast in the form of a dialogue between two unnamed personages, 'Hic' ['This man'] and 'Ille' ['That man']; a contemporary quip, attributed to Ezra Pound, suggested that 'Hic' and 'Willie' (i.e. Yeats) might have been more appropriate. 2. Keats's father managed a livery stables in Moorfields; the poet lacked the education shared by most of the other famous early-19th-century English poets, and died of tuberculosis. 3. Dante, *La Vita Nuova*, III.

Alfred, Lord Tennyson (1809–92)

367 Tennyson's poetry of grief

I sometimes hold it half a sin
   To put in words the grief I feel;[1]
   For words, like Nature, half reveal
And half conceal the soul within.

But, for the unquiet heart and brain,
   A use in measured language lies;
   The sad mechanic exercise,
Like dull narcotics, numbing pain.

In words, like weeds,[2] I'll wrap me o'er,
   Like coarsest clothes against the cold;
   But that large grief which these enfold
Is given in outline and no more.
    ((1850) Alfred, Lord Tennyson (1809–92), from *In Memoriam*)

1. alluding to the death of Tennyson's friend Arthur Hallam in 1833, the direct subject of *In Memoriam*, and the indirect inspiration of many of Tennyson's most famous poems. 2. clothes.

368 Wapentake[1] to Alfred Tennyson

Poet! I come to touch thy lance with mine,
   Not as a knight who on the listed field
   Of tourney touched his adversary's shield
In token of defiance, but in sign
Of homage to the mastery, which is thine
   In English song; nor will I keep concealed,
   And voiceless as a rivulet frost-congealed,
My admiration for thy verse divine.
Not of the howling dervishes of song,
   Who craze the brain with their delirious dance,
   Art thou, O sweet historian of the heart!
Therefore to thee the laurel leaves belong,
   To thee our love and our allegiance,
   For thy allegiance to the poet's art.
    ((1877) Henry Wadsworth Longfellow (1807–82)[2])

1. an Old Norse word, meaning 'the brandishing of weapons in assent, at an assembly'; Longfellow was a Professor of languages, and a keen student of Scandinavian literature. 2. as an American poet, Longfellow comes, strictly speaking, outside the scope of the present volume; this poem, however, has been included as an interesting tribute to Tennyson by one of his more distinguished English-speaking contemporaries.

369 On the Death of Lord Tennyson

Silence! 'The best' (he said) 'are silent now,'[1]
That younger bearer[2] of the laurel bough,
Who with his Thyrsis,[3] kindred souls divine,
Harps only for Sicilian Proserpine;[4]

For Arnold died, and Browning died,[5] and he –
The oldest, wisest, greatest of the three –
Dies, and what voice shall dirge for him today?
For the Muse went with him the darkling way,
And left us mute! ... Peace! who shall rhyme or rave?
The violet blooms not on the new-made grave,
And not in this first blankness of regret
Are eyes of men who mourn their master wet.
New grief is dumb; himself through many a year
Withheld the meed of his melodious tear
While Hallam slept.[6] But no! the moment flies!
And rapid rhymers, when the poet dies,
Wail punctual, and prompt, and unafraid,
In copious instant ditties ready made.
Oh, peace! Ye do but make our loss more deep,
Who wail above his unawaking sleep.

((1892) Andrew Lang (1844–1912)[7])

1. Matthew Arnold, 'Stanzas from the Grande Chartreuse', 1.114. 2. Arnold (1822–88). 3. Arthur Hugh Clough (d. 1861); see 378 n.1. 4. like Orpheus (see 12 n.12). 5. in 1889. 6. Tennyson's *In Memoriam* (see 367 n.1) was not published until 1850. 7. see 271 n.7.

370 To Lord Tennyson (with a Volume of Verse)

Master and mage, our prince of song, whom Time
In this your autumn mellow and serene,
Crowns ever with fresh laurels, not less green
Than garlands dewy from your verdurous prime;
Heir of the riches of the whole world's rhyme,
Dowered with the Attic[1] grace, the Mantuan[2] mien,
With Arno's[3] depth and Avon's golden sheen;
Singer to whom the singing ages climb,
Convergent; if the youngest of the choir
May snatch a flying splendour from your name,
Making his page illustrious, and aspire
For one rich moment your regard to claim,
Suffer him at your feet to lay his lyre,
And touch the skirts and fringes of your fame.

((1890) Sir William Watson (1858–1935)[4])

1. Greek. 2. see 293 n.6. 3. the river of Florence, birthplace of Dante. 4. popular minor poet, who flourished in the 1890s; his *Lachrymae Musarum* (1892) consists of verse on the death of Tennyson.

371 The Passing of Tennyson

As his own Arthur fared across the mere,
With the grave Queen,[1] past knowledge of the throng.
Serene and calm, rebuking grief and tear.
Depart this prince of song.

Whom the gods love, Death doth not cleave nor smite,
But like an angel, with soft trailing wing.
He gathers them upon the hush of night,
With voice and beckoning,

The moonlight falling on that august head,
Smoothed out the mark of Time's defiling hand,
And hushed the voice of mourning round his bed –
'He goes to his own land'.

Beyond the ramparts of the world, where stray,
The laureled few o'er field Elysian,[2]
He joins his elders of the lyre and bay,
Led by the Mantuan.[3]

We mourn him not, but sigh with Bedivere,[4]
Not perished be the sword he bore so long,
Excalibur, whom none is left to wear –
His magic brand of song.
((1915) Ernest Dowson (1867–1900)[5]

1. King Arthur, in Tennyson's 'Morte d'Arthur' (1842; later incorporated into *Idylls of the King*) is borne away on a black barge, attended by three queens. 2. see 12 n. 11. 3. Virgil (see 293 n, 6.); Tennyson greatly admired Virgil, and addressed a celebrated poem to him in which Virgil is described as a 'wielder of the stateliest measure/ever moulded by the lips of man' and as 'majestic in [his] sadness/at the doubtful doom of human kind'. 4. Sir Bedivere, King Arthur's companion at his passing, entrusted by Arthur to throw the royal sword Excalibur into the lake; an arm appeared, clothed in white samite, and a mysterious hand caught Excalibur, brandished it, and conveyed it to the depths. 5. *fin de siècle* aesthete; friend of Wilde and Beardsley and contributor to the magazine, *The Yellow Book*.

Robert Browning (1812–89)

372 *Browning and 'Men and Women'*

I shall never, in the years remaining,
Paint you pictures, no, nor carve you statues,
Make you music that should all-express me;
So it seems; I stand on my attainment.
This of verse alone, one life allows me;
Verse and nothing else have I to give you.
Other heights in other lives, God willing;
All the gifts from all the heights, your own, Love!

Yet a semblance of resource avails us –
Shade so finely touched, love's sense must seize it.
Take these lines, look lovingly and nearly,
Lines I write the first time and the last time.[1]
He who works in fresco, steals a hair-brush,
Curbs the liberal hand, subservient proudly,
Cramps his spirit, crowds its all in little,
Makes a strange art of an art familiar,
Fills his lady's missal-marge[2] with flowerets.
He who blows through bronze, may breathe through silver,
Fitly serenade a slumbrous princess.
He who writes, may write for once as I do.

Love, you saw me gather men and women,³
Live or dead or fashioned by my fancy,⁴
Enter each and all, and use their service,
Speak from every mouth, – the speech, a poem.
Hardly shall I tell my joys and sorrows,
Hopes and fears, belief and disbelieving;
I am mine and yours – the rest be all men's,
Karshish, Cleon, Norbert⁵ and the fifty.
Let me speak this once in my true person,
Not as Lippo, Roland or Andrea,
Though the fruit of speech be just this sentence:
Pray you, look on these my men and women,
Take and keep my fifty poems finished;
Where my poor heart lies, let my brain lie also!
Poor the speech; be how I speak, for all things.
((1855) Robert Browning (1812–89), from 'One Word More : To E.B.B.'⁶ in *Men and Women*)

1. Browning is using a metre (trochaic pentameter) which he had never used before and would never use again. 2. the margins of her missal (Roman Catholic prayer book); these were often beautifully illuminated. 3. alluding to the title of the volume in which this poem first appeared, which mainly consists of dramatic monologues by various characters, historical or imaginary, some of whom are named in the following lines. 4. imagination. 5. the hero of 'In a Balcony'. 6. Elizabeth Barrett Browning (see 67 n.1).

373 *Browning's active mind*

There is delight in singing, though none hear
Beside the singer; and there is delight
In praising, though the praiser sit alone,
And see the praised far off him, far above.
Shakespeare is not *our* poet, but the world's,
Therefore on him no speech; and short for thee,
Browning! Since Chaucer was alive and hale,
No man hath walked along our roads with step
So active, so inquiring eye, or tongue
So varied in its discourse. But warmer climes
Give brighter plumage, stronger wing;¹ the breeze
Of Alpine heights thou playest with, borne on
Beyond Sorrento and Amalfi,² where
The Siren waits thee, singing song for song.
((1845) Walter Savage Landor (1775–1864),³ 'To Robert Browning')

1. Browning had sailed to southern Italy in the autumn of 1844. 2. towns on the Italian coast near Naples, legendary resting place of one of the Sirens, the seductress-maidens of Greek myth. 3. see 152 n.3; Landor met Browning in 1836 and was one of his most fervent early admirers.

374 *Browning and common life*

All of us have the opportunity of mastering the common facts of nature and human life; yet it is precisely in these departments of knowledge that Browning's pre-eminence appears to me most decided. With the great majority of us, the senses are dull, the perceptions slow and vague and confused; Browning drinks in the living world at every pore. There exist, in fact, some men so rarely endowed, that their minds are as revolving mirrors, which, without effort, reflect clearly everything that passes before them and around them in the world of life, and without effort retain all the images constantly ready for use; while we ordinary men can only with fixed purpose and long endeavour catch and keep some very small fragments of the whole. Chaucer, Rabelais,[1] Shakespeare, Ben Jonson, Goethe,[2] Scott, Balzac,[3] are familiar examples of this quietly rapacious, indefinitely capacious acquisitiveness, men of whom we can say, 'They have learned everything and forgotten nothing;' and the star of Browning is of the first magnitude in this constellation.

((1882) James Thomson ('B.V.') (1834–82),[4] from 'Notes on the Genius of Robert Browning')

1. early-16th-century French humanist and satirical writer, author of the fantastic tales of the two giants, Gargantua and Pantagruel. 2. see 324 n.2. 3. Honoré de Balzac (1799–1850), French novelist, author of the large collection of novels and stories, *La Comédie humaine* (1827–47). 4. see 73 n.3.

375 *Browning's energy*

I look up to Browning as one of the very few men known to me by their works who, with most cordial[1] energy and invincible resolution, have lived thoroughly throughout the whole of their being, to the uttermost verge of all their capacities, in his case truly colossal; lived and wrought thoroughly in sense and soul and intellect; lived at home in all realms of nature and human nature, art and literature; whereas nearly all of us are really alive in but a small portion of our so much smaller beings, and drag wearily toward the grave our for the most part dead selves, dead from the suicidal poison of misuse and atrophy of disuse. Confident and rejoicing in the storm and stress of the struggle, he has conquered life instead of being conquered by it – a victory so rare as to be almost unique, especially among poets in these latter days.

((1882) James Thomson ('B.V.') (1834–82),[2] from 'Notes on the Genius of Robert Browning')

1. invigorating. 2. see 73 n.3.

376 *Browning's rapid intelligence*

He is something too much the reverse of obscure; he is too brilliant and subtle for the ready reader of a ready writer to follow with any certainty the track of an intelligence which moves with such incessant rapidity, or even to realise with what spider-like swiftness and sagacity his building spirit leaps and lightens to and fro and backward and forward as it lives along the animated line of its labour, springs from thread to thread, and darts from centre to circumference of the glittering and quivering web of living thought, woven from inexhaustible stores of his perception, and kindled from the inexhaustible fire of his imagination. He never thinks but at full speed; and the rate of his thought is to that of another man's as the speed of a railway to that of a waggon, or the speed of a telegraph to that of a railway. It is hopeless to enjoy the charm or apprehend the gist of his writings, except with a mind thoroughly alert, an attention awake at all points, a spirit open and ready to be kindled by the contact of the writer's.

((1875) Algernon Charles Swinburne (1837–1909),[1] from *George Chapman*)

1. see 123 n.4.

Emily Brontë (1818–48)

377 Emily Brontë[1] : 'Du hast Diamanten'[2]

Thou hadst all passion's splendour,
    Thou hadst abounding store
Of heaven's eternal jewels,
    Belovèd; what wouldst thou more?

Thine was the frolic freedom
    Of creatures coy and wild,
The melancholy of wisdom,
    The innocence of a child,

The mailed will of the warrior,
    That buckled in thy breast
Humility as of Francis,[3]
    The self-surrender of Christ;

And of God's cup thou drankest
    The unmingled wine of love,
Which makes poor mortals giddy
    When they but sip thereof.

What was't to thee thy pathway
    So rugged mean and hard,
Whereon when Death surprised thee
    Thou gav'st him no regard?

What was't to thee, enamoured
    As a red rose of the sun,
If of thy myriad lovers
    Thou never sawest one?

Nor if of all thy lovers
    That are and were to be
None ever had their vision,
    O belovèd, of thee,

>   Until thy silent glory
>   Went forth from earth alone,
>   Where like a star thou gleamest
>   From thy immortal throne.³
>   ((wr. 1921; pub. 1925) Robert Bridges (1844–1930)⁴)

1. best known for her novel, *Wuthering Heights* (1847), Emily Brontë was also a considerable poet, writing usually in the short-line stanzas here imitated by Bridges. 2. 'You have diamonds' (the opening line of one of the poems in the *Buch der Lieder* ['Book of Songs'] by the German poet, Heinrich Heine (1797–1856)). 3. St Francis of Assisi. 4. made Poet Laureate in 1913; friend of Gerard Manley Hopkins and the first editor of his work; now little read, but once highly regarded, particularly for his long philosophical poem, *The Testament of Beauty* (1929).

Arthur Hugh Clough (1819–61)

378 *Clough's stormy note*

>   What though the music of thy rustic flute
>   Kept not for long its happy, country tone;¹
>   Lost it too soon, and learnt a stormy note
>   Of men contention-tossed, of men who groan,
>   Which tasked thy pipe too sore, and tired thy throat –
>   It failed, and thou wast mute!²
>   Yet hadst thou alway visions of our light,
>   And long with men of care thou couldst not stay,
>   And soon thy foot resumed its wandering way,
>   Left human haunt, and on alone till night.
>   ((1866) Matthew Arnold (1822–88), from 'Thyrsis: A Monody to
>   Commemorate the Author's Friend, Arthur Hugh Clough, who
>   Died at Florence, 1861')

1. Clough was an Oxford friend of Arnold; he is best known today for *The Bothie of Tober-na-Vuolich* (1848), a poem in hexameters about a student reading party in Scotland, and for 'Amours de Voyage' (1858), an epistolary poem recounting a frustrated love affair; Arnold's elegy on Clough is cast in pastoral form, and contrasts the peace and happiness enjoyed by Clough and Arnold as undergraduates with Clough's later life, which was tormented by religious doubt and social anxiety; in fact, Clough's doubts date back to his Oxford days. 2. Clough published no new poems in England after 1849. 'Amours de Voyage' was published in an American magazine.

George Meredith (1828–1909)

379 George Meredith (1828–1909)¹

>   Forty years back, when much had place
>   That since has perished out of mind,
>   I heard that voice and saw that face.
>
>   He spoke as one afoot will wind²
>   A morning horn ere men awake;
>   His note was trenchant, turning kind.

> He was of those whose wit can shake
> And riddle to the very core
> The counterfeits that Time will break. ...
>
> Of late, when we two met once more,
> The luminous countenance and rare
> Shone just as forty years before.
>
> So that, when now all tongues declare
> His shape unseen by his green hill,[3]
> I scarce believe he sits not there.
>
> No matter. Further and further still
> Through the world's vaporous vitiate air,
> His words wing on – as live words will.
>
> ((1909) Thomas Hardy (1840–1928))

1. mainly remembered today as a novelist, but once famous for his *Modern Love* (1862), a sequence of fifty sixteen-line poems, recounting the souring of an initially happy marriage. 2. blow, sound. 3. Meredith's home on Box Hill, Surrey.

William Morris (1834–96)

380 *Morris's[1] pictures of childlike happiness*

All he writes seems to me like the make-believe of a child who is remaking the world, not always in the same way, but always after its own heart; and so, unlike all other modern writers, he makes his poetry out of unending pictures of a happiness that is often what a child might imagine, and always a happiness that sets mind and body at ease. Now it is a picture of some great room full of merriment, now of the wine-press, now of the golden threshing-floor, now of an old mill among apple-trees, now of cool water after the heat of the sun, now of some well-sheltered, well-tilled place among woods or mountains, where men and women live happily, knowing of nothing that is too far off or too great for the affections. He has but one story to tell us, how some man or woman lost and found again the happiness that is always half of the body; and even when they are wandering from it, leaves must fall over them, and flowers make fragrances about them, and warm winds fan them, and birds sing to them, for being of Habundia's[2] kin they must not forget the shadow of her Green Tree even for a moment, and the waters of her Well must be always wet upon their sandals. His poetry often wearies us as the unbroken green of July wearies us, for there is something in us, some bitterness because of the Fall, it may be, that takes a little from the sweetness of Eve's apple after the first mouthful; but he who did all things gladly and easily, who never knew the curse of labour, found it always as sweet as it was in Eve's mouth. All kinds of associations have gathered about the pleasant things of the world and half taken the pleasure out of them for the greater number of men, but he saw them as when they came from the Divine Hand. I often see him in my mind as I saw him once at Hammersmith holding up a glass of claret towards the light and saying, 'Why do people say it is prosaic to get inspiration out of wine? Is it not the sunlight and the sap in the leaves? Are not grapes made by the sunlight and the sap?'

((1902) William Butler Yeats (1865–1939), from 'The Happiest of the Poets')

1. most of Morris's poetry consists of retellings of Greek, Norse, and Arthurian myths; his *Life and Death of Jason* (1867) and *The Earthly Paradise*, a collection of tales (1868–70), established him as one of the most popular poets of his day. 2. the Lady of Abundance in Morris's prose romance, *The Well at the World's End* (1896), in which Morris tells of the quest of Ralph, youngest son of King Peter of Upmeads, for the well whose waters save 'from weariness and wounding and sickness' and win 'love for all, and maybe life everlasting'; on his journey, Ralph meets and falls in love with the Lady of Abundance, who has herself drunk from the well, which is situated in a remote region, likened by Morris to Eden.

Algernon Charles Swinburne (1837–1909)

381 *Swinburne's lyre*

And now in turn see Swinburne[1] bent
Above his favourite instrument –
He strikes the trembling wire.
Let horn and flute at once be mute
Before the new lascivious lute,[2]
Little man and great lyre –
I had him there! l-i-a-r!

((wr. 1868; pub. 1974) Robert Browning (1812–89), '[Lines on Swinburne]')

1. see 123 n.4; Browning's epigram was composed in response to a review of Matthew Arnold by Swinburne, in which Swinburne had noted the 'characteristic instruments' of several contemporary poets. 2. Browning alludes to *Richard III*, I.i.14 ('the lascivious pleasing of a lute'), in his reference to Swinburne's *Poems and Ballads* (1866), which had provoked outrage for their masochism, sexual luxuriance, and atheism.

382 *Swinburne's song*

The passionate pages of his earlier years,
Fraught with hot sighs, sad laughters, kisses, tears;[1]
Fresh-fluted notes, yet from a minstrel who
Blew them not naïvely, but as one who knew
Full well why thus he blew.

I still can hear the brabble[2] and the roar
At those thy tunes, O still one, now passed through
That fitful fire of tongues then entered new!
Their power is spent like spindrift[3] on this shore;
Thine swells yet more and more.

– His singing-mistress verily was no other
Than she the Lesbian,[4] she the music-mother
Of all the tribe that feel in melodies;
Who leapt, love-anguished, from the Leucadian steep
Into the rambling world-encircling deep
   Which hides her where none sees.
      ((wr. 1910; pub. 1914) Thomas Hardy (1840–1928), from 'A
         Singer Asleep (Algernon Charles Swinburne, 1837-1909)')

1. see 123 n.4 and 381 n.2. 2. uproar. 3. driving spray. 4. Sappho, Greek poetess (b. *c.*612 BC) who lived on the island of Lesbos; Sappho is fabled to have thrown herself into the sea because her love for Phaon the boatman was unrequited.

Thomas Hardy (1840–1928)

383 Birthday Poem for Thomas Hardy

Is it birthday weather[1] for you, dear soul?
Is it fine your way,
With tall moon-daisies[2] alight, and the mole
Busy, and elegant hares at play
By meadow paths where once you would stroll
In the flush of day?

I fancy the beasts and flowers there beguiled
By a visitation
That casts no shadow, a friend whose mild
Inquisitive glance lights with compassion,
Beyond the tomb, on all of this wild
And humbled creation.

It's hard to believe a spirit could die
Of such generous glow;
Or to doubt that somewhere a bird-sharp eye
Still broods on the capers of men below,
A stern voice asks the Immortals why
They should plague us so.[3]

Dear poet, wherever you are, I greet you.
Much irony, wrong,
Innocence you'd find here to tease or entreat you,
And many the fate-fires have tempered strong,
But none that in ripeness of soul could meet you
Or magic of song.

Great brow, frail frame – gone. Yet you abide
In the shadow and sheen,
All the mellowing traits of a countryside
That nursed your tragi-comical scene;
And in us, warmer-hearted and brisker-eyed
Since you have been.

                      ((1948) Cecil Day Lewis (1904–72)[4])

1. Hardy was born on 2 June 1840. 2. ox-eyed daisies. 3. an allusion to Hardy's references to the malign deities of ancient Greece (e.g. in the last paragraph of *Tess of the d'Urbervilles* [1891]). 4. one of the 'left-wing' poets of the 1930s (his later work was less political); translated Virgil and Valéry; became Professor of Poetry at Oxford in 1951 and Poet Laureate in 1968; Day Lewis was buried at Stinsford, Dorset, next to the resting-place of Hardy's heart.

Robert Bridges (1844–1930)

384 *Bridges's delicacy*

There is poetry that is like the white light of noon, and poetry that has the heaviness of woods, and poetry that has the golden light of dawn or of sunset; and I find in the poetry of Mr Bridges[1] in the plays,[2] but still more in the lyrics, the pale colours, the delicate silence, the low murmurs of cloudy country days, when the plough is in the earth, and the clouds darkening towards sunset; and had I the gift of praising, I would praise it as I would praise these things.

((1914) William Butler Yeats (1865–1939), from 'Reveries over Childhood and Youth')

1. see 377 n.4. 2. Bridges wrote eight verse-plays between 1885 and 1894.

Gerard Manley Hopkins (1844–1889)

385 *Hopkins's flagging inspiration*

The fine delight that fathers thought; the strong
Spur, live and lancing like the blowpipe flame,[1]
Breathes once and, quenchèd faster than it came,
Leaves yet the mind a mother of immortal song.

Nine months she then, nay years, nine years[2] she long
Within her wears, bears, cares and combs[3] the same;
The widow of an insight lost[4] she lives, with aim
Now known and hand at work now never wrong.

Sweet fire the sire of Muse, my soul needs this;
I want[5] the one rapture of an inspiration.
O then if in my lagging lines you miss

The roll, the rise, the carol, the creation,
My winter world, that scarcely breathes that bliss
Now, yields you, with some sighs, our explanation.

((wr. 1889; pub. 1918) Gerard Manley Hopkins (1844–89), 'To R.B.'[6])

1. a flame blown by a glassblower which (as Hopkins himself put it) 'darts out into a jet taper as a lance head and as piercing too'. 2. In his *Ars Poetica*, Horace had suggested that a

poem should be kept for nine years before publication; Hopkins's poems were, indeed, left in rough copy for months, sometimes years. 3. as a mother grooms her child's hair. 4. the original spark of inspiration (the poem's 'father') is lost, but mind (its 'mother') knows that it is her task to bring it into the world. 5. lack. 6. Robert Bridges (see 377 n.4); Hopkins wrote this poem to his lifelong friend when depressed and burdened with his teaching and administrative duties at University College, Dublin, where he was Professor of Greek.

William Butler Yeats (1865–1939)

386 *Yeats's naked style*

I made my song a coat[1]
Covered with embroideries
Out of old mythologies[2]
From heel to throat;
But the fools[3] caught it,
Wore it in the world's eyes
As though they'd wrought it.
Song, let them take it,
For there's more enterprise
In walking naked.[4]

((wr. 1912; pub. 1914) William Butler Yeats (1865–1939), 'A Coat' in *Responsibilities*)

1. I made a coat for my song. 2. much of Yeats's early work treated subjects from Irish myth and folklore. 3. Dublin hack poets who imitated Yeats's early 'Celtic' manner. 4. 'Yeats's later style was altogether sparer and less consciously 'literary' than the idiom of his earlier poetry.

387 *The aged Yeats and his themes*

I

I sought a theme and sought for it in vain,
I sought it daily for six weeks or so.
Maybe at last, being but a broken man,
I must be satisfied with my heart, although
Winter and summer till old age began
My circus animals were all on show,
Those stilted boys,[1] that burnished chariot,[2]
Lion and woman[3] and the Lord knows what.

II

What can I but enumerate old themes?
First that sea-rider Oisin[4] led by the nose
Through three enchanted islands, allegorical dreams,
Vain gaiety, vain battle, vain repose,
Themes of the embittered heart, or so it seems,
That might adorn old songs or courtly shows;
But what cared I that set him on to ride,
I, starved for the bosom of his faery bride?[5]

And then a counter-truth filled out its play,
The Countess Cathleen[6] was the name I gave it;
She,[7] pity-crazed, had given her soul away,
But masterful Heaven had intervened to save it.
I thought my dear[8] must her own soul destroy,
So did fanaticism and hate enslave it,
And this brought forth a dream and soon enough
This dream itself had all my thought and love.

And when the Fool and Blind Man stole the bread
Cuchulain fought the ungovernable sea;[9]
Heart-mysteries there, and yet when all is said
It was the dream itself enchanted me:
Character isolated by a deed
To engross the present and dominate memory.
Players and painted stage took all my love,
And not those things that they were emblems of.

III

Those masterful images because complete
Grew in pure mind, but out of what began?
A mound of refuse or the sweepings of a street,
Old kettles, old bottles, and a broken can,
Old iron, old bones, old rags, that raving slut
Who keeps the till. Now that my ladder's gone,
I must lie down where all the ladders start,
In the foul rag-and-bone shop of the heart.

((1939) William Butler Yeats (1865–1939), 'The Circus Animals' Desertion' in *Last Poems*)

1. the Celtic characters in Yeats's early work (see 386 n.2). 2. belonging to the Ulster hero Cuchulain, a character in several of Yeats's early poems and plays. 3. perhaps a reference to the sphynx figure who appears in several of Yeats's poems. 4. the hero of Yeats's early poem *The Wanderings of Oisin* (1889); Oisin was carried off to faeryland by Niamh, daughter of the sea god. 5. Yeats alludes to his own early love, Maude Gonne, momentarily identifying her with Niamh. 6. Yeats's play, written for Maude Gonne and published in 1892. 7. in Yeats's play, the Countess Cathleen sells her soul to the demons to relieve a famine among her own people, but is forgiven because of the nobility of her motives. 8. Maude Gonne became deeply (fanatically, Yeats thought) involved in Irish politics, and in 1903 married the political activist, John MacBride. 9. in Yeats's play *On Baile's Strand*, Cuchulain dies fighting the sea.

388 In Memory of W.B. Yeats

1

He disappeared in the dead of winter:[1]
The brooks were frozen, the air-ports almost deserted,
And snow disfigured the public statues;
The mercury sank in the mouth of the dying day.
O all the instruments agree
The day of his death was a dark cold day.

Far from his illness
The wolves ran on through the evergreen forests,
The peasant river was untempted by the fashionable quays;
By mourning tongues
The death of the poet was kept from his poems.[2]

But for him it was his last afternoon as himself,
An afternoon of nurses and rumours;
The provinces of his body revolted,
The squares of his mind were empty,
Silence invaded the suburbs,
The current of his feeling failed: he became his admirers.[3]
Now he is scattered among a hundred cities
And wholly given over to unfamiliar affections;
To find his happiness in another kind of wood
And be punished under a foreign code of conscience.
The words of a dead man
Are modified in the guts of the living.

But in the importance and noise of to-morrow
When the brokers are roaring like beasts on the floor of the Bourse,[4]
And the poor have the sufferings to which they are fairly accustomed,
And each in the cell of himself is almost convinced of his freedom;
A few thousand will think of this day
As one thinks of a day when one did something slightly unusual.

O all the instruments agree
The day of his death was a dark cold day.

2

You were silly like us:[5] your gift survived it all;
The parish of rich women, physical decay,
Yourself; mad Ireland hurt you into poetry.
Now Ireland has her madness and her weather still,
For poetry makes nothing happen: it survives
In the valley of its saying where executives
Would never want to tamper; it flows south
From ranches of isolation and the busy griefs,
Raw towns that we believe and die in; it survives,
A way of happening, a mouth.

3

Earth, receive an honoured guest;
William Yeats is laid to rest:
Let the Irish vessel lie
Emptied of its poetry.

Time that is intolerant
Of the brave and innocent,
And indifferent in a week
To a beautiful physique,

Worships language and forgives
Everyone by whom it lives;
Pardons cowardice, conceit,
Lays its honours at their feet.

Time that with this strange excuse
Pardoned Kipling and his views,[6]
And will pardon Paul Claudel,[7]
Pardons him for writing well.

In the nightmare of the dark
All the dogs of Europe bark,
And the living nations wait,
Each sequestered in its hate;[8]

Intellectual disgrace
Stares from every human face,
And the seas of pity lie
Locked and frozen in each eye.

Follow, poet, follow right
To the bottom of the night,
With your unconstraining voice
Still persuade us to rejoice;

With the farming of a verse
Make a vineyard of the curse,
Sing of human unsuccess
In a rapture of distress;

In the deserts of the heart
Let the healing fountain start,
In the prison of his days
Teach the free man how to praise.

((1939) Wystan Hugh Auden (1907–73))

1. Yeats died on 28 January 1939. 2. because they survived him. 3. because his works – all that now remain of him – have a powerful effect on those who read them. 4. the Paris Stock Exchange. 5. in his article 'The Public v. the Late Mr. William Butler Yeats' (1939), Auden has the Public Prosecutor list among Yeats's 'sillinesses' his eccentric editing of *The Oxford Book of Modern Verse*, his sentimentality about the Irish peasantry, his snobbish frequenting of rich people's (particularly rich ladies') houses, his youthful belief in fairies, and his elderly addiction to obscurantist spiritualist 'mumbo-jumbo'. 6. the poet and story-writer Rudyard Kipling (1865–1936) had been criticised for his jingoistic, pro-imperialist views. 7. the French poet and dramatist Paul Claudel (1868–1955), a fervent Catholic, held extreme right-wing political views; Yeats had himself often seemed to support authoritarian and anti-democratic political positions. 8. Auden's poem was written on the eve of the Second World War.

INDEX

1 General Topics

References are to item numbers; only main treatments are indexed

acrostics 17, 251
adventurousness of poets 189, 190, 198, 199, 200, 203, 207, 267, 319, 339, 340, 346, 350, 373
alexandrine 26

blank verse 37, 190, 192, 193, 196, 258
burlesque 219

civilisation, poetry and 18, 25, 30
comedy 171, 176, 177, 178
comprehensiveness of poet's soul 38, 87, 128
conceits 158, 159, 165, 168, 229
consolation, poetry as 10, 108, 282, 307, 308, 310, 320, 324
correctness 186, 232
couplets, heroic 37, 64, 221, 232, 236, 248, 250, 253
creator, poet as 2, 7, 15, 16, 27, 29, 32, 36, 38, 57, 62, 63, 67, 133, 198, 199, 223, 243, 317, 336, 340, 347

demands of poetic calling 11, 20, 24, 33, 71, 222, 385
diction, poetic 26, 28, 350
didacticism 60, 318
divine nature of poetry 5, 6, 9, 14, 16, 59, 62, 67, 68, 73, 164, 172, 206, 232, 330, 347, 348, 352, 353, 361, 369

egotism of poet 65, 211, 317, 318
empathy, poet's power of 60, 65, 92, 135, 142, 159, 311, 372
enchanter, poet as 3, 55
English language, poetry and the 77, 79, 83, 85, 88, 97, 115, 118, 181, 243, 265
envy provoked by poets 230, 245, 265, 271, 340, 349, 359, 361, 364
epic 98, 99, 189, 190, 192, 193, 214, 217

fashion, poetry and 45, 64, 66, 93, 134, 169, 230, 241, 245, 345

fire, poetical 27, 63, 247, 248, 347
fusing power of poet 17, 52, 60, 62, 242, 247, 310, 317, 324
future, poetry and the 61, 62, 63, 302, 307, 308, 346, 350

genius, poetic 44, 247, 267, 274, 291, 292, 310, 311, 319, 341

heroic plays 241

imagery 52, 280, 283, 307, 358
imitation 11, 15, 56, 165, 171, 176, 226
immortality, poetic 1, 8, 15, 25, 30, 40, 58, 59, 61, 62, 64, 66, 80, 83, 84, 89, 102, 126, 127, 156, 179, 223, 224, 230, 249, 269, 270, 292, 308, 341, 364, 365, 379
inspiration 6, 7, 11, 17, 19, 23, 62, 99, 113, 116, 129, 189, 190, 285, 307

judgement, poetic 23

legislator, poet as 33, 63

memory and the poet 205, 307
metre 42, 93
mock-heroic 31, 263
morality, poetry and 55, 60, 72, 96, 103, 105, 108, 214, 255, 256, 259, 260, 261, 266, 268, 269, 270, 273, 277, 282, 307, 320, 388
music, poetry and 3, 12, 13, 14, 16, 53, 69, 101, 116, 117, 186, 216, 243, 244, 350, 352, 353, 355, 371, 382, 383

nature, poetry and 16, 23, 27, 33, 35, 39, 40, 48, 52, 56, 57, 64, 70, 87, 89, 129, 132, 134, 136, 146, 172, 174, 177, 178, 233, 236, 272, 274, 275, 276, 278, 281, 285, 287, 288, 295, 296, 298, 306, 307, 308, 311, 316, 317, 319, 320, 321, 323, 324, 325, 326, 344, 348, 349, 350, 354, 356, 360, 361, 375, 380, 383, 384 'negative capability', poet's 153

obscenity in poetry 17, 234, 237, 238, 239
octosyllabics 219, 220
ode 49, 220, 248, 286, 329
organism, poem as 7, 27, 28, 32, 43, 50, 51, 54, 73, 146, 358

panegyric 185, 187
passions, poetry and the 21, 33, 106, 129, 132, 133, 134, 166, 233, 243, 301, 307
past, poetry as dialogue with 4, 56, 87
pastoral 99, 278, 293, 294, 378
philosophy, poetry and 2, 10, 39, 73, 75, 80, 148, 206, 223, 233, 328
pleasure, poetry and 3, 10, 39, 42, 59, 62, 73, 307
pictorial poetry 112, 144
pindarics 224, 225, 226, 248, 279
prose, poetry and 41
public poetry 98, 240, 257, 332

quibbles 139, 197

reincarnation, poetic 20, 83, 223, 224, 265, 359
religious poetry 35, 91, 110, 116, 163, 165, 166, 182, 183, 184, 189, 206, 218, 256, 277, 289
Restoration, poetry and the 231, 233, 234, 237
rhyme 6, 26, 64, 190, 238, 337
rhythm 74

satire 22, 31, 162, 234, 240, 246, 251, 253, 255, 257, 259, 260, 261, 262, 266, 290
science, poetry and 2, 40
sonnet 47, 97, 113, 286
sound and sense 26, 352, 353
sublime, the 35, 37, 65, 159, 190, 192, 193, 195, 196, 198, 201, 203, 212, 282

tragedy 13, 34, 76, 122, 233
transcendental truths of poetry 33, 39, 40, 52, 58, 59, 61, 62, 64, 68, 89, 134, 137, 308, 310, 351
translation 18, 20, 117, 118, 119, 120, 188, 223, 224, 226, 265
transporting power of poetry 27, 141, 147, 154

vision, poetic 75, 298, 303, 307, 319, 323, 363, 366

wit 17, 23, 116, 158, 159, 160, 164, 165, 167, 168, 169, 170, 176, 183, 225, 226, 227, 228, 229, 231, 238, 290

2 Authors

Mentions of particular English poets outside main author entries

Arnold, Matthew 369

Beaumont, Francis, and Fletcher, John 126, 239
Blackmore, Sir Richard 245
Blake, William 325
Browning, Robert 369
Bryan, Sir Francis 95
Buckingham, George Villiers, Duke of 252
Butler, Samuel 177, 283
Byron, George Gordon, Lord 296, 304, 324, 363

Campbell, Thomas 304, 305
Carew, Thomas 164, 231
Chaucer, Geoffrey 13, 77, 96, 104, 126, 287, 359, 373, 374
Coleridge, Samuel Taylor 153, 304, 314
Congreve, William 260
Cowley, Abraham 30
Crabbe, George 304, 305

Davies, Sir John 52
Denham, Sir John 26
Donne, John 64, 246

INDEX

Dorset, Charles Sackville, Earl of 252
Dryden, John 37, 190, 232, 235, 253, 259, 260, 315, 327
Duck, Stephen 293

Flecknoe, Richard 251

Garth, Sir Samuel 260
Godolphin, Sidney 252
Gower, John 77

Herbert, George 251
Hobbes, Thomas 265
Hood, Thomas 335

Jonson, Ben 12, 222, 239, 374

Keats, John 319, 335
Kipling, Rudyard 388
Kyd, Thomas 126

Landor, Walter Savage 335
Lansdowne, George Granville, Lord 260
Lydgate, John 77
Lyly, John 115, 126

Marlowe, Christopher 112, 126
Milton, John 27, 30, 37, 47, 148, 240, 260, 287, 307, 327, 334
Moore, Thomas 305
Ogilby, John 265

Oldham, John 246
Otway, Thomas 232

Pope, Alexander 31, 64, 93, 247, 315, 327, 363
Procter, Bryan Walter ('Barry Cornwall') 335

Rogers, Samuel 304, 305

Scott, Sir Walter 304, 305, 374
Scroope, Sir Car 252
Sedley, Sir Charles 231, 239, 252
Shadwell, Thomas 252
Shakespeare, William 12, 27, 32, 34, 40, 65, 169, 232, 239, 260, 287, 344, 358, 370, 373, 374
Shelley, Percy Bysshe 335
Southey, Robert 304, 305
Spenser, Edmund 30, 47, 60, 126, 287, 334, 359
Sprat, Thomas 231
Surrey, Henry Howard, Earl of 95
Swift, Jonathan 260

Thurlow, Edward 335

Waller, Edmund 26, 30, 204, 232
Wordsworth, William 65, 90, 108, 296, 297, 304, 305
Wyatt, Sir Thomas 95
Wycherley, William 252